"I have watched Scott lead so many couples through this message, and lives have been changed! Take every encouragement and challenge he has written, have the conversations, and I guarantee your marriage will be better for it."

Jennie Allen, author of *Nothing to Prove*; founder and visionary of IF:Gathering

"Our generation needs this book. We need to learn the truth about love, sex, and covenantal marriage. Even more than that, we need to be reminded that marriage is a good gift from a good God who has designed it with our absolute best in mind. Scott does an incredible job undergirding timely, practical application with the timeless principles of God's Word. Highly recommended!"

Ryan and Selena Frederick, authors of *Fierce Marriage*; founders of FierceMarriage.com

"Whether you're single, dating, or engaged, this book is a must-read. Scott Kedersha's warm writing style is conversational, comprehensive, and caring. No matter where you find yourself, you'll feel heard, you'll be challenged, and you'll have a plan to move toward marriage. I have a feeling I'll be buying copies of *Ready or Knot?* to give away for years to come."

Clay Scroggins, lead pastor of North Point Community Church; author of *How to Lead When You're Not in Charge*

"In the past decade of ministry at The Porch I've had the privilege of watching hundreds of couples get married. I've seen the ones who have done it right and the ones who have struggled. Those who have had the most 'success' in their new venture are the couples that gleaned from Scott's wisdom and premarriage ministry, Merge. This book is that wisdom in written form and, might I add, is very entertaining. It should be required reading for every seriously dating and engaged couple. Learn from Scott as thousands of others have."

Jonathan "JP" Pokluda, teaching pastor of Watermark Community Church; author of *Welcome to Adulting*

"If we were friends, and I could give you any wedding gift, it would be twelve weeks in a room with Scott and his bride to help you prepare for your marriage. Since I can't give you that, give yourself the gift of twelve chapters with him and the wisdom he has waiting for you."

Todd Wagner, senior pastor of Watermark Community Church; author of *Come and See*

"If we had to go to one person for sage marital advice, it would be Scott Kedersha. Scott is able to communicate God's truth in such a loving way, and he doesn't skirt around the tough issues while doing so. *Ready or Knot?* is the book every prospective married couple needs to read before their big day. Communication, forgiveness, in-laws, finances, sex—Scott covers these and so much more with God's heart at the center of it all."

Sean and Catherine Lowe

"A much-needed resource, *Ready or Knot?* is a book every couple who is preparing for marriage should read *and* discuss together! It's packed full of biblical wisdom, practical advice, personal stories, and must-have conversation ideas. We highly recommend!"

Patrick and Ruth Schwenk, founders of FortheFamily.org; coauthors of *For Better or For Kids: A Vow to Love Your Spouse with Kids in the House*

"If you are engaged or thinking about becoming engaged, next to the Bible, *Ready or Knot?* might be the most important book you could ever read in this season of your life. Scott's book is full of inspiring true stories, thought-provoking discussion questions, and life-changing principles to help you build a Christ-centered foundation for a lifelong marriage full of love and laughter. This book will also help you prepare to create a legacy that will positively impact your future children and grandchildren. If every engaged couple would read this book, divorce rates would instantly drop!"

Dave and Ashley Willis, authors and speakers; TV hosts for *MarriageToday*

"Many couples will undertake a DIY home improvement project on their house. Scott Kedersha has given you something much more valuable: a DIY relationship improvement project for your home. If you are planning on getting married—or even just considering it—this do-it-yourself guide will help get you ready for life after the wedding."

Ron Deal, family author, speaker, and therapist;
bestselling author of *The Smart Stepfamily*
and *Dating and the Single Parent*

"This is a wonderful book about deep conversations to have with yourself, with God, and with your intended. It's written with warmth and insight for Christians and seekers who want to discern the best path for the biggest adventure in life."

Scott Stanley, coauthor of *A Lasting Promise: The Christian
Guide to Fighting for Your Marriage*

"In a culture that worships extravagant weddings but does little to prepare people for actual marriages, Scott Kedersha writes a practical, biblically based book to equip couples for a lifetime of oneness. He is honest about his own failures and victories in marriage, which makes *Ready or Knot?* relatable for today's generation—one that craves authenticity and transparency. It is the book I wish I'd read when I was engaged and a must-read for anyone about to walk down the aisle."

Elizabeth Oates, speaker and author of several books,
including *Mending Broken Branches*

"In *Ready or Knot?* Scott Kedersha provides a relevant, practical, and biblical resource for those who want to prepare well for marriage. He doesn't shy away from potential landmines or difficult topics, which makes this a resource I'll be recommending highly to premarried couples in our church."

Christine Hoover, author of *Searching for Spring*
and *Messy Beautiful Friendship*

"On many a Saturday, I stand before a couple as they commit their earthly lives solely to one another. In most situations there is one significant problem . . . the couple has not talked enough. Plenty of words have been said between them, but they have not truly discussed the details of marriage. *Ready or Knot?* is a gift for these couples, as it gives the framework to have the truly important conversations necessary to prepare for marriage. Don't just read this book. Talk through it—and you will have a better marriage because of it."

Kevin A. Thompson, author of *Friends, Partners, and Lovers* and *Happily*

"*Ready or Knot?* prepares couples to experience high levels of marital satisfaction. Scott delivers great content and touching stories with a pastor's heart. Before you walk down the aisle, read this book. If you don't have plans to walk down the aisle anytime soon, this book paints a beautiful picture of marriage for you."

Ted Cunningham, pastor of Woodland Hills Family Church, Branson, MO; author of *Fun Loving You*

"*Ready or Knot?* is a great resource! Scott does a wonderful job of communicating essential questions that are relevant for couples considering marriage! His practical, thoughtful communication style and insightful questions will definitely help them in this process!"

Doug Goodwin, COO, Kanakuk Ministries

"For the last thirteen years, Scott has been given the unique opportunity to focus on helping premarital couples. Through his ministry at Watermark Community Church, he has worked with thousands of couples. In *Ready or Knot?*, he brilliantly weaves together biblical principles, research, wisdom, expertise, and real-life stories in a way that will leave couples feeling understood, empowered, and known. I highly recommend this book for any couple who wants to start their marriage off right!"

Ted Lowe, director of MarriedPeople.org; author of *Your Best US: Marriage Is Easier Than You Think*

Ready or Knot?

12 Conversations Every Couple
Needs to Have before Marriage

SCOTT KEDERSHA

BakerBooks

a division of Baker Publishing Group
Grand Rapids, Michigan

© 2019 by Scott Kedersha

Published by Baker Books
a division of Baker Publishing Group
PO Box 6287, Grand Rapids, MI 49516-6287
www.bakerbooks.com

Printed in the United States of America

Library of Congress Cataloging-in-Publication Data
Names: Kedersha, Scott, 1973- author.
Title: Ready or knot? : 12 conversations every couple needs to have before marriage / Scott Kedersha.
Description: Grand Rapids, MI : Baker Books, [2019] | Includes bibliographical references.
Identifiers: LCCN 2018027344 | ISBN 9780801077937 (pbk.)
Subjects: LCSH: Marriage—Religious aspects—Christianity.
Classification: LCC BV835 .K43 2018 | DDC 248.4—dc23
LC record available at https://lccn.loc.gov/2018027344

Some names and details have been changed to protect the privacy of the individuals involved.

19 20 21 22 23 24 25   7 6 5

To Kristen

We dated.
We were "knot" ready.
We broke up and fell in love with Jesus.
We dated again, I put a ring on it, you said "Yes!"
(among other things), and we tied the knot.
I love you more.

Contents

Foreword

As a Boy Scout, I never made it past Tenderfoot. The next rank up was underwhelmingly called Second Class. It just didn't seem worth the effort to work toward something as humble as Second Class, so I switched my focus to baseball.

One of the things that held me back was that I was so terrible with knots. I momentarily learned one or two in an attempt to get a merit badge, but I forgot how to retie them fifteen seconds later. Nobody in the entire troop trusted me to tie down the tent we'd be sleeping in. While I knew the names—the slip knot, the trucker's hitch, the bowline, the double fisherman's knot—all my fellow scouts would have chosen a Brownie over this Tenderfoot in order to secure our shelter.

God, on the other hand, excels at knots. He can take the two most diverse substances on this planet—man and woman—and tie them together in a ceremony so that the two become one: "'For this reason a man will leave his father and mother and be united to his wife, and the two will become one flesh.' So they are no longer two, but one flesh" (Matt. 19:5–6).

There's something about such "knot tying" that delights the heart of God. Remember what Jesus did with James and John? A seemingly offhand comment packs a powerful punch when you reflect on what it means. After mentioning James and John, Mark tells us that Jesus "gave [them] the name Boanerges, which means 'sons of thunder'" (Mark 3:17). Jesus gave two brothers, two different people, *one name*. They were something *together* that they weren't individually.

Such unity is so undervalued in our individualistic times that pursuing true unity as a married couple can be a prophetic act of faith. Psalm 133:1 proclaims "How good and pleasant it is when God's people live together in unity," which Jesus emphasized with his famous prayer: "I pray . . . that all of them may be one, Father, just as you are in me and I am in you" (John 17:20–21).

More than marriage is about sex and children, it's about unity. Time-wise, sex takes up less than 1 percent of a married couple's time, and nobody else witnesses it. Unity covers everything the couple does and says, even when they're not together, and everyone can see it. And while you can have a marriage without children, you cannot have a marriage without unity. Christian marriage is a humble, ironclad, surrendered commitment to a God-inspired and God-tied unity.

Scott Kedersha has written the "marital scout's guide" to what knots need to be tied, how to tie them, and, on occasion, when to know that these two strands of rope should actually *not* be tied together (or at least not yet) in order to achieve such unity. He's even thrown in the occasional illustration to teach you how to tie the knots of conflict resolution, communication, finances, friendship, extended family dynamics, sexual intimacy, and spiritual intimacy.

Don't skip a step. I know from past experience that skipping a step can make your knot look like a tangled phone cord by the time you're through. To get the most out of this manual, pray for God's enlightenment, surrender to His words, and pursue His agenda and design for marriage (which Scott so ably captures here) and you'll experience the true blessing and miracle of being tied into an indissoluble knot whose craftsman is none other than God Himself.

Few experiences on earth match the beauty, wonder, and fulfillment of an intimately connected marriage. *Ready or Knot?* will show you how such a knot is tied.

Gary Thomas,
author of *Sacred Marriage* and *Cherish*

The Best $20 You Will Spend on Your Relationship

September 15, 2001, was one of the greatest days of my life. It was the day Kristen and I became husband and wife. Four days after the tragedy of 9/11, our wedding ceremony provided some good news in a week when we all needed something to smile about.

I still remember almost every detail about that day. The white pews in the chapel of Peachtree Presbyterian Church in Atlanta were decorated with purple, red, and maroon flowers. The candles on the groom's side looked as if they were about to fall over. I felt goose bumps rising on my arms as our friend Todd played "You Are Awesome in This Place" on his guitar.

Then I straightened my tuxedo and nervously walked with my groomsmen to our designated spot at the front of the sanctuary. My best man, my brother Chris, stood by my side. Turning to face the pews, I was grateful to see our friends and family who had gathered to celebrate our marriage and lavish us with love on our wedding day.

After what seemed like an eternity, the organ finally began to play the first few familiar notes of the wedding march—and the large wooden doors opened to reveal my stunning bride. I remember being awestruck by Kristen's beauty as she walked down the aisle to marry me. I admired her splendor and poise and grace. I wasn't able to restrain my tears of joy as the love of my life joined me to exchange our marriage vows.

Why This Book?

I love a good wedding. I still get a little choked up every time I see a father walking his daughter down the aisle to meet her adoring groom. She usually holds it together while the groom can't restrain his tears. I enjoy the conversations, the food, the dancing—and of course, the wedding cake! I've been to morning weddings, evening weddings, indoor weddings, outdoor weddings in the 100-degree Texas heat, and even a wedding on the eighteenth hole of a prestigious golf course! One of my favorite parts of my job as a marriage pastor is getting to attend and officiate so many weddings.

But the best weddings are the ones when I'm excited and hopeful for the bride and groom. We've all been to weddings when we're anxious about the couple's future. I don't want that to be your story. I want you to be ready to tie the knot! When you share your vows and say "Till death do us part," I want you to know what and who you are committing to.

Lately, I've noticed many couples spend more time planning their wedding than preparing for their marriage. The pressure to have an amazing wedding has increased significantly since Kristen and I said "I do." Today, many engaged couples spend hours and hours looking through bridal magazines and websites, poring over details and pinning images that tend to pull the focus off the marriage and onto the wedding day. Because our society, and even our churches, put a lot of pressure on couples to have a beautiful wedding, far too many couples slide by important conversations and questions that beg to be asked.

Don't misunderstand me: there is nothing wrong with having a great wedding—unless it's at the expense of a great marriage.

In 2017, the average price of a wedding in America landed at a whopping $25,764.[1] This average cost doesn't even include some of the extraneous expenses such as the rehearsal dinner and honeymoon.

In contrast, the book you're holding probably cost you, at most, twenty bucks. I wrote *Ready or Knot?* to help seriously dating and engaged couples take the best next step in your relationship. Whether you are considering marriage for the first time or thinking through the realities of remarriage, reading this book can be the best investment you will make in your relationship.

Let's be honest: no one plans to end up divorced or stuck in a lifeless marriage. Every couple comes into marriage with the best of intentions. Yet we continually see couples, both inside and outside the church, whose marriages end in divorce or misery.

This book guides you through twelve essential conversations you need to have with your significant other before you tie the knot, including ones you've been avoiding and some you probably didn't even know you should have. When you and your future spouse take the time to talk through each of these issues honestly and thoughtfully, you will be well prepared for a healthy, successful marriage.

Who Is Scott Kedersha, and Why Should I Care What He Says?

Since 2006, I have served as a marriage pastor at Watermark Community Church in Dallas, Texas. I love my job and am grateful that I get to help couples prepare for and start their marriages well.

During the past thirteen years, I've helped lead thousands of seriously dating and engaged couples, and I've officiated close to one hundred weddings. I've served alongside couples with successful marriages, and I've counseled struggling couples who wish they had never gotten married in the first place. Along the way, I have learned countless lessons about dating, relationships, and marriage that I want to pass on to you.

How Will This Book Help You?

Before I tell you how to prepare for marriage, we need to talk about traffic lights. Imagine driving your car and approaching a traffic light. Based on the color of the light, you either move forward (green), slow down (yellow), or stop (red). The light is designed for your safety and lets you know the best next step.

After reading *Ready or Knot?* you should know whether the status of your premarried relationship is green, yellow, or red.

- Most of you will come to a green light. You will realize you are ready to tie the knot as you move forward, confirmed in your decision to get married.
- Some of you will come to a yellow light. You might decide to tap the brakes on your relationship. You will know what questions need to be answered and what issues need to be resolved before the two of you move forward. You are not ready to break up, but you're also not ready to tie the knot until you make some changes.
- Others will come to a red light. After you and your significant other have the essential conversations described in this book, you will realize that the best decision you can make is to break up and go your separate ways.

What You'll Find in This Book

Each chapter of *Ready or Knot?* features the inspiring story of a real couple, combined with God's view of marriage from the Bible. These stories take an honest look at challenges faced by couples just like you, whose marriages have been transformed by applying the biblical truths you are about to discover.

As you read this book, you'll see what makes successful couples stick out from those whose marriages ultimately fail. You will find answers to many of your questions and learn things like how to deal with each other's differences, how to love difficult in-laws, and how to share the less glamorous parts of your past. Most importantly, you will learn about the gift of marriage and the One who created and designed this gift.

In every chapter, you will find a Knot-Tying Tip with practical ideas to help you strengthen your relationship. At the end of each chapter, look for the following three sections:

- **Am I Ready?** These questions are intended for individual reflection. They give you the opportunity to think through and personalize what you have learned so you can walk away with a better handle on the topic and your relationship.
- **Strengthening Our Knot.** These questions are designed to be discussed with your significant other. Share your individual responses to the Am I Ready? questions and then spend some time talking through the Strengthening Our Knot questions together.
- **Closing Prayer.** Each chapter includes a short prayer for you and your significant other to pray together as you finish the chapter and discussion.

James 1:5 says, "If any of you lacks wisdom, you should ask God, who gives generously to all without finding fault, and it will be given to you." As followers of Christ, we need to humbly admit when we need help and then seek God's wisdom. As a couple getting ready for engagement or marriage, you and your future spouse will need all the help, guidance, and wisdom you can get!

What's the Best Way to Read This Book?

The information in this book is helpful on its own, but you would be wise to read it alongside someone who can help you prepare for marriage. I encourage you and your significant other to read *Ready or Knot?* with a married mentor couple you love and respect.

I'm proud of you for taking the time to prepare for marriage. I have prayed, many times, for you as you read this book. I want you and your significant other to pursue each other in the best possible way as you prepare for engagement and marriage. If you are humble, open, and teachable, then it will go well for you.

Ready or knot, here we go!

Am I Ready?

- What do you hope to get out of reading *Ready or Knot?* Of all the relationship books out there, why did you choose to read this book?
- What are you most excited about in your relationship? What are some of your concerns about yourself, your significant other, or marriage in general?
- How would you define a successful marriage?
- Who do you know who has a successful marriage? What specific things do you admire about their relationship?

Strengthening Our Knot

- Discuss your answers to the Am I Ready? questions about your excitement and/or your fears and concerns about your relationship.
- How do you think that you, as a couple, will get the most out of reading this book?

- Write down the names of some couples you might ask to help you talk through this book. Then make a plan to contact at least one couple this week and schedule a time to meet together.

Closing Prayer

Lord, we need Your help as we process next steps together as a couple. Please grant us the wisdom to discern how You are leading us as a couple. Help us to be honest, open, teachable, and pure as we prepare for whatever You have planned for us in our relationship. Thank You for the gift of marriage and for Your perfect design for relationships. We need You. In the name of Your Son, Jesus, we pray. Amen.

1

What Is the Point of Marriage Anyway?

Why "You Complete Me" Is a Big, Fat Lie

"Happily ever after" did not turn out the way they thought it would.

Dan and Tracy had been married for twenty-five years, and they hated each other. One night they started throwing things at each other—pillows, coasters, and whatever else they could get their hands on. She even took her favorite marriage book and tossed it into the fireplace. The pages of *Sacred Marriage* burned up in the fire along with all their dreams for the future.[1]

Yet twenty-five years earlier, Dan and Tracy had been so in love. They couldn't wait to tie the knot! What happened?

Dan: We met in 1983 at a Campus Crusade for Christ meeting, when one of my roommates brought Tracy to a campus event.

Tracy: He stuck his name tag on my back, and the flirting began. A few days later, dressed in all black, I doorbell-ditched his house and left him a plate of cookies.

Dan: She was beautiful, smart, and everything I had dreamed about in a wife. She laughed at my jokes and played the piano. She only knew one song, but she knew it well! When I heard her play, I dreamed of the days our future family would spend singing around the piano.

They started dating and got engaged. Tracy and Dan met one time with the pastor who would marry them, and he warned them that they, like all other couples, would argue about in-laws and money. They decided they did not need further counsel. After all, they loved each other.

Unfortunately, things didn't go like they imagined.

They never dreamed that someday their daughters would catch Tracy in the middle of an affair. Neither did they dream that Dan would confess to his own affair. They never imagined that their evenings would consist of yelling, arguing, and blaming, followed by lonely nights in separate bedrooms.

When they walked down the aisle, Dan and Tracy envisioned the American dream of marriage, 2.5 kids, a dog, and a home with a white picket fence. Neither of them thought much about their past hurts, habits, or families of origin.

Dan: I really didn't know the woman I was marrying, and Tracy didn't know me. I didn't know about her sexual abuse. She didn't know about the alcoholism in my family, my passive dad, or that I had no idea how

24

to be a husband. We dragged our messed-up past into marriage and had no clue how to deal with it.

Tracy: We also learned not to call 911 to stop a big fight when we were naked. It turned out the police were right around the corner. I had no idea they could arrive so quickly!

What went wrong? And how can you prevent a heart-breaking journey like theirs?

There's nothing wrong with wanting a few kids, a comfortable home, and a happy life together. What this well-meaning couple lacked—and what so many other couples miss before getting married—is a deeper understanding of marriage and the commitment necessary when a husband and wife say "I do."

Dan and Tracy didn't have parents who modeled a godly marriage. They never saw their parents open up God's Word and live out the truths of the Bible. Dan's father had cheated on his mom, and Tracy followed the unhealthy patterns she saw modeled in her parents' home. They simply continued the cycle.

Why Start with Bad News?

This might seem like a depressing place for a premarried book to start, but before you can fully grasp the good news of marriage—and believe me, there is good news—you must understand the whole picture. Your view of marriage will affect how you walk through every part of married life.

Let's get back to Dan and Tracy.

Dan: We got pregnant five months into marriage, and for the next twenty years, we threw ourselves into parenting, careers, and playing pretend at church week after week. Even though everything looked good on the outside, our marriage was rotting from the inside out. Without authentic friendships, an abiding faith in Christ, or any spark in our relationship, I looked for satisfaction in the wrong places.

Tracy: After twenty-three years of marriage, I decided it was time to get what I thought I deserved. I was done with our boring life and started looking for satisfaction outside of Jesus and outside my marriage. I threw myself headfirst into working out and started caring a whole lot more about what I looked like than I cared for my husband. One day I made eye contact with another guy in the gym, and before long it turned into flirting, an emotional affair, and then a full-blown affair.

Dan: I knew our marriage lacked physical, spiritual, and emotional intimacy. I wasn't caring for Tracy and soon followed in the footsteps of my father by having an affair of my own. Things weren't great at home, and I thought I deserved to get what I wanted, so I pursued intimacy with someone who wasn't my wife.

After two decades of marriage, Dan and Tracy had become roommates. No more flirting. No more songs around the piano. Their kids were grown, and all they had was a shell of a marriage. They were isolated, bored, and looked elsewhere for their satisfaction.

They forgot what it meant to be married.

What Is Marriage?

There is a lot of confusion and misunderstanding in our world about marriage. For example, I've heard the following questions from couples thinking about marriage:

- Is marriage temporary?
- Is marriage the same as cohabitation?
- Most couples I know seem pretty miserable, so is this what I should expect?
- Can't marriage be like a contract you sign for a few years and then decide to either re-up or move on with someone different?[2]

We need to look at God's Word to answer these questions. From cover to cover, the Bible addresses relationships—God's relationship with humanity, family relationships, friendships, and much more. While the Bible doesn't address every facet of marriage, it does give us a firm foundation for the most important aspects of marriage.

Marriage Is Created by God

From the beginning, the Bible shows us that God created and designed marriage. After God brought Eve to Adam in the Garden of Eden, Scripture says, "That is why a man leaves his father and mother and is united to his wife, and they become one flesh. Adam and his wife were both naked, and they felt no shame" (Gen. 2:24–25). Ephesians 5:21–33 gives further explanation of God's purpose and design for marriage (more on that in chapter 6).

God is worthy of our trust, and He didn't make a mistake when He created the marriage relationship. God's Word provides the final word about marriage, but too often couples choose to follow their own design and purpose of marriage.

Marriage Is a One-Flesh Relationship

In Matthew 19:5–6, Jesus said, "'For this reason a man will leave his father and mother and be united to his wife, and the two will become one flesh.'. . . So they are no longer two, but one flesh." What does it mean for marriage to be a one-flesh relationship?

Oneness is emotional. Adam and Eve were fully naked and felt no shame around each other (Gen. 2:25). There is a level of emotional intimacy exclusively intended for marriage (more on this in chapter 7).

Oneness is physical. The man and woman were naked in the Garden of Eden, and they enjoyed the benefits of nakedness. They didn't need a talk about the birds and bees. They didn't need pornography to show them what to do. The man woke up from a deep sleep and realized God had given him a great gift: a woman with no clothes. They became one flesh and enjoyed the fruits of sex and physical intimacy. This is huge! When you understand the physical nature of oneness, you realize that in the marriage relationship, sex is not dirty, wrong, or sinful. God created physical oneness for us to enjoy in marriage (more on this in chapter 8).

Marriage Is Permanent

God intends marriage to be a permanent, lifelong relationship. In Matthew 19:6, Jesus said, "Therefore what God has joined together, let no one separate."

We often have to fight against a common perception in culture and even in the church that the marriage relationship can be temporary. Yet the Bible clearly teaches that God intends marriage to be a permanent relationship, separated only by death.

Marriage Is Mysterious

Something significant, supernatural, and mysterious takes place when a man and woman become husband and wife. The apostle Paul said in Ephesians 5:31–32, "'For this reason a man will leave his father and mother and be united to his wife, and the two will become one flesh.' This is a profound mystery—but I am talking about Christ and the church."

A wedding is not just a ceremony and then cake and a honeymoon. In marriage, a man and a woman leave their families (more on this in chapter 9). And then, in some mysterious way, God makes their marriage a permanent relationship that reflects Christ's relationship with the church.

Marriage Is Companionship

In Genesis 2:18, God said, "It is not good for the man to be alone. I will make a helper suitable for him." Marriage is designed to fill our human need for companionship.

Your spouse should be your closest and best friend. Friendship and companionship may be the most underdiscussed and undervalued aspect of marriage (more on this in chapter 10).

This companionship is enhanced when you and your spouse strengthen relationships with friends who can provide both of you with counsel and biblical community (more on this in chapter 11).

Marriage Is an Opportunity to Multiply and Fill the Earth

In Genesis 1:27–28, God blessed Adam and Eve and then commanded them, "Be fruitful and increase in number; fill the earth and subdue it."

Of course, you don't have to be married to have children, and certainly not every married couple is required to have kids. But the Bible teaches that God's ideal way to "be fruitful and increase in number" is by having and parenting children within a marriage relationship (more on this in chapter 12).

Marriage Is a Covenant Relationship

Some couples think marriage is a limited, conditional contract where either spouse can exit the marriage when these conditions aren't met. Some denominations believe marriage is a sacrament where God mystically dispenses divine grace upon the husband and wife. In my faith tradition, marriage is viewed as an unbreakable, unconditional covenant relationship.[3] A covenant view of marriage is built upon a foundation of trust and provides the greatest opportunity for safety and intimacy in marriage.

I believe the Bible teaches that the unconditional, unbreakable covenant relationship of marriage is similar in many ways to God's covenant relationship with His children (Mal. 2:14; Ezek. 16:8; Gen. 2:18–25).

Learn What Marriage Is Not

God did not create marriage to make you happy. In his excellent book *Sacred Marriage*, Gary Thomas writes, "What if God designed marriage to make us holy more than to make us happy?"[4] Anytime you look to marriage to make you happy or to satisfy you fully, you will be disappointed.

One of my favorite movies when I was in my twenties was *Jerry Maguire*, starring Tom Cruise as Maguire and Renee Zellweger as single mom Dorothy Boyd. In one of the more famous scenes from the movie, after talking about the complex and cynical nature of the world, Jerry expresses his true feelings for Dorothy. He looks across the room and says three dramatic words: "You complete me."

That scene gets me every time. It makes for a powerful, albeit cheesy, dramatic moment. But the theology is terrible, and it sets up the viewer for false expectations. No human relationship will ever fulfill you, bring you ultimate happiness, or complete you.

Happiness might be the by-product of a godly marriage, but God never promised that marriage will make you happy. When the going gets tough, it's easy to think you married the wrong person or that an affair will make things better. Some turn to alcohol, gambling, work, hobbies, or even their own children to find happiness. But only Jesus Christ will satisfy you.

So before you think your significant other will fulfill you or make you happy, think again. Find your ultimate satisfaction in a relationship with Jesus.

Marriage Provides a Picture of God's Love for the Church

Your marriage communicates a message. In Ephesians 5:21–33, the apostle Paul describes how a healthy marriage relationship illustrates Christ's relationship with the church (more on this in chapter 6).

Putting all the above aspects of marriage together leads to the following definition: *marriage is designed by God to be a lifelong, covenant relationship between one man and one woman that gives a picture of Christ's loving relationship with His bride, the church.*[5]

Why a Bible-Based Understanding of Marriage Is Important

Your understanding of marriage will determine how you respond when your spouse disappoints you. When you want to quit and move on, you have to deal with the fact that marriage is permanent. When you want to stop working on your marriage, you need to remember that your marriage is a picture of Christ's love for the church. Just as Jesus's love for you doesn't end, so your love for your spouse shouldn't end either.

If you don't have a biblical view of marriage, then you will seek a way out as soon as your spouse disappoints you. You *will* have unmet expectations—every couple does. Your spouse will let you down, and you will let your spouse down. When it happens, your foundational view of marriage will impact the actions you take and the way you respond.

Fortunately, God's love for us is not dependent on our actions. Your commitment to your spouse shouldn't be either.

The Rest of the Story

Despite all the pain in their relationship, Dan and Tracy didn't want a divorce. But they knew their marriage couldn't remain in its current state. They decided they needed help.

They started to do some hard work on their marriage and heart work in their own lives. They invited others into their mess and started the healing process of confession, grief, forgiveness, and reconciliation. They met with a professional Christian counselor, went to a marriage recovery ministry called re|engage, studied their Bibles, and read marriage books together.[6]

> **Dan:** Even with our problems, from the beginning, we said divorce was never an option. I encourage all couples to make this decision before you say "I do." If you're not in alignment on this one, then you're not ready to get married.

> **Tracy:** Whenever we talk with premarried couples, we tell them to do all the hard work they can before marriage so they understand what they are getting into when they decide to tie the knot.

Today, Dan and Tracy have one of the most exciting, life-giving marriages I've ever seen. They have fun and serve the Lord together.

Not long ago, Tracy, Dan, and their daughters flew to Hawaii to celebrate their thirty-year anniversary, where Dan and Tracy renewed their marriage vows. Their daughters read from Ephesians 5:22–33 and Colossians 3:12–17 and celebrated with their parents. This time Dan and Tracy understood what they were getting into as they said "I do, again."

Am I Ready?

- Do you tend to think of marriage as a temporary, conditional contract you can get out of if you become unhappy or unsatisfied? Or do you see marriage as a permanent, unconditional covenant designed by God, intended to mirror His love for us? Why did you answer this way?

- What did you grow up believing about marriage? How did your parent(s) model for or teach you what marriage should or shouldn't look like?
- If you commit to marriage, what could your spouse do that would lead you to seek a divorce? Read Malachi 2:16. What does this verse say about God's attitude toward divorce?
- What did you learn in this chapter about what God's Word says about marriage?
- What encourages you the most about Dan and Tracy's story?

Strengthening Our Knot

- Discuss your answers to the Am I Ready? questions about the meaning of marriage.
- What would you do if you found yourself in a similar situation to Dan and Tracy? Would you agree to move forward together and heal your marriage, or would you look for a way out? Who would you call to help you process your next steps?
- Review the aspects of marriage listed in this chapter and discuss each one with your significant other. What excites you and what concerns you about marriage?

Closing Prayer

Lord, thank You for offering us a relationship with Yourself through Your Son, Jesus. We are grateful for the incredible gift of marriage and for our dating relationship. Please help us understand the nature of Your relationship with us and the meaning of marriage. Thank You for Your sacrificial, unconditional, selfless love, and help us model this same type of love for each other if we get married. Help us avoid any dangers that could lead to isolation or divorce. Thank You for Your endless love for us. In the name of Your Son, Jesus, we pray. Amen.

2

Are We Looking to Win or Seeking to Understand?

The Most Important Skill You Need in Your Relationship

Sometimes I don't want to talk to or listen to my wife. Even though we've been married since 2001 and I've served as a marriage pastor since 2006, I admit I sometimes strongly dislike communicating and resolving disagreements with Kristen.

The reality is, most married couples don't love to communicate or resolve conflict. We're not good at it, it's rarely modeled well, and it takes so much time and effort to do it with success. Our selfish desires get in the way, and most of the time we are radically different from our spouse in the ways we prefer to communicate and resolve disagreements. All our lives we're taught to win, defend, and prove our point. We often do this by speaking more than the other person, by talking in a raised voice, or by becoming master debaters and crushing our opponent. These tactics might work in a debate, argument, or sporting event, but they won't work in a marriage relationship. If you act like this with your spouse, you will end up with a mess of a marriage. You and your spouse won't truly know each other, and you'll end up resenting the person you are intended to love most.

What if things could be different? What if the two of you were able to engage in awkward and difficult conversations, which are inevitable in any relationship, and come out of them better off and closer than ever? Imagine learning to value understanding each other rather than winning. Marriage calls for a different type of communication, where if one person "wins" an argument, then no winner truly exists.

Next to your decision of whether or not to follow Christ and trust Him as your Lord and Savior, how you communicate and resolve conflict will play the biggest role in determining the strength and health of your relationship.[1] If you can't communicate, then the rest of this book will not benefit you.

To help you determine if you and your significant other are ready for marriage, you need alignment in your views about effective communication and conflict resolution.[2]

Meet Jason and Kelly

To help us navigate this topic well, let's turn to a couple with one of the strongest and most intentional marriages I've ever seen. Jason and Kelly tied the knot in 1995 and have served and led in marriage ministry in the church since 2002.

Jason: The first five years of our marriage were good. But once we learned how to communicate and engage in healthy conflict, our marriage went from good to great. Everything changed when we realized we could discuss any and every topic. Nothing was off-limits for us as a couple. We started to talk about our sexual desires, dreams for the future, and hopes to better parent our kids.

Kelly: We watched many other couples struggle, and we knew we didn't want to end up like everyone else. So we started to admit areas of insecurity, talk about our sin struggles, and grow in emotional intimacy. We learned the value of humility and forgiveness and communicated in a way that allowed us to move toward oneness instead of running away from each other.

Jason: The turning point for us came when Kelly's parents wanted to come visit us for the weekend. I was in the middle of an extremely busy season with work and travel, all while trying to raise two little kids.

Kelly: Jason's parents were in town the prior weekend, so when my parents wanted to visit, I thought it was a great idea. We'd get to see my family, and I knew we'd get a date night since they could watch our kids. When Jason told me he didn't want my parents to visit, I immediately assumed he didn't like my family. Why was it okay for his family to visit but not mine?

Jason: I remember telling Kelly I didn't want her parents to visit, but I never gave any explanation or other options. I got frustrated and couldn't understand why she couldn't see why I was right and she was wrong!

Kelly: Later that night, Jason apologized to me and asked for forgiveness for being short with me. We slowed down and allowed each other to share our thoughts. This argument helped us realize the importance of listening, asking good questions, and humility.

When Jason and Kelly learned to communicate and resolve conflict in a biblical, God-honoring way, they started to attain the marriage God intends for us each to have and the marriage about which they dreamed and hoped.

Jason: Outside of intimacy with Jesus, nothing will help you improve your relationship more than how well you communicate and resolve conflict.

Kelly: Communication is both a way to connect as a couple and a way to resolve issues you need to discuss. Marriage is not just long talks on the sofa or hours and hours of sex. Yes, both of these should be a part of marriage, but so much more of your relationship will be the day-to-day communication with your spouse to discuss things such as meals, money, and what God is teaching you.

In other words, if you're following Christ and can communicate and resolve conflict, then you will do well in marriage.

Healthy Marriages Require Healthy Communication

If you get married, you'll soon realize that you and your spouse will need to talk about many important topics every day. You each bring different styles of communication into the relationship, and you'll need to make decisions about crucial topics such as money, sex, spiritual intimacy, and kids. If the two of you can't communicate and resolve conflict related to these areas of marriage, then you will always be stuck.

Your Spouse Will Help You Grow

You will look to your spouse for feedback and advice in every part of life. They will give you feedback on the clothes you wear, how you parent, your tone when you communicate with others, and much more.

> **Jason:** Kelly sees deficits in my life and communicates those to me. She'll help me see when I'm harsh in my tone or when I don't listen. I think I'm doing great until she encourages me to speak with more gentleness and to pay better attention.

Healthy skills related to communication and conflict allow you to be authentic with each other. In marriage, the husband and wife are "one flesh" (Gen. 2:24), which compels them to be 100 percent open and real with each other (more on this when we discuss emotional intimacy in chapter 7). If you and your spouse can't communicate with each other, then you will never experience oneness as God intends.

Create a Safe Place for Your Spouse

Since your spouse will help you grow in areas where you need help, you need to create a safe space. You and your significant other need to build safety in your relationship so you can talk freely about the big and little things in life.

For example, I've struggled with my weight and health for as far back as I can remember. As a young boy, swallowing was painful for me. The doctor told my parents my tonsils were swollen and had to be removed. Once they removed my tonsils, my difficulty with eating stopped. Now I face a different kind of eating problem. Kristen knows my weight and health issues impact my life in a negative way. Because of this, I've asked her to help me keep accountable and make good decisions when we go out to eat.

An unsafe marriage when it comes to communication might look like this:

Kristen: How about if we go eat at SuperChix (a restaurant near our house) tonight?

Scott: That sounds great, but please make sure I order the salad with dressing on the side and no tortilla chips.

At the restaurant:

Scott: I'll have the fried avocado sandwich, black rosemary pepper fries, and a large custard.

Kristen: I thought you were going to get the salad.

Scott: Leave me alone. I'm a big boy and can make my own decisions. I'm paying, and you're not my mom, so back off!

While I exaggerate for the sake of creating an example, the above scenario is not too big of a stretch. When I speak with a defensive posture after I ask my wife to help me, I'm not creating a safe place for communication and conflict resolution in marriage.

Five Nonnegotiables of Communication and Conflict Resolution

How can you communicate in a healthy way, help your spouse grow, and create a safe environment in your relationship for communication and conflict resolution? Many books present great tips and tricks on how to talk and fight well. I don't want to offer you worldly wisdom. Each of these five essential components of healthy communication and conflict resolution comes directly from God's Word.

1. Seek to Understand, Not Win

Perhaps no verse better captures both the problems and opportunities in communication and conflict resolution than Proverbs 18:2, which says, "Fools find no pleasure in understanding but delight in airing their own opinions."

The book of Proverbs often speaks about the actions, behaviors, words, and patterns of a foolish person.[3] When it comes to communication, the foolish person wants to win every argument and always expresses their opinion. On the other hand, the wise person chooses to understand and put the thoughts, feelings, and desires of their spouse before themselves.

The couple who seeks to understand each other knows that effective communication takes effort. We work hard in just about every other aspect of our lives. If we want to run a marathon, we train by getting up early and running in the mornings and on the weekends. If we want to improve in our jobs, we take classes and read books. In marriage, if we want to grow and move toward our spouse, we also must work hard. We need to be intentional to understand and communicate with our significant other.

The chart below contrasts the foolish person with the wise one. Which will you be?

The Foolish Person	The Wise Person
Expresses their opinion before listening	Listens and seeks mutual understanding
Is quick to speak	Is slow to speak
Is slow to listen	Is quick to listen
Is quick to get angry	Is slow to anger
Seeks to win	Desires to serve
Knows the right way but doesn't care	Knows the right way and chooses it
Gives an answer before they hear	Listens before they speak

Often, we'd rather be right and win than seek to understand. We miss the goal of mutual understanding and therefore choose not to communicate with our significant other.

2. Learn to Communicate and Resolve Conflict in a Selfless Way

In 2004, Kristen gave birth to our twin boys, Duncan and Drew. I was a graduate student, and Kristen was the breadwinner of the family. When Kristen had the twins, we lost our primary source of income. I worked as a part-time physical therapist, took classes as a full-time seminary student, and served part-time as an intern at our church. This was an extremely challenging season for our family.

To make things worse, one of our babies was colicky. This meant he cried all the time. It didn't matter what you did, Drew cried. We joke that we don't know how Duncan survived this season because Drew demanded all our time and attention. This made a challenging season of life even more stressful.

One day, when the twins were around four months old, Kristen and I got into an argument. To this day, neither of us has any clue what we argued about. It started with a little bickering, but before you know it, we were yelling at each other. The level and intensity of the jabs became louder and more personal, and the yelling culminated with me banging my hands on the counter, repeatedly screaming, "My life is over! My life is over! My life is over!"

See what I did there? This argument over who knows what became an example of how everything was ruined in *my* life. It didn't matter that our four-month-old baby was in constant pain. It didn't matter that Kristen hadn't slept in months, always had one or two babies attached to her, or struggled with real fears and concerns about our kids and the mess of our lives. It became all about me.

We fought because I was selfish. I *am* selfish. I'm the most selfish person I know.

And you're selfish too. You may not think so, but you are. Just ask your significant other, friends, coworkers, or parents.

The conclusion to my shining star selfish moment? Kristen set crying baby Drew down in the crib, ran across the room, and jumped on my back. For those of you who know Kristen and me, you realize she is a whole lot smaller than I am. The scene probably looked like a fly trying to knock over a gorilla. I did what any godly husband would do at that moment: I laughed at my wife. In retrospect, this might not have been the best decision. But we both laugh now at our classic selfish fight.

While we don't deal with crying infants in our home any-more, my selfishness still screams out every day. The cause is usually food, lust, anger, impatience, pride, insecurity, and much more. In marriage and relationships, selfishness swoops in and tries to break down the marriage and destroy God's picture of intimacy and oneness.

I'm sure you can think of many examples of how you and your significant other are selfish. Our culture has a very low threshold for pain, and when the going gets rough, we want out. But getting out is not the solution.

Fortunately, God's Word provides the solution. The book of James, written by Jesus's brother, is filled with practical wisdom. It points to the fact that our lives as followers of Jesus should align with the ways we think, the decisions we make, and the way we live.

James 4:1 says, "What causes fights and quarrels among you? Don't they come from your desires that battle within you?" We fight because we want something, and our passions and desires rule over and control us. While we try to blame our significant other or the circumstances around us, the real reason we fight is because our selfish desires wage war within us. If you are going to succeed in your marriage, then you are going to have to deal with your selfishness. That's why James goes on to say, "'God opposes the proud but shows favor to the humble.' . . . Humble yourselves before the Lord, and he will lift you up" (vv. 6, 10).

In Philippians 2:2–5, the apostle Paul instructs us to be "like-minded, having the same love, being one in spirit and of one mind. Do nothing out of selfish ambition or vain conceit. Rather, in humility value others above yourselves, not look-ing to your own interests but each of you to the interests of the others. In your relationships with one another, have the same mindset as Christ Jesus."

So what should we do whenever we have a conflict or difference of opinion with our significant other? The Bible is clear: act like Jesus. Humble yourself in your relationship with the Lord and toward your spouse. Put the needs of the other before yourself. This is definitely easier said than done, but the only way to overcome our selfish desires is to humble ourselves and become more like Jesus.

3. Be Quick to Listen

James 1:19 says, "Everyone should be quick to listen, slow to speak and slow to become angry." This verse is simple to understand but much more complicated to apply. Most of us want to get our point across and win instead of stopping to listen to our spouse.

Choose to listen. It's a lot easier for me to run my mouth than it is to listen to someone else. Most of the time when I'm supposed to be listening, I'm actually thinking through how I'm going to respond whenever the other person stops talking. We need to pray and apply Psalm 141:3: "Set a guard over my mouth, LORD; keep watch over the door of my lips." At times, we just need to shut our mouths. We can pray for the Lord to keep watch over what and how much we say.

Learn to be an active listener. When you slow down and listen to what the other person says without arguing, being defensive, or thinking through your rebuttal, you serve the other person by choosing to understand. When we listen, we act like Christ, who put the needs of others before Himself.

In most cases, one individual in the relationship tends to use more words than the other. If your significant other uses more words, then you can serve them by giving more details. On the other hand, if you're the one who tends to use more words, you can serve your significant other by giving them highlights instead of details. This is how the gospel plays out in marriage. Whenever we put the needs of the other before our own, we exemplify Christlike behavior.

Pay attention to your nonverbal communication. It's been said that *what* you say makes an impact 20 percent of the time. On the other hand, *how* you say it makes 80 percent of the difference. In other words, your nonverbal behavior plays a large role in your relationship and the ways you communicate and resolve conflict. We often can't hear our tone. While we think we are speaking with gentleness, our significant other might hear defensiveness, anger, or pride.

Think about your posture, your hands, and your facial expression. One of my friends has a listening face that looks as if he is mad. In reality, it's just the face he makes when he's concentrating or trying to pay attention. Pay attention to your body language and facial expressions whenever you talk or listen to your significant other.

4. Change the Way You View Conflict

Most of us do whatever we can to steer clear of awkward and challenging conversations. We pretend issues don't exist, or we brush them under the rug to run away from conflict.

Instead, you and your future spouse can be intentional about growing in your ability to communicate and resolve conflict. Couples who do well in marriage view conflict resolution as an opportunity for growth with God and with each other. When you handle conflict in a biblical way, as Jason and Kelly did when her parents wanted to visit, conflict resolution can and should draw you closer together. Disagreements can become a means to help you become more like Jesus and develop oneness in your relationship.

5. Become an Expert in Forgiveness

No relationship will provide you with more opportunities to seek or grant forgiveness than marriage. For this reason, you need to become an expert in seeking and granting forgiveness.

Get really good at apologizing and asking for forgiveness. Be specific in your apologies. Saying "I'm sorry for whatever I did" is not helpful. Rather, get specific and say, "I'm sorry I snapped at you yesterday at lunch. I was prideful and defensive, and I don't want that pattern in our relationship. Will you forgive me for my pride and defensiveness?"

Be a good forgiver. If you're a follower of Christ, then you know we live as forgiven people. Read the parable of the unmerciful servant in Matthew 18:21–35. Live out Ephesians 4:32: "Be kind and compassionate to one another, forgiving each other, just as in Christ God forgave you." We forgive because we are forgiven people.

If your future spouse never asks for forgiveness, you need to move on. People who don't seek or grant forgiveness don't make good spouses. You remember the relationship traffic light? This one is a red light.

A few years into our marriage, Kristen and I developed a sincere belief that God created marriage for oneness. We learned that when we have a difference of opinion or a conflict of some kind, it's not about being right or winning but rather about us being one flesh together. When one of us

How Does Technology Affect Communication and Conflict Resolution?

While many advantages certainly come with technology, we need to learn to turn away from our smartphone, computer, tablet, and television. In spite of the great communication benefits of technology, they can also be a barrier to oneness and growth in communication.

Quit constantly checking Instagram, Facebook, and sports scores. I'm not saying you need to delete all social media and sports apps off your phone, but don't let them dominate your life. When you talk face-to-face instead of with a device in your hand, you communicate to your significant other you care about what they say and how they're saying it.

One of the downsides to our obsession with our phones is we're losing the ability to communicate spontaneously. Most of our thoughts are premeditated and calculated instead of on the fly. While this might prevent you from saying something you'll later regret, it also changes the dynamic of your relationship. Marriage involves a great deal of face-to-face time. Put down the phone and communicate in person.

When we don't look the other person in the eye or when we speak to them with our eyes on our phones, we communicate indifference. Even if you *say* the right thing, if you're not looking at your significant other with your full attention, you diminish who they are to you and the importance of what the two of you are talking about.

Embrace the positive benefits of your phone and technology:

- Text messages allow for quick, transactional conversations, such as, "Can you pick up dinner on the way home?" "I'm going to the gym after work—see you around 6:15."
- You can send quick "I love you!" messages or emojis that communicate your love and care for your significant other.
- Take advantage of the "Do Not Disturb" feature on your phone. Or, if you're prone to check your phone while you're out on a date, give your phone to your significant other so you're not tempted.

wins an argument in marriage, we really hurt ourselves. We learned it's no longer "you" or "me" but rather "us."

In marriage, we've got to be careful of the words we use with the person we love. Know that you will be deeply affected by the words and tone your spouse will use, and they will be impacted by the words and tone you use.

What If You Rarely Struggle with Communication and Conflict?

Not all couples are created equal. Depending on the personality and temperament of you and your significant other, you might not be apt to struggle in this area as much as other couples. For instance, Kristen and I both tend to be laidback. We don't have polarizing opinions about many topics, and we tend to resolve conflict quickly. But we have several sets of married friends who seem to argue about everything. It's not that they don't love Jesus or have a great marriage; they just have strong opinions.

You might be one of those couples who have it a little easier than others. If that's the case, be grateful. However, make sure the absence of arguments isn't because you stuff your thoughts and opinions or give in because you'd rather avoid conflict than have a hard conversation.

One of the warning signs I've seen in premarried couples is a tendency to avoid anything that might break up the relationship. Some couples live in such fear of ruining a relationship that they stuff their feelings or thoughts because they don't want to upset the other person.

If you want to best prepare for marriage, you must learn to have difficult, sometimes awkward, conversations. Pushing through the tough stuff will allow you to honor God and each other.

The Rest of the Story

Today Jason and Kelly teach others about communication and conflict resolution. I've learned more about communication from them than any other couple. They model it well in their marriage, and they're raising their kids to communicate and argue according to biblical principles. When you get this right, it affects so much more than just you and your significant other. The work you do to grow in this area can impact your children, friends, coworkers, and other family members.

If you and your significant other can't (or choose not to) communicate and resolve conflict, then you are not ready for marriage. If your future spouse is not willing and able to improve the ways they communicate and resolve conflict with you, then they're not ready to take the next step in your relationship.

The good news is that you can learn to resolve conflict in a way that honors God and each other. Healthy communication is the means by which you and your spouse will grow in oneness.

Am I Ready?

- Why do you think communication and conflict resolution are challenging for many couples? What do you think will make you and your spouse different than other couples when it comes to communication and conflict resolution?

- Identify your undesirable communication habits and pitfalls, confess to what you do poorly, and think through ways you can grow and improve.
- What types of communication patterns did you see in your parents? If you were married previously, what challenges did you face in communication and conflict resolution?
- Ask others what kind of nonverbal communication your posture communicates. Does it make you seem warm and likable, or cold and prickly?
- Ask your friends and family what they consider to be your strengths and weaknesses when it comes to communication and conflict.

Strengthening Our Knot

- Discuss your answers to the Am I Ready? questions about communication and conflict.
- Ask your significant other how you are doing with the five nonnegotiables listed in this chapter. Which ones are your strengths, and which are weaknesses? As they share their responses with you, do not argue or respond with a defensive posture.
- In what ways does your significant other think you need to grow as a couple when it comes to communication and conflict resolution?

- Go on a date night with each other and leave your phones behind. Laugh, play, and talk about what you are learning through reading this book.

Closing Prayer

Lord, thank You for the ways You communicate with us through Your Word, Your Spirit, and Your people. Please help us communicate in a way that honors You and each other. Show us when we foolishly seek to win an argument instead of seeking to understand. Give us wisdom to be quick to listen, slow to speak, and slow to become angry. Help us to forgive one another as we learn how to communicate and resolve conflict well as a couple. In Jesus's name, we pray. Amen.

3

How Much Does Our Faith Really Matter?

Building Your Marriage on the Right Foundation

On February 15, 2015, Tim and Sonja celebrated their fortieth anniversary with a vow renewal ceremony. Friends and family gathered in the chapel, and I officiated the renewal. The happy couple walked down the aisle and then stood at the front of the chapel surrounded by their grown children and their spouses. They reaffirmed their love, committed to continue to pursue Jesus together, and sealed it with a kiss.

The ceremony was filled with cheers, laughter, and a Christlike joy. Tim fought hard to keep it together because he was overwhelmed by God's goodness. Sonja walked around bubbly and happy, as if floating on air. We danced, ate cake, and toasted to their wedded bliss. All the guests declared our desires to be like Tim and Sonja.

It wasn't the same way when Tim and Sonja said "I do" the first time.

In 1975, they got married in a small ceremony in front of a handful of friends and family. Against the wishes of their families, Tim and Sonja shared their vows. There was no cake, no dancing, and no toasting.

Tim: We each made a profession of faith at a young age, but it didn't change or direct our lives. We did what we thought was right and had no one to model a healthy marriage for us. We didn't look to God's Word to see what marriage and relationships should look like. Instead, I looked at culture and allowed my personal desires to drive my decisions and our marriage.

Sonja: Our families thought we were way too young to get married. Tim was twenty-one at the time, and I was twenty-two—an older woman! Tim's parents wanted him to accomplish some career goals before getting hitched. We didn't care what they thought and had no idea what we were doing, but we *felt* in love.

Tim: We were superficial Christians, living for ourselves and no one else. We didn't read the Bible, pray, or go to church, and we definitely didn't have any close Christian friends. Both sets of parents made it abundantly clear they didn't support our marriage.

Sonja: When we got married, Tim was still in school, I was working full-time, and he didn't have a job. His family gave us six months before we got divorced.

As I listened to their story, I thought of the people of Israel during the time of the judges in the Old Testament. Judges 17:6 says, "In those days there was no king in Israel. Everyone did what was right in his own eyes" (ESV). Like God's people described in this verse, we often do what is right in our own eyes.

The problem is, what is right in our own eyes is often wrong in every other way.

What happened to Tim and Sonja between 1975 and 2015 that led to such a profound difference between their wedding day and their fortieth anniversary vow renewal? When so many other couples have broken or miserable marriages, why is Tim and Sonja's story so different?

Sonja: About eight years into marriage, some neighbors invited us to come to their church. While we didn't necessarily want to go to church, we liked this couple and watched the ways they raised their kids and lived out their faith. There was something different about them.

Tim: We had hit rock-bottom and realized our faith couldn't just be a marginal add-on to our marriage on Sunday mornings. We couldn't allow ourselves to be swayed by the lure of culture and selfishness. We knew we needed to figure out how to make Jesus the center of our lives and our marriage. We rededicated our lives to Christ, got baptized, started reading and learning the Bible, and haven't looked back since.

Build Your Marriage on the Foundation of Faith

In Matthew 5–7, Jesus gave radical thoughts about some of the most important topics in our lives: marriage, divorce, murder, lust, prayer, conflict resolution, and much more. He told us to love our enemies, to pray for those who persecute us, and to gouge out our eye or cut off our hand if either of them causes us to stumble.

At the end of His sermon, Jesus challenged His listeners to decide what kind of foundation to build their lives on:

> Everyone who hears these words of mine and puts them into practice is like a wise man who built his house on the rock. The rain came down, the streams rose, and the winds blew and beat against that house; yet it did not fall, because it had its foundation on the rock. But everyone who hears these words of mine and does not put them into practice is like a foolish man who built his house on sand. The rain came down, the streams rose, and the winds blew and beat against that house, and it fell with a great crash. (Matt. 7:24–27)

What foundation will you choose for your marriage? Will you choose to build your marriage on the rock-solid words of Jesus Christ, or will you build it on the shifting sand of what this world says about marriage?

Not by the Hair of My Chinny Chin Chin

Remember the fairy tale about the three little pigs who somehow were also homebuilders? One of them built his house with straw. The second built his house with sticks. But the third little pig wisely chose to build his house with bricks. It took more work on the front end, but his house was the only one able to withstand the threats and attacks of the big, bad wolf.

The lesson for you from this story is to build your marriage on a solid foundation. Like the third little pig, it might take more time and expense to invest in your spiritual lives, but you will build a foundation of marriage that will not be swept away by the enemy's attacks.

If you get married and can balance a budget, communicate like champions, and have amazing sex but aren't on the same page about Jesus and matters of faith, then none of the rest really matters. Jesus said, "Apart from me you can do nothing" (John 15:5). While you may succeed in the short term, eventually your house will crash down like the house built on the sand. The storms will come and destroy your home.

Sometimes the storm may come in the form of the death of a loved one, the loss of a job, or infidelity. Other times the storms might include financial hardship, a challenging child, or a struggle with parents and in-laws. Sometimes the storms will be the direct result of sinful or foolish decisions such as pornography or addiction. Other times the cause of the storm might be completely out of your control, such as infertility.

For us, a storm came in the form of newborn twin boys who challenged our sleep, finances, and communication. Kristen and I loved Jesus, worked hard on our marriage, and did all the right things we should have done. But our lives were completely rocked by our babies. Words can't capture the challenges we faced with our twins. I know that if we hadn't relied on our faith and lived in a home built on the rock-solid foundation of faith in Jesus Christ, then our marriage might not have survived this season.

What If You and Your Significant Other Don't Share the Same Faith?

The Bible doesn't tell us whom we should marry. It would make life much easier if we could chapter/verse it and say something like "Scott 3:16 says 'Thou shalt marry Kristen.'" It would take away our questions and remove angst from our lives.

Even though the Bible doesn't say whom we *should* marry, it does tell us whom we *shouldn't* marry. God's Word is abundantly clear a believer in Christ should not marry someone who doesn't share the same beliefs. Whether the other person is a Buddhist, Muslim, atheist, or has any other worldview, a follower of Christ should marry only another follower of Christ. In 2 Corinthians 6:14, Paul writes, "Do not be yoked together with unbelievers. For what do righteousness and wickedness have in common? Or what fellowship can light have with darkness?"

In this passage, Paul instructs the follower of Christ to marry another follower of Christ. It doesn't mean you must end all relationships with non-Christians, but it does mean you shouldn't marry someone who doesn't have faith in Jesus. Married life centers around a shared faith, and all the decisions you make revolve around your beliefs. As 2 Corinthians 6:14 says, righteousness and wickedness have nothing in common. How will you and your spouse make decisions about money, parenting, work, and intimacy without operating from the same beliefs and worldview?

I can't tell you whom you should marry. But I will tell you if you're a follower of Christ and you're dating or engaged to a non-Christian, then you must hit the eject button and get out of the relationship. This is a clear red light in the relationship. I don't care how much money she makes, how much fun you have together, or how good-looking he might be. If you are a Christian who is unequally yoked to an unbeliever, then you should move on.

Four Questions about Spiritual Intimacy You Should Ask before You Say "I Do"

How does spiritual intimacy affect your relationship as a premarried couple, and how should it affect your lives when you get married? There are four conversations you need to have to know whether you are building your relationship on the same foundation.

1. What Is Your Story of Faith?

Although I grew up in a great home with a mom and stepdad who loved me, we didn't talk about our faith, attend church, or center our lives on Jesus Christ. I assumed I was a Christian because I wasn't Muslim, Buddhist, or Jewish. We sometimes attended church, and for the most part I thought I was a pretty good person.

When I went to college at Wake Forest University in North Carolina, I quickly realized I wasn't a Christian. I made a lot of poor decisions and didn't believe God existed. And I didn't think I needed saving from my sins. I believed that people didn't have a soul or need to think about eternal questions.

In spite of worldly success, I felt empty and purposeless. Then God brought a follower of Christ into my life named Will. He shared the gospel with me and spent time with me. After many hours of discussion, Bible study, and early morning meetings, I realized I was a sinner in need of a Savior. On the evening of February 13, 1998, I surrendered my life to Christ.

Even though I still struggled with sin (and still do!), my life and worldview changed. I realized that my life was not my own. Rather, I knew I needed to live for Christ and build my life on the solid foundation of Scripture.

Kristen and I share a common faith in Christ, and our relationship is built upon our shared trust in Jesus. You need to become comfortable talking about your faith, especially with the person you will spend the rest of your life with.

Here are a few questions to guide your discussion with your significant other:

- Do you consider yourself a follower of Christ? Are you saved by grace, through faith, as Ephesians 2:8–9 describes? Are you trusting in anything besides your faith and the life, death, and resurrection of Christ to earn God's love and affection?
- When did you start following Jesus? What is your conversion story? (Note: some people don't have a specific moment they remember trusting in Christ, but they know they are saved. Either way, if you're a follower of Jesus, your story is a beautiful one and should be shared with others.)
- What's your view of baptism? Do you believe that you need to be baptized to be saved, or do you think getting baptized is an act of obedience for the follower of Christ?[1]

2. What Is Your View of Church?

There are many churches and denominations to choose from. Where will you and your spouse go to church when you get married? This becomes especially challenging if the two of you come from different church backgrounds. The church you choose as a couple will hopefully be a major catalyst in your faith and friendships.

Here are a few questions to get the conversation started:

- What do you look for in a church? What's important to you about the church and its mission?[2]
- Do you expect your church to provide community and friendships?
- Do you participate regularly in a small group or Bible study?
- Do you prefer a contemporary service, or one with liturgy and tradition?
- If you and your spouse come from different denominations, how will you decide what your home church will be?

The church has been a tremendous source of growth and community for Tim and Sonja and for me and Kristen. We spend so much of our time, resources, and gifts with our church family. Like us, you'll have some big decisions to make when it comes to choosing a church home. Make sure you discuss your view of church before you tie the knot.[3]

3. How Will Jesus Impact Your Day-to-Day Married Life?

Spiritual intimacy is one of the most challenging aspects of many marriages. Most husbands and wives don't know how to discuss their faith, what they're learning in church, or what they're reading in their Bibles. The majority of married couples don't pray together, and even fewer share their faith with others.

Even though I'm a marriage pastor and tell other couples they need to pray together, I don't often practice what I preach. Kristen and I have always struggled with making prayer together a priority. I do pray throughout the day on my own, but for whatever reason, it's hard for me to make praying with Kristen a priority. I know I'm not alone—I've heard this same sentiment many times from other married couples.

But I hope you will do better than we have. I encourage you to start on the right foot and make your faith central to your relationship. You have many opportunities in front of you to read your Bibles and share what you're reading and learning. You'll be able to pray together every day and challenge each other to grow in your faith. You'll get to invite non-Christians over to your house, and you'll serve on mission together.

Before you get married, discuss with your significant other how you will make your faith central to your relationship with each other. For example, set an alarm on your phone as a reminder to pray with your spouse. Kristen's birthday is May 3, so every Sunday I pray for Kristen at 5:03 p.m. I pray for her more than once a week, but this practical suggestion provides a cue to help me pray for my bride. You will need to decide how you will help each other become more like Christ.

Should a Couple Pray Together before Getting Married?

This is one of the most frequently asked questions in our premarried class. Some people say yes, while others say no. Here is a brief summary of each perspective.

Yes, you should pray together before you get married.

You can pray before meals and you can pray God allows you to have a great date night and helps keep you pure. You can let your significant other know how they can pray for you and what causes anxiety in your life. You can pray with each other when you have big decisions to make. How someone prays provides a window into their relationship with Christ and can help you discern how your significant other is doing spiritually.

No, you shouldn't pray together before you get married.

Prayer is one of the most intimate aspects of a relationship. Some couples even say prayer is more intimate than sexual intercourse. While I don't agree with that personally, I know what they mean. When you pray together with someone, you gain deep insight into the condition of their soul. You get to know them on an intimate level. You hear the cries of their heart and the depth of their pain. For this reason, you need to make sure you "guard your heart, for everything you do flows from it" (Prov. 4:23).

Whether to pray together is something each couple has to decide for themselves. If you and your significant other do pray together, make sure you don't unwittingly create an environment for sexual temptation. It can be difficult to run from temptation when you're connected spiritually while cuddling in a dark, private place. Sometimes those types of prayers end with clothes flying off or with one partner on top of the other fully clothed, enjoying some of the benefits of a relationship intended for married couples only.

4. How Will Your Faith Impact Your Wedding Day?

I've been to weddings where Scripture isn't read and the name of Jesus isn't even mentioned. I've also been to weddings where I walk away with a deeper love for the Lord. What do you want people to say and think when they leave your wedding?

If you are a Christian, you want your guests to be more wowed by the goodness of God than by the beauty of your flowers and decor. You want them to walk away strengthened in their own marriages more than intrigued by how much you spent on your wedding dress. Don't just prepare for your wedding day. Instead, prepare for your marriage. You're doing that right now—that's why you're reading this book!

Discuss with your significant other what your wedding day will be like and how your shared faith in Jesus will impact the decisions you make about your special day.

How Can You Grow in Spiritual Intimacy before the Wedding?

The best way to prepare for marriage is by growing in your own relationship with Christ.

- Start with reading your Bible. Consider a guided Bible reading plan such as Join the Journey or download a Bible app such as YouVersion and choose a reading plan you can go through.[4]
- Count down to your wedding date by reading a psalm a day.

- There are thirty-one chapters in the book of Proverbs. Read one every day of the month and look for personal applications. For example, if the date is March 9, then read Proverbs 9.
- Serve in your church, pray throughout the day, and join a community group with other followers of Jesus Christ.

How Can You Grow in Spiritual Intimacy as a Couple?

Talk to your future spouse, and decide together what you're going to read in the Bible. Do the psalm countdown or proverb of the day together. Share with each other what you're learning. Take some notes and journal about your time in God's Word, and share your thoughts with your significant other.

Most married couples I know struggle with being spiritually intimate with each other. They're often insecure about what they're learning, and they don't know how to share what God is teaching them. You can start developing some habits before marriage that will yield fruit down the road.

As I mentioned earlier, Kristen and I struggle to make prayer a priority in our marriage. I've set reminders on my phone, printed notes with the word *pray* and placed them all over my bedroom, and asked friends to text me to remind me to pray. None of my plans have worked beyond a few days at a time. On the other hand, I know many young couples who started praying and sharing with each other from day one of marriage and have had a much easier time establishing healthy spiritual habits as a couple.

There are plenty of great books out there for couples to read, but nothing will be better for your soul or for your relationship than reading the Bible together. Plus, it will help you establish strong patterns for married life.

The Rest of the Story

So, how are Tim and Sonja doing today?

Sonja: On our fortieth anniversary vow renewal, we celebrated all God had done in our lives. We marveled at His goodness, knowing that apart from Christ we wouldn't be celebrating four decades of marriage. Now we love spending time together, have healthy relationships with our children and grandchildren, and lead couples in our church's premarried ministry.

Tim: As we look back and see what God has done since we allowed Him to be the center of our relationship, we are simply amazed. The first eight years of our marriage were built upon culture's plan for our lives and our selfish desires. Everything changed when we truly trusted in Jesus to be our Savior and rebuilt our marriage on the rock-solid foundation of Christ.

What will you choose to build your marriage on? Will you be like the wise builder who built his house on the solid rock? Or will you be like the fool who chose to build his life and relationships on sand? The problems of the world may huff and puff and try to blow your house down, but no storm will destroy your marriage if you build it on the rock-solid foundation of Jesus Christ.

Am I Ready?

- Why do you think couples have a hard time discussing spiritual matters? What are a few steps you and your significant other can take to distinguish yourselves from couples who struggle in this area?
- What excites you about the possibility of being married to your significant other for over forty years? What most concerns you?
- What can you do right now to help build your life on the rock-solid foundation of Christ? What can you and your future spouse do to grow in your relationship with Christ before you say "I do?"
- When it comes to spiritual intimacy, are you running at the same pace as your future spouse? Why or why not?

Strengthening Our Knot

- Discuss your answers to the Am I Ready? questions about spiritual intimacy in marriage.
- Spend some time discussing the "Four Questions about Spiritual Intimacy You Should Ask before You Say 'I Do'" in this chapter.
- Share your dreams and hopes for your wedding day with your significant other. What elements do you want to include to make sure your ceremony is focused on Christ?[5]

Closing Prayer

Lord, help us to build our lives as singles on the rock-solid foundation of Jesus Christ. And if we get married, help us build our marriage on the foundation of our shared faith in Christ. Help us to know You more, to prayerfully depend on You, and to continually seek to become more like Your Son, Jesus. Help us to find godly friends who will spur us on and a healthy church where we can plug in and serve You for Your glory. In Jesus's name, we pray. Amen.

4

What If You Say Tomato and I Say Tomahto?

Learning to Live with Each Other in an Understanding Way

Kristen and I are different in just about every way. While we share the same spiritual convictions and values, our personalities and temperaments are almost polar opposites. For example:

- She keeps everything, and I like to throw it all away.
- She has over fifteen thousand emails in her inbox, and I try to keep less than twenty.
- She grew up in a military home with one sister, while I grew up in a blended family with one brother.

- She's tall, slender, and has brown hair and blue eyes. I'm average height, stocky, and have no hair and brown eyes.
- She's emotionally steady, and I'm highly emotional (aka a drama queen).

We complement each other well even though we sometimes drive each other crazy. Sometimes our differences are attractive, while other times they're annoying and difficult.

Kristen and I have had to learn how to live with each other in spite of our differences. In marriage, all couples need to learn to live with each other in an understanding way. This learning process needs to start before you tie the knot.

Living Proof of the Power of Genetics

In May 2004, my wife gave birth to our twin sons. Our twins couldn't be more different from one another. Even though they are both boys, were conceived at the same time by the same parents, and entered the world two minutes apart, they're still radically different from each other. One is tall like Kristen, while the other is average height like me. One has lighter features like my wife, while the other has darker hair, skin, and eyes like me. Their personalities are different as well, with each of them possessing some characteristics of both Kristen and me.

I am amazed by how God's beauty and creativity are reflected in our twin sons. They are "fearfully and wonderfully made" (Ps. 139:14), and before they were even formed in the womb, the Lord knew them and all their differences (Jer. 1:5).

If twins can be so different from each other, how much more different do you think a man and a woman are when they come together in marriage?

Think about your relationship. You and your significant other come from different parents. You probably also come from different cities or states, went to different schools, and have different families of origin. You each have unique personalities, temperaments, and gifts. One of you might be more introverted or extroverted, and you probably have different vocational skills and dreams. Furthermore, one of you is a male and the other is a female. You are in a relationship with someone who is a completely different person.

Sometimes those differences are very attractive—that might be what initially brought you into a dating relationship. Yet sometimes those differences will drive you nuts. You'll question their sanity and wonder what planet they are from—and what was wrong with their parents!

In her book *Reading People*, Anne Bogel shares some great wisdom: "When you understand yourself better—your strengths and weaknesses, emotional needs, and driving motivations—it is much easier to understand others as well, especially when they aren't like you."[1] Your spouse probably isn't like you, so once you admit this truth, you will have a much better opportunity to deal with your differences.

How will you and your future spouse handle your differences? Will they push you apart, or can you work through them in a way that might actually draw you closer together as a couple? Fortunately, God's Word gives us the solution to how we can survive, and even thrive, being married to someone who is different than ourselves.

Sometimes Opposites Attract

My friends Eric and Julie met in 1982 at a church party where friends played a game, won fake money, and then bid on prizes with their winnings. When the time came to bid on prizes, they pooled their winnings to buy some Dallas Mavericks basketball tickets.

Eric: Right off the bat, I liked how much Julie enjoyed sports. A woman who picked the prize of NBA tickets was all right in my book! She coached basketball, was quite feisty, and was no stranger to technical fouls. I really appreciated that she wasn't high maintenance, was easy to please, and could cook like nobody's business!

Julie: I loved how funny Eric was and how he could easily make me laugh. I also loved his blond hair, blue eyes, and big smile. He had a great friend group of Christian guys, was fun to be with, and had a unique ability to put me at ease.

Over a golf game with some guys, Eric realized he loved Julie and wished he was with her and not sweating in the August heat with a bunch of dudes.

Eric: I was ready to take the next step in my relationship with Julie. When I talked to her dad about marriage, he warned me, "Julie can't tell time and can't tell distance, but if you can handle that, you'll be good!" Her family was amazed that someone was able to tame Julie! I knew we were very different from one another.

Julie: He's a planner, and I'm spontaneous. He likes to be on time (better yet, early), while I am just fine getting there late. I live life full of grace, while he holds high expectations. He looks at life through the lens of reality, whereas I tend to look at life through rose-colored glasses.

Each knew the other wasn't perfect, and they knew plenty of challenges lay ahead of them because of their differences. They married in 1984, and love each other more now than when they said "I do."

Living with Each Other in an Understanding Way

Whether you're similar to each other or as different from each other as Eric and Julie are, you and your significant other will need to work through some challenges related to your personality and wiring. How can you live with your future spouse when so many differences exist between you? Will you be able to handle those differences in a way that allows you to grow in oneness, or will you drive each other crazy?

In 1 Peter 3, the apostle Peter discusses how spouses should respect each other in marriage. In verse 7, Peter writes, "Husbands, live with your wives in an understanding way, showing honor to the woman as the weaker vessel, since they are heirs with you of the grace of life, so that your prayers may not be hindered" (ESV).

In his notes on 1 Peter, Dr. Tom Constable said the following:

By comparing a wife to a "weaker" vessel, Peter was not implying that wives or women are inferior to husbands or males, or that they are weaker in *every* way or *most* ways. Obviously, in many marriages the wife is the *stronger* person: emotionally, mentally, spiritually, morally, socially, and/or physically. Nevertheless, *physically* the wife is usually weaker than her husband. Men tend to choose as their wives women who are not as strong or muscular as they are. Furthermore, men are generally physically stronger than women. In view of this, husbands need to treat their wives with special consideration.[2]

In no way did Peter see the wife as inferior to her husband. Rather, he highlighted the fact that usually the woman is weaker physically. The man and woman are equal in value and worth and are coheirs of the grace of life but play different roles in marriage as defined by God (more on this in chapter 6).

The principle from this passage applies equally to men and women: live with your spouse in a way that shows you understand them. This means you must make the effort to get to know them. If you don't, Peter said, your prayers will be hindered. If you choose to not live with your spouse in a way that shows you know and understand them, your spiritual life will be affected.

Five Ways to Get to Know Each Other

How do you learn how to live with your spouse in an understanding way? Here are five ways to get to know each other before you tie the knot.

1. Be a Student of Your Significant Other

When you studied for a test in school, you did research, read, asked questions, took notes, and put effort into learning about the subject matter. In a similar way, when you're pursuing someone with a view toward engagement and marriage, you need to make some effort and learn more about them.

Ask fun questions and serious questions. Put down your phone and spend time being a student of your future spouse. The more you do this before you get married, the better. You'll learn more about your significant other, which will allow you to better prepare for marriage. For example, ask them:

1. What do you like to do for fun?
2. What is God teaching you these days?
3. What's your favorite movie? Book? TV show?
4. What's your favorite holiday? Why?
5. What kind of gifts do you like to get?
6. What's your love language?[3]
7. What's your favorite sport? Your favorite team? Even more fun: What's your least favorite team?
8. What do you love most about your job? What do you dislike the most?
9. What's your favorite book of the Bible?
10. What's your favorite restaurant? Favorite type of food? Beverage?

That's just a brief list; I'm sure you can think of many more. Ask questions and get to know your significant other.

Note that this process does not end after you get married. Hopefully you will continue to have these conversations on a consistent basis as a married couple. You must be intentional. Without effort or intention, you will not grow in this area. Being a student of another human being takes effort, so be prepared to make some effort to know your significant other.

2. Don't Hide Your Differences

You've done some work and learned more about your future spouse. What happens when you discover just how different you are from your significant other?

When we hide or minimize our differences because we don't want others to reject us, problems arise. We don't let each other see our struggles, sins, or quirks because we believe the relationship will end if they see our faults. However, when you get married, you become "one flesh" with your spouse (Gen. 2:24). This means you must no longer hide or minimize your problems. When you unconditionally love and accept one another, the relationship will be safe.

I see big warning signs when an individual has something they don't want to tell their spouse. For example, if you were sexually abused as a child, you need to share this with your spouse, preferably before getting married. You're a victim of a terrible sin done to you by someone else and understandably might be reluctant to talk about your past abuse. But when love, acceptance, and safety are not present in the relationship, you might not feel safe sharing about the past. This would be a yellow or red light.

Most of the time when we're afraid to share something with a person we're dating, it's because we live in fear that they might break up with us after we tell them. Don't give the Swiss cheese version of the truth. Choose to give your significant other the truth, the whole truth, and nothing but the truth. Without truth, you prevent oneness.

Knot-Tying Tip

How Do You Know If a Difference Is Too Big to Overlook?

Maybe you and your significant other root for different sports teams or have different methods of filtering email. Maybe you have different views on how to spend a vacation. Most of the time, married couples will work through their differences by communicating about them and compromising.

Proverbs 19:11 says, "It is to one's glory to overlook an offense." If it's not a sin issue, sometimes you simply need to overlook the difference and let it go, knowing you trust each other. Remember, you have minor issues that annoy your future spouse as well.

But other differences are too big to ignore or pretend they will go away. Hopefully you and your significant other can talk about any topic. If your future mate is unwilling to talk about differences or a situation, then I would be concerned. If you bring something up and they push it off, this is a reason to potentially call off your engagement. If either of you think you can bring secrets into a marriage relationship, then you are not ready for marriage.

Many guys, and increasingly more women, bring a pornography and masturbation addiction into marriage. They think once they get married, their secret problem will go away. Most of the time this is not the case. If you have a pet sin you think you can hide from your significant other, think again. When you are one flesh, you choose not to keep secrets from one another.

Sometimes engaged couples realize their differences are so big that they break up, especially if the differences are spiritual ones. Remember, the Bible doesn't tell us whom to marry but does tell us whom *not* to marry. This truth bears repeating because it's that big of a deal-breaker. Second Corinthians 6:14 says, "Do not be yoked together with unbelievers. For what do righteousness and wickedness have in common? Or what fellowship can light have with darkness?"

If you are a follower of Christ and you are dating someone who's not, then God is very clear: the relationship needs to end. For the follower of Christ, all of life is seen through the lens of Jesus. If you're dating someone who is not a Christian, then you will never be aligned on the most important aspects of life.

Premarried couples often see the world through rose-colored glasses. Choose to take off those love goggles and see your relationship rightly. If not, someday you and your spouse may be like strangers.

3. Embrace Your Differences

Once you and your significant other understand how you are different from each other, what's the next step? You must embrace your differences.

Most of our differences are not wrong, and typically our differences are characteristics of how God made us as individuals. When you have issues with your spouse and the way they are made, your issues aren't really with your significant other but with the God who made them.

Look for the good in your differences. There is a reason you were attracted to your significant other in the first place!

4. Celebrate Your Differences

After you understand and embrace your differences, you celebrate them. Celebrate your Maker for the ways He created each of you. Your differences don't surprise God. Celebrate the ways you are different from each other and thank God for those differences.

In addition, celebrate the fact that the Lord can use your differences to help make each of you more like Jesus. It is not good for us to be alone (Gen. 2:18), and by design He chooses to use others to help shape each of us to become more like Christ (Rom. 8:29; Eph. 5:25–28).

Eric: We can't expect our significant other to change. Most of our differences will not change. For example, I'll more than likely always like to be on time. But I've learned to put Julie's desires before my own. I don't pace the house stomping my feet or sit in the car honking the horn when I'm ready to leave. Rather, I choose to live with Julie in an understanding way, knowing I can better love her by putting her needs and desires first.

Julie: I do the same thing for him in different areas of marriage. We get to follow the example of Jesus when we consider the other person as more important than ourselves (Phil. 2:3). I can do the same thing for Eric by getting ready earlier even when I don't want to.

5. Listen Well and Show You Care

In 1 Peter 3:7, Peter challenges spouses to live with each other in a way that communicates you understand your significant other. This is the challenge you will face every day after you say "I do."

My friends Greg and Lori shared a great story that illustrates this challenge. When Greg and Lori had a one-year-old boy, they were invited to an out-of-town wedding. It was the first time they left their son with friends for longer than a few hours on a date night. As you can imagine, they were filled with anxiety about leaving their son overnight. Their conversation that day went something like this:

Lori: I'm concerned about leaving our son because we've never left him with anyone this long. And he's still having some eating issues.

Greg: He'll be fine. Our friends know what they're doing—they have three kids of their own and will be able to take good care of him.

Lori: I know, but I'm still concerned. Plus, I'm worried—

Greg: (Cutting her off) You're getting anxious about nothing. They'll be fine, and it will be good for us to get away.

While Greg was right, he did not live with his wife in an understanding way. He cut her off and didn't listen well.

When Greg realized he was trying to fix the problem instead of listening to his wife, he apologized and asked for forgiveness. He realized he wasn't living with Lori in a way that showed he cared for her.

When you live with each other in an understanding way, you become more like Jesus Christ. You don't conform to the image of your spouse but to the image of Jesus. When you marry someone, God intends for you to grow in holiness and to become more like Christ.

The Rest of the Story

Eric and Julie are about to celebrate thirty-five years of married life. Over the years, they have learned to understand and celebrate their differences. They're one of the funnest couples I know, and everyone they meet loves spending time with them largely because of how their differences strengthen their marriage. And like their first date many years ago, they still love going to Mavericks games together.

Marriage provides us with the opportunity to address our struggles, selfishness, and sin. And when we slowly chip away at those areas, we begin to look more like Jesus. Marriage will change you. I pray your future spouse, as you live with them in an understanding way, will help you become more like Jesus.

Am I Ready?

- What are some of the biggest differences between you and your significant other? Identify them and prepare to discuss these differences with each other.
- What are some of your characteristics or traits that might make you a challenging spouse? For example, if you almost always run behind schedule, how might that make life challenging for your spouse?
- What concerns do you have about your significant other's personality and wiring that might make things challenging in your marriage?

Strengthening Our Knot

- Discuss your answers to the Am I Ready? questions about living with each other in an understanding way.
- Take some time to talk about your differences. What excites you about some of your differences? What concerns do you have about your different wiring?
- Go to 5LoveLanguages.com and discover each of your love languages. Discuss specific ways that you can best serve each other according to your love language.

Closing Prayer

Lord, thank You for the ways You have made each of us in a unique way. Thank You that we're made with different wirings and gifts. Help us to live with each other in an understanding way after we get married, and please help us start that process right now. Help us to understand, embrace, and celebrate our differences. Please help us to look for ways to serve each other according to our unique wiring. We pray our differences will help us become more like Christ. In Jesus's name, we pray. Amen.

5

Will We Clip Coupons or Max Out Credit Cards?

A Biblical View of Money and Financial Stewardship

At twenty-two, without a full-time job and while headed to grad school, I decided to lease a new Ford Explorer. When that lease ran out, while still in grad school and *still* without a job, I decided to lease yet another new Ford Explorer. Clearly, I started college as a financial idiot and I finished grad school an even bigger financial idiot.

I didn't have a clue about managing my finances. I was really good at using my credit cards and increasing my debt, but I didn't know about the dangers of debt and credit cards.

I came into marriage with car debt, school debt, and consumer debt. I bought a house that maxed out my resources, and I had no plan to get out of debt or to be generous. I saw things I wanted and bought them. I'm a spender.

Kristen, on the other hand, came into marriage with no debt. She left home with a ten-page, single-spaced document instructing her how to spend, save, give, and invest. Her father prepared her for life by helping her make decisions about retirement, cars, and homes. She followed the plan just as her dad recommended. Kristen is a saver and learned how to make wise financial decisions.

Kristen had her stuff together. I just had a lot of stuff.

When you combine an impulsive spender with a conservative saver in marriage, you are going to experience some financial challenges. Were finances a challenge for Kristen and me after we got married? Are they still a challenge for us with four kids to feed, a house, cars, and medical bills? You better believe it.

After thirteen years of working with thousands of couples, I know we're not alone. You'd better get this area of your relationship right, or it might lead to a boatload of destruction in your relationship. But if you do get it right, financial health can be a great source of joy and blessing to your family and others.

Whether you and your significant other have a lot of money, a lot of debt, or something in between, your view of money will be one of the most important parts of your relationship. Every couple I know faces challenges with regard to financial decisions. And perhaps no other aspect of your marriage will lead to tougher times and harder conversations than money.

When Life Doesn't Turn Out Like You Hoped It Would

Married life didn't turn out the way my friends Kyle and Meghan planned it.

Kyle: In 2002, I helped lead a ministry at our church for young adults. For our Christmas party, we planned a series of progressive dinners that culminated at someone's house. Andrea, one of the leaders of the event, secretly played matchmaker by putting Meghan and me in charge of one of the dinners.

Meghan: Our planning sessions started on the phone and over email and soon led to a one-on-one meeting at Starbucks. We struck up an immediate friendship and started a running group together with some friends. We began doing more ministry as a couple, and our relationship grew.

Kyle: I didn't marry her for the money, but I thought I'd hit the jackpot when I found out Meghan was an attorney! In the beginning of our relationship, I didn't realize my wife-to-be came with a large chunk of law school debt. I brought some of my own debt into the relationship, but not nearly as much debt as Meghan brought into our marriage.

Meghan: We got married in December 2003, and together we brought over $120,000 worth of debt into marriage. We knew it was a big deal, but we didn't realize how much it would affect our relationship.

Kyle: At the time we married, I was making around $1,000/month as a ministry intern, and Meghan made a modest attorney salary as a pro bono lawyer. Since I'm a CPA, I love numbers and Excel spreadsheets. One day I crunched some numbers and realized it would take us over twenty-five years to pay off our debt. We had a big problem on our hands, and it started to affect our marriage.

Money: One of the Largest Sources of Relational Tension

Kyle and Meghan are not alone in their financial and relational struggles. A study by the American Institute of CPAs discovered that "financial matters are the most common source of discord among American couples."[1]

Fortunately for Kyle and Meghan, none of their financial debt was a surprise to the other before they got married. Each of them brought some financial challenges into their relationship, but they were purposeful to discuss these areas with each other. They discussed their debt and financial background as part of their marriage preparation.

When they sat down and discussed their areas of shame, they responded to each other with Christlike grace and mercy. Paul wrote in Ephesians 2:4–5, "Because of his great love for us, God, who is rich in mercy, made us alive with Christ even when we were dead in transgressions—it is by grace you have been saved." When we receive each other with mercy and grace, we are following in the footsteps of Christ.

Six Questions to Ask about Money before You Get Married

There are six conversations you and your significant other need to have about money before you get married—four are financial in nature, and the other two are related to your background and personality. When you have these conversations, share details and don't intentionally leave out specific aspects you're not proud of or don't want to share. See these conversations as a great way to build trust. For most couples, the right timing of these conversations would take place around the time of engagement. If you're already engaged, then better late than never.

1. What's Your Financial Picture?

What assets do you possess, and what value do they hold? Think about cars, homes, valuables, and things that are tangible and intangible. How much do you have in your checking, savings, and retirement accounts? Do you own any stocks or bonds? You ought to each have a good picture of your financial assets and accumulations. As you discuss this, remember that it is not a competition, and your worth is not determined by how much stuff you own. Rather, this conversation provides an opportunity for you to share with your significant other what kind of assets you will bring into marriage.

2. What Debt Do You Have?

Keep track of and discuss any money you owe someone or something else. How much money do you owe, and to whom do you owe it? What are your interest rates and maturity dates? What is your current plan for addressing your debt? Do you have a way you keep track of your debts and payments (e.g., Excel spreadsheet, Quicken, Mint)?

3. Where Does Your Money Go?

Your conversation about spending habits doesn't have to be a line-by-line, "tell me where every dollar goes" discussion. Rather, this should be a higher-level discussion of income and giving. The outflow will change—whether you spend fifty dollars or five hundred dollars on groceries doesn't matter at this point. Rather, do you give money to a church or other organization? What are your high-ticket expenses (such as a car or home), and how do you spend the money you bring in? This conversation should give each of you a better understanding of the other person's view of stewardship and generosity.

In His Sermon on the Mount, Jesus shared some challenging truths about money and how we spend it. In Matthew 6:19–21, He said, "Do not store up for yourselves treasures on earth, where moths and vermin destroy, and where thieves break in and steal. But store up for yourselves treasures in heaven, where moths and vermin do not destroy, and where thieves do not break in and steal. For where your treasure is, there your heart will be also."

Jesus gives us two choices with our money. Either we invest in the stuff of this earth, or we invest in things of eternal value. Until both you and your significant other develop a mindset focused on eternal things, you will always struggle with how to best manage the resources and possessions you have as a couple.

During the early years of our marriage, I was in seminary full-time and Kristen was the primary breadwinner, working full-time as a physical therapist at a hospital downtown. Our church met at a local high school on Sunday mornings, and the church's leadership presented the members an opportunity to buy some land a few miles away that would be used to build a permanent facility we'd get to use seven days a week. Every member was challenged to pray about giving money to buy this land.

When the opportunity arose, Kristen and I had to decide if we were going to give to the church and how much we'd give. We knew a few months down the road Kristen would no longer be the breadwinner and instead would be a stay-at-home mom to our twin boys. Finances were tight and would become even tighter, but we had a little nest egg saved away in the bank.

As we prayed, we both realized we wanted to give toward the land purchase. Kristen and I both knew that our savings wasn't *our* money; it was *God's* money, entrusted to our management for a season. We kept a small amount of money as an emergency fund and decided to give the rest to our church. I don't think we've ever given more money at any one time than we did with this opportunity.

When the money was in the bank, it was our treasure. It provided a sense of safety and security. But when we gave the money away, God's work and His church became our treasure. We could make this decision together because we believed and lived out Matthew 6:19–21. We knew we were accountable for how we spent every penny of our resources.

The Bible is filled with verses encouraging us to be generous. For example, in 1 Timothy 6:18–19, Paul said, "Command them to do good, to be rich in good deeds, and to be generous and willing to share. In this way they will lay up treasure for themselves as a firm foundation for the coming age, so that they may take hold of the life that is truly life."

Be generous. Give to your church or to others in need. I've never heard anyone say at the end of their life they wish they hadn't given away so much. In fact, it's usually the opposite. Are you and your future spouse aligned in your desires for where you want your money to go?

4. What's Your Family History with Money?

Our family's view of money has a huge impact on the way we grow up and how we currently steward our resources. Think through what your family did with finances growing up and discuss it with your significant other. Did you purchase new or used cars? Did you go on expensive family vacations, or did you visit other family members for your vacation? Did both of your parents work growing up, or did one parent work and the other stay at home?

This conversation becomes even more significant when you think about the fact that many people grew up in broken homes or single-parent homes. For example, the boyfriend who grew up in a dual-income family will view money in a very different light than the girlfriend who grew up with her mom and two brothers in a single-parent family. We often view the way we grew up as normal and right, and anything else seems strange to us.

How did you handle money in a previous relationship? If you're previously married, how did you and your former spouse handle money? Discuss with your significant other what you did well and what needs to change. I know some of these conversations can be hurtful, especially when you have to think of prior relationships, but they provide great opportunities to make different and better decisions in the future.

5. What's Your Personal History with Money?

This conversation gives you insight into each other's day-to-day habits with money. This could be as small as how often you buy a latte at Starbucks to how often you buy new cars. We each have personal habits that seem normal to us but might seem bizarre to our future spouse.

6. Do You View Yourself as an Owner or a Steward?

Each one of us is given different amounts of money and possessions with which to work and live. Are you the owner, and do you get to decide how to spend it? Or does it belong to God, and you are a steward of all your resources?

We don't often hear the word *steward* anymore. A steward is "someone entrusted with another's wealth or property and charged with the responsibility of managing it in the owner's best interest."[2] Psalm 24:1–2 tells us, "The earth is the LORD's, and everything in it, the world, and all who live in it; for he founded it on the seas and established it on the waters." The earth is the Lord's, and we are stewards (or managers) of whatever He has entrusted to us. When you get married, you and your spouse are stewards of the resources God has entrusted to you as a couple.

These discussions about money are not just numbers and equations in a spreadsheet. These numbers represent how we view the resources God has entrusted to us while on earth. We each possess some level of hurt and baggage around how much we spend and how little we might give. Or we might feel a sense of pride because we live off a little and give away a lot.

Before you tie the knot, you need to decide if you view yourself as an owner or a steward of money. If you are an owner, then you get to make the decisions and call the shots. If you are a steward, then you are accountable to God to manage well the resources He has entrusted to you. If you're not aligned with your significant other in your view of whether you are owners or stewards, then you're going

Knot-Tying Tip

What's the Best Way to Keep Track of Your Finances and Develop a Budget?

We have an abundance of options to keep track of income and expenses and how to develop a budget. To name just a few:

- Keep a handwritten ledger of expenses and bills.
- Use a simple Excel spreadsheet.
- There are many software/app options to help budget and track expenses. Use software such as Mint, Quicken, or YNAB (You Need A Budget). If you don't know where to start, look into the resources from Dave Ramsey and Financial Peace University.[3] Some of these are free, while others come with a small cost.

What's the best method to budget and track expenses? Whichever one you'll use. Try out several formats and use the one that works best for you as a couple. Kristen and I use Quicken, but we've tried several others over the years. Pick a system and look for an option you're both able to easily access.

to struggle with money. This decision guides the way you think about giving, saving, spending, debt, and everything else related to finances.

The Rest of the Story

When we last saw Kyle and Meghan, they were starting out their marriage with a whopping $120,000 debt. What did they decide to do about it?

Kyle: We knew we needed to make some drastic changes, or else we would be stuck paying off our debt for decades. We wanted to buy a house and have kids, but we feared moving in that direction with the large amount of debt we carried.

Meghan: We brought together a group of friends and mentors and shared our full financial picture. We asked for wisdom and counsel and asked them to help us see what we couldn't see and to help where we needed help. We realized we needed to invite others in so that we didn't cut off part of God's provision in community to help us steward the resources God had entrusted to us.

Kyle: We made some significant decisions to attack our debt. Instead of wallowing in debt for twenty-five years, we challenged each other to pay off the entire debt in less than five years. Meghan switched to a higher-paying job, and I dropped out of seminary and ended my ministry internship so I could take a full-time job as a CPA.

Meghan: Kyle never viewed my debt as just *my* debt. He always saw it as *our* debt and that we would attack our financial challenges as a couple. We worked as a team to knock out our debt, and in five years we paid it all off! Everything changed in our relationship. We no longer were a "slave to the lender" (Prov. 22:7) but were able to live in financial freedom. Our debt no longer held us back from growing our family and eventually buying our first home. Kyle is back in full-time vocational ministry, and I'm able to work part-time at our church and stay at home with our two boys the rest of the time.

Kyle: We still invite others in to help us make financial decisions. We don't make major financial decisions in isolation. Most people don't want others to see how they spend their money and how little or much they give. But we've realized the benefit of community and how wise friends can help us make good decisions.

To best help you get ready for marriage, make sure you have the six conversations about money recommended in this chapter. When couples fail to discuss finances or align financial expectations, they often face marital strife and discord. When you take the time to align your beliefs and expectations, money can become a source of great joy and generosity.

Am I Ready?

- Answer the six questions above and be ready to discuss them with your significant other.
- Do you consider yourself to be a spender or saver? What about your significant other? What makes you answer the way you responded?
- What are some future hopes and dreams you have when it comes to spending money? What are some hopes you have about being generous with your money?

Strengthening Our Knot

- Set aside a few hours to talk through the six questions outlined in this chapter.
- Discuss your answers to the Am I Ready? questions about money and financial stewardship.
- If you have children (or plan to), do you both plan on working after the kids are born, or do you plan on one of you staying home with your children? If you plan on having one of you stay home, then do the best you can

to live off one income as a married couple before you have children. This will help you budget and prepare to live off the income of the one who will continue to work.

Closing Prayer

Lord, thank You that You are the owner of everything and trust us with resources to steward during our time on earth. Help us to be willing to have honest conversations about money and possessions. Give us wisdom to quickly resolve arguments about money. Help us to develop a stewardship mindset and see resources as "Yours" first and "ours" second—and not "his" or "hers." Help us to be generous as a couple. Thank You for Your generosity toward us, best exemplified in the way You gave Your Son for us. In His name, we pray. Amen.

6

Who's in Charge, and What Are Our Biblical Roles?

The Part of Marriage TV Shows Never Get Right

Based on stereotypes seen on TV, how would you describe the typical husband? He'd probably be lazy, passive, weak, indifferent, selfish, and checked out of the marriage.

How would you describe the typical wife? She'd probably be dominant, assertive, overworked, underpursued, whiny, and unhappy. She does everything in the house while he sits on the couch watching *SportsCenter* all night.

Culture does us no favors in helping us understand God's ideal for a godly husband and wife. Most of us lack role models to help point us in the right direction, and chances are good you didn't grow up in a home with solid models of biblical roles in marriage.

Roles in marriage are among the most misunderstood concepts in marriage. Most people don't know what the Bible says about the roles of husband and wife, so we tend to choose according to our *desires* rather than God's *design* for marriage. A proper understanding of God's design will best help you get ready for marriage.

Meet Andy and Heather

Andy and Heather have been married for thirty-seven years and have two adult children.

Heather: Andy and I met during our freshman year at Oklahoma State University in History 101. My friends and I scoured the room for cute guys, and I immediately noticed Andy. We met in person a few weeks later at a sorority event before a football game—I knew his sister, so I got to meet him.

Andy: I wasn't a believer at the time, but Heather was a follower of Christ. I thought she was beautiful and seemed like a fun girl to party and hang out with. We were interested in each other, but she wouldn't date or spend too much time with me because I wasn't a follower of Christ. Over time we started to develop a friendship, and I eventually trusted in Christ as my Savior during our junior year in college.

Heather: I was interested in him early on, but I knew we didn't live off the same spiritual foundation. I knew Jesus needed to be the center of everything we did and believed. Once Andy trusted in Christ, our relationship changed. We did a Bible study together and had a fun first date. We ate, and then he taught me how to play backgammon. He was fun, different than other guys I knew, and he made me laugh.

Andy: From that point on, we did everything a premarried couple should do: we met with a pastor, listened to some teachings on marriage, and had everything we needed to have a long-term, successful, thriving, Christ-centered marriage. We joyfully said "I do" to each other in 1982.

Heather: We had a deep friendship, no debt, and good jobs. Both sets of parents liked each other and liked us—we had it made! We had healthy relationships with siblings, no divorce in either of our immediate families, and weren't sexually active before marriage. We soon realized, however, that our relationship was performance-based and we didn't understand the picture of biblical, Christlike, sacrificial love.

Andy: Because we were immature in our faith and because no one really told us what roles in marriage should look like, we didn't understand God's design for marriage. I didn't know what it meant to love Heather like Christ loved the church, and there was no way Heather was going to submit to my poor leadership.

Heather: From our honeymoon, we struggled. At times, Andy's communication was explosive, and he wanted to control everything. I worked for a bank and got lots of affirmation from others at work but wasn't getting much at home. I found my significance in the wrong things, and we were ill-equipped to deal with our problems. Before long, I sought comfort from a coworker and we had an affair. I never, ever thought this would happen to me. I thought I was bulletproof, so I flirted with other guys. I couldn't deal with the problems at home and sought happiness with someone who wasn't my husband.

Andy: Meanwhile, I was a terrible spouse. I was passive, checked-out, weak, and addicted to pornography and masturbation. I worked long hours because work was easier than home, and I didn't cherish or value my wife. While Heather was the one who had the affair, I take responsibility for the weak, broken condition of our marriage. If I had loved her as Christ loves the church, I believe our story would be completely different.

I hope you see from their story why a proper understanding of roles in marriage is so crucial to helping you get ready for marriage.

Three Prominent Views on Marriage Roles

At the risk of oversimplifying a very complex topic, most Christian couples view biblical roles in marriage in one of three ways:

1. *Traditional.* The husband does everything outside the house, and the wife does everything inside the house. He does the yard, the cars, earns the money, and makes the decisions. She stays at home with kids, does housework, cooks meals, and does most of the shopping.

2. *Egalitarian.* The husband and wife lead the marriage and household equally. They both work (before and after kids) and share responsibilities around the home. They make decisions together as a couple, and if things fall apart, they are equally responsible for making the mess and cleaning things up.

3. *Transitional.* The man and woman are each made in God's image and likeness (Gen. 1:27) and are equal in God's eyes (Gal. 3:28). The husband and wife share tasks both inside and outside the home, primarily based on preference or willingness to serve their spouse in areas where they don't

like to spend their time and efforts. This view requires a selfless and humble spirit but sees the ultimate good in glorifying God with their efforts and serving their spouse in the process. Even though the husband and wife are equal in God's eyes, the husband is the leader of the relationship and the wife submits to his leadership. Even if a problem is not his fault, as the leader the man is responsible for making sure the issue is resolved.

I most closely align with the transitional view of marriage roles. This is what Kristen and I do in our marriage: we both shop, cook, and do tasks inside and outside of the home. I work full-time at our church, and Kristen works part-time as a physical therapist. She has more margin than I do, so she does the majority of the shopping, cleaning, and cooking. This division of responsibilities is not because she's a woman and I'm a man but because our schedules better allow for her to do those tasks.

You and your significant other will need to have many discussions around roles and your expectations of who will do what in your marriage. Here are a few examples:

- Who will do the laundry? Cooking? Cleaning? Oil changes? Mow the grass?
- Who will pay the bills and balance the budget?
- Even more important, how will you decide the answers to all these questions? How will you handle arguments or disagreements related to roles and expectations?

This is just the tip of the iceberg. Much of this will change over the years as you discover new tasks and better discern how you each can best use your time, gifts, and resources.

Look for the One Best Way to Serve Each Other

You probably have one task that you really hate doing. You know you have to do it, but you only do it because it absolutely has to be done. Perhaps you have a dog, and the least favorite part of your day is when you need to throw the leash on your dog and walk it around the block. You know if you don't, the problems might pile up (pun intended).

For some people, it's doing the dishes or cleaning the bathroom. For others, it might be taking out the trash or mowing the lawn. For me, it's doing laundry. Our laundry room is not built for people of my large size, and I especially struggle with sorting my boys' clothes (especially all their socks). For Kristen, it's deboning rotisserie chicken. She doesn't like the smell or the feeling of pulling chicken off the bone. You might love doing laundry and deboning chicken, but you have something you don't like to do, and your significant other has something they dislike as well.

In Philippians 2:3–4, Paul wrote, "Do nothing out of selfish ambition or vain conceit. Rather, in humility value others above yourselves, not looking to your own interests but each of you to the interests of the others." Here's a Knot-Tying Tip that will serve you well in marriage: find that one thing your spouse hates to do, and do it for all the days of your marriage. Put your spouse's needs before your own, and look for ways to serve them in the task they don't like to do.

Equal in Rank, Different in Role

To understand God's design for roles in marriage, we need to dive into a short lesson on the Trinity. A right understanding of the Trinity is relevant to a discussion about biblical roles.

I believe there is one God (Deut. 6:4–5). I also believe that the Father, the Son, and the Spirit are each God, and that the Father and the Son and the Spirit are each a distinct person.[1] While the Father, Son, and Spirit are equal to each other, they still play different roles. The Son is the only One who is fully God and fully human. The Spirit dwells in all who believe in Jesus. The Son submits to the Father (John 4:34, 8:28; Heb. 10:7; 1 John 4:10). Likewise, the Spirit is sent by Jesus and proceeds from the Father (John 14:26; 15:26).

Even though they are equal in nature, the Father does not submit to the Son or Spirit. The Son and Spirit submit to the Father. They each have unique roles but are still equal in rank.

Ephesians 5 helps us understand how the unique roles and equal rank in the Trinity inform our view of marriage. Ephesians 5:22–24 says the wife is to submit to the husband. Most people don't like the word *submit* in marriage because it has a negative connotation. Many think *submissive* means *inferior*. Likewise, when Genesis 2:18 says the Lord created the woman as a "suitable helper," many believe this to mean the wife is in an inferior role. This couldn't be further from the truth.

If you have any negative connotation about these roles, it's not because there's a problem with the roles. It's because these roles have been abused or misunderstood. The role of the husband and wife are equally Christlike; they just have different responsibilities and opportunities.

In a biblical marriage, the wife joyfully submits to her husband's leadership because he loves and serves her. When the husband cares for her as Christ loves the church, the wife will gladly follow his leadership. This especially holds true when the husband and wife both apply Ephesians 5:21, which says we are to mutually "submit to one another out of reverence for Christ."

How Do Biblical Roles Play Out for the Seriously Dating or Engaged Couple?

When does submission start—before or after the wedding day?[2] A relationship leading to marriage should, over time and as the couple gets closer to the wedding date, resemble a marriage. After all, in a normal Christian relationship, they are beginning to function as "one" in many respects, with the obvious exception of sexual intimacy. They begin to spend money with the other's interest in mind, make housing decisions thinking of their future together, and work through future in-law issues as a couple.

When big decisions or conflicts arise during the dating and engagement period, the couple should work through those issues with each other's interest in mind. The man should want to increase in his ability to lead and love the woman in the same way that Christ loves the church. The woman should want to respect his leadership in the relationship and should want to be the helpmate in a greater capacity.

By the time they reach the altar, ideally most couples are already functioning relationally as husband and wife. I wouldn't say to a guy, "Today you can be a jerk. You can act in your own selfish interests. Don't worry about your future wife. But tomorrow, after your wedding, you'll need to love and serve her as Christ did the church." Nor would I say to a woman, "Today, you're allowed to be disrespectful and are within your rights to usurp your future husband's leadership. But tomorrow, after your wedding, you'll need to respect and honor him as the head of the home."

I encourage you to continue to grow in your roles as future husband and wife. He should continue to learn more about what it means to lead well, and she should continue to learn about what it means to be a God-honoring wife.

While you are dating, talk about these roles and make sure you're aligned in your view of them. The decision you make regarding your roles in the relationship will help determine how you function as husband and wife. It will impact the way you make decisions and the ways you practically process counsel from others. If you and your spouse disagree on how you will handle roles in marriage, you will want to get counsel from someone else. Talk to a mentor, pastor, married couple, or biblical counselor. You will make decisions in your marriage every day, so you will want alignment on how you make decisions and handle roles in marriage. If you continue to disagree about marriage roles, then you are staring at a yellow or red relational traffic light.

By the way, I've never told my wife that, since I'm the leader, I'm making the decision and she needs to step in line because she's my wife and submits to my leadership. In fact, no God-honoring couple I know has ever played this card. Any guy who leads this way borders on being a bully and a manipulator. The husband is to love like Christ and lead like a servant. No godly husband would ever force his wife to "fall in line."

The Rest of the Story

How are Andy and Heather doing today? The last we heard from them, Andy was looking at porn, and Heather had an affair with an acquaintance from work.

Heather: Things got worse before they got better. I knew I wasn't going to divorce Andy, but on several occasions, I prayed he would die so I would be free to marry someone else. I'm not proud of my prayers, but I felt trapped and he didn't love me as Christ loves the church.

Andy: When I found out about the affair, I knew I needed to make some changes in our marriage and in my life. I'd made our marriage so performance-based—almost as if Heather had to earn my love and affection. I realized how I fell short when I looked at Christ's example of love toward us. He doesn't wait for us to initiate; rather He "demonstrated his own love for us in this: While we were still sinners, Christ died for us" (Rom. 5:8). He didn't wait but initiated. It was time for me to do the same.

Heather: Everything changed for us when we got plugged into a healthy church and started applying Paul's marital wisdom from Ephesians 5. I realized I needed to work with Andy, like Genesis 2:18–25 says, and not compete against him. We were on the same team and needed to start acting like it.

Andy: The fruit of the Spirit (Gal. 5:22–23) did not flow from my life. I wasn't a horrible person, but I wasn't nearly as kind and loving as I thought I was. I didn't lighten Heather's load, serve her, or value and cherish her. I began to understand why she went outside of our marriage for affirmation. I didn't excuse or justify the infidelity, but I gained a better grasp of why she prayed for my death! I started to work through my pornography issue and knew that if I was going to lead my wife and fully follow Jesus, then I needed to work through all my sin struggles.

Heather: I wasn't thrilled to learn about Andy's struggle with porn, but I knew I needed to forgive him, as he forgave me for my infidelity and as Christ forgave us for all our sin—past, present, and future. I noticed a new desire in him to love and serve me and our kids. For the first time in our marriage, he started to love me as Christ loves the church. I knew I could follow his lead wherever he took us in marriage.

When I think of a man I want to be like when I grow up, the first person I think of is Andy. He is humble, kind, and knows God's Word as well as anyone I know. He didn't become a follower of Christ until his junior year of college but has more than made up for lost time. He's serious about his faith, and his marriage began to thrive when he and Heather began to do what God's Word instructed. When he started to love like Christ and lead like a servant, everything changed.

Heather is as strong a woman as I've ever met. She's a gifted teacher and communicator. God gave her the gifts of leadership and teaching, and she has used them well. She could easily dominate any marriage and any husband. But when she grasped what it meant to help and submit in marriage to Andy, her life began to change.

One of the most important decisions you will need to make about your relationship is how you view roles in marriage. I pray your conversations will allow you to serve and love one another as husband and wife.

Am I Ready?

- Think of examples of how roles in marriage are portrayed on television and in the movies. What's healthy and not healthy about the way culture portrays marriage?
- How did your parents live out biblical roles in your home as you were growing up? Did your parents provide a good or bad example of how a couple should function together in marriage?
- What's your view of roles in marriage? Do you hold to a traditional, egalitarian, or transitional view of roles? What Scripture can you use to support your view?

Strengthening Our Knot

- Discuss your answers to the Am I Ready? questions about biblical roles in marriage.
- Discuss with your significant other what your family was like as you were growing up. Share how your parents made decisions. What would you like to incorporate into your marriage from your parents, and what would you like to leave out?
- How will you make decisions as a married couple? Discuss together.[3]

Closing Prayer

God, we thank You for Your beautiful design of marriage. Thank You for making man and woman in Your image and likeness and for creating us with different roles in marriage. Thank You for the ways You perfectly live out being equal in rank but different in roles in the Trinity. Help us be aligned in the ways we pursue each other and the ways we view our roles in marriage. When we lack wisdom, may we come to You and ask, knowing You will joyfully give us all the wisdom we need. In Jesus's name, we pray. Amen.

7

How Can We Pursue Emotional Intimacy?

How to Be Completely Naked while Fully Clothed

When I was six, my dad passed away from heart disease. When I was nine, my mom remarried a man we called "Mic" (rhymes with *tick*).

For over thirty years Mic worked as a sporting goods representative, a middleman between the retailers who sold sporting goods and the manufacturers. For example, he worked with Nike and helped retailers like DICK'S Sporting Goods know what new products would be released in the upcoming season.

Every year, many of the sporting goods manufacturers gathered for national conferences where they highlighted their new product lines. For example, these days Nike would promote a new line of LeBron James shoes or Under Armour would promote a new line of clothing from Steph Curry. The coolest part of these shows, for me, was that companies often brought in famous athletes to promote their products. Sometimes Mic brought me to the shows, and I'd get to walk through row after row of booths filled with company employees and famous athletes.

When he finished a show, he almost always brought me home a stack of pictures, index cards, or random pieces of paper signed by famous athletes. They wrote me personalized notes such as, "Good luck in your baseball game on Saturday against the Cheetahs."

For years, I saved all my autographs in a scrapbook. I held a deep-seated hope that one day I could sell those autographs and try to make some money to go toward my kids' college fund.

A few years ago, I looked more closely at all the autographs. I noticed they looked similar to one another. Sure enough, after confirming with my mom and brother, I concluded Mic, who died of Alzheimer's disease in 2017, had forged almost every one of those autographs. No real notes wishing me luck in the game. No future college fund. Just a scrapbook of pictures signed by my stepdad.

I don't harbor any ill feelings toward Mic. I think he was simply looking for a way to connect with me and make his stepson happy. But in the end, I was reminded of a great object lesson—fake is worthless.

Often, in fact, fake turns others away. It can build walls between people. And if it's the spiteful and mean-spirited kind, fake is even detested by the Lord (Prov. 12:22). You and I both desire what is genuine and real in life, not forgeries and fakes. And nowhere else in life is this truer than in the arena of relationships. Even more specific, in marriage, God's ideal is for the man and woman to be naked together without shame (Gen. 2:25).

The Nakedness Goes beyond No Clothes

I can't even fathom the concept of being physically naked and not feeling shame. I'm embarrassed and insecure about the way I look. If you're like almost every other person I've ever met, you probably struggle with some level of insecurity about your body and the way God made you as well. Most of us feel this way—body-image issues, comparison, and neglect of the body lead us to feel shame and to hide.

You might think you are too short, too tall, too big, or too little. Your curves are too wide or not wide enough. The possibilities are endless. And unfortunately, this extends far beyond just our physical appearance. Our entire lives are marked by shame, even when we're fully clothed.

Genesis 2:25 says that Adam and Eve were without clothes yet felt no shame. This is a beautiful picture of what we can long for on earth and will ultimately experience in eternity. While it's certainly true that the man and woman were physically naked, they were also emotionally naked. This meant they kept it real with one another and felt no shame. They communicated without insecurity. The woman expressed her feelings without wondering what her husband thought about her. The man didn't judge her body, and neither of them had to compare themselves to anyone else.

Imagine the scene. The Garden of Eden was filled with beautiful colors, vegetation, and animals of every variety. In the middle of it all stood a naked man and a naked woman. They didn't need to hide, and they were completely exposed and felt no shame. It was good and right!

I love the way my friend Dave Willis describes this scene:

> The first picture of sex and marriage the Bible paints for us tells us that the couple was naked but felt no shame. This is a beautiful image of the vulnerability, trust, honesty, transparency and intimacy that should create a healthy foundation for every marriage. God wants a husband and wife to be "naked" physically, spiritually and emotionally with one another. When you have a "naked marriage" with no secrets and total vulnerability, you can experience perfect intimacy without shame or fear.[1]

Then Genesis 3 comes along. The serpent deceived the man and woman, and they ate the fruit from the tree in the middle of the garden. Genesis 3:7 says, "Then the eyes of both of them were opened, and they realized they were naked; so they sewed fig leaves together and made coverings for themselves." *Everything* changed in this moment. Adam and Eve went from naked without shame to hiding, covering, blaming, and selfishing (yes, it's a made-up word, but you get the point). In that moment, emotional intimacy was lost.

But marriage calls us back to the Garden of Eden. Marriage is designed to create a safe place for a husband and wife to be exposed and without shame, and it is intended to be different from any other relationship. We mess this thing up big-time, and we pay the price. When couples hide, lie, and pretend in front of each other, it's the exact opposite of the oneness God intends and we desire.

I'm Hot for Teacher

When I was growing up, I loved the song "Hot for Teacher" by rock band Van Halen. In 1997, when I started my third internship in graduate school for physical therapy, I was "hot for teacher." I sat on the exercise mat on the third floor of the Shepherd Center (a comprehensive rehabilitation center), and in walked the woman who would eventually become my wife. That day Kristen appeared was love at first sight for one of us. For the other? Let's just say it took Kristen a few years to get with the program!

Kristen: I met Scott in 1997, and I thought he was a nice guy and a really good physical therapy student. He made me laugh, and we hung out together with a great group of friends. I was a brand-new follower of Christ, and Scott was in the searching phase of his faith. I was dating another guy, and to be honest, I had no attraction toward Scott.

Scott: I can tell you exactly what Kristen wore the first day we met. She was tall, confident but not cocky, beautiful, and clearly had her stuff together. I whispered a quick "Thank You, Jesus" under my breath, stood up, and shook her hand. It took everything in me to not throw her down on the mat and start kissing her!

Kristen: Scott finished his internship, graduated from physical therapy school, and took a job working with me and our other friends at the Shepherd Center. Even though I was still dating this other guy, Scott and I started spending a lot of time together. We ran together, did a coed Bible study with coworkers, and went to church together almost every week.

Scott: I trusted in Christ a few months before starting my job as a physical therapist and started to develop a voracious appetite for God's Word. One day I professed my deep affection for Kristen. She was probably the last to know! She was on-again, off-again with this other guy, but I didn't care.

Kristen: My attraction for Scott started to grow. I saw his faith and his love for people, and took note of the way he cherished and valued me. We started to date but really didn't know what we were doing. We crossed lines physically and emotionally, and our relationship did not honor the Lord. Even though we weren't having sex, we didn't honor each other well.

Scott: To make a long story short, I struggled with my past: pornography, insecurity, people-pleasing, self-hatred, guilt and shame over sexual sin, and so much more. I was afraid of opening up to Kristen and didn't want to deal with my past. I didn't want her to know my deep, dark secrets. Like Adam and Eve covered themselves in the garden, I covered myself around Kristen. I didn't want her to see the parts of my life I was ashamed of.

Kristen: In the spring of 2000, Scott and I broke up. Apart from each trusting in Christ as our Savior, it might have been the best thing that ever happened to Scott and me.

Before I finish the story, you need to learn more about emotional intimacy.

What Does It Mean to Be Naked without Shame?

Often when we hear the word *intimacy*, we think first of sexual intimacy. While this is certainly a component of intimacy, it's not the only facet we need to discuss. Emotional intimacy is about sharing our thoughts, feelings, hopes, dreams, past, struggles, and much more without fear of rejection. Over the years, I've come to define *intimacy* as "to fully know and be fully known without fear of rejection."

Emotional intimacy looks different depending on the person or group of people with whom you're relating. I like to think about it in terms of concentric circles.

- The outermost ring of the circle contains people such as acquaintances and coworkers. I want to be honest with them and not lie, but they also don't need to know my struggles or feelings.

- The next ring toward the center consists of close friends. This might be your best friends, other people in your small group, or close family members. This would be the group of men or women who will soon stand by your side as groomsmen or bridesmaids. I share more and more with this group of friends. They don't know everything about me, but I'm honest, transparent, and desire to know them and be known by them.

- The next circle is your significant other. As you move closer to the altar and after you become husband and wife, you will share just about everything with each other. This is what it means to be naked and without shame. Because of sin, insecurity, communication issues, or perception problems, you may be tempted not to share everything with your significant other, but this level of emotional intimacy should be as good as it gets in a human relationship.

- The center of the circle is God. He knows everything about you anyway, whether you let Him or not. He is all-knowing (Job 34:21; Ps. 139:2–3; Matt. 10:30) and all-loving (John 3:16; Rom. 5:8; 1 John 4:10).

Concentric Circle of Emotional Intimacy

As a seriously dating or engaged couple, you are in a crucial stage of your relationship as you get ready to tie the knot. You're learning new things about each other every day and discovering more about yourself and about marriage. You should feel the comfort and freedom to move closer and closer toward the center of these concentric circles as you share without fear of rejection.

Three Areas of Emotional Intimacy

Emotional intimacy consists of three main areas of life.

Your Past

Each of you has a story before you came together in your relationship, and your past affects you much more than you realize. In marriage, if you're going to be intimate emotionally, then you need to be able to share all aspects of your past. Your spouse should know your past hurts, struggles, and addictions (we'll talk more about sexual past in the next chapter). You should also know about the great parts of each other's past: the wins, terrific memories, and achievements. We all have many aspects of our lives in the past. Are you willing to share those with each other?

If you're going to be naked without shame, you ought to be able to share your past with your significant other.

Your Present

I can tell Kristen everything about my life. She knows my stress points, prayer requests, and sin struggles. In particular, Kristen knows all about my battle with food and weight. As I mentioned earlier, I've struggled with overeating for almost my whole life. Kristen prays for me, helps me, encourages me, and challenges me. She also knows my wins—when I have a good day of eating, when I'm not obsessed with food, and when I experience victory in my battle with eating.

Every one of us struggles with something. Are you honest about your struggles, and have you shared them with each other? If you're going to be emotionally naked without

Don't Date Each Other's PR Departments

The role of a Public Relations Director (PRD) is to help someone manage their reputation. Their job is to "promote clients and make them seem as successful, honest, important, exciting or relevant as possible."[2] Professional athletes and celebrities often need a PRD to help create a favorable public persona. Sometimes PRDs have to take the bad from someone's past and help make it seem better than reality.

Although you've probably never hired a PRD, you've more than likely indirectly benefited from their services. When we start dating someone, we act like a PRD. We manage our reputation, and we do whatever we can to seem as successful, honest, important, exciting, and relevant as possible. We want our significant other to be impressed by us, so we put our best face forward. We watch what we eat, work out more than ever, and share only what we want the other person to know about us. We excel in letting others see only what we want them to see.

In other words, when we date, we're often filled with lies and half-truths. And guess what? So is the other person we're trying to impress. We date and pursue each other's PRDs. Unfortunately, this is the exact opposite of what we're called to be in marriage—naked without shame.

Fire your PRD, and be honest and authentic with each other.

shame, you should be able to share your present struggles and victories with each other.

Your Future

One of my dreams in life is to write a book. I'm living out my dream as I type these words. I want to leave a legacy and make my life count. I want my kids to grow up with a deep love for Jesus, and I want them to get married and give me lots of grandkids (all perfectly behaved, of course).

Kristen has dreams as well. She also wants to make her life count. She wants to share her faith and develop deep friendships. She wants to continue to have an impact on the patients she sees as a physical therapist. She wants to travel and to do a triathlon with our kids.

We each have fears about the future as well. I have no idea how we are going to afford to send four kids to college. We have fears about health concerns and the direction of our nation and world. Some of our fears are rational, whereas others might stem from a weak faith and trust in God.

Emotionally intimate couples can share their future dreams and fears with each other. They don't all have to come to fruition in the future, but we should be able to share them without fear of mockery or rejection.

The Rest of the Story

So, what happened after Kristen and I broke up in the spring of 2000? Here's a brief glimpse at the rest of our story.

Scott: After breaking up, we both got serious about our faith. We dealt with our past, worked on our struggles, and got more involved at church. We both began to lead our small groups and serve at church. Kristen and I still worked together and went to the same church, but we were friends and that was it. I was ready to move on.

Kristen: I watched Scott grow in his relationship with Christ, and I saw how he led others at our church. The tables turned as I started to get hot for my (former) student! Some friends encouraged me to get back together with Scott. I had a gift certificate for a really nice restaurant, so I asked him out and we had a blast together. Our relationship did a complete 180.

Scott: The second time around was different. We had each dealt with our hurts and struggles. I opened up to Kristen about my past sexual sin, my struggles with pornography, and my dreams of going into ministry. I apologized for my sexual sin and for not honoring her when we dated the first time around. She listened, granted forgiveness, and didn't reject me when I shared the "yuck" of my past. I knew I could be real with her, and she knew the same about me. We started dating, got engaged in February 2001, and tied the knot on September 15, 2001.

Kristen: We've developed the type of marriage where we can be naked without shame, emotionally and physically.

Kristen and I by no means have emotional intimacy figured out. At times, I still struggle with guilt and shame over my struggles with lust or overeating. At other times, Kristen struggles with sharing her feelings with me. But we are on the journey together and enjoy the challenge of being fully naked with each other.

"If You Have a Problem, We Will Fix It Together"

One of my favorite TV shows is *This Is Us*. Two of the central characters in the show are a married couple named Jack and Rebecca. In the season 1 finale, Jack and Rebecca separate due to some marriage struggles. Rebecca kicks Jack out, and their three kids stay with Rebecca in their home.

In the first episode of season 2, Rebecca goes to the house where Jack is staying, knocks on the door, and tells Jack she wants him to come home. She apologizes for kicking him out and says, "That's not what we do. That's not who we are. That's not us." She tells him they need to come back together and work on their marriage. Jack looks at her, and through slurred words tells her she doesn't know everything about him. He hasn't been emotionally intimate with her (my words, not his). He confesses to a major drinking problem and tells her, as he closes the door, that he needs to work through his problems on his own before he comes home.

The next scene makes me tear up even as I type the words. She knocks on the door again. When he opens it, she says, "You are my husband and I am your wife, and if you have a problem, we will fix it together."³

That's it, my friend. When you tie the knot, you agree to work on your marriage together. It's not his problem or her problem. It's *our* problem, and we work on it together. Emotional intimacy says we will pursue oneness as God intends. We will share our dreams, hurts, problems, and struggles. And when we do, we do so without shame, fear, guilt, rejection, or mockery.

Imagine what could happen if you and your significant other shared your challenges with each other and solved them together. You'd be on mission together. You'd be a picture of the gospel as you love each other without measured communication or fear of rejection. It's the way God loves us, and it's available to us in marriage.

Test the waters of emotional intimacy now as a premarried couple, and completely dive in after you say "I do." Whether you're fully naked (after you say "I do," please), or fully clothed, be emotionally naked without shame as God intends and you desire.

Am I Ready?

- Read Genesis 2:18–3:21. What was different before and after the fall of Adam and Eve? How does their sin affect you and your relationship today?
- How are you doing at being emotionally intimate? What are some of your fears about being emotionally intimate with your future spouse? What are you most excited about when it comes to emotional intimacy?
- What are some specific areas in which you're afraid to be intimate with your significant other? Are there some parts of your story, your current struggles, or future dreams or fears you are afraid of sharing? How can you "test the waters" of emotional intimacy by sharing a few things with your significant other?

Strengthening Our Knot

- Discuss your answers to the Am I Ready? questions about emotional intimacy.
- Do you feel accepted, respected, and admired by your significant other? If not, why not? If so, let them know what makes you feel this way.
- What are some specific aspects of your past, present, and future you need to discuss together? Create time

and space to have honest conversations with each other about some aspects of your relationship you may not have already discussed.

• Discuss how you think you are doing at listening without judgment or rejection.

Closing Prayer

Lord, thank You that You know everything about us and still choose to love us. We pray that we would live out this same love in our relationship. Help us to not hide, pretend, or fake it. Help us to communicate about our past, present, and future, and to be naked without shame. God, we pray that through this season of dating and engagement we would get a glimpse of what it means to know and be fully known without fear of rejection. In Jesus's name, we pray. Amen.

8

What Do We Need to Know about Sex?

Finding Fulfillment between the Sheets

From 2002 to 2006, I worked on and completed my master of theology degree from Dallas Theological Seminary. One year after I graduated and started my job at Watermark, I audited a class called Human Sexuality, taught by Dr. Douglas Rosenau from the Institute for Sexual Wholeness.

I profoundly remember when Dr. Rosenau asked the class to think of all the words, both clinical and slang, that each of us knew for sexual activities and body parts. If grades were awarded for knowing the most words, I would've broken the curve and received an A+. My mind was flooded with so much slang, because for most of my life I lived far from the Lord. My sexual vocabulary sure proved it.

I don't share this story to brag about how many words I knew. Rather, I share it because I, like many of you, have cheapened a great gift from a loving God. Dr. Doug had deeper motives with his question. He wanted us to realize how our vocabulary, and the distorted values it portrayed, reduced something beautiful and intimate down to a bunch of crude, crass terms that were so far from God's intent for sexuality and true lovemaking.

I knew those terms because I looked at way too much porn and lived out too much of what I saw. I took God's gift of sexual intimacy and did everything I could to ruin it and ruin my life. Porn. Manipulation. Selfishness. Pleasure-seeking. Sin.

It's time to talk about sex. This might be the hardest chapter to write and to rightly capture the heart of God. I want to start by telling you God loves you. Whether you've sinned sexually for as far back as you can remember or you've never looked at porn or crossed any boundaries physically and have repressed your sexual feelings, each of us walks into relationships and marriage with some level of pain, guilt, and shame connected to sex. Wherever you fall in this spectrum, remember God loves you, He is good, and He is worthy of your trust.

I'm encouraged by your desire to seek God's best in your relationship. That's why you're reading this book. I hope this chapter helps you grow in your relationship with Christ and your significant other as we discuss a topic that might be marked by guilt and shame in your life.

Meet Rob and Crystal

For years, Rob and Crystal each lived far from the Lord. They both brought a decent amount of sexual baggage into their dating and marriage relationship. Their story is one of hope and redemption.

Rob: Crystal and I met when I was in the middle of an "I'm not dating anyone" season of life. I saw this beautiful brunette sitting across from me in Starbucks and told my friend she was my type of girl. She was with a friend of mine, so of course I needed to go say hey to my friend. Crystal and I shook hands, and that was it. For now.

Crystal: Rob was my type of guy. Fortunately, the gal I was sitting with was my mentor, and she immediately knew I was attracted to Rob. She said to me, "No, you're not going to date him. We're studying the Bible together and that's all you need to know right now." She was right, so I moved on. A few years later I took a job at our church working with our young adult ministry and re-met Rob when we started working together on a young adult event.[1]

Rob: Even though I was attracted to her in every way, I chose not to pursue anything with her. One day I was with my friend in his truck, and we had one of the windows half-open. We drove by Crystal, who was holding a football in her hands. She zinged the football at my friend's truck and the ball went right through the window. Game changer—she's attractive, she loves Jesus, and she can throw a football! A few days later, I asked her out for coffee.

Crystal: God ordained that football throw—it might have been the best pass I've ever thrown in my life! I was super attracted to Rob, so I was pretty pumped when he asked me out. We had a great first date and talked for hours. Soon after, we became an official couple and started dating. We went through our church's premarital class, got engaged in July 2009, and got married in November 2009.

Rob: We both knew we wanted to date each other in a different way than we had dated other people in the past. Both of us had been sexually active in other relationships, and we each had a significant history with pornography.

Rob and Crystal have a story similar to many couples reading this book. Over the last six years, our church has done anonymous surveys with men and women in our pre-married class. Over 75 percent of all individuals in the class have been sexually active in the past. Most of the guys look at pornography at least one time per month, and around 20 percent of the women have been sexually abused. I don't want to assume this is your story or your past, but one common denominator among all dating or engaged individuals is we all have some level of fear, anxiety, or pain to work through when it comes to sexual intimacy. That's why we need to talk about God's design and plan for sexual intimacy, both before and after the wedding day.

What Does the Bible Say about Sexual Intimacy?

The Bible says a lot more about sexual intimacy than you probably think it does, and these verses should have direct implications on your relationship.

Sex Is Good, and the Body Is Good

God created our bodies and created us male and female. When He finished this work, He said it was not just *good* but "very good" (Gen. 1:31). He told the man and woman to "be fruitful and multiply" (Gen. 1:28 ESV). You don't have to be married to have sex and make babies, but the Bible shows us this is the ideal way God intends humanity to fill the earth.

God made sex pleasurable. He could have made it feel mildly enjoyable, like a good sneeze or the joy we feel when we laugh with friends. But he made it much better than that. He created our bodies to experience pleasure when we are sexually intimate with each other. Sex should lead us to worship and praise God.

We Can Have Sex to the Glory of God

In 1 Corinthians 10:31, Paul said we should do everything to the glory of God. Eat to the glory of God. Drink to the glory of God. Work to the glory of God. And have sex to the glory of God. It's easy for me to understand how to pray and study my Bible to the glory of God, but hard to imagine how we could have sex to His glory. But when enjoyed within the right context (of marriage), we can have sex and bring God glory.

Sex Is an Opportunity to Serve Your Spouse

According to 1 Corinthians 7:3–5, the husband's body belongs to the wife, and the wife's body belongs to her husband. Paul writes,

> The husband should fulfill his marital duty to his wife, and likewise the wife to her husband. The wife does not have authority over her own body but yields it to her husband. In the same way, the husband does not have authority over his own body but yields it to his wife. Do not deprive each other

except perhaps by mutual consent and for a time, so that you may devote yourselves to prayer. Then come together again so that Satan will not tempt you because of your lack of self-control.

Sex gives us the opportunity to serve our spouse and put their needs and desires before our own (Phil. 2:3–4). Your spouse is your only outlet sexually, so choose to serve them in that way even when you don't feel like it.[2]

You Were Bought at a High Price

God created sexual intimacy for couples to enjoy together within the context of marriage. Genesis 2:24 says, "That is why a man leaves his father and mother and is united to his wife, and they become one flesh." As discussed in chapter 1, physical intimacy is part of the one-flesh relationship. While you don't have to be married to enjoy the pleasures of sex, God intends for intimacy to be reserved for a couple after they commit to one another in marriage.

Before couples say "I do," God calls them to pursue each other with purity. There is to be no hint of sexual immorality in a couple (Eph. 5:3), and the "marriage bed" (aka sexual intimacy) is to be "kept pure" (Heb. 13:4). It is God's will that we, as followers of Jesus, "avoid sexual immorality" (1 Thess. 4:3). God is not silent on intimacy, and He cares very much for us. He's not trying to rip us off or withhold good from us. Rather, He is trying to set us free from the bondage of sexual sin.

In 1 Corinthians 6:12–20, Paul writes about intimacy. In verse 18, he tells the church to flee from sexual immorality because of the potentially devastating consequences of sexual sin. He goes on to say in verses 19–20, "Do you not know that your bodies are temples of the Holy Spirit, who is in you, whom you have received from God? You are not your own; you were bought at a price. Therefore honor God with your bodies."

You and I were purchased at a high price. No dollar amount can capture what God paid for our bodies—the high price of Jesus's death, burial, and resurrection. My body is not my own—it belongs to the Lord. He paid for it, so I will choose to honor Him with my body. This means I should honor God in what I eat, how I exercise, my sleep habits, and how I treat my body with regard to drinking, nicotine, and drugs. I want to honor God in what goes in my mouth and how I take care of my body. Part of honoring God is to remember that because Christ's death paid for my sin and my body, I will choose to honor Him in every way, including sexual intimacy and physical boundaries.

I believe we often misspeak about sexual intimacy. When couples cross boundaries, they say they made a "mistake" or "slipped." A mistake is when you forget something; for instance, if you forget to carry the one in long addition, you can call it a mistake. But when you engage in any kind of sexual activity before marriage, it's called *sin*. We need to call our actions what God calls them. We prefer to call it a mistake because we believe this diminishes its significance or impact. Sin is a big deal.

Some of you may have a story that is very different from the majority of premarried couples. Some of you will come into marriage without having crossed physical boundaries with anyone else. Maybe you've never seen or been directly affected by pornography. If this is your story, praise God! Thank Him that He has spared you from making poor decisions and from being on the receiving end of abuse. I'm encouraged by your faithfulness in trusting the Lord and not giving in to the lies society tells you about sex. You believe His promises hold life, and you have been willing to die to your sexual desires in order to most honor God. I pray my children will have your testimony.

What Are Some Healthy Physical Boundaries before Saying "I Do"?

Some of the most frequently asked questions in our premarried class are about purity. We often hear the question, "How far is too far?" Often what couples are trying to figure out with this question is how close they can get to the edge of sin without really sinning. I had the same question when I was in your shoes, so I understand well the question you might be asking. However, it's not a good question to ask, because you're really asking (without even knowing it) how far you can get away from God but still be in His good graces. You're asking how close to the edge you can get without falling over it.

Rather, I challenge you to stay as close to God as you can. I want you to choose to honor Him with every part of your life, including your body and your sexual desires.

Let's get explicit on some boundaries you can put in place to help you honor God with your body and honor each other before you say "I do." I care about you and your relationship and don't want to see you mess things up with sexual sin. Consider these loving words of wisdom from a guy who wants God's best for you.

1. *Don't open-mouth or tongue kiss.* In 1 Timothy 5:2, Paul instructs men to treat younger women as sisters, with absolute purity. You wouldn't open-mouth kiss your sister, so don't do the same with your significant other. Kissing can be the "gateway drug" that leads to other sexual activity. When you kiss someone in an intimate way, it causes you to be aroused. Your body is preparing for sexual activity, and you don't want to train your body to prepare for something God only intends for marriage.

2. *Don't get horizontal with each other.* Don't lie down together on the couch, on the floor, or anywhere else. This won't go well for you, and could lead to you getting horizontal on top of each other.

3. *Don't spend time alone in each other's house or apartment.* If you're alone, cuddled on the couch and watching a movie, stuff might happen. You may not intend for it to go anywhere, but isolated time on the couch, watching Netflix, could lead you to cross boundaries. Rather, go eat someplace in public or go see a movie in the theater. Crystal never even saw Rob's bedroom until she helped him and some friends pack up his stuff to move into their apartment after they got married.

4. *Avoid any substance that could cloud your judgment or lead you to compromise your boundaries.* This is not a moral rant against alcohol. But I do recommend you exercise caution when it comes to drinking and your relationship. Any substance that alters your judgment or leads to compromising behavior could lead you to cross boundaries you don't want to cross.

5. *Get a life—don't cut off all other relationships.* Spend time with friends and include them in your dates. Allow your community and friendships to be a part of your relationship (more on this in chapter 11). They will hold you accountable, and they can help keep you from crossing sexual boundaries.

6. *Take the long-term view.* You have your whole life together to enjoy the awesome gift of sexual intimacy. Don't compromise long-term satisfaction for short-term pleasure. Just as you don't want to be intimate with someone who is not your spouse after marriage, choose not to be intimate with someone who is not your spouse before marriage.

7. *Acknowledge the challenge of purity.* I know purity is a very legitimate challenge for premarried couples. It's completely understandable to struggle with sexual boundaries; in fact, if you don't struggle, that might be a problem. If you're not attracted to the other person or don't desire to be with your significant other sexually after marriage, then talk to a friend and get some help. This can be even more challenging if you've been sexually active in the past. Remember you are a new creation in Christ (2 Cor. 5:17), and you are under control of the Holy Spirit, not your fleshly desires (Gal. 5:16–18).

8. *Understand the why of purity.* Don't just take my word for it—search God's Word for His best with regard to physical intimacy (see Prov. 6:27–28; Eph. 5:3; 1 Cor. 6:12–20; 1 Thess. 4:3–8; Heb. 13:4). Couples who enjoy the benefits of intimacy before marriage (whether it's sexual intercourse, oral sex, or even grinding/dry humping), probably don't see the relationship as clearly as they think they do. If you're enjoying the fruits of intimacy, then you can easily overlook the faults or shortcomings in your relationship. It's as if you're

wearing love goggles that blind you to the problems. The orgasm and fun of intimacy tend to lead couples to minimize the problems and shortcomings in the relationship.

It's okay to want to be involved physically with your significant other. But I challenge the two of you to demonstrate self-control (Gal. 5:23) and to not mess around with temptation (1 Cor. 10:12–13). Before marriage, treat one another as you would a sibling (a brother or sister in Christ), in all purity. And then, after you get married, have all kinds of fun![3]

Choose to Honor God with Your Body

I beg you, if you are crossing boundaries with regard to purity, choose to honor God with your body. Have a conversation with a trusted friend or pastor and choose to exercise self-control. To be clear, you *should* struggle and *should* have desires to cross boundaries with your significant other. If you're not sexually attracted to them, then that's a whole different issue. The desire is not the problem; it's what you do with the desire.

One of the most comforting verses in the whole Bible to me is Hebrews 4:15, which says, "We do not have a high priest who is unable to empathize with our weaknesses, but we have one who has been tempted in every way, just as we are—yet he did not sin." Jesus gets it! He was tempted in many of the same ways you and I are tempted, yet He managed not to sin in the process.

I encourage you to choose to put in place boundaries that will help you and your future spouse pursue each other with purity. If you know you're going to struggle, as most couples

Knot-Tying Tip

Why Is Pornography So Destructive to Relationships?

Much has been said about the negative effects of pornography, and that's beyond the scope of this book.[4] But for your immediate benefit, I'll share a few dangers of pornography.

Many people don't see pornography as a big deal. They think everyone else is looking at it, and they could be doing much worse, like having an affair or going to prostitutes. Some see it like drinking a glass of wine with dinner: "No big deal; it's just part of my day."

It's easy to access pornography today. When I was growing up, you had to drive to a movie store to rent it, buy a magazine at a store, or subscribe to a magazine. Now, porn is pervasive—it's affordable, available 24/7, and anonymous. No one knows what you are doing or looking at. In the process, it numbs us and creates a false sense of reality. We compare our spouse to what someone else looks like in pornography.

Before you think porn is not that big of a problem, read Jesus's words in Matthew 5:27–30. Jesus compares looking at a woman with lustful intent to committing adultery. Even though Jesus addresses men in this passage, the principle applies to women as well. Whenever a woman looks at a man with lustful intent, she also has committed adultery in her heart. For women, it might not be movies, websites, or magazines but rather romance novels like *Fifty Shades of Grey*.

Increasingly over time, pornography is not just a men's issue. More women in our premarried class confess to looking at and struggling with pornography. It's caused so much damage in my own life, and I hate the day I saw pornography for the first time.[5] If pornography is not part of your story, then praise God. If it is, I strongly encourage you to confess to the Lord and to others, and get some help through a recovery ministry like re:generation recovery or Celebrate Recovery.[6]

do, then put the line way back so that you're far away from crossing boundaries.

The Rest of the Story

Rob and Crystal both had some struggles with pornography, and each brought a large amount of sexual baggage into marriage. Here's the good news: in God's remarkable grace and kindness, He enabled Rob and Crystal to pursue each other in a different way than either had dated in the past.

Rob: For the first time in my life, I dated someone well. I chose to honor God and honor Crystal by pursuing her with purity. Every other relationship in my past was marked by my selfish sexual desires. Crystal was different, and I was a different man than I had been in the past.

Crystal: Rob always let me know where we stood. He was clear about the boundaries we needed to set in place so we didn't cross lines sexually. He cared for me by not giving me everything I wanted. I wanted to stay out later on dates, and I wanted to hang out more. There's nothing wrong with spending more time together, but he did everything in his power to keep us from crossing lines we didn't want to cross. He dated and pursued me selflessly, and because of the way he cared for me, I knew I could trust him as my husband.

Rob: I knew we needed to talk about our past with each other. Our past didn't define us, but I wanted us to discuss anything that could possibly impact us in the future. I prepared a few questions for us to discuss together and made sure we created a safe place to talk about our sexual past. I didn't want or need all the details, but I did want to know what I might expect in the future. For example, I got a girl pregnant in the past, and we chose to get an abortion. I hate that I made that decision, but I wanted Crystal to know this part of my story. I know I'm forgiven and would never make that decision ever again. God has allowed me to encourage others with my story so that they don't choose to end a life like I did.[7]

Crystal: We had to remember Romans 8:1. Paul said, "There is now no condemnation for those who are in Christ Jesus." There's no sin so horrific that Jesus didn't already pay the price for it. It was finished, and we were not going to allow guilt and shame to rob us of intimacy as God intended and we desired. Satan will try to use the guilt of your past against you, and we chose not to let that happen in our relationship.

If you have crossed physical boundaries in your current or past relationship, I encourage you to read the story of the adulterous woman in John 7:53–8:11. Jesus did not condemn the woman for her sexual sin, but He commanded her to go and sin no more. God's best is for you to do the same. There is no condemnation if you are in Christ Jesus, but go and sin no more sexually.

The questions of when, why, and how to share about your sexual past might be the hardest questions I get asked in our premarital ministry.[8] Kristen and I sat down together and talked about our sexual past a few weeks before I proposed to her. I wanted her to know some of the details of my past, and I wanted to give her the opportunity to ask me any questions. I confessed to her my sexual sin, cried, and asked for her forgiveness. The way she forgave me and cared for me provided the confirmation I wanted and needed to put a ring on her finger. She showed me grace, and I knew she would be a safe place for me to share in the future.

Most married couples don't know how to discuss sexual intimacy with each other. They don't know they *should* talk about it, and many don't even know they *can* talk about it! If you set some good communication patterns now as a pre-married couple, it can help you down the road. Remember what you learned in chapter 2—create a safe place for each other, and be the kind of couple who can talk about anything and everything, including sexual intimacy. You shouldn't be more afraid to confess something to your significant other than you would be to confess it to the Lord.

Who Are the Most Sexually Satisfied Couples?

What couples are the most satisfied sexually? The answer to this question might surprise you. I assumed it would be couples in their twenties. They're young, flexible, have fewer kids and less stress, and probably are in the best shape of their lives.

If it's not the twenties (and it's not), then surely it must be couples in their thirties or *maybe* the forties. It can't be beyond that!

Oh, but it is. According to a recent study, the most sexually satisfied couples are in their fifties and sixties.[9] Guess what? That's probably your mom and dad, and they're home alone right now. While you recover from your nausea, let me tell you why I agree with this survey.

When Kristen and I are in our fifties and beyond, we will have shared many years of love, communication, trust, spiritual intimacy, and commitment. We'll know we love each other without condition. We will have decades of memories together, and for years we'll have pursued Jesus together.

While our stress might be higher and our health might be declining, I believe the intimacy we will have developed outside the bedroom will help our intimacy in the bedroom.

God gave us a great gift in sexual intimacy. It feels amazing, and it's a whole lot of fun. In *The Meaning of Marriage*, Tim Keller says every time you are sexually intimate with your spouse, you are reminded of the covenant commitment you made to each other in marriage.[10]

Exercise self-control now, remember God's not trying to steal your joy, and then renew that covenant every chance you can after you get married!

Am I Ready?

- What influences have shaped your view of sexual intimacy? For example, if porn is part of your story, when was the first time you looked at pornography, and how has it affected your view of intimacy? What did your parents teach you (or not teach you) about sexual intimacy?
- What are some of your biggest fears or anxieties about marital sexual intimacy?
- What are you most excited about when it comes to sexual intimacy?
- Spend some time thinking back through your sexual past. What can you think of that might lead to some challenges down the road? Pornography? Abuse? Abortion? Sexual immorality? What would be helpful to share with your significant other?

- What expectations do you have for your wedding night? What are your expectations for your honeymoon?

Strengthening Our Knot

- Discuss your answers to the Am I Ready? questions about sexual intimacy and marriage.
- Discuss what boundaries you will put in place in your relationship to help best pursue each other with purity. Ask trustworthy Christian friends for help, encouragement, and accountability.
- As you get near your wedding day, discuss your expectations about your wedding night and your honeymoon—and remember to apply the listening skills you learned in chapter 2. Honestly admit any concerns you may have about sex with your future spouse and talk through ways your significant other could help you feel more comfortable (such as taking it slow, etc.) However, I encourage you to not have this conversation in a dark apartment, all by yourselves, with no roommates around!

Closing Prayer

Lord, thank You for creating us as sexual beings and for giving us good, healthy desires. Help us honor You first and honor one another. Help us to put in place boundaries You've established and to exercise self-control in this part of our relationship. Give us courage to confess when we fall short. We give You all the glory You deserve as we seek to honor You with our bodies. Thank You that You purchased our bodies through the blood of Your Son, Jesus. We pray we would live as people who know we have been bought at a very high price. Amen.

9

Do I Have to Visit Your Parents?

How to Thrive in Your Relationships with Family and In-Laws

If you believe what the world says, in-law relationships are a source of pain and struggle. But if you apply some simple strategies, you and your future spouse can do a whole lot more than just tolerate each other's families. Rather, you can thrive in your relationships with family and in-laws.

Unfortunately, the Bible doesn't talk a whole lot about in-laws. We only have a few examples to learn from:

- The book of Ruth shows us the very healthy relationship Ruth has with her mother-in-law, Naomi. After

Ruth's husband dies, Ruth professes her devotion to her mother-in-law (Ruth 1:16).

- Genesis 2:24 gives us the clearest picture of our relationship with our parents and family of origin: "That is why a man leaves his father and mother and is united to his wife, and they become one flesh."

- And thank the Lord for this one: Deuteronomy 27:23 says, "'Cursed is anyone who sleeps with his mother-in-law.' Then all the people shall say, 'Amen.'"

Meet Jay and Ashley

In 2009, I met Jay and Ashley when they took the premarried class at our church. They got married a year later, and we've been friends ever since.

Ashley: We met when I started my freshman year at the University of Texas. Jay transferred in as a sophomore, and we met during new student orientation. I invited him to a party. He said no, but he did ask for my number.

Jay: I thought she was really cute, and I liked that she had a meal plan and didn't use all her money. We started spending time together, but I wasn't really walking with the Lord, so I was hanging out with a few other women at the same time. Fortunately, one of my roommates challenged me to start acting like a Christian instead of playing around. I was acting like a jerk, and I'm glad he called me out on it.

Ashley: We started dating a few weeks later. My mom got married at a very young age, so she wasn't excited about me dating someone so early in my time at school. Jay and I struggled a fair amount when we started dating. We were both young and immature and argued often about anything and everything.

Jay: I still remember sitting on the swings on campus and arguing about how we spent our time, physical boundaries in our relationship, and college stuff. I wasn't growing spiritually nearly as fast as Ashley was, so we had multiple arguments over my lack of spiritual growth. We had an on-again, off-again relationship for a few years.

Ashley: We worked hard to resolve most of our challenges and decided to take some intentional steps toward engagement and marriage. I moved to Dallas to finish physical therapy school while Jay stayed in Austin to finish his undergrad degree. We signed up for the premarital preparation class at my church in Dallas in the summer of 2009. Jay was my hero—every week, for eight weeks, he left Austin after class, drove over two hundred miles to Dallas to take our class, and then drove back home that night.

Jay: Those drives were not fun, but they were totally worth it. We loved the class, had some great leaders, and actually ended up breaking up after the class. I know it doesn't sound like a good end result, especially after all those long drives, but it was completely worth it because the class revealed some significant challenges Ashley and I needed to work through before getting married.

Ashley: I had it all planned out—when we'd get engaged, the perfect wedding at my parents' house, and what married life would look like. But our premarried class revealed all kinds of things we needed to resolve individually and as a couple. We weren't ready for marriage.

Sometimes the Best Outcome in Marriage Prep Is to Break Up or Pause

Earlier in this book, I shared the traffic light analogy. Many readers will get a green light and move forward toward engagement and marriage. Some will hit a yellow light and need to pause and work out a few things. This might mean the postponement of a wedding.

I've walked alongside many couples who made the wise decision to slow things down and work through some challenges before moving forward toward marriage. They decided to resolve personal sin struggles or relational challenges before getting married. Personally, I believe this is one of the bravest and wisest things a couple can do. It might be embarrassing, but it could be the best thing for you.

Some of you might call things off completely, and that's okay. I know it is painful and disappointing, but if you are sparing yourselves from a miserable marriage or a divorce down the road, then it's definitely worth the short-term pain.

If you're feeling some anxiety about moving forward toward marriage, then talk with your significant other, trusted friends, mentors, and pastors.

Jay: We called things off in the fall of 2011 but still remained friends. We each worked on some of the personal sin struggles we identified through the premarried class, and both got more serious about our faith. I started studying my Bible, finally, and got connected with a strong group of other Christian guys. I think Ashley and I both knew we'd get back together, and sure enough, we started dating again a few months later.

Ashley: Our relationship changed in so many ways the second time around. We didn't argue like we used to, and we put some good physical boundaries in place and asked for some accountability from friends so that we didn't spend the night with each other. All was good until we restarted talks about marriage. When we did, the problems started up again. We had arguments about wedding planning, costs, and location, especially between me, my mom, and Jay's mom.

Jay: The biggest mistake we made was saying hurtful things and choosing sides. I thought my family was right, and Ashley thought her family was right. This led to conflict with each other.

Five Principles for Relating to Your Family and In-Laws

Jay and Ashley's story demonstrates five principles that will guide you through your relationship with your family and your significant other's family.

Principle #1: Don't Choose Sides

When you run to your family of origin and bad-mouth your significant other, it will not go well with you. Let's be honest: most families think their child is right. Moms tend to think no woman is good enough for her son, and dads tend to think no man can ever be good enough for his daughter.

Whenever you run to your parents and criticize your significant other, you're perpetuating their belief that no one is good enough to marry their child. It's okay to be honest and ask for counsel from your parents, but unless you want to create a lot of tension, be careful how you talk to your family of origin about your significant other.

Kristen and I have a rule in our marriage—we never talk badly about each other to either of our families. If we have issues to resolve, then we work them out together or we bring in friends. We don't ever bring in our families unless they're part of the problem or part of the solution.

Ashley: With all the blaming, finger-pointing, and arguing, it's no wonder my family didn't like Jay and his family didn't like me. At times I wondered which "team" Jay was on. We eventually had to apologize to each other and to our families for the ways we had talked badly about one another.

Jay: I lovingly stood up to my parents and told them they would not talk to Ashley or about Ashley in a negative way. It was the first time I made her a priority. She finally knew I cherished and cared for her when I had some hard conversations with my parents. Ashley did the same thing with her parents. We both knew if we were going to move forward toward marriage that our relationships with both sets of parents needed to change.

I often see couples show favoritism to one set of parents over the other, especially if one family gives better gifts or has a nicer home. Be sure you don't let gifts sway you in any one direction. This especially can play out if you have children.

Here's a pro tip for you: seek to build your relationship with your in-laws. My father-in-law loves all things military. He served in the US Navy for years and still holds a deep interest in the military. To help strengthen our relationship, I've read some books about Navy SEALs and the military. We don't have a lot in common, so I look for ways to proactively build our relationship. Take some time to get to know your future in-laws and develop your relationship with them.

Principle #2: Your Significant Other Becomes the Priority Relationship

When you get married, the priority of your relationship changes. Your parents are no longer the top human relationship in your life. Genesis 2:24 says, "That is why a man leaves his father and mother and is united to his wife, and they become one flesh."

Knot-Tying Tip

What Does It Mean to "Leave and Cleave"?

You might have heard the phrase "leave and cleave" when it comes to parents and in-laws. What does this mean, exactly? The phrase comes from Genesis 2:24, where the man leaves his father and mother and cleaves to his wife (your translation might say something like "hold fast" or "become united" instead of "cleave").

Leave. You will establish independence from your parents. In the premarital ministry at our church, we like to say children are arrows, not boomerangs (Ps. 127:4–5). In other words, they are shot out into the world to create their own lives, independent of their parents. By no means does this mean the parent/child relationship ends. Rather, it transforms into a new kind of relationship. If you don't leave your parents, then you can't possibly cleave to your spouse.

Cleave. As a married couple, you establish your commitment to one another. When you leave your parents' support, you go somewhere else to find it or have it provided for you. God intends you to find this provision in your spouse. Most children will move out of their parents' house before they get married for college or jobs, so they will establish some semblance of leaving before marriage. The cleaving part takes place when you make your marriage commitment.

After you leave and cleave, you become one flesh with your spouse (as discussed in chapter 1).

Outside of your personal relationship with Christ, your spouse must be your priority relationship. This doesn't mean you shun your parents and in-laws, but your priorities change.

Ashley: We struggled to make it through our challenges in dating, but engagement was the hardest season of our relationship, by far. Neither of us was prepared to handle the mess we found ourselves in. Thankfully, Jay said he wanted to fully pursue me and move toward marriage, and he had some definitive steps we were going to take.

Jay: I knew we needed to rebuild our relationship with each other and rebuild trust as a couple. We went back to the basics and applied what we learned about communication and conflict resolution from our premarried class and mentors.

Ashley: We apologized and sought forgiveness from both sets of parents. We spoke with one voice instead of blaming, and we talked to them with respect and honor. We shared some decisions we made as a couple, and we made sure they heard why we loved each other and wanted to move toward marriage.

Principle #3: Communicate with Parents and (Future) In-Laws Like You Want Them to Communicate with You

Before our twins were born, I had a decent relationship with my mother-in-law. I knew she loved me, but I allowed all my insecurities to shine when I spent time with her. I made some poor assumptions about her, and I would imagine she didn't always assume the best about me either.

She came to Dallas and stayed with us for six weeks when our twins were born. We needed all the help we could get, but six weeks is a very long time—that's forty-two nights and days, and over a thousand hours! The days leading up to their birth were busy with the typical prebaby preparations: baby showers, crib assembly, and much more. They were also filled with tension between my mother-in-law and me. I know it drove my wife crazy.

On May 25, 2004, the night before the twins were born, Kristen, my mother-in-law, and I sat down at the kitchen table for a heart-to-heart. I apologized for being defensive, argumentative, and short-tempered. I asked for my mother-in-law's forgiveness and told her we needed to be on the same team so that we could best support Kristen and care for the twins.

This conversation changed the direction of our future. It still wasn't an easy six weeks, but at least we were all on Team Kristen. Today, my in-laws and I are quick to apologize and ask for forgiveness.

Communicate with your parents and in-laws like you want them to talk with you.

Jay: Our arguments and challenges got much worse when our families got involved. We wanted to move toward marriage, but we walked through some significant family challenges, especially with Ashley's family. My family wasn't easy at times either, but we still have some major challenges with her family.

Ashley: Without question, this is the hardest part of my life. My relationship with my parents, especially with my mom, has been the toughest relationship I've ever had. For as far back as I can remember, we've struggled. I still don't know just what to do.

Jay: Fortunately, we have a very healthy relationship with Ashley's sister and her family. But Ashley's right—we've struggled with the relationships with her parents since day one of our relationship. But we can honestly say we've done everything we can to build these relationships. We've met with friends and pastors from our church, we've sought counsel from God's Word, and we've done the hard work of humbling ourselves and seeking forgiveness. At the end of the day, we can't control how Ashley's family will respond—we can only do our part.

Principle #4: Do Whatever You Can to Live with Others in Peace and Unity

We want Scripture to be our guide in the area of relationships. Ephesians 4:1–3 says, "Live a life worthy of the calling you have received. Be completely humble and gentle; be patient, bearing with one another in love. Make every effort to keep the unity of the Spirit through the bond of peace." And Romans 14:19 tells us to "make every effort to do what leads to peace and to mutual edification." These passages encourage us to seek peace and unity whenever possible.

At our church we often say, "Draw a circle around yourself and work on everyone inside the circle." The image provides a great illustration of getting the plank out of your own eye before focusing on the speck in someone else's eye (Matt. 7:3–5). Before you worry about what someone else has done wrong or how they have wronged you, do the hard work of drawing a circle around yourself and work on the person inside that circle. This will help you in marriage and will go a long way toward helping you grow your relationship with your family and in-laws.

Principle #5: Discuss Holidays with Your Significant Other and Both Sets of Parents

When you get married, you might spend Christmas or another major holiday away from your family. Make sure you and your significant other communicate about holiday expectations.

Many couples switch between families every year. For instance, one year they will go to his family's house for Thanksgiving and her family's house for Christmas, and then they'll swap the following year. Part of it might depend on how many families you need to visit. If your parents are divorced and remarried, then you might have more homes to visit. And if you have children from a prior relationship, you may need to consider scheduling holidays with your child's other parent. Another factor is the distance you need to travel. For instance, Kristen's parents live a lot closer to us than mine do, so we visit her family for Christmas every year. The six of us need to fly to see my family, so we look for other opportunities outside of Christmas to visit them.

Regardless, ask your parents and (future) in-laws what they'd like you to do for holidays, and consider their counsel along with your preferences as a couple. With proper communication and expectation-setting, holidays don't have to be stressful. You can truly enjoy them if you plan ahead and work together as a team.

The Rest of the Story

I've walked alongside Jay and Ashley for years as they have tried to heal their relationships with Ashley's parents. To be honest, I struggled about whether Jay and Ashley were the right couple for this chapter. Every other chapter in this book ends with a (more or less) happily-ever-after story. The other couples in this book worked through their affairs, resolved their conflicts, and learned to live with each other in an understanding way. But this chapter doesn't end on a good note. Jay and Ashley still don't have a healthy relationship with her parents.

Jay: Eight years later, things are even tougher and we are in a worse spot than when we walked through our engagement and marriage drama. But I'm loved and supported by Ashley, and we operate as a team. We've grown so much as a family through this, and we've learned how to care for each other in our trials.

Ashley: I wouldn't wish our struggles with my parents on anyone. But my tough relationship with my mom has been the single biggest catalyst in my growth in my relationship with Christ. Do I wish our relationship was better? Of course. But I see evidence of Romans 8:28 in my life through my strained relationship with my mom. I see how God indeed works all things together for our good and His glory. Paul also said in 2 Corinthians 12:10 that when we are weak, God is strong. I've learned to lean on the Lord and rely on His strength, not my own.

This is the reason that I think Jay and Ashley are the best couple for this chapter. Sometimes you can do everything right and things still don't end up where you want them to land. Sometimes you act like Jesus over and over and over—you humble yourself, you apologize, you get the log out of your own eye—and you still struggle. Their story is the right story for this chapter because it's real, and I want you to be ready for reality when you tie the knot. No matter what your story of your family and future in-laws looks like, I hope your faith in Christ can sustain you as a couple.

Am I Ready?

- Spend some time thinking about your family of origin and what it was like to grow up in your home. You've been shaped and influenced more than you probably realize by your parents and the ways they communicated and resolved conflict. Think through the patterns you grew up watching and responding to.
  - » Did your parents divorce, or did you grow up in a single-parent family? How did your parents communicate and resolve conflict?
  - » Did your parents model humility? Did they apologize and ask for forgiveness?
  - » Did they yell and scream at each other, at you, and/ or at your siblings?
- Take some time to write a letter to your future in-laws. Let them know why you are excited about marrying their child. Thank them for the ways they've intentionally poured into their child and why you are grateful this person will be your spouse.

Strengthening Our Knot

- Discuss your answers to the Am I Ready? questions about family and in-laws.

- What do you want to bring into your marriage from your family of origin? Share this with your significant other. Ask the same thing of them about their family.
- What do you want to make sure you leave out of your new family from your family of origin? Ask the same of your significant other and share your responses with each other.
- If you and your future spouse come from different ethnic or cultural backgrounds, discuss some of the opportunities and challenges the future may bring.

Closing Prayer

God, help our story be different from the typical story of family and in-laws. Thank You for guiding us with Your Word, Spirit, and people to help us love our families. Shape us to be different than the pattern of the world, so we can maintain loving, Christlike relationships with both of our families. Give us wisdom to be humble, teachable, and caring with our families. Thank You for your model of leaving, cleaving, and living as one flesh. We pray we'd do that well and still have strong relationships with our families. In Christ's name, we pray. Amen.

10

Are We Roomies for Life or Best Friends?

Doing Life with Your Constant Companion

Marriage is not easy. Selfishness, busyness, schedules, kids, and other factors creep in and make something beautiful very challenging at times. Even though you are not yet married, I know I don't need to convince you of this.

- Your parents' marriage might be all the evidence you need. Or maybe it was your own first marriage, if you're previously married.
- You've seen the challenges on television or heard about them on social media.
- You know friends who have difficult marriages.

While I can't deny that marriage brings its fair share of trials, we (your friends, family, culture, and even the church) have not served you well. We've talked far too often and with too much gusto about the challenges of marriage. When I hang out with fellow married couples, we often discuss the ordeals of married life and the difficult world we are navigating as parents.

We haven't spent enough time talking about the greatness of marriage and the fun you're about to have as a married couple. Perhaps the most undervalued and underdiscussed quality of great marriages is friendship and companionship.

In the Beginning, God Created

Have you ever thought about what Genesis 1 and 2 looked like? In the beginning, God created the heavens and the earth, and He filled the world with birds, trees, and animals—including possums (Why, God, *why*?!). He then created man, and God gave him a job to do—to work the garden and take care of it. He told the man, "Rule over the fish in the sea and the birds in the sky and over every living creature that moves on the ground" (Gen. 1:28).

In the process of naming the animals, Adam noticed God had created two of every creature: male and female. I imagine he marveled at each animal with its own distinct characteristics, size, and shape. He watched them go by, two by two, and realized he did not have a similar human companion. In Genesis 2:18, God said, "It is not good for the man to be alone. I will make a helper suitable for him."

I can't imagine what it was like for Adam. I hate being alone. A few days ago, I got attacked by a combination of a head cold and end-of-summer Texas allergens. My nose ran nonstop, and I couldn't stop sneezing. I made the wise decision to stay away from the church office and work from home. My kids were all in school, and Kristen was at a Bible study. For four hours, I saw no other human being, and I hated it. God creates us with a need and desire to be with others. It's not good for us to be alone.

The Bible goes on to say the Lord put the man into a deep sleep, removed one of his ribs, and fashioned a woman out of the rib. I don't know how He did it, but God created the most beautiful part of His creation (in my opinion) in that moment. The man woke up and said, "This is now bone of my bones and flesh of my flesh; she shall be called 'woman,' for she was taken out of man" (v. 23). Even though they looked different from each other, the man knew he had found someone just like him.

The man was no longer alone. Human companionship began.

Your friendship with your spouse can be a sweet gift. That's what this chapter is all about—helping you develop a friendship with your future spouse that will benefit your lives as long as you both shall live.

Meet Tim and Emily

Tim and Emily met while working at a Christian youth camp called Kanakuk in Branson, Missouri. Emily was serving in leadership, and Tim was serving as a first-year counselor the summer they met.

Emily: Tim caught my eye as soon as I saw him that summer. I started scouting him out, but we had not yet met face-to-face. We'd seen each other around camp, but that was it. The first time we met in person was during a twenty-four-hour break between camp sessions.

Tim: Emily was reading *My Utmost for His Highest*, by Oswald Chambers. I thought she was cute, so I told her I loved the book and that we should get together sometime and talk about it. Kind of cheesy, but it worked! She believed me, and next thing I knew, I found a note on my car from Emily—she wrote a quote from the book on a page she tore from some magazine. The rest of the summer we talked more and more at camp, and even left notes for each other on a regular basis.

Emily: When camp ended, we went our separate ways, but this was the beginning of our friendship. I moved to Dallas to start my first full-time job, and Tim went back to Tulsa to finish school. We began to write notes to each other and mailed letters back and forth. The distance helped us grow our friendship through letters and phone calls.

Tim: I'm so glad we grew our friendship over the miles. We shared and talked about school, work, friendships, and what God was teaching us through Bible study and church. To this day, thirteen years into marriage, we are still best friends. This initial time of getting to know each other formed the foundation of our friendship.

While your story might not be the same as Tim and Emily's, you and your significant other still need to focus on becoming friends and companions. Even though your spouse will not provide for your every relational need, they still need to be your closest friend and someone you love sharing your life with.

In Proverbs 5, King Solomon wrote about the disappointing nature of sexual sin. He warned his son about adultery and described how sexual sin can move at lightning speed from sweet to bitter (vv. 3–4). He instructed his son to drink water from his own cistern (v. 15). In other words, get your lovin' from your spouse, not from someone else's. "May your fountain be blessed, and may you rejoice in the wife of your youth. A loving doe, a graceful deer—may her breasts satisfy you always, may you ever be intoxicated with her love" (vv. 18–19).

Solomon told his son to delight in his wife. While there's certainly a sexual element to these wise words, it was also a call to enjoy the relationship. In the book of Ecclesiastes, Solomon instructed the reader to "Enjoy life with your wife, whom you love" (Eccles. 9:9). Even though this specific command is written to males, the principle works both ways. Ladies—enjoy life with your husband!

How can you, as a seriously dating or engaged couple, best get ready for marriage, and how can you delight in your spouse during the days you have together on this earth?

Five Ways to Grow in Friendship

Here are five different ways you and your significant other can best grow your friendship. The benefits will start now, before marriage, and will continue decades into marriage.

1. Find Your Silly Side and Have Fun!

When Kristen and I first dated in 1999, we had so much fun together. We ran up and down Peachtree Street after work, ate at new restaurants, and created unique shared experiences together as a couple. While running together now sounds miserable to me, in 1999 running was a blast! We talked and grew our friendship on our runs together.

Try something new. Do things you've never done before. Invite your significant other into your hobbies and experience them together.

> **Tim:** We went fishing on our first date as a couple. I hate to admit it, but I was terrified of baiting a hook. Emily was a good ol' girl who knew how to fish, so she helped me out on our first date. I'm surprised she let me ask her out for a second date!

Ironically, Tim and Emily are now both expert fly fishermen. She must have taught him well.

Even though I love eating fish, I hate the thought of smelling or touching a fish. Fishing is not fun to me or to Kristen, but to Tim and Emily it's a big part of their marriage. What's fun to one couple might be boring to another. Regardless, figure out what's fun for you.[1]

2. Be Intentional to Build Your Friendship

The key word here is *intentional*. As you do these fun activities, eat meals, and spend time together, be intentional about getting to know each other in your conversations. Take time to ask some interesting questions.

While not every conversation needs to be deep, emotional, and personally revealing, we can't just sit in front of the TV or a movie without any intentionality. Life as a married couple consists of both the intentional *and* the ordinary day-to-day moments together.

These intentional conversations could and should start right now for you. Talk with each other about what you're learning from the Lord, what you're learning in church, and how you're being challenged spiritually. Talk about how to love others well, how your job is going, and the most recent conversations you're having with your family.

Your friendship should be so strong that you can have some hard conversations. Because of the depth and uniqueness of your friendship, you should be able to discuss anything and everything with your significant other.

Emily: Tim asked me out a few weeks after we met, but I told him I wouldn't date him because I thought he was too prideful. I wanted to date and marry a humble guy, not one who thought too highly of himself.

Tim: No one ever shared with me in this way. No one ever told me I was a prideful guy. In fact, no one ever really challenged me on any sins or struggles in my life. To be honest, they may have, but I didn't hear it as clearly as when Emily told me I was a prideful dude.

Emily: Over the next six months, as we continued our long-distance friendship, I watched God chip away at his pride. I knew that the person I wanted to date or marry had to be able to listen to wise counsel and make changes in his life to help him become more like Christ. After six months of watching him grow, I told Tim I was ready to begin dating if he still wanted to pursue me.

Tim: When Emily told me about my sin problem and watched me pursue humility with Christ, I knew I wanted to pursue her. I wanted my spouse to be the kind of person who cared enough about me to challenge me, and to be someone I could challenge in turn.

When Tim and Emily lived long-distance from each other, there were some challenges they could sweep under the rug. When they hung up the phone, they could choose to ignore their frustrations or hurts. But when Tim moved to Dallas and they saw each other much more often in person, they could no longer hide or ignore their problems.

Emily: When Tim moved to Dallas, I knew we needed to work through some challenges. We handled money in different ways, and I was concerned about the ways he dealt with some challenges in his family. Even though he wasn't the prideful man I'd met at camp, he still struggled with anger, control, and remnants of pride. I knew he could never be sinless and perfect like Jesus, but he had a little too far to go.

Tim: In a similar way, I really cared for Emily, but it felt like her people-pleasing tendencies caused problems in our relationship. She worked with high school students, and we always had a third wheel with us on our dates. She couldn't say no to anyone's requests and didn't want to let anyone down. She didn't seem to make our time together a priority, and I wondered if she liked her students more than she liked me.

Emily: Our first few months of living in the same town were filled with hard but necessary conversations we needed to have as a couple. I'm so thankful we were each open to working through these challenges as friends.

Tim and Emily got married in 2005. To help keep their friendship strong, they've developed a set of weekly questions.[2] Every week they go for a walk and ask each other the following five questions:

1. How did you feel loved this past week?
2. What does your upcoming week look like?
3. How would you feel most loved and encouraged in the days ahead?
4. How would you best feel pursued in sexual intimacy this week?
5. How can I pray for you this week?

You might develop your own set of questions to give you and your significant other the opportunity to connect with each other in an intentional way.

3. Go on a Date!

Couples whose marriages are marked by boredom often look for fun outside their marriage relationship. Someone once said, "Let the wife make her husband glad to come home and let him make her sorry to see him leave."[3] I love this quote. I want Kristen to be glad when I get home and sad when I leave. I want our marriage to be marked by fun, excitement, creativity, and adventure.

One of the best ways to create that gladness is by pursuing your significant other and by letting them know how much you enjoy their friendship. The married couples who do this well are the ones who don't quit having fun after their wedding day.

- Jason and Kelly chose to do or learn something new on their date nights. Every month, for one year, they did something they've never done before. For example, one month they blew glass. The next month they took a cooking class.

- Tim and Emily like to build forts with each other and then watch a movie in their homemade fort.
- Brian and Rachel love being on the lake. Every weekend they wakeboard, water-ski, or just take the boat out.
- Chad and Lisa love board games. In reality, Chad loves board games, but because she loves him, Lisa has also learned to play them.

Bottom line: "fun" is different for every couple, so don't just copy everyone else. Figure out what is fun for the two of you, and make it happen![4]

4. Find a Hobby as a Couple

Several times over the last few years, friends have asked me what Kristen and I do together for fun as a couple. Usually, I blurt out some lame answer about watching TV together or doing stuff with our kids. While these are legitimate, good answers, I've realized we don't have any great hobbies as a couple. Kristen and I have discussed this and plan to find a hobby to do together, although in our busy season of life as parents, time with our family is our most fun and important hobby!

I know friends who fish together. Others ride their bikes together every weekend. Some friends love to travel, dance, cook, refinish furniture, or work in the garden.

Shared activities for couples create shared memories. Agree now before you say "I do" that you will be a couple who creates special memories through hobbies you do together. You'll laugh, spend some quality time together, and get more time to communicate with each other.

5. Be on Mission Together as a Couple

Your relationship is much bigger than the two of you. I've seen many premarried and newly married couples become isolated and self-focused in the beginning stages of their relationship. Look for ways to serve together as a couple: lead and teach kids in Sunday school, go on a mission trip, or reach out to neighbors who don't have a relationship with Christ. Make your relationship about something or someone else.

Kristen and I lead small groups of newlyweds together, mentor premarried couples, and teach in various marriage ministry environments. We know our relationship is much larger than the two of us, so we seek ways to remind ourselves life is not just about Kristen and Scott.

In what ways can you and your future spouse build your friendship while serving together in your church or community? Choose to be on mission together as a couple instead of simply wanting others to serve and pour into you.

Bonus: Do the Things You Did in the Beginning

File this one away for the future. You'll definitely need to remember it years down the road after you get married and have kids (and you'll probably need the reminder in the first year of marriage as well). In his message to the church in Ephesus as recorded in Revelation 2:4–5, John records Jesus's words: "Yet I hold this against you: You have forsaken the love you had at first. Consider how far you have fallen! Repent and do the things you did at first."

As a married couple, you will need to remember to do the things you did in the beginning. When couples get stuck in routines and the busyness of life, they often forget to do the things they did when they first met. Don't forget to do all the things I recommended above—keep dating each other, have intentional conversations, and serve together as a couple.

Don't Build Your Companionship on the One Part Guaranteed to Fade Away

Can we have some honest talk for a minute? I don't want to make any assumptions about your relationship, and I don't know where you're doing well or how you're struggling. But for over a decade, I've watched premarried couples all too often build their relationship on the wrong foundation of looks, attraction, and sexual chemistry.

If that's your story, you are building on the one part of your relationship guaranteed to fade. In Proverbs 31:30, King Lemuel reminds us that "beauty is fleeting." Your body will eventually sag, droop, wrinkle, and much more. Have lots of amazing sex after you get married, but please don't build your relationship only on sexual attraction and intimacy. If you are currently unmarried and sexually active, reread chapter 8, and share with and confess to a trusted mentor couple or pastor.

I love that Kristen is my companion in college football, in watching TV shows, in raising our boys, in leading and

Knot-Tying Tip

Can You Continue Opposite-Sex Friendships after Marriage?

Should you have friendships outside of marriage? Of course! We'll talk further about community and couple friends in chapter 11. But how about friends of the opposite sex? Maybe you have some friends of the opposite sex from high school, college, or work. Should those relationships change when you say "I do"?

When you are intentionally dating, it should be clear that you are no longer looking for any other opposite-sex relationships. Marriage must be built on the foundation of relational trust, so be careful of friendships, old or new, that could erode your future marital trust.

You want to live "above reproach" (1 Tim. 3:2). This means you live in such a way that your actions are consistent with your character. Just because you are spending time with someone of the opposite sex doesn't mean you're having an affair or that you have ill intentions. But be cautious about spending time with someone of the opposite sex who isn't your spouse.

In our marriage, Kristen and I have established a few guidelines to protect our marriage and to live above reproach. We don't drive, share a meal, or sit behind a closed door alone with someone of the opposite sex. We minimize the amount of texts, phone calls, and emails with someone of the opposite sex who isn't our spouse. We know each other's passwords and aren't afraid of the other reading our texts or messages.

We both actively post on social media, but we know each other's passwords and have no fears of our spouse looking through our history and friends/followers. Some of our friends have husband-wife joint accounts. You'll want to make sure you spend some time discussing how you want to handle different types of social media. Look for ways to build trust and strengthen your one-flesh relationship (Gen. 2:24).[5]

I'm not telling you to end old friendships. But I do think you'd be wise to have some conversations with your future spouse about how you can best protect and guard your marriage.

I do everything I can to speak highly of Kristen in front of her and behind her back. I don't want anyone to be confused on whether or not I love my wife. Michael Hyatt calls this "adultery repellant."[6] I highly suggest you invest in some adultery repellant!

serving together, in sexual intimacy, in spiritual intimacy, and much more. She is my best friend.

The Rest of the Story

Tim and Emily are almost a decade younger than me, but they are the couple I want to be like when I grow up. Over ten years into marriage, they are still best friends. They take adventures together, and having a child has not slowed them down as a family. They're living proof that the fun of relationships does not and must not end when you get married or have kids.

When I look at the ways they love each other, it makes their God look really good. So often Christian married couples seem boring, stuck, and complacent. Out of their love for the Lord, Tim and Emily love each other so well and still can say they're married to their best friend.

One way to know if you are ready for marriage is that you and your significant other enjoy a deep friendship with each other.

Am I Ready?

- One of my favorite parts of Tim and Emily's story is when she challenged him on his pride. Can you speak the truth in love and grace to your significant other? Are you willing to listen to input from your significant other?

- Do you see fun as a central part of your relationship, or do you consider it nonessential?
- How do you think your friendship with your spouse will be different from your same-gender friendships?
- Spend a few minutes reflecting on your use of social media and technology. Is there anything you don't want your significant other to see on your phone, in your email, or in any of your social media accounts? If so, then you need to discuss this with your future spouse. Please don't hide secret sin from the person you're going to marry.
- Each of you should plan a date night for the other. Do something they would enjoy! Get creative and try something you've never done before as a couple.

Strengthening Our Knot

- Discuss your answers to the Am I Ready? questions about friendship and companionship.
- Look over Tim and Emily's weekly questions. Do you think this is something you would consider adding to your relationship? Discuss with each other if you'd keep the questions or change them.
- Discuss your hobbies with each other. Each of you should share what you like to do or what you'd like to try in the future. Agree to try a new hobby together as a couple.

Closing Prayer

Lord, thank You that You knew it was not good for us to be alone and that You created us for relationships. We pray that we would develop and strengthen a deep friendship with each other. Help us to have fun, find hobbies, pursue each other, and live on mission together as a couple. We pray that our marriage will be marked with fun, creativity, and companionship. In the name of Your Son, Jesus, we pray. Amen.

11

None of Their Business or Better Together?

Pursuing Community as a Couple

When I lived in Atlanta, God used a group of friends to transform my life as a new Christian. I grew up far from the Lord and didn't even hear the gospel until I was twenty-two. When I finally grasped the truth of the gospel, the grace of God rocked my sinful world. The gospel changed every part of my life—except for one nasty sin habit I didn't want to give up right away.

After almost two decades of hiding an addiction to pornography, I finally confessed my struggle to a group of single male friends. I fully expected condemnation, judgment, and a swift kick out of the church after I confessed. Instead, I found grace, love, and truth from a group of fellow strugglers.

Fast-forward a few years to my first Christian dating relationship (Kristen). Once again, my Christian community played a huge role in helping me navigate the ups and downs of this relationship. My friends encouraged me to end the dating relationship because of some unhealthy dynamics, including a lack of purity. The bigger problem was that my life revolved around Kristen. If she was nice to me, it was a good day. If she didn't give me attention, I'd get sad. I was pretty pathetic! My friends challenged me to pursue greater intimacy with Jesus.

Also in Atlanta, Kristen's life transformed because of the women in her community group. Kristen was on-again, off-again dating a nonbeliever and consistently chose less than God's best because of her people-pleasing personality and insecurities. She dated me during the off-again seasons. Her friends challenged her to end her relationship with this other guy and with me so she could pursue a deeper, obedient relationship with Christ.

From there, Kristen and I both grew in our relationships with Christ. We dove deeper into our friendships and started to serve in our church. After around six months, with the encouragement of our community groups, Kristen and I started dating again, this time radically transformed by God's Word, His people, and His Spirit. The same friends who had urged us to end our prior relationship now encouraged us to start dating again.

Because of the important role our friends played in our lives, Kristen and I have made a commitment to never live apart from biblical community. Your view on community and friendships as an individual and as a couple will play a massive role in helping you get ready for marriage and helping you get established after you tie the knot.

Can you imagine having a group of friends who love and "spur [you] on toward love and good deeds" (Heb. 10:24)? A group of friends God could use to change every part of your world? How different would your life and relationship with Jesus be? Good, faithful friends are hard to find. It's important to walk through your premarried and married seasons of life with a loving, caring group of friends.

Meet Kevin and Brittany

Two of my closest friends are a couple Kristen and I met when we first moved to Dallas in 2002. Their story sobers me every time I hear it, and I'm thankful for the ways God has used community and friendships to help save their marriage.

Kevin: Brittany and I met our freshman year in college and married each other at the ripe old age of twenty. We met at a Christian school, were active in our churches, hung out with the same friend group, and had each been a follower of Christ for many years. We dated for four months (several of which were long distance), got engaged, and then married in 1997. In some ways, we were the ideal couple. We were both music majors, and I planned on going into full-time ministry after graduating college.

Brittany: We didn't really have any close community or friendships around us and developed most of our views on love and marriage from television. But we were young and in love—what else did we need? My mom, our premarital counselor, and the pastor who married us assumed that since we pursued each other with purity and because Kevin was going to be a pastor that we would do really well in marriage. What could possibly go wrong?

Kevin: We were the envy of all our friends—we got to live in a house, have guilt-free married sex, and could enjoy wild and crazy Friday nights where we rented movies, ate pizza, and did laundry together. We were living the dream! The simple things of life brought us so much pleasure. We grew up together and got to experience our first jobs, first budget, and much more as a couple. We looked forward to all the things married couples do together, and we had fun doing them.

Brittany: None of our friends really challenged us in our relationship with Jesus or in our marriage. We did have some church friends, but when we tried to help encourage each other to grow, it was like the blind leading the blind. We had no concept of biblical community. We started to have some problems, but we didn't know how to deal with them and didn't have anyone around us who could help us navigate our challenges.

Kevin: Our marriage problems started the day after our wedding, as we were about to head out on our honeymoon. We couldn't find $1,000 in traveler's checks (yes, dating myself here), and I started to lose my cool. I threw a fit and blamed Brittany, but we never found the money. More important, this response started a pattern of anger, screaming, and animosity between us.

On the outside, Kevin and Brittany looked like they had it all together. Behind closed doors, they were a mess.

Brittany: Things escalated to where Kevin would physically restrain me and wouldn't let me leave the house or call someone. I wanted to bring others in to help, but Kevin wouldn't let me. We tried meeting with counselors, but that didn't work. We told friends part of the truth, but Kevin never let me share the full extent. Our friends knew some of the details but didn't know how to help us.

Kevin: I told Brittany we didn't need help and could handle it on our own. My pride and fear of what others would think held me back. What would others say? What about my desire to be a pastor? What would our friends and family think if they knew we were arguing and fighting?

Kevin and Brittany isolated themselves and hid their problems from others. They were headed in a very dangerous direction as a couple. I pray this won't be your story. Take note from their story and the lessons below, and you'll be ready to tie the knot.

The Dangers of Isolation and the Benefits of Community

Anytime we think we can handle life on our own, it's a problem. A quick look at some of the Proverbs shows us the dangers of isolation and the benefits of community.

Listen to Others

Proverbs 12:15 says, "The way of fools seems right to them, but the wise listen to advice." And in Proverbs 19:20, we learn this: "Listen to advice and accept discipline, and at the end you will be counted among the wise." The Bible teaches that a wise person sees the benefits of accepting input from others instead of thinking they can do things on their own. Individuals and couples who do well in life and marriage open themselves up to counsel from friends.

Be Open to Counsel

If you want your marriage to fail, then avoid seeking the counsel of others. It sounds harsh, but without counsel, plans fail. Solomon tells us, "Plans fail for lack of counsel, but with many advisers they succeed" (15:22). Anytime we tell God, "I got this," we're acting like a fool and operating out of our own abilities.

As you and your significant other process your relationship, invite others in to give you counsel and feedback. Fight the temptation to think or claim that "I got this," and instead choose to live in dependence on God and on His provision of godly counsel through other believers. Before saying "I do" is an ideal season to bring wise counsel into your life and relationship. Most couples in your stage of life walk through the same challenges, issues, and questions you are walking through, and there is great benefit in knowing you're not alone. Life is better together, and community is one of God's greatest gifts He provides to His people.

The Value of Friends

Here are a few of the benefits a great group of friends could bring to your life right now.

Friends Help You Grow Wise

Proverbs 13:20 says, "Walk with the wise and become wise, for a companion of fools suffers harm." This proverb is both a promise and a warning. It promises we will make good decisions if we hang out with wise people, yet warns us that we will suffer harm if we hang out with a bunch of fools. We need wise people around us to help us grow in our relationship with Christ and with one another. I've heard it said that we are essentially a combination of the five people closest to us. Who are the five people you spend the most time with?

Friends Will Wound You

We don't need a bunch of people to tell us how awesome we are. Rather, we need friends who will challenge and lovingly wound us when we need it. Proverbs 27:6 says, "Wounds from a friend can be trusted, but an enemy multiplies kisses."

To wound someone means a friend takes the initiative to help you see your blind spots. The word *wound* has a negative connotation, but in this passage, it's a very positive thing for someone to wound you. In the last month alone, friends have lovingly wounded me about my schedule, my weight, my parenting, and my pride. It's never fun, but I am so thankful for friends who help me become more like Christ. Who is lovingly wounding you right now?

Friends Will Sharpen You

We need someone who will help us grow in our faith and intimacy with Jesus. Proverbs 27:17 says, "As iron sharpens iron, so one person sharpens another." Sometimes I get so used to my stench that I don't think I smell bad anymore. We need people who will point out the areas where we can grow to become more like Christ. And we need people to help us grow in our faith and encourage us to grow spiritually.

Allow Others to Ask You Hard Questions

One of the best decisions Kristen and I ever made was to let others ask us really hard questions. My pride often gets in the way, and I don't like it when I'm wrong and someone else is right, or when someone else lovingly challenges me about an area of sin in my life. But Kristen and I both realize we have some blind spots in our lives. We all do, so we need others to help us see clearly.

To be specific, here are three challenging questions you and your friends should ask each other on a regular basis.[1]

1. What are you reading in God's Word?

This should never be asked as a "gotcha" question but rather as a way to encourage each other to read, study, meditate, and apply God's Word to your life. On the other hand, we never share what we are learning with each other in a bragadocious way. Rather, we ask each other questions about what we're learning in the Word so that we can help encourage each other to grow spiritually.

2. How are you doing at loving, encouraging, and serving your spouse?

When my friends ask me how I'm doing at loving and serving Kristen, it communicates to me that they care about me and about my wife. They are willing to ask the hard questions, since we often know we can do a better job in our marriage. Whether I have to confess to falling short or get to celebrate the wins in our marriage, I'm thankful for friends who are willing to challenge and spur me on in my marriage.

3. What's eating your lunch?

In what ways are you struggling right now? Is it at work, with your spouse, with your kids, or your pet sin? In community, you open up your lives to the input and counsel of others, asking each other the questions maybe no one else will ask. Over the years, my close friends have asked me how I'm eating, exercising, sleeping, loving and prioritizing my wife and kids, and so much more.

I'm grateful for the gift of community and the ways my friends help me grow. Community is God's provision and His Plan A to help us grow in our relationships with the Lord and our spouse.

Friends Will Encourage You

Sometimes we just need a friend to hug and encourage us. The Scriptures are filled with exhortations to love and spur each other on (Heb. 3:13; 10:24–25). Sometimes we need a friend to encourage us when we're discouraged. Proverbs 25:11 says, "A word fitly spoken is like apples of gold in a setting of silver" (ESV). A friend knows exactly what we need to hear, whether it's a word of encouragement or challenge.

Why Don't We Invite Others into Our Lives?

Marriage doesn't create the problems; it merely exposes them. In his book *The Meaning of Marriage*, Tim Keller tells the story of a ten-ton truck crossing an old, faulty bridge with hard-to-see structural defects. The truck crosses the bridge, and the pressure causes hairline fractures in the bridge to be seen. The truck didn't cause the defects but rather exposed them. In many cases, marriage doesn't cause the problems in your lives but, like the bridge, reveals them to the eye so we can deal with them.[2]

So why don't we open up and invite others into our lives to seek wise counsel?

We Don't Want Accountability

Sometimes we don't want to ask community to speak into our lives because we don't want the accountability. Some of you reading this book are crossing sexual boundaries, and even though you know it's not God's best, you're still choosing to pursue each other without purity. You know if you ask someone to help or invite someone else into your relationship, you're going to have to either confess your sin or lie to cover it up. You don't want to do either of these things. Believe me, I've done both too many times to count, and it never works out well for me.

Our Pride Gets in the Way

Other times, we don't invite others into our lives because of pride. We either think we know better or we know we've messed up and don't want others to know.

Some readers will compromise in their marriage choice. They think life will be better with a spouse, and they're not getting any younger. Their biological clock is ticking, and they think if they don't marry this person, then they might not get another chance at marriage. So they compromise, even though they know the relationship is not God's best. They know if they invite others to speak into their life, they might have to give up the relationship.

We Are Afraid to Admit We Are Weak

Sometimes our pride gets in the way because we don't want to admit we are weak. "I'm the one who has all their stuff together! I did great in school, I have six-pack abs, I drive a nice car, and people like me. If I let people see what's really going on in my life, they might realize I'm not perfect." We don't want to admit that we are weak, so we shut the door on community.

One of the Best Gifts We Can Give to Others

Sometimes the best gift we can give others is the gift of vulnerability. Vulnerability means you let into your life someone who puts you at risk.[3] This tears down walls and shows a humility that will serve you well in marriage. We often think being vulnerable should lead us to shame, isolation, and loneliness. But what we find when we're vulnerable with others is that we build a bridge that helps us connect with them.

When I've been vulnerable in my life and in my writing, I have been met with love, compassion, empathy, and grace. Others want to help us when we demonstrate and live with vulnerability. Don't be afraid to be open with a close group of friends. They will encourage you, pray for you, and appreciate your willingness to trust them with your struggles. However, make sure these friends are *trustworthy* friends. A trustworthy friend, among other things, doesn't gossip, is willing to tell you the truth even when it hurts, comforts you and celebrates with you, and helps you become more like Jesus Christ.

When my friend Mark went to school, he told his parents his goal was not to meet a bunch of pretty girls, get the best grades, or join the most popular fraternity with the biggest parties. Rather, his goal was to make the best friends possible. He knew the greatest gift he could add to his life was a group of friends who would help him make wise decisions, hold him accountable, and celebrate the wins of life by his side. These men eventually became the guys who stood by his side on his wedding day. I pray my four sons will develop friendships like Mark's.

Do you have friends like Mark's friends? Do you desire to walk alongside men and women who will help you become more like Christ? Does your group of friends help you, right now, make decisions about your relationship?

One of the biggest problems I see in premarried couples looks something like the following:

- Boy gets plugged in at church by serving and hanging out with a great group of guys.
- Meanwhile, a friend invites Girl to the same church. She makes some quality friendships and grows in her faith.
- Boy meets Girl at church one day, Boy asks Girl out for dinner, and then Boy and Girl spend every waking moment together.
- Boy and Girl no longer serve at church and don't hang out with their friends, and no one has any idea how they're doing as a couple.

I recently heard a term for couples who do this: *submarining*. Couples who submarine retreat beneath the water level when they start dating and don't come up for air again until the relationship is in trouble or until they get married.

If this is your story, you're missing out on one of the greatest gifts in your life. Please don't be that couple who isolates themselves from all sound wisdom and counsel. If you date in isolation, no one will be able to give you feedback on your relationship—and you will miss out on the gifts and provision of community.

The Need for Community Doesn't End When You Say "I Do"

After you get married, you will still need wise friends around you. I can't think of a season of life where couples need to make more major decisions than when they are newly married. You'll have decisions to make about growing your family, jobs, cars, school, where to live, and so much more.

Kristen and I have experienced the benefits of community in many ways. Here is a small smattering of the countless ways our community has spoken into our lives as a married couple:

- They help us make decisions about our schedule and commitments.
- They've helped us parent our kids, especially when we don't know how to best encourage or discipline our children.
- They've helped us process job frustrations, financial challenges, issues with our parents and in-laws, sin struggles, and so much more.

I hate to be the bearer of bad news, but there will be times when you and your spouse will be in conflict and you'll want someone else to help. Whether you disagree on a major decision or are arguing because of sin struggles, you will want others to help you navigate those challenges. If you don't have a community, then you will miss out on the help and wisdom you can get from an outside perspective. And if you choose to marry someone who doesn't value community or the input of others, you're in for a never-ending challenge as a couple. Solomon tells us, "For lack of guidance a nation falls, but victory is won through many advisers" (Prov. 11:14). If the person you want to marry doesn't seek or desire any input from others, I'd run from the altar. This is a red light.

Know you should play this role for others as well. As a single or married person, you can counsel, encourage, and spur others on in their relationship with Jesus and with their significant other. You might not always have the right words to say, but sometimes simply being there for them goes a long way.

The Rest of the Story

In 2005, the fighting between Kevin and Brittany reached a peak. While on the outside they still looked like they had it all together, behind closed doors things continued to crumble. Now they had two children, and Kevin served in full-time ministry at a church in Dallas. The stakes were higher than ever for my friends.

Brittany: One night we called a friend to come over because the arguing and fighting was getting out of hand. The "D Word" (divorce) was thrown around, and we argued over who would get each of our kids and how we'd work through custody. Our friend didn't know exactly what to do or say, but he listened, loved us, and prayed for us. We widened the circle and began the healing process.

Kevin: I took a step back from my ministry job for a season. Instead of leading from the front, I took a job behind the scenes. I stacked chairs, set up rooms, and took out trash among many other things. I went through our church's recovery ministry and began to address, with the help of community, my anger and pride issues.

Brittany: We witnessed the body of Christ do what the church is supposed to do. Our friends loved us, prayed for us, challenged us, and walked alongside us. Without our community, I'm not sure we'd still be married today.

Today, Kevin and Brittany have four kids and an incredible ministry together as a family. They're among my closest friends and my strongest community. Kevin is one of the first guys I call when I want to celebrate and when I need to confess, need prayers, or want wisdom. I'm thankful my friends widened the circle, as Matthew 18:15–20 instructs, and invited others into their relationship. Whether single, engaged, or married, we need all the help we can get!

Why would you willingly choose to miss out on one of life's greatest provisions? As a married couple, you'll need others to speak into your lives, so why not start now, before you even get married? Will you choose to isolate yourselves, or do you think life is better together?

Am I Ready?

- Who are the five people you spend the most time with?
- Who are the individuals you turn to when you want to celebrate something in life?
- Who are the individuals you turn to when you need to confess, seek accountability, or ask for wisdom?
- Do you think your significant other will invite others into their life when you get married, or do you think they would flee or run from wise counsel? Why did you answer this way?

Strengthening Our Knot

- Discuss your answers to the Am I Ready? questions about creating community as a couple.
- Discuss with your significant other your biggest fears about community, both as a single person right now and as a married couple in the future.
- What couples do you and your future spouse spend time with now? Discuss the community (or lack thereof) you have cultivated around you while you are dating.
- Discuss your plan for community in the future after you say "I do." What couples will you spend time with?
- Who are some people from whom you can gain wise counsel? Can you identify a mentor couple who is further down the road than you and from whom you can learn?

Closing Prayer

Lord, we pray we would be a couple who has great friends, before and after marriage. Help us walk with the wise and grow wise. Shape us to be humble and teachable as a result of the input of others in our lives. Give us the wisdom and opportunities to make great friendships in every stage of life as a married couple. Thank You for the ways Your Word informs us about the importance of relationships. In Jesus's name, we pray. Amen.

12

What about the Kids?

Figuring Out the Future of Your Family

Most of the challenges Kristen and I face in our marriage can be boiled down to four primary reasons: Duncan, Drew, Carson, and Lincoln.

I love my four boys, and I hope they love their old man, but nothing takes more of my energy, time, and money than our sons. I don't know what it's like to have a daughter, but I know sons are loud, smelly, and messy. They fight and complain, and they are selfish and inconsiderate. I know because I was one (and still am).

Kristen and I struggle with how to discipline, encourage, motivate, and educate our kids. Most of our arguments involve our kids, and our highest levels of stress come when we have problems with our kids.

Life used to be much simpler. We could travel for the weekend whenever we wanted. The average Saturday did not start at 7:45 a.m. and end at 8:00 p.m. and consist of nineteen soccer, basketball, and baseball games along with two band competitions and three birthday parties (slight to moderate exaggeration). We didn't have to restock our fridge and pantry every forty-eight hours because all the food had been devoured by four growing boys.

Being a father has provided the biggest challenges in my life. At the same time, Kristen and I are rich in love, laughter, and experiences with our children. Our boys keep us entertained, they are fun to play games and snuggle with, and there's nothing like being on mission with your spouse to raise godly kids.

Because of the challenges and joy kids bring to married life, every couple needs to figure out the potential future of their family. Whether you have children from a previous relationship, want a whole army of kids, or are terrified of children (like I was), you and your significant other must spend some time talking about children before you say "I do."

Meet Josh and Betty

Josh and Betty have been married over fifty years and are among the most intentional parents and grandparents I've ever met. They have been involved in full-time ministry for almost two decades. Because of their wisdom in marriage, parenting, and following Jesus, as well as some challenges they have walked through as parents, they are the perfect couple to guide us in thinking about children and parenting.

Josh: Betty and I met when I was a senior in college, and she was a freshman. We met on a blind double date when my roommate was taking out Betty's friend from her dorm.

Betty: I came from a Christian family, so I was thrilled that Josh took me to church on our first date. Little did I know that he didn't have faith in Christ—he just knew I wouldn't go out with him again if he didn't at least act like a Christian!

Josh: I conveniently forgot to mention to Betty that this would be my first time going to church in college. I brought her some chocolates and somehow convinced her to go out with me on a second date. I was a nice enough guy and told her dad I would take her to church and be her spiritual leader.

Betty: After we got married, Josh took me to church for six months and then stopped. He kept finding reasons not to go to church— work projects, yard work, or an early Cowboys football game, among other excuses.

Josh: Fast-forward a few years. A friend from church shared the gospel with me, and I finally trusted in Christ. Betty had been praying for me for years!

Betty: Around the same time Josh trusted in Christ as his Savior, we brought home our first of four children.

Josh: I grew up as an only child, and I wanted to have a big family after I got married. I hated being home alone with my parents—there were times when they wouldn't talk to each other or to me, and the worst part of every day was coming home to my quiet, lonely house. Even as a young boy, I knew I wanted my home as a married guy to be very different from my childhood home.

Betty: My upbringing couldn't have been more different than Josh's. Whereas Josh tried to stay away from his house, I couldn't wait to be with my family. I was one of four kids and always shared a room with one of my siblings. We had a lot of fun together, and I couldn't wait to have four kids of my own.

Josh: The one thing we had in common was that we both wanted to have a bunch of kids.

Perhaps the idea of having kids sounds like a distant dream to you. Or maybe you already have children, and you and your future spouse are trying to figure out how to blend your families. Wherever you are in the parenting spectrum, you and your significant other need to be aligned on some major issues regarding children before you get married.

Eight Questions to Discuss about Kids

Before you tie the knot, there are eight questions you and your significant other need to discuss about kids, parenting, and figuring out the future of your family.

1. How Do You View Children?

Confession: I don't like kids. I like my own, but I do not relate well to children in general—to be honest, they scare me. I don't know how to relate to them. There's a reason why I serve in adult marriage ministry and not children's or student ministry.

But I know children are a gift from God. The Bible is clear about how God views children. Psalm 127:3–5 says,

"Children are a heritage from the LORD, offspring a reward from him. Like arrows in the hands of a warrior are children born in one's youth. Blessed is the man whose quiver is full of them." The psalmist reminds us children are not an inconvenience but a heritage (a blessing or gift) from the Lord. Throughout Scripture, we see the way Jesus celebrates children (Mark 10:13–14) and values the faith and humility of children (Matt. 18:3–4; Luke 18:17).

How do you and your significant other view children? Do you see them as a necessary burden to married life, something to keep you busy as you get older, or as a blessing from the Lord?

I'll never forget one couple who came through the premarried class at our church. He had been previously married and was in his midthirties, while she was in her late twenties and had never been married. On the surface, they seemed like a great couple. Their marriage mentors, parents, and friends were all excited about them getting married. As I observed their relationship, I had no concerns about their future.

About one year after they got married, I heard through a mutual friend this couple was getting divorced. The problem? She wanted kids, and he didn't. They had just assumed they were aligned with each other, so they never discussed the future of their family before tying the knot. After they married, they argued about whether to have kids, prayed about it, discussed it, and processed it with their community, but they never came to any alignment as a couple. As a result, about eighteen months after they said "I do," their marriage ended in divorce.

It is imperative that you and your significant other discuss your view of children before you get married. If you don't, your story could end as this couple's did.

2. How Many Kids Do You Want, and When Do You Want to Start Having Them?

Even though your ideal number of children will probably change after you get married, it's still important to discuss your hopes and desires about the number and timing of children.

If you want two children, and your significant other wants three, then it's not that big of a deal. You'll figure it out. If, however, you want only one child and your spouse wants four or five or more, then you've got a problem. You need to work toward alignment in this area before you get married. If you and your future spouse are too far apart on this one, then the traffic light just turned yellow or red, and you might not be ready for marriage.

Kristen and I both come from families with two biological children. Before we got married, we said we wanted two children or *maybe* three. But when we moved to Texas, we saw many large families with three to six kids and started to open our eyes to the possibility of having a larger family. Granted, we got two for one with our twins! But in spite of the loud, messy chaos we live in, we love having four kids.

Make sure you also discuss your thoughts on when you want to try to start having children. Know that you can have some control of the timing, but the Lord ultimately controls when the womb will open and close. Discuss your expectations so you can make sure you're at least on the same page regarding timing.

3. What Will You Teach Your Children to Value?

What is the most important thing for you to build into your children?

Betty: We know that a lot of people value achievements like academic or athletic success. We made a decision early on in our relationship that we would value character development and spiritual progress more than home runs, baskets, and grades.

Josh: We still wanted our kids to be active in sports and music and do everything they could to succeed in school, but we know following Christ is more important than anything the world values. We were okay with our kids not going to college as long as they developed godly character.

Betty: We decided to reward things like serving in the church and memorizing Scripture. We still do this with our adult children and grandchildren!

What do you and your significant other want to reward and value in your future children? If either of you already has kids you are bringing into marriage, what conversations do you need to have today to better parent your children and set you up for success in the future after you get married?

4. What Are Your Views on Education?

You and your significant other might have different views on how you will educate your children. Make sure you discuss some of the options for the future. Will you choose public school, private school, or homeschool? Your answer

Knot-Tying Tip

Share about Your Upbringing
and How Your Parent(s) Parented You!

One of the most helpful conversations you will have with your significant other is talking about your family of origin and how you were raised. Here are a few questions to get you started.

- How many children are in your family? Where do you fall in the birth/adoption order?
- What were some of the best ways your parent(s) raised you? How about some of the decisions they made that you don't want to bring into your marriage?
- What kind of activities did you do as a kid—sports, dance, gymnastics, music? How many activities did your parents allow you to do at a time?
- What did you do for family vacations? What were some of your favorite memories as a family?
- How did your parents discipline you? Did they provide consequences? Spank you? Ground you? Give you time-outs? Turn the other cheek?
- Who did the majority of the discipline? Your mom, dad, or both parents?

Spend a few minutes talking about how you think you will discipline your children in the future. When parents discipline their child, it's a sign of parental love. In the same way, the Lord disciplines us as a sign of His love for us (Prov. 13:24; Heb. 12:4–12).

Know that every child will need to be disciplined in different ways. For example, one of our children responds best when we take away his privileges (such as restricting the use of his electronics or not allowing him to play in a soccer game). For another one of our kids, all I have to do is look at him and *very lightly* tap his hand, and he knows he made a bad decision. Each of your children will respond in different ways, so make sure you understand each of your children so you can best parent them. For those of you with children from a previous relationship or marriage, you'll need to discuss the role of the stepparent in discipline.

to this question might influence where you choose to live and raise your kids.

Kristen and I chose public school for our children, but every couple needs to make this decision for their own family and children. Perhaps the wisest advice I ever heard was to keep your options open for each of your children, and instead of choosing one solution for all your kids, be open to what's best for each child. For example, maybe one of your children would thrive in a larger school, whereas another might benefit from more individual attention at homeschool or private school. You don't need to make a final decision before marriage, but make sure you at least discuss your preferences.

5. What Will You Do If You're Unable to Conceive Children Biologically?

I've walked alongside many couples during the past thirteen years who have either been unable to conceive children or have suffered through multiple miscarriages. Many couples walk through seasons or lifetimes of infertility challenges.

> **Betty:** We visited doctors and tried every option the doctors presented to us, but we couldn't get pregnant. So we ended up adopting our first two children as babies two years apart from each other. We had never discussed adoption before marriage, but I'm thankful our hearts were aligned as a married couple.

Are you open to foster care, adoption, or fertility treatments? Are you open to adopting a child of a different ethnicity or background? How will your families respond to you adopting a child? Remember, every child of God is adopted into the family of the Lord (Eph. 1:5). Adoption is a beautiful picture of our heavenly Father's relationship with us. Again, you don't have to have your final answer right now, but at a minimum discuss with your significant other some options you might consider in case infertility is in your future.

6. Will You Both Work, or Will One of You Stay Home with Your Child(ren)?

Every married couple needs to decide if one parent will stay home with kids or if both parents will work and leave your children with a nanny or in some kind of day care. We have friends on all ends of the spectrum here; in some families, the father continues to work full-time while the mom stays home with the kids either full-time or part-time. We also know families where both parents work and families where the mom works full-time and the dad stays home with the kids.

I encourage you and your significant other to process this decision with your community. If you decide that both of you will continue to work, make sure you're doing it for a significant reason and not only so you can make more money and buy newer, nicer stuff. Too often, I see both parents outsource the parenting to someone else just so they can support a higher standard of living.

7. What's Your View of Birth Control?

Every couple needs to discuss their views and preferences on birth control. There are many options to choose from, but any type of birth control that leads to an intentional or unintentional abortion is completely out of bounds according to a biblical view of life. Most men don't know much in the arena of birth control outside of condoms, so make sure you do some research and talk to a doctor to find out more about different birth control options.[1] It might also be helpful to ask a mentor couple or other Christian friends what they have done so you can learn from others.

8. What If One or Both of You Have Children from a Prior Marriage or Relationship?

I've heard as many as one out of every three marriages in 2019 will be blended marriages in which at least one adult will bring a child (or children) into their new marriage. Blended families present many incredible opportunities and challenges for newlyweds, so you want to make sure you do all you can to prepare for your blended family before and after you say "I do." Make sure you equip yourself by reading some stepfamily books and checking out other blended family resources.[2]

Single parents, you are doing much more than preparing for a wedding day or marriage. In addition to thinking through how to merge your lives as adults, you and your future spouse need to think through how you will best parent your child as newlyweds and with your child's other biological parent. Here are a few questions to discuss:

- How will you split the week with the other parent/family?
- How will you figure out holidays and summer plans?
- How will you handle discipline of your child? Will the stepparent discipline the child or just the biological parent?

- If you both have kids, how will you handle differences in the way you parent your child (rules, expectations, etc.) and the way your future spouse parents his or her child?
- How will you discuss your new marriage with your child, especially if they are younger and don't have a full understanding of the changes headed their way?
- How will you walk through disagreements with the other biological parent?

Blending families can be a tremendous challenge. But if you do everything recommended in this book and continue to be humble and open to learning along the way, you can change the trajectory of the average blended family. I've seen many families do this well. You can do it!

The Rest of the Story

Josh and Betty are more than fifty years into marriage and love being both parents and grandparents. They've had many struggles along the way—financial, discipline, wayward children, and much more. They've also had many great moments. But in the great moments and the challenging ones, they've been aligned and have parented as a team.

The most important thing you can do right now for the future of your family is to discuss the questions and topics introduced in this chapter. You won't be able to have accurate conversations about many of these issues until you're already married and making real-time decisions. For this reason, you want to make sure you are marrying someone with whom you can have honest, biblical conversations.

Amos 3:3 says, "Do two walk together unless they have agreed to do so?" You and your future spouse must be aligned on the important issues about kids and parenting. Be able and willing to say, "I don't know what's in the future, but we will walk through it together." If you marry someone with a humble, teachable spirit, these conversations will go much better for you.

Am I Ready?

- What is your view of children? How do you feel about having kids in the future? What makes you anxious or excited about the possibility of having kids?
- What are some of your favorite memories of your family while you were growing up? What did your parent(s) do well?
- If you have children from a prior relationship or marriage, what are you most excited about in blending your families? What makes you most anxious? If you don't have any children but your significant other does, what are you most excited and anxious about?

Strengthening Our Knot

- Discuss your answers to the Am I Ready? questions about children.
- Spend some time talking through each of this chapter's eight questions about kids that you need to discuss before saying "I do."

- Share with your future spouse three traits you are excited to see in them as they parent any future children the Lord gives you.
- Who are some parents you could learn from on how to parent children well?

Closing Prayer

Heavenly Father, thank You for providing the greatest example of how to parent well. Thanks for the ways You unconditionally love us and the ways You discipline us out of love when we need to be disciplined. We pray You would bless us with children in the future, either biologically, with medical intervention, or through foster care or adoption, and we pray we would love and parent our children well. Help us be unified when we parent, and surround us with wise friends who can help us be better parents. Thank You for being a perfect, good Father. In the name of Your Son, Jesus Christ, we pray. Amen.

How Do We Break Up, Stop Having Sex, and Eight Other Frequently Asked Questions

As bonus content, I'm answering ten frequently asked questions we get in our premarried class at my church. Each question will be answered with biblical truth and honest, authentic counsel.

1. What If We Have Been Sexually Active with Each Other but Want to Stop?

Many couples assume once they have crossed sexual boundaries, it's too late to go back. I assure you this is not the case. If you are a follower of Jesus Christ, then you are indwelled by the Holy Spirit, and you have the ability and self-control to abstain sexually until marriage (Gal. 5:16, 22–23).

Here are a few suggestions:

- First, pray. Ask God to help you and give you self-control to honor each other without crossing boundaries. God will give you wisdom and help if you ask Him for it (James 1:5).
- Second, don't put yourself in situations where you are likely to cross boundaries. For instance, don't travel alone together or spend the night at each other's place. Don't snuggle on the couch in a dark room and watch a movie together. You will have plenty of opportunity to do these things after you get married.
- Third, get some accountability from a trusted friend, mentor, or pastor. Ask others to check on you and pray for you.
- Fourth, choose to be different from the pattern of the world. Just because other couples sleep together before getting married does not mean you need to make the same decision (Rom. 12:1–2).

Read the story of the adulterous woman in John 7:53–8:11. Jesus didn't condemn the woman for her sexual sin, but He told her to "go, and from now on sin no more" (John 8:11 ESV). Can you imagine the power of this scene? This woman was caught in the act of adultery, and the people wanted to stone her. Yet Jesus told this woman He didn't condemn her, but she was to go and leave her life of sin.

I encourage you to do the same. Jesus loves you and does not condemn you for your prior sexual activity. Romans 8:1

assures us, "There is now no condemnation for those who are in Christ Jesus." But go, and from now on sin no more.

2. What If Our Friends and Family Don't Approve of Our Relationship or Engagement?

Outside of the Lord, your family and friends should be the loudest voices in providing relationship counsel. If your close family and friends oppose the relationship, then I urge you to pay attention and find out why they don't approve.

Here are a few questions you should ask:

- Do I trust their counsel in general?
- Are they followers of Christ?
- What reasons are they providing for why they don't approve?

If your family and friends don't approve of your relationship, you are in a tight spot, and I'm sorry this is your situation. Instead, I wish those around you would celebrate your engagement or upcoming marriage. The Bible says you are to honor your father and mother (Exod. 20:12; Eph. 6:2–3), but at the same time, you and your signficant other are adults and don't require parental approval before saying "I do."

I can't speak for every parent, but most parents love their children and desire God's best for them. I suggest you pay close attention to the voice of your parents. But if your church community and other Christian friends around you approve, then you may proceed with caution.

3. If We Don't Think We Should Move Forward toward Marriage, How Do We Break Up?

I'm glad you're asking this question, because this means you are being honest about the state of your relationship or concerns you have about next steps. Whether you are the one who initiates or receives the breakup, no matter the reason, breakups are tough. In her book *The Real Thing*, Ellen McCarthy wrote, "Maybe it's a tiny bit better when you're the dumper and you know what's coming and have some sense of control. But then you also have to deal with the anxiety leading up to the split and the tidal wave of guilt that comes after. And you still have all the garden-variety sadness besides."[1]

During my thirteen years in marriage ministry, I've walked alongside hundreds of couples who decided to end their relationship. For many, especially for those who are engaged, the breakup is tougher because they have already made decisions about their wedding, had wedding showers, or sent wedding invitations.

If you are thinking about breaking up or postponing your wedding, make sure you widen the circle and ask trusted mentors, family, and friends for counsel and prayer. Just as you don't want to propose without wise people speaking into your life, so you don't want to end the relationship without wise counsel.

If you do end the relationship, do all you can to leave your significant other in a better place than when you first started dating. In other words, honor them in your dating and your breakup. This is another reason it's important to not cross physical boundaries in a dating relationship.[2]

4. What If One of Us Wants to Sign a Prenuptial Agreement?

Be very cautious when it comes to prenuptial agreements. Marriages are built on trust, and most prenups disregard trust from the very beginning of the marriage. If you can't trust your significant other before you get married, then you need to ask whether you should move forward. A prenuptial agreement essentially lays out who gets what in case your marriage doesn't last. In some ways, it is as if you are arranging for your divorce before you even get married.

Sometimes there are complications and exceptions regarding an inheritance for kids from a prior relationship or marriage. If there are financial or legal issues related to children from a prior marriage or relationship, then widen the circle and get feedback from a trusted family law attorney.

A friend of mine once said he's all for prenups—as long as your prenup says, "I will never, ever leave you or divorce you. No matter what you say and how many times you do it, I will stay with you until death do us part."[3] Then you both sign it and live happily ever after.[4]

5. Should We Combine Bank Accounts or Keep Them Separate?

Although the Bible does not address this question specifically, there are a few principles to think through when it comes to marital money management. Whenever a couple tells me they want separate bank accounts, I ask them why they want to do this. Separate accounts lead to a greater chance of hiding or deceit. When the two of you get married you become one flesh, so I strongly encourage you to combine all your assets into one account. Anything else increases the opportunity to view your resources as personal possessions instead of shared. In marriage, you always want to look for ways to build trust, and joint bank accounts provide an opportunity to grow, not divide.

What if I said to Kristen, "Since I'm the one who gets paid to work full-time, and you don't get paid to be a stay-at-home mom, I'll keep the majority of the money and you can get a small amount. I will give you enough to buy groceries and an occasional grande nonfat mocha with whip." That would be ridiculous, and I shouldn't be writing a marriage book if that were the case! Kristen and I share all our resources. We are one flesh, so we act like it in every way. A joint bank account communicates that you view your resources as "ours," not "yours" and "mine." You have some built-in accountability since you can see each other's transactions, and you communicate an all-in oneness with each other.

6. Why Is Porn Such a Big Deal?

No issue I'm aware of has hurt or destroyed more relationships than pornography. I don't think we've even begun to see anywhere near the full detrimental effects of pornography.

You need to know pornography is sin. Every time you look at pornography, you are lusting and committing adultery in your heart (Matt. 5:27–30). You are supporting an evil industry that enslaves women and feeds the pockets of greedy manipulators. It sets you up for comparison, insecurity, and counterfeit intimacy. The woman often compares herself to women in pornography; and the man, even more often, can't perform sexually without thinking of or bringing porn into the bedroom.[5]

Pornography is available twenty-four hours a day, seven days a week on our computers, tablets, and phones. We can find it all over the web, on many television stations, and in many romance novels. Porn is killing relationships in every stage of life. It nearly destroyed my life.

We can't solve this problem in a few paragraphs, but full books have been written on porn, and I've compiled a list of recommended resources for you to help battle this struggle if you have a history with pornography.[6]

7. Should We Move In Together before Getting Married?

Studies show that 60 to 80 percent of couples will move in together before they say "I do." In a worldly way, I know it makes sense. You and your significant other want to make sure you are compatible and try things out before you get married. Before I trusted in Christ, I walked through life with the same perspective.

However, let me warn you. Women often think moving in together is a sign of future marital commitment. Guys, on the other hand, know it means they can enjoy the benefits of marriage without the commitment marriage requires. Most couples who move in together will not get married.

Cohabitation is sin. God designed marriage in a way that says the man leaves his father and mother, unites to his wife, and then they become one flesh. They don't leave their home and live with their future spouse until they become one flesh.

If you're looking for ways to test the relationship, let me give you a few better ways:

- Build your friendship. Spend time together on dates, and spend even more time communicating with each other.

- Pray that the Lord would help you make a great decision about next steps.

- Ask others to give you feedback on your relationship. Are they excited or concerned about the prospect of the two of you getting married?

- Serve and study the Bible together. Get to know your significant other's heart, and pray it is the heart of a servant. Spend time talking about your spiritual lives and discovering what each other is learning from God's Word.

8. Does God Guarantee a Great Sex Life after Marriage If We Abstain before Marriage?

Some of you have been told a lie that holding out before marriage means God owes you amazing sex as a married couple. On behalf of other Christians and the church, I'm so sorry. The Bible includes no promise that if you abstain sexually before marriage, then God owes you anything after marriage. The reward comes in the obedience of trusting what God says about marriage and intimacy.

If you do have problems in your sex life after getting married, then make sure you seek help from a trusted friend, pastor, professional counselor, or even a medical doctor. Couples are often too scared to ask for help when it comes to intimacy, but I encourage you to seek wise counsel if this becomes a challenge in your marriage.

9. Is It Wrong for My (Future) Spouse and I to Attend Different Churches?

The precursor to this FAQ is covered in chapter 3: Are you building your lives on the same spiritual foundation? Assuming you and your significant other are both Christians who are aligned in your views on Jesus and salvation, then you should make sure you discuss a church home.

Before you tie the knot, the two of you might live in different towns or attend different churches. But you should do everything you can to get counsel from a healthy church and plan on building your marriage and family at the same church (Prov. 13:20; 15:22; 19:20).

Your church home should play a huge role in helping you build your spiritual foundation (Matt. 7:24–27). Where you go to church is a much more important decision than where you get your daily cup of coffee or what college football team you root for. If you don't attend the same or similar type of church, you will be receiving counsel from two different sources. In addition, you and your spouse will be cared for and underneath the authority of two different sources.

All the healthy, thriving couples I know attend the same church. They serve, worship, and learn together at the same church. They raise their children in the same church. For Kristen and me, most of our strongest friendships also come from our church. If the two of you cannot agree on teaching or worship style, one of you might need to put the preferences of the other before your own for the lasting benefit of your marriage.

Can you be married, attend different churches, and still have a good marriage? Possibly, but the chances of staying strong in your marriage are much greater if you attend the same church.

10. How Much Should We Spend on Our Wedding?

I started this book by challenging you to place a lot more time, money, and effort on your marriage than on your wedding day. But I also know weddings cost money. So how much should you spend on your wedding?

The pressure to throw an expensive wedding is intense, much more so today than when Kristen and I got married in 2001. Comparison, social media, and the influence of parents all work to increase the pressure you face as a couple.

As you think through how much to spend, ask yourselves this question: "What is the purpose of our wedding day?" The purpose of marriage is to be a picture of God's love for the church (Eph. 5:22–33), so your wedding day should help illustrate this picture. Make sure you spend more time focused on fulfilling the picture of God's purpose for marriage than you do the pictures you will have from your wedding.[7]

At the same time, it is right to celebrate, laugh, and dance at your wedding (Eccl. 3:4). Your wedding day should be a celebration—just don't conform to the patterns of the world to simply impress others. I'd rather hear your wedding guests talk about the beauty of your relationship than about the beauty of the flowers or décor.

One last principle: don't go into debt for your wedding. Debt in and of itself is not sinful, but the borrower is a slave to the lender (Prov. 22:7). Don't put yourself into a position where you have to pay off debt for months and months just for a one-day wedding. Process with God's Word, wise friends, and family how much you will spend on your wedding.

I've saved my favorite story for last. Let's wrap up this book and help you tie the knot!

Final Word

Till Death Do Us Part

As we wrap up our discussion of marriage, I want to leave you with an image from my stepdad's funeral. I promise you it's not as bleak as it sounds. In fact, it's one of the most beautiful pictures of marriage I've ever seen.

As I shared earlier, my biological father passed away from heart disease when I was six years old. My brother was three and a half at the time, and he and I grew up in a single-parent home with our mom. A few years later, our mom remarried, and we became a stepfamily.

My stepdad was diagnosed with Alzheimer's a few years before he died. I'm not going to sugarcoat it—as many of you know, Alzheimer's is a terrible disease. It's horrible for the individual and brutal on the family and loved ones. Over the years, we watched my stepdad progressively decline in verbal and cognitive function. The disease process became a huge challenge to my mom, as she had to make many sacrifices to care for him. She couldn't travel or even leave the house without bringing my stepdad. He needed around-the-clock care and supervision. My mom cooked every meal, drove everywhere they went together, and made sure he took his pills. She changed his diaper and cleaned him up after he made a mess of himself. Even though she grew weary at times, she still sacrificially cared for and supported him.

I watched as my mom loved my stepdad all the way until the day he died. Their marriage was far from perfect, but they loved each other until the end. My stepdad's funeral was one long testimony to my mom's love for him. That's the kind of marriage I want to build with my wife and the lifelong love I want for our lives.

A Reflection of God's Love for Us

As I reflect on how my mom loved my stepdad selflessly and sacrificially, I can't help but think of the ways God loves us. His love for us is the perfect model for how to love without expecting anything in return. The Lord knows we can never repay Him or show Him the proper gratitude for His many gifts. Thankfully, His love is not contingent upon our proper or worthy response.

I'm thankful for all the marriage books I've read and married couples I've learned from over the years. Yet the best picture of love I have ever seen was the way my mom loved my stepdad during the last years of his life. It's the type of unconditional, sacrificial love I hope to live out in the ways I care for and serve Kristen.

I hope that you won't have to walk through the same circumstances as my mom and stepdad did. But there will still be many ways for you to love and serve your spouse in practical ways. If you have a baby, you can be the one to take the lead in changing her diapers. If you have a toddler who cries at 3:00 a.m., you can be the one to console him. Or maybe it's as simple as finding out the chores your spouse dislikes and doing them with a joyful and content heart.

I am confident that if you apply the truths my friends and I have shared in this book, then you and your significant other will be ready for marriage. We are cheering you on as you say "I do" and tie that knot!

Acknowledgments

There are so many to thank who have helped make this dream come true and this book come to fruition.

Thanks to the five-thousand-plus couples who have been through the Merge premarried class at Watermark during the last thirteen years. I've learned so much from you, and I hope we prepared you well for marriage.

Thanks to my book team: Sarah Fultz, Allen Hankins, David Liggitt, and Derek Scott. You helped me shape this book from the beginning; you challenged me, supported me, prayed for me, and even gave me the title. Thanks for sticking with me from the beginning until the end.

Thanks to Gary Thomas for writing the foreword for this book! Much more than that, thank you for all the ways you've allowed the Lord to use you to help the body of Christ grow in their love for Jesus and in our understanding of marriage and family. Words can't express my gratitude for how much your words have grown, challenged, and encouraged me.

Thank you to my friends who let me use their lake house to get away from the noise of the big city to write this book.

Your generosity and kindness is not lost on me. I hope you celebrate this book and see the role you played in making it happen! Thanks as well to my friends at Pine Cove for giving me a place to write and dream for a few days.

Thank you to the Alexanders, Campions, Liggitts, and Sperrings. I am so grateful for our friendship and for the ways you sharpen and love me. Many verses come to mind when I think of our community group, but especially Proverbs 13:20 and 27:6. Thank you for helping me grow wise and for "wounding me" when I need to be wounded.

Thanks to Chad Allen, my writing coach. How can I find the ~~write~~ right words (pun intended) to thank you? You helped grow me, sharpen me, and encourage me, and you got my foot in the door at Baker! Somewhere along the way, you went from being my coach to my friend. I look forward to all the Lord has for us in the future.

Thank you to my all-star team at Baker—Brian Vos, Erin Smith, Patti Brinks, and so many others. I've loved working with you and appreciate your giving me this opportunity. Thanks also for bringing Jennifer Stair on the project and for the work she did as well.

Thanks to my friend Ethan Pope. Seven years ago, you sat down with me over some good Texas barbecue, and we talked writing, books, and next steps. You've helped me with every step along the way. You've coached me, encouraged me, and prayed for me. Let's go eat some more barbecue and celebrate together!

Thank you to the elders and staff at Watermark Community Church. For some crazy reason you hired this insecure, inexperienced guy thirteen years ago, and being a part of this staff has been one of the greatest blessings in my life.

Thanks for the opportunity to serve alongside a team of worldchangers and to serve marriages. Most churches do very little to support marriages from the staff side, so thank you for your strong belief in biblical marriage and relationships.

Speaking of working on marriages, thanks to the marriage staff team and leaders at Watermark—I love you and love serving with you. I'm so thankful for every day we get to be on mission together to help prepare nearlyweds, establish newlyweds, and enrich and restore all marriages. Let's keep running together for a long time.

Thanks to John McGee. We've been working on marriage ministry together every day for thirteen years! Thanks for taking me to IHOP many moons ago. I've learned more about marriage from you than any other human being. Thanks for your wisdom and friendship.

Only one guy has his name on the front of the book, but this book was really written by the twelve couples I interviewed for *Ready or Knot?* Combined, you have 314 years of marriage wisdom, and I'm thankful we get to benefit from your mistakes and successes in marriage. Thank you for being open and honest and for sharing your stories with the world!

Thank you to Duncan, Drew, Carson, and Lincoln—I love being your daddy. Thanks for the times you've sacrificed so I could work on this book. I owe you some hoops, baseball catches, guitar/vocal duets, and some daddy dates. I pray you read these words and apply them to your lives when you're ready to date! I love you.

Thanks to my wife, Kristen. You have carried the rock more times than I can count, and you never complain. Even though you didn't write one word in this book, you've been a part of every single one of them. I love you more.

Above all, thank you to my Lord and Savior. Twenty-one years ago, You saved this guy. I'm not sure why, because I certainly did not deserve it. I was an absolute mess, and I still would be without You. Thanks for taking my mess upon Yourself and making something beautiful out of it.

Notes

The Best $20 You Will Spend on Your Relationship

1. "Average Wedding Cost," *Cost of Wedding*, accessed June 26, 2018, http://www.costofwedding.com.

Chapter 1 What Is the Point of Marriage Anyway?

1. Gary Thomas, *Sacred Marriage: What If God Designed Marriage to Make Us Holy More Than to Make Us Happy?* (Grand Rapids: Zondervan, 2010). *Sacred Marriage* is among my favorite marriage books. It's a great book to read after you get married.

2. It's hard to believe, but this is a real question people ask. See my blog post "The Most Frustrating Marriage Article I Have Ever Read," *Scott Kedersha*, April 13, 2016, http://www.scottkedersha.com/frustrating/.

3. Andreas Köstenberger provides an excellent discussion on the contract, sacrament, and covenant views of marriage in his helpful book, *God, Marriage, and Family*, 2nd ed. (Carol Stream, IL: Crossway, 2010).

4. Thomas, *Sacred Marriage*, 11.

5. For further study, see Genesis 2:24–25; Matthew 19:4–6; Ephesians 5:31–32.

6. For more information about re|engage, see http://www.reengage.org.

Chapter 2 Are We Looking to Win or Seeking to Understand?

1. Throughout the book I use the terms *Christian* or *follower of Christ* synonymously. Someone who is a Christian is a person who realizes they

need a Lord and Savior. They realize their sin separates them from the perfect, holy, loving God. We're all sinners (Rom. 3:23), and because of our sin we fall far short of the glory of God. Our sin leads to death, both physical and spiritual (Rom. 6:23). But God demonstrates His love for us by sending His perfect Son, Jesus Christ, to die on the cross for our sins (Rom. 5:8). If you admit you're a sinner, then all you need to do is *believe* in what Jesus did on the cross for you and me. You can't behave your way into a relationship with God; you simply believe in what Jesus did, and afterward you choose to follow Him all the days of your life.

2. When I use the word *conflict*, I do not mean physical fighting. I am using *conflict* synonymously with *argument* or *disagreement*.

3. For example, see Proverbs 10:14, 12:15, 15:15, and 26:11, among many others.

Chapter 3 How Much Does Our Faith Really Matter?

1. My church, Watermark Community Church, provides a helpful guide on baptism that you can find at http://cms-cloud.watermark.org/WM-Baptism-Guide-2017_09.pdf?mtime=20170922113103. Also, Romans 6:1–14 provides a great description of baptism.

2. For a funny video on picking your church home, watch "meChurch 2" from my friend Rob Thomas and Igniter Media, available at http://www.ignitermedia.com/products/4559-mechurch-2.

3. I recorded a short video with Todd Wagner, the lead pastor of my church, answering the question, "Is It Important That I Go to the Same Church as the Person I'm Dating?" at *Real Truth Real Quick*, October 15, 2016, http://realtruthrealquick.com/important-go-church-person-dating.

4. Join the Journey: http://www.jointhejourney.com. YouVersion: http://www.youversion.com.

5. If you are looking for extra reading on how to most honor Christ on your wedding day, check out Catherine Parks, *A Christ-Centered Wedding: Rejoicing in the Gospel on Your Big Day* (Nashville: B&H, 2014).

Chapter 4 What If You Say Tomato and I Say Tomahto?

1. Anne Bogel, *Reading People: How Seeing the World through the Lens of Personality Changes Everything* (Grand Rapids: Baker, 2017), 24.

2. Tom Constable, "Notes on 1 Peter, 2017 edition," Plano Bible Chapel, accessed June 27, 2018, http://www.planobiblechapel.org/tcon/notes/html/nt/1peter/1peter.htm.

3. To learn more about your love language, see "Discover Your Love Language," *The 5 Love Languages*, http://www.5lovelanguages.com.

Chapter 5 Will We Clip Coupons or Max Out Credit Cards?

1. American Institute of CPAs, "AICPA Survey: Finances Causing Rifts for American Couples," AICPA, May 4, 2012, http://www.aicpa.org /press/pressreleases/2012/finances-causing-rifts-for-american-couples .html.

2. Ben Patterson, *The Great Essentials* (Waco, TX: Word, 1987), 17.

3. For more information about Dave Ramsey and Financial Peace University, see http://www.daveramsey.com.

Chapter 6 Who's in Charge, and What Are Our Biblical Roles?

1. From Watermark Community Church, "What We Believe," http://www.watermark.org/dallas/about/beliefs (Deut. 6:4; Matt. 28:19–20; 2 Cor. 13:14; see also 1 Cor. 8:6; Col. 2:9; Acts 5:3–4).

2. Thanks to my friend David Leventhal for his input on this question.

3. Blake Holmes, director of Dallas Campus Ministries and the Watermark Institute at Watermark Community Church, did an excellent two-part series on how to make decisions. I encourage you to check it out at http://www.watermark.org/message/2612.

Chapter 7 How Can We Pursue Emotional Intimacy?

1. Dave and Ashley Willis, *The Naked Truth about Sex and Marriage* (Augusta, GA: Willis Family Media, 2017), 20.

2. Robert Wynne, "What Does a Public Relations Agency Do?" *Forbes*, April 10, 2013, http://www.forbes.com/sites/robertwynne/2013/04/10 /what-does-a-public-relations-agency-do/#4558a40275d9.

3. *This Is Us*, season 2, episode 1, "A Father's Advice," directed by Ken Olen, written by Dan Fogelman, aired September 26, 2017, on NBC.

Chapter 8 What Do We Need to Know about Sex?

1. Watermark has an incredible ministry for young adults called The Porch. I highly recommend you check out their website, blog, and sermon library: http://www.theporch.live.

2. Choosing to serve your spouse sexually does not mean you *ever* allow them to abuse you or do anything to you against your will. If your spouse forces you to do anything with them sexually, against your will, please get some help from a trusted friend, mentor, pastor, or counselor.

3. For more on this question, check out this video by my pastor, Todd Wagner: "How Far Is Too Far in a Dating Relationship?" *Real Truth Real Quick*, June 21, 2014, http://www.realtruthrealquick.com/how -far-is-too-far.

4. I've compiled a list of helpful resources (sermons, books, articles) about pornography on my blog. See Scott Kedersha, "Stuff I Like Saturday: I Hate Porn Edition," *Scott Kedersha*, July 25, 2015, http://www.scottkedersha.com/sils7.

5. I share my story about my struggle with porn in my blog post "How Porn Nearly Ruined My Life," *Scott Kedersha*, July 13, 2015, www.scottkedersha.com/pornography.

6. re:generation recovery: http://www.regenerationrecovery.org; Celebrate Recovery: http://www.celebraterecovery.com.

7. If abortion is part of your story, please check out some of the resources Watermark has made available for men and women at "Someone Cares," http://www.watermark.org/someonecares.

8. For resources about discussing your sexual past, check out the following posts: Jonathan Pokluda, "Dating Questions—Discussing Your Sexual Past," *The Porch*, March 16, 2015, http://www.theporch.live/blogs/discussing-your-sexual-past; Jonathan Pokluda, "Dating Questions: When Should I Share My Past," *The Porch*, February 27, 2015, http://www.theporch.live/blogs/when-should-i-share-my-past.

9. Jud Wilhite, *That Crazy Little Thing Called Love: The Soundtrack of Marriage, Sex, and Faith* (Colorado Springs: Standard, 2007), 75.

10. Timothy Keller with Kathy Keller, *The Meaning of Marriage: Facing the Complexities of Commitment with the Wisdom of God* (New York: Dutton, 2011), 215.

Chapter 10 Are We Roomies for Life or Best Friends?

1. My friend Mike wrote a great guest post on my blog about inside jokes and rituals in marriage. Check it out at "How Inside Jokes and Rituals Can Strengthen Your Marriage," August 21, 2017, *Scott Kedersha*, http://www.scottkedersha.com/marriage.

2. Emily Loerke, "Weekly Questions," *Today's Letters*, November 8, 2015, http://www.todaysletters.com/p/tuesday-questions.html.

3. This quote has been attributed to various sources, but it is most often attributed to Martin Luther.

4. I've accumulated a collection of date night ideas for any couple. To download your own killer date night list, go to "124 Killer Date Night Ideas, 2017 Updated & Revised," *Scott Kedersha*, May 1, 2014, www.scottkedersha.com/datenight.

5. For some more practical suggestions on how to handle opposite-sex friendships and how you can strengthen your relationship and build trust, check out this post I wrote on the Watermark Community Church marriage blog: "6 Ways You Can Strengthen Your Marriage," May 19, 2017, http://www.watermark.org/blog/6-ways-you-can-strengthen-your-marriage.

6. Michael Hyatt, "Why Speaking Well of Your Spouse Is So Important," MichaelHyatt.com, February 12, 2016, http://www.michaelhyatt.com/why-speaking-well-of-your-spouse-is-so-important.

Chapter 11 None of Their Business or Better Together?

1. Thanks to my friend and coworker Scott Coy for these helpful questions.
2. Keller, *The Meaning of Marriage*, 153.
3. Clay Scroggins, "Naked and Afraid: Opening Up without Falling Apart," message delivered March 12, 2017, North Point Community Church, Alpharetta, GA, http://www.npnights.org/connect/naked-afraid.

Chapter 12 What about the Kids?

1. Check out Todd Wagner's video, "Is It OK for a Christian to Use Birth Control?" *Real Truth Real Quick*, April 9, 2016, http://www.realtruthrealquick.com/birth-control. Additionally, The Village Church in Flower Mound, Texas, has written a helpful position paper on contraception and reproductive technology, "Should Christians Use Contraceptive Methods and Reproductive Technologies?" February 7, 2013, http://www.tvcresources.net/resource-library/articles/should-christians-use-contraceptive-methods-and-reproductive-technologies.
2. Ron Deal has written several books on stepfamilies that are outstanding. In particular, check out *The Smart Stepfamily: Seven Steps to a Healthy Family* (Bloomington, MN: Bethany House, 2014).

How Do We Break Up, Stop Having Sex, and Eight Other Frequently Asked Questions

1. Ellen McCarthy, *The Real Thing: Lessons on Love and Life from a Wedding Reporter's Notebook* (New York: Ballantine, 2015), 131.
2. For more input on when and why to break up, listen to this message from David Marvin: "When to Break Up," *The Porch*, September 20, 2016, http://www.theporch.live/messages/4260.
3. I am *not* giving license for any kind of abuse here. If your spouse/significant other abuses you, get help. Widen the circle, protect yourself, and get counsel from people who love you and will help you.
4. For more on this very relevant question, check out the video from my pastor, Todd Wagner, "Is It OK for a Christian to Get a Prenuptial Agreement?" *Real Truth Real Quick*, June 15, 2014, http://www.realtruthrealquick.com/prenuptial-agreement.
5. Belinda Luscombe, "Porn and the Threat to Virility," *Time* (April 11, 2016): 40–47.

6. As mentioned in chapter 8, I've compiled a list of helpful resources (sermons, books, articles, etc.) about pornography. You can find this list at Scott Kedersha, "Stuff I Like Saturday: I Hate Porn Edition," *Scott Kedersha*, July 25, 2015, http://www.scottkedersha.com/sils7.

7. Thank you to my pastor, Todd Wagner, for this genius play on words.

About the Author

Scott Kedersha is a follower of Jesus Christ, husband to Kristen (since 2001), dad to four boys (Duncan, Drew, Carson, and Lincoln), and an overly proud graduate of Wake Forest University. He also earned his master of theology degree from Dallas Theological Seminary.

Scott serves on staff at Watermark Community Church in Dallas, Texas, as the director of marriage ministry. Since 2006, Scott has helped prepare nearlyweds, establish newlyweds, and enrich and restore all marriages with an incredible staff and leadership team. Scott has worked primarily with the Merge premarital ministry, where he's helped guide more than five thousand seriously dating and engaged couples.

The first twenty-four years of Scott's life were marked by academic, relational, and professional success. Those years were also marked by incredible loneliness and worship of anything other than God. His poor decisions brought him to a point of desperation, and God brought some key people into his life at exactly the right time. Life dramatically changed for Scott in 1998 when he placed his faith and trust in Jesus Christ as his Lord and Savior.

Scott writes about marriage, ministry, leadership, and much more at ScottKedersha.com. You can also find Scott on:

Twitter: www.twitter.com/skedersha

Instagram: www.instagram.com/skedersha

Facebook: www.facebook.com/AuthorScottKedersha

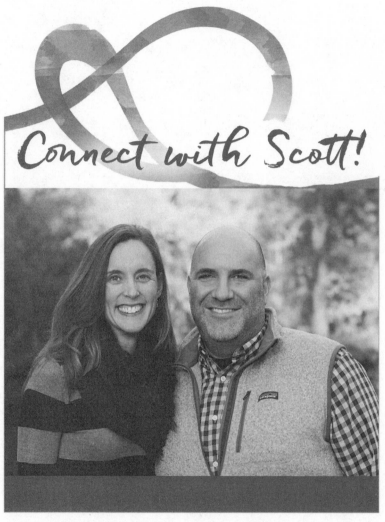

Connect with Scott!

Visit Scott online to subscribe to emails, read blog posts, and more!

f @SKedersha　**◎** @SKedersha　**◆** @SKedersha

If you'd like to learn more about the marriage ministries at
Watermark Community Church mentioned in this book,
please visit watermarkresources.com.

LIKE THIS
BOOK?
Consider sharing it with others!

- Share or mention the book on your social media platforms. Use the hashtag **#ReadyorKnot**.

- Write a book review on your blog or on a retailer site.

- Pick up a copy for friends, family, or strangers— anyone who you think would enjoy and be challenged by its message!

- Share this message on Twitter or Facebook: **I loved #ReadyorKnot by @SKedersha // @ReadBakerBooks**

- Recommend this book for your church, workplace, book club, or class.

- Follow Baker Books on social media and tell us what you like.

 Facebook.com/ReadBakerBooks

 @ReadBakerBooks

Corporate
Conversations

Corporate
Conversations

A Guide to Crafting Effective and
Appropriate Internal Communications

Shel Holtz

AMACOM

American Management Association

New York • Atlanta • Brussels • Chicago • Mexico City • San Francisco
Shanghai • Tokyo • Toronto • Washington, D.C.

Special discounts on bulk quantities of AMACOM books are available to corporations, professional associations, and other organizations. For details, contact Special Sales Department, AMACOM, a division of American Management Association, 1601 Broadway, New York, NY 10019.
Tel.: 212-903-8316. Fax: 212-903-8083.
Web site: www.amacombooks.org

This publication is designed to provide accurate and authoritative information in regard to the subject matter covered. It is sold with the understanding that the publisher is not engaged in rendering legal, accounting, or other professional service. If legal advice or other expert assistance is required, the services of a competent professional person should be sought.

Library of Congress Cataloging-in-Publication Data

Holtz, Shel.
    Corporate conversations : a guide to crafting effective and appropriate internal communications / Shel Holtz.
        p.   cm.
    Includes bibliographical references and index.
    ISBN 978-0-8144-1549-8(paperback)
    1. Communication in personnel management.   I. Title.

HF5549.5.C6H63   2004
651.7'9—dc21
                                                      2003006503

Printing number

10   9   8   7   6   5   4   3   2   1

For my mother, Sally Schwimer Holtz.

You always believed.

Contents

Preface

EMPLOYEE COMMUNICATION is the most important type of communication in which a company can engage. These days, as organizations rely more and more on information—and as organizations undergo continuous metamorphosis—leaders at all levels recognize the need to communicate with employees but are not certain how to go about it. Formally, employee communications departments are often the least important communication function within an organization.

Corporate Conversations explains the link between internal communications and business success, and it offers advice about how to organize and manage the process for the best results. It is based on more than twenty-five years of personal experience, along with a great deal of study and research.

Over the years, I have accumulated hundreds of case studies showing how to—and how *not* to—conduct communications. Many of these examples are scattered throughout this book. In nearly all cases, however, I have placed these situations in two fictitious companies. Amalgamated Pulp & Paper is a clueless company, making classic mistakes with deleterious results. Allied Gate & Fence has its communication act together, taking advantage of the fruits of effective internal communication. While the companies are not real, the case studies ascribed to them are.

Acknowledgments

A BOOK LIKE THIS is never the work of one person. In the twenty-five years I have spent in the communications business, I have learned from some of the very best, and I continue to be inspired by their vision and dedication to the practice and theory of communicating with employees.

Dave Orman was my first boss when I joined the employee communications staff at ARCO. Dave was one of a small group of visionaries who set the standard for strategic, business-oriented communication back when most internal communication departments cranked out house organs. At the same time, I worked directly for the late Ken Estes, one of the best editors who ever lived.

Another one of those visionaries is Roger D'Aprix, who continues to counsel organizations and whose books continue to inform the profession.

Among others who have influenced and motivated me are Lester Potter, ABC, one of the masters of strategic planning; Angela Sinickas, ABC, who made internal communication measurement a practice deserving of respect; and Ron Martin, ABC, who showed how to meld the various elements of communication—strategic and tactical—into a practical program that works from day to day.

My NetGain partners deserve special note, since I speak with them often and seek their advice. Tudor Williams, ABC, is another measurement guru and an expert in the application of knowledge

management to internal communications; Peter Shinbach, APR, focuses on external communications, but brings that perspective to any
discussion of employee communications. Former NetGainer Craig
Jolley has also been a source of ideas and information.

I doubt many internal communicators would be as good at their
jobs as they are without the support of the International Association
of Business Communicators (IABC). Whether they belong to IABC
or not, communicators have benefited from the association's decades-
long support of the profession. My admiration and respect is unend-
ing for Chris Grossgart, Natasha Spring, Joseph Ugalde, Suzanne
Byron, Shahana Alam, Vicky Yim, Gloria Gordon (retired), and
Elizabeth Allan, ABC, CAE (former president, now heading another
association). Also, from Ragan Communications are Dan Oswald,
Mark Ragan, Ralph Gaillard, Cristin Clifford, David Murray, and
Kasia Chalko.

Other names I'd be remiss to exclude are Lou Williams, ABC,
APR; Charles Pizzo; Wilma Mathews, ABC; John Gerstner, ABC;
Sheri Rosen, ABC; Jerry Stevenson; Carol Kinsey Goman; Dan
Janal; John Clemons, ABC, APR; Ed Robertson; Marcia Vaughan,
ABC; Dave Seifert, ABC; Robert Holland; Steve Crescenzo; Robert
Holland, ABC.

And of course, I would be nowhere and nothing without the
love and support of my family: Michele, my wife of twenty-seven
years and the person who always reminds me what life is all about;
and my children, Ben (serving with the Screaming Eagles, the U.S.
Army's 101st Airborne) and Rachel. I love you all beyond expression.

CHAPTER ONE

Getting Employees
on the Same Page

EVERYTHING COMMUNICATES, like it or not. Words obviously communicate, but actions and even silence also send strong messages. It sounds like something Yogi Berra might have said (but did not): *You can't not communicate.* It's this notion that communication simply happens that leads many organizations to dismiss the importance of employee communications as a management function. Few people would tell a doctor how to operate, or a structural engineer how to build a bridge so that it won't collapse, or a CPA how to account for inventory on a profit-and-loss statement.

"If I want something communicated to everyone in this company, I know exactly which three secretaries to tell," a company president once told me, explaining why he didn't see a need to develop comprehensive internal communications programs. (One must wonder whether he ever played the telephone game as a child. The first child whispers a message to the next, who whispers it to the next, on down the line until the last child announces the message he heard, which rarely sounds like the message the first child uttered. Did the message that reached front-line employees through the company grapevine accurately reflect the one the president confided to those three administrative assistants?)

In that same company, the chief financial officer expressed disgust when a survey revealed that a hefty portion of the employee population was blissfully unaware of a major reorganization. "We sent them the company magazine," he growled, referring to a special issue devoted to the change. "If they're going to work for us, they should be expected to read it."

Remember quality improvement training from back in the 1970s and 1980s? Quality improvement gurus used to teach a concept called "right things right." You can do the right thing right, the wrong thing right, the right thing wrong, or the wrong thing wrong. For example, consider a fast-food customer ordering a hamburger well-done:

RIGHT THING RIGHT	RIGHT THING WRONG
A hamburger well-done	A hamburger, rare
A chicken burger, well-done	A chicken burger, rare
WRONG THING RIGHT	WRONG THING WRONG

Employee communication is like the hamburger. The goal is to always communicate the right things in the right way. Consider the following example: A company is about to implement a cost-reduction program that will require employees to obtain the insurance company's permission before they can proceed with a medical procedure their doctor has recommended. Using the burger matrix, let's look at the communication in the table on page 3.

How do you know what the right thing is? How do you know whether you're communicating it in the right way and in a manner that will build trust between employees and the company? Are you communicating in a manner that will lead employees to dedicate their efforts to company goals and represent the company to various public audiences in a manner that can only bolster the organization's repu-

The right thing:

Tell the truth. The slump in the economy, coupled with changing buying habits among our core customers and manufacturing delays, has put us in a position where we need to cut costs. This was one way to reduce expenses with the least impact on employees. You will still receive the health care you need, but we may head off unnecessary procedures. It is a trend in benefits many companies have adopted. The alternatives would have been worse.

Done right:

- Benefits meetings in which the financial rationale is explained.
- Print publication covering the change so employees can study it and take it home to share with family.
- Communication directly to supervisors so they can answer employee questions.
- Channels for addressing employee issues and concerns.

The right thing:

Tell the truth. The slump in the economy, coupled with changing buying habits among our core customers and manufacturing delays, has put us in a position where we need to cut costs. This was one way to reduce expenses with the least impact on employees. You will still receive the health care you need, but we may head off unnecessary procedures. It is a trend in benefits many companies have adopted. The alternatives would have been worse.

Done wrong:

The whole thing is covered in standard-issue benefits materials employees receive as a routine part of their benefits enrollment.

The wrong thing:

This is a new benefit we're providing you to make sure you don't find yourself having unnecessary surgery performed by an unscrupulous doctor interested only in the fees. We're doing this out of entirely altruistic motives.

Done right:

- Benefits meetings in which the financial rationale is explained.
- Print publication covering the change so employees can study it and take it home to share with family.
- Communication directly to supervisors so they can answer employee questions.
- Channels for addressing employee issues and concerns.

The wrong thing:

This is a new benefit we're providing you to make sure you don't find yourself having unnecessary surgery performed by an unscrupulous doctor interested only in the fees. We're doing this out of entirely altruistic motives.

Done wrong:

The whole thing is covered in standard-issue benefits materials employees receive as a routine part of their benefits enrollment tation? That's where an understanding of the principles of employee communications—and leaders' roles in fostering effective communications—comes in. It is your job as a leader to foster an environment in which communication is effective, because communication that simply happens rarely achieves measurable, bottom-line results.

Lest you think this is merely another management-practice-of-the-month, consider the growing trend toward taking strategic internal communication more seriously:

- A 2002 survey by the Society of Human Resource Management (SHRM) concluded, "Companies making headlines for financial wrongdoings could cast a long and lingering shadow of doubt on corporate America's respect for employees. At a time when public distrust of big business is at an all-time high, organizations should strive to appreciate and place a high value on their employees. Many are relying on employee communication to influence internal perceptions of organizational reputation and credibility. By doing so they hope to increase employee morale, productivity, performance, and retention. Is it working? Human resource professionals and employees around the U.S. believe it is."[1]
- A British study, reported in the *Financial Times,* noted that internal communications used to consist mainly of "low-budget company newsletters, often by public relations or human resources specialists." But its role, the *Times* reported, is rising to the top of the leaders' agendas. Internal communicators build relationships with employees and deliver feedback to management. CEOs, according to the *Times,* have traditionally failed to appreciate the business benefits of having professional communicators. "Today, particularly in organizations where the CEO is very dialogue-oriented, he is starting to understand more about the commercial value of employee communications and is looking to expand the internal communications role accordingly."[2]
- Hewlett Packard CEO Carly Fiorina was quoted in *The Wall Street Journal* as saying, "Employee communication is as vital right now as shareholder communication."[3]

This book is about how to communicate the right stuff the right way. The short answer is simple: Companies that communicate well with their employees perform better in the measures that count, such as profitability, customer acquisition and retention, and reputation. Companies that don't . . . well, they don't.

Employees Are an Organization's Most Important Audience

Companies pour scads of money into communication—only not *employee* communication. Advertising usually gets the lion's share of the budget allocated to communication. Advertising creates awareness of a company's products or services, leading targeted customers to differentiate those products from what the competition offers. It creates *brand,* which is generally defined as the way someone feels about a company or its offerings.

Marketing is closely related to advertising, using somewhat subtler methods than advertising to gain exposure for products in the marketplace. Media relations ensures that the press covers the company and its operations accurately and (one hopes) positively. Investor relations helps the financial community understand the value of the company as an investment. Government relations represents the company's interests to legislators with the power to create laws that could either ease the organization's burdens or increase them. All these activities generally fall under a common heading such as "public relations" or "public affairs."

But the fact is, media relations efforts—or any of the other kinds of communication—will not succeed if employees don't understand and agree with the messages the company is delivering, and act accordingly. There are two reasons for this:

1. Employees are a company's face to all its various constituencies.
2. Employees execute the business plan that is at the heart of all the communication aimed at other audiences.

A few years ago, a major nationwide bank launched a public relations effort that was unique and compelling enough to generate coverage on the front page of the business sections of daily newspapers across the country. I imagine it was an easy pitch for media relations reps at the bank: Employees would volunteer to "adopt" ATMs. As part of the team-focused culture the company was promoting, these employees would care for their ATM, ensuring they were presentable by washing the screens, wiping down the surfaces, and keeping the area free of litter. Employees were so dedicated to this effort (so the story went) that they were going to spend their own money buying paper towels and bottles of cleaning solutions and care for these ATMs on their own time.

That's a pretty good story. Who wouldn't want to do business with a bank that supported such a participatory employee culture?

While conducting a transaction at one of this bank's branches shortly after the story appeared, my wife asked her teller if she had adopted an ATM. In a voice dripping with cynicism, the teller said, "Oh, sure. After working here all day for a teller's salary, with all the crap I have to put up with, I'm going to spend my own money to take care of the bank's ATM when I could be home with my kids just so the bank can save a few bucks." She turned to the teller working the window next to her, and asked, "How about you, Mary? Have you adopted an ATM?" Mary broke out laughing. Within minutes, every teller in the bank was actively disparaging the program.

Funny how I never heard about the program again. No follow-up stories appeared in the press. Despite the time, energy, and money expended to create and promote the program, cynical employees who hadn't bought into the message killed it. In fact, their vocal ridicule of the program probably did more damage than if the program had never been launched in the first place.

To be effective, employee communication must achieve the following three results, which are critical to an organization's success:

1. *Employees represent the company to external audiences in a manner consistent with the image the company's leaders want the outside world to see.*

They walk the talk. They are brand ambassadors. Their behavior represents the ideal that company leaders desire. Instead of covering breeches of ethics or wrongdoing by employees, the press winds up covering employee involvement in the community or tales of employee innovation.

2. *Employees produce quality work that satisfies the needs of customers.* They innovate and collaborate to produce what the company needs them to produce, helping the company achieve competitiveness and profitability.

3. *Employees don't quit to go work someplace better.* Companies that experience high turnover (or "churn")—particularly among higher-level staff and key contributors—struggle to find the talent required to execute the company's plans.

The World of Work Has Changed

Strategically managed employee communications is a relatively new phenomenon. When I first started working in the field in 1977, I had never heard of it. I had been a newspaper reporter with a degree in journalism. I figured my job with a big oil company's employee newspaper was merely another twist on being a reporter—same job, different audience. That would have been the case if I had taken an employee communications job in any other company. ARCO, however, was one of a few companies (such as Xerox, Westinghouse, and a few others) blazing the trail toward more strategic communications. I was there not to report on the news but to produce content consistent with the department's goal of reinforcing or changing employee behaviors. Those behaviors we were trying to influence were the ones that would support the company's bottom-line business efforts.

Most communication going on at that time (and earlier) was a mixture of reactive news reporting and happy talk. The dreaded four *B*'s of internal communication littered the pages of company publications: *b*irthdays, *b*abies, *b*rides, and *b*owling scores. There was nothing strategic or business-focused about these communications. If times got tough and money got tight, communications were scaled back or eliminated. And yet, companies managed to succeed in spite of this haphazard approach to communication. What changed between the good old days and now?

Nearly everything, for example:

- Nobody's loyal anymore.
- Business has become more complex.
- Command-and-control structures stopped working.

Nobody's Loyal Anymore

Not long ago, employees tended to march in lockstep with their employer's goals and objectives out of a sense of loyalty. Loyalty is an emotional characteristic, not a rational one. Nobody decides to be loyal. Rather, loyalty bubbles up out of a sense of deep connection, out of gratitude, or from a host of other reactions to conditions.

An understanding existed between employees and employers: "If you come to work every day, do your job, and follow the rules, this company will employ you, pay you, and provide you with benefits until you retire, at which time the company will give you a gold watch and a pension so you can live comfortably for the rest of your life." (We'll go into more detail on this issue in Chapter 2.)

Most of the leaders of today's organizations started their careers as part of the world in which this pact was an unwritten rule; they succeeded, rising through the ranks to the heights of leadership within the context of those types of assumptions. The employees who report to them, however, are part of a different world. While leaders expect to receive the same loyalty they gave their organizations, today's employees feel no such emotional connection to their companies. Because a job for life is no longer a guarantee—in truth, it is a rarity—loyalty to one's employer has vanished.

Information and Knowledge Drive Business

Many factors that drive business today are more complicated than they were fifty years ago. But that's nothing new. Up until the Industrial Revolution, business was remarkably simple. With the exception of a few oddities (such as the East India Trading Company), most businesses were ridiculously small. Craftsmen worked at their trades, cobbling shoes or printing books or thatching roofs. They employed apprentices who hoped to spend ten to fifteen years learning their trade before they could open their own shop. The biggest organizations were the trade guilds, which regulated individual trades or occupations; they set pay rates and established quality standards.

The Industrial Revolution meant the end of that way of life. Not that the change came easily to those who were accustomed to— and comfortable with—the way things were. Ned Ludd—a vocal opponent of industrialization—led his followers in a fruitless attempt to hold back the tide of change. They destroyed the machines that symbolized the transition to an industrial world, engaged in mass protests, and lobbied against the adoption of the new tools that threatened their way of life. (Today, those who resist new technology are referred to as Luddites, a backhanded homage to Ned Ludd.)

In a manner similar to the way the world shifted gears with the Industrial Revolution, the information revolution has forced us to shift gears again. The cornerstones of business in the Industrial Era were land, labor, and capital. Nobody would suggest that business today does not need these things. Even for the most industrial companies, though, information is the *most* important element of production in this new era.

Consider Wal-Mart, the most successful company of its kind. Wal-Mart buys goods from producers and sells them to consumers. The company stocks its shelves with *stuff*. Land is critical; without it, there would be no stores in which to stock that stuff the customers want to buy. Labor is critical; without it, there would be nobody to stock the shelves or work the cash registers. Capital is critical; without it, Wal-Mart wouldn't be able to purchase the goods it resells or pay the labor that handles all those processes.

Yet, Wal-Mart is more successful than any of its competitors because of *information*. Its supply chain systems are renowned for identifying what customers are going to want before they even know it, ensuring the suppliers are producing the right goods and delivering them in time to meet those customer needs. All the land, labor, and capital in the world wouldn't make Wal-Mart the darling of the retail world if the company didn't have the information necessary to make the kinds of decisions the company is capable of making. Information is at the heart of Wal-Mart's business model; it is the fuel that propels the Wal-Mart engine.

In the information-driven world, the command-and-control structure is an obstacle to success.

Command-and-Control Structures Stopped Working

During a panel discussion at a conference on intranets, a panelist suggested that the notion of knowledge sharing was flawed. Organizations are necessarily hierarchical, he said; those people occupying boxes higher up on the chart need information those lower on the totem pole don't need and, in many cases, shouldn't have. There will always be hierarchy, the panelist insisted; "need-to-know" will always be a part of the world of work.

Certainly those leaders who ascended the corporate ladder under the industrial model have a hard time envisioning any other type of structure. But the hierarchical org chart is a relic of an industrial economy. Org charts are based on the notion of command-and-control, a military concept popularized in the post–World War II business world. The org chart works on several principles:

• The person at the top knows everything and doles information out to subordinates based on what they need to know to achieve their discrete and independent objectives. These subordinates in turn distribute their knowledge on a need-to-know basis to *their* subordinates. This military concept was designed to safeguard mission-critical information so that it wouldn't fall into the hands of the enemy. Low-ranking soldiers on the front lines knew only their most immediate tactical goals; they would not give too much information away if they were captured. The higher up the chain of command you were, the less likely you were to fall into the hands of the enemy. Generals, with a thorough understanding of strategy, are the least likely to find themselves in a position where they can be tortured into divulging that strategy.

- Each layer in the cascading chart is designed to be able to perform its tasks and achieve its objectives on its own, using only the resources it has and not depending on knowledge, information, or resources from others. A foot patrol is assigned to capture a hill. The troops can achieve this task with the weapons they carry with them and the information they have been given. Someone higher up the chain knows that the capture of the hill is necessary to accomplish some other part of a broader strategy, which in turn supports an even more crucial effort. But the foot patrol does not need to know that. All they need to know is that they are supposed to take that hill.

- Nobody is supposed to deviate from his or her assignment without the approval of somebody higher up the chart. Because of the independent nature of departments (or, in military terms, squads), members of those departments do not know the big picture. Any action or decision that strays from the authorized path could affect the outcomes sought by leadership.

Work occurs now in an information-driven economy, in which information must get into the hands of the people who need it on demand. Knowledge needs to be *just in time*.

Trust Is at Its Lowest Point

The corporate scandals of 2001 and 2002 have left virtually all constituent audiences skeptical and distrustful of business. Investors have suffered terrible losses, making many people reluctant to invest. Employees, though, were hurt most of all. At Enron, retirement nest eggs evaporated overnight. Employees in other organizations doomed by the greed and malfeasance of their leaders are disoriented and confused. They have learned the hard way to watch out for themselves first; their employers, they know now, are not to be trusted. Companies that have not experienced the catastrophic effects of executive wrongdoing are nevertheless painted with the same brush, and employees wonder when the other shoe will fall on them.

Employee Communication Is About Business

Given all these changes to the world of work, the function of communicating to employees has evolved from the kind of reporting that populated most "house organs"—the name given to fluff-filled company publications—to a strategic business activity, the kind that (in the words of a 2002 study by the Society of Human Resources Managers), "influence internal perceptions of organizational reputation and credibility."

The goal of employee communication is influence. The company has goals, and leaders need employees to focus their energy and effort on doing the kind of work that helps the company achieve those goals. While good communication will not produce profits for a company with a bad product or a lousy business plan, it *will* yield considerable benefits to organizations with a solid business foundation. More to the point, a solid business foundation will not necessarily ensure success *unless* the organization communicates its plans, strategies, aspirations, vision, and expectations to the employees who must make it happen through their day-to-day efforts. (According to a study by human resources consulting firm Watson Wyatt Worldwide, a clear correlation exists between high-performing companies and the extent to which they communicate with their employees.)

Companies, then, need to influence employee opinions, the degree to which they commit themselves, and their behaviors so that they perform in a manner consistent with the business plan.

How often have you heard leaders lament that employees simply aren't on the same page they are? They're not singing from the same hymnbook; they're not rowing in the same direction?

In the following chapters, you will learn how employee communications gets employees on the same page—that is, how it can influence employee commitment to helping the company achieve its goals. Your job, as a leader, is to see to it that these principles are implemented and that all leaders—from the executive suite to supervisors at the front lines of the business to leaders of formal communication functions—live these principles.

Notes

1. "Corporate Credibility and Employee Communications Survey," Society of Human Resources Management, 2002.
2. British executive search consultancy Watson Helsby, "The Rise of the Internal Communicator," *Financial Times,* January 30, 2003, "Inside Track" section, p. 14.
3. Pui Wing Tam, "Boss Talk: The Chief Does Double Duty—How H-P's Fiorina Manages to Run Global Corporation While Waging Proxy Fight," *The Wall Street Journal,* February 7, 2002, p. B1.

CHAPTER TWO

What We Know About Employees

"Employees should read the employee magazine/newsletter/ intranet because they work here and it's part of their job."

"We put it in the magazine/newsletter/intranet, so it's been communicated."

"Employees get a paycheck. In exchange, they owe us their best efforts, including the effort it takes to know what's going on in the company."

IF YOU EVER CATCH yourself saying one of these phrases, dock yourself a week's pay. It means you are utterly clueless about what motivates employees, why they pay attention to company messages, and how they absorb messages into their work habits. Write one hundred times on a dry erase board, "Nothing's that simple."

As a leader, is your paycheck your only motivation? Is it even your primary motivation? Is it among the *top five* motivators? Do you spend hours with the *Wall Street Journal* and trade journals just because you have a job and ought to know what is going on? Human motivation—whether you are a line employee or a senior executive—is inspired by more complex drivers.

Psychologist Abraham Maslow identified a hierarchy of human needs. Maslow's Hierarchy of Needs was introduced to the business world in response to management expectations that employees should start a new job at the top of the pyramid, a pinnacle at which employees declare, "I'm ready to do whatever management asks of me." According to Maslow, basic needs must be satisfied before employees can turn their attention to someone else's needs. At the most fundamental level, for example, people need food and shelter. Imagine focusing on means to enhance shareholder value while wondering how you are going to feed your homeless family.

Once food and shelter have been taken care of, individuals can move to the next level, and the next, until finally they can ask, "Okay, now tell me; what can *I* do for *you*?"

Communication with employees functions on a similar hierarchy of its own.

The Pyramid of Communication Quality

The communication hierarchy was mapped by former FedEx internal communicator Ed Robertson, who dubbed it, "The Pyramid of Communication Quality." At the base of the pyramid—the first level—is logistics.

The Logistics Level

Logistics represent the only step on the pyramid over which you and your professional communicators have any control. They can ensure that the publication is distributed on time, that the intranet page displays correctly on the browser, that the video cassette sent to the sales office in Singapore is in the proper format, or that the translation for the workers at the plant in Puerto Rico includes the proper words to convey the benefits concepts.

These may seem like basic tactics, hardly worth the consideration of company leadership. However, if the publication doesn't arrive on time, the Web page isn't viewable, the tape won't play in an

Asian tape player, or the translation makes no sense, employees simply cannot ascend to the next level. Put another way, like anything in business, you must have the fundamentals down cold if you hope to achieve complex goals.

The Attention Level

Assuming that the logistics have been achieved, the next challenge is for communication to capture employees' attention. Like most employee communication, grabbing employee attention is contingent upon recognizing that different things appeal to different people. What is compelling to members of the management committee would bore a mine worker to tears. What makes an administrative assistant sit up and pay attention would cause a middle manager to roll his or her eyes. One size never fits all. (Hence, the failure of communication strategies that rely on a single vehicle.)

At Amalgamated Pulp & Paper

A quarterly managers meeting is the primary means of communicating business issues and initiatives. The company produces a monthly newsletter, but its focus is on employee features. One issue, for example, was released shortly after the company nearly went bankrupt. Its key division had its best year ever, but another division suffered such spectacular losses that the company was forced to divest everything *except* its core business. Thousands of employees lost their jobs, and only an investment bank's intervention saved the corporation from extinction (in exchange for which the bank obtained multiple seats on the board of directors). Employees of the core division—which had a phenomenally successful year—were disoriented, rudderless, and afraid. What was the lead story in the monthly newsletter? It was a feature about a secretary who would be performing with hundreds of other square dancers during the opening ceremonies of the Olympic Games.

The company's woes, and plans for revitalization, were outlined at the quarterly managers meeting. All employees with the title of manager or higher were expected to attend the session, which was held in the employee cafeteria. The chairperson spoke first, reading from a prepared script, eyes trained downward over the rims of his glasses, never looking at the individuals gathered before him, the people who were supposed to lead the charge when they got back to their offices. His remarks focused on the company's performance over the previous quarter.

Next up was the chief financial officer. "Please pick up the press release that was on your chair when you came in the room," he instructed. Then he *read* the quarterly earnings press release, highlighting key numbers in the financial section.

Finally, the president spoke about the challenges facing the company in the next quarter.

By the end of the meeting, barely a manager was awake. Those who managed to keep their eyes open were numb with boredom. Managers sleepwalked out of the cafeteria. It was hardly the type of communication that would capture their attention.

The employees whose attention you need to capture are the ones whose reactions will determine whether you will, in fact, get them to (as flight attendants say) put down their reading materials, cease their conversations, and give you their complete and undivided attention.

The rationale for grabbing attention is obvious: If they're not paying attention, they won't hear the underlying message.

Think about what captures *your* attention. Not just at work. Anywhere. In order for you to focus on something you didn't think you were interested in, it must be:

- *Compelling.* Did it make you turn your head? Did it grip you? Startle you? Make your jaw drop?
- *Understandable.* You won't pay much attention to a message that's vague, indecipherable, or hopelessly complex.
- *Credible.* Even if you understand it and it grabs you, your attention

will waver quickly if you know it's a lie. Credibility is a tough nut to crack for business leaders for a couple of reasons. First, credibility isn't automatic; it is earned. Employees need to *trust* you in order to believe you. Even more difficult to understand is this: What one employee finds credible another will find *in*credible. Consider a labor negotiation. Management representatives take it as a matter of faith that the issues supporting the company's position are factual. The managers of the airline companies, for example, know in their gut that the financial situation is every bit as dire as the company's leaders have said it is. Why can't those selfish, disloyal, treacherous union bosses understand that? Why can't they be team players and work with us to save this airline? The union, though, does not inherently believe management. They see things from a different perspective. "We've been lied to before, the bosses will twist the numbers so they say what they want them to say, they want us working stiffs to make concessions that will affect our families while they continue driving their Mercedes, flying the corporate jet, staying at the Ritz-Carlton, and sending their kids to Princeton." "Absurd!" cries management. It is difficult to see, from either perspective, that management is from Venus and labor is from Mars. You cannot communicate to the union the same way you communicate to management and hope to be credible with both audiences.

Getting attention, then, is not a cakewalk. Audience segmentation is critical. Management/labor is not the only differential. There is the headquarters/field, staff/profession, corporate/business unit, and many other distinctions that you must recognize to appeal to employees' attention.

If all this seems a little overstated, consider what is needed to gain *your* attention. According to Seth Godin, the man behind the idea of opt-in (or permission) marketing, the average North American consumer sees or hears approximately three thousand marketing messages each day. How many of those messages do *you* remember from yesterday? As we are assaulted by more and more messages, we establish stronger and stronger defense mechanisms that allow us to block them out, filter them, screen them, and hear only the ones that are—let's say it together—compelling, understandable, and credible. Add to those three thousand daily marketing messages the 130 or so messages office workers send and receive each day (according to a study conducted by the Institute for the Future for Pitney Bowes). The same study notes that the average office worker is interrupted eleven times per hour by messages that have nothing to do with the task he or she is performing at the time. (This issue is addressed in the discussion about managing message overload in Chapter 11.)

None of which is intended to discourage you from trying to get employees' attention. Gimmicks work well. One company, for example, kicked off a quarterly employee meeting with the chief operating officer and a business unit leader taking the stage as the Blues Brothers, belting out a blues song about a new corporate initiative. At Amalgamated Pulp & Paper, the CEO might have considered breathing some life into those dreadful quarterly managers meetings, for example, by presenting the quarterly numbers as a rap tune, backed up by the administrative assistants from the executive suite. Now that would have captured managers' attention! It wouldn't work at *every* meeting. In fact, Amalgamated would need to employ a different gimmick each quarter, but managers would be eager to attend the meeting to see what the CEO had up his sleeve *this* quarter.

The Relevance Level

Okay, so you presented the material to the audience on time, in the right language. It was legible. It was understandable. It was interesting and credible. So what?

FedEx's Ed Robertson calls this stage the relevance level. It might as well be known as the "So What?" level. What in the world, employees are bound to ask, does this have to do with me?

Just as the audience itself controls what it will pay attention to, you must understand employees to know what matters to them. In order to be relevant, communication must be:

- *Germane.* That is, it must relate to the environment in which the employee works. Imagine standing in front of a group of employees who spend all day on an assembly line, safety goggles securely in place, hard hats protecting them from chunks of metal that could fall from an overhead conveyor belt, and saying, "This company needs to meet Wall Street expectations for earnings in the next quarter. We're counting on you." Wall Street expectations? So what?
- *Helpful.* Everybody asks, "What's in it for me?" If the communication does not help employees achieve their objectives, why should they waste their time? There already are too few hours in the day and they've been asked to do more with less repeatedly over the last several years. Somehow, your communication needs to lead employees to think, "If I think/believe/do what this message asks me to, I can (fill in the blank)." What might be important to employees? A partial list includes:

  - It will help me do my job better or faster so that I can meet my targets and earn my bonus.
  - It will reduce hassle in my life.
  - It will earn me recognition.
  - It will help me move up the promotion track.

Advertisers understand the "So what?" concept implicitly. Back in the 1960s when it was common for women to stay at home as homemakers, household products were advertised based on what they could do for the full-time homemaker. Homemakers didn't buy a bottle of floor cleaner because it had the extrapowerful ingredient X or because a team of engineers labored for years to develop it. They bought the product because it *eliminated waxy yellow buildup* with *less work.* Silly as that may seem, it's clear what the benefit was to the consumer who bought that product. The product was:

- *Germane.* "I work in the kitchen, so a product that will help me keep the kitchen clean is germane to the work I do and the environment in which I do it."
- *Helpful.* "If I use *this* product, I'll expend less energy and get the floor clean in less time, leaving me ample time to work on those stubborn toilet bowl stains."

Of course, the homemaker would never arrive at this point if the logistics criteria were not met—for example, if the commercial's music was so loud she couldn't hear the narrator, or if it didn't grab her attention to begin with, or if it wasn't credible. "Oh, *that* company? I've bought into their crap before and been burned. I'm going to tune out anything they have to say."

As fundamental as these age-old advertising principles are, the same concepts apply to employees. What does shareholder value have to do with going down into the mine? Why should a roughneck in the oil patch or a dockworker or a janitor care about cash flow return on investment? You can give me a hundred arguments why they should, but until you make it relevant to them where they work, you will never succeed in getting the message across in a meaningful way.

At Allied Gate & Fence

Recognizing the need to make a shareholder value initiative relevant to employees, the employee communications and training departments worked together to devise a flexible training program that brought the notions of shareholder value to life for workers at different levels. Did it work?

Jim Cook worked in the facilities department. He walked around the company wearing a tool belt; he was the company's handyman, the fix-it guy. One day, the president called Jim to his office, which featured a large plate-glass window overlooking the campus. A bird had flown into the window at near-warp speed, leaving an unsightly crack. "I need this fixed," the president said.

"Right away," Jim replied. He left the office and was back in minutes, a can of caulk in hand. He dipped his finger into the caulk and smeared it into the crack, then wiped away the residue with a rag. "All fixed," he said.

The president, stunned momentarily into silence, finally shook his head and said, "Jim, I want a *new window.*"

"A new window?" Jim asked. "But how does *that* enhance shareholder value?" Jim understood what shareholder value meant to him in his environment with the kind of tasks he was required to perform. He was able to translate lofty concepts into actions he could take.

And the president couldn't argue. "You're right, Jim," he said. "It doesn't."

The Influence Level

The influence level is where most leaders think employees should start. "We pay them," the reasoning goes, "so they should be focused on what we want from them." As we've seen, though, you must ensure that any communication is logistically sound, captures the employees' attention, and is relevant to the employee. Only after those levels have been reached are employees willing to say, "Okay, what do you want from me?"

There are three degrees of influence for employees—or any other audience, for that matter:

What They Think

You can affect employee opinions about work-related issues.

Employees may be skeptical, for example, about the need for a change that has been introduced, but effective communication can lead them to believe the change is the right thing for the company.

Some might question the need to influence opinions. As long as they are doing what they are supposed to, who cares *what* they think? Opinions, however, drive performance. Employees might work without enthusiasm, performing only the work they must to stay employed. But when a better offer comes along from another company, they are out of there. In the meantime, they certainly are not innovating or excelling on behalf of a company whose values and actions are inconsistent with their own beliefs.

Companies are forever promoting their values, but without a concerted effort to convince employees of the fundamental rightness of those values, they are little more than words framed on walls—and can often become a source of derision.

Commitment

How much energy is an employee willing to commit to a company initiative, value, or activity?

At Allied Gate & Fence

Allied Gate & Fence Design Group is a subsidiary of a larger company. Because designers of gates and fences are an elite group, they have for years enjoyed a retirement package different from the employees in Allied Building Materials' other business units. Because of a variety of factors, management has made the decision that the gate and fence designers will be rolled into the company's larger retirement plan.

Gate and fence designers are routinely courted by competitors. The company fears that the change to the company-wide retirement plan may be the enticement some designers need to make the jump to a competitor. The company considers several ways to communicate with this elite group to encourage them to remain committed to continued employment with Allied. General communications are considered, in which every employee receives the same message. But finally, the company decides to produce comparison sheets for *each* employee. The comparison sheet shows how much their retirement accounts would have grown under the old plan over five, ten, and twenty years. Right alongside appears their retirement balance for the same periods under the company-wide plan. It is obvious when looking at the comparison that the company-wide plan is at least as good as the old plan and, in some cases, even better.

The comparison sheet is delivered in a four-page brochure that covers the highlights of the designers' new plan along with an explanation of the rationale for the change (which is direct and candid).

Ultimately, not one designer left the company. They remained committed to their work with Allied Gate & Fence.

Action

Will employees actually *do* what you want them to do? This is the kind of influence most leaders want to wield. It's nice that employees are on the same page with you, and it is even better if they're willing to commit themselves to a course of action. Ultimately, however, actual employee behaviors are what make or break a company.

Simply stated, getting employees to behave in a manner consistent with company goals is the driving force behind nearly all strategic internal communication efforts. Examples of desired behaviors include:

- Contributions to the 401(k) retirement savings plan are lagging among nonexecutive employees. The low level of investment is threatening to suspend matching-fund contributions to the executives' plans. The desired behavior: *Inspire employees to contribute to the 401(k) plan.*
- The cost of health care coverage for employees is cutting into earnings. Most employees have stuck with the old indemnity plan, even though the health maintenance organization (HMO) would cost the company—not to mention individual employees—much less. Because HMOs have a bad reputation, employees are reluctant to give up their current doctors for the unknowns associated with an approach to health care about which they have heard only bad things. The desired behavior: *Get a significant number of employees to switch from the indemnity plan to the HMO during the next enrollment period.*

- The regional Air Quality Management District has announced it will fine companies that don't reduce employee vehicle trips to and from the office. The desired behavior: *Get employees to carpool.*
- Too many products are shipping with defects. The company implements a quality program, the linchpin of which is a system that allows any employee to stop production when detecting a problem that will lead to flaws. For years, pressure has been put on employees to crank out as much product as possible and as quickly as possible; meeting shipping deadlines has meant bonuses and raises while missing deadlines has led to recriminations and even firings. The desired behavior: *Convince employees to live the principles of the quality program despite a culture that promotes shipping product over any other concern.*
- The discovery process accompanying a couple of lawsuits has led to public embarrassments for the company. These problems never would have cropped up if employees adhered to a document retention policy. Since the issue had never arisen before, the policy has descended into obscurity. The desired behavior: *Employees rigorously adhere to the document retention rules.*
- The competition is suddenly burning up the marketplace with a flood of innovative new products. Meanwhile, your product teams haven't rolled out a hit in more than a year. Realizing that an outmoded command-and-control structure is hindering innovation, you unveil a new organization chart designed to inspire greater collaboration and idea sharing. The culture, however, is one in which knowledge is power and employees are reticent about sharing what they know without getting something in return. The desired behavior: *Get employees innovating through the open exchange of ideas and information.*

What Leads to Commitment?

In the old days of the Industrial Revolution, companies bought employee loyalty through an unspoken promise: "Come in every day, work hard, do your best, and you'll retire with a pension and a gold watch."

The cold reality of the 1980s swept away the unspoken agreement; job security does not exist. No company can guarantee lifetime employment—even those that had made vows to never lay off employees had to back down on their promises. Without job security, employees will not blindly give a company their loyalty. Instead, companies must earn the commitment of employees (the operative word is *earn*). Commitment is the voice inside us that says, "Since the company is making an effort for me, I'll make an effort for the company as long as I'm employed here." Think of loyalty as an emotion, like love. Nobody decides to fall in love. But commitment is a rational decision, which is why we say that someone "made a commitment."

Unfortunately, many companies believe they earn commitment with a paycheck. Most research conducted on this subject does not list compensation among the top ten reasons employees are committed to their organizations.

What does it take to earn employee commitment? While different studies have approached the issue in different ways, we can lump all the results into the following three basic categories:

1. Trust
2. Involvement
3. Role knowledge

Trust

How would you define trust? Would you use either of the dictionary definitions of "firm reliance on the integrity, ability, or character of a person or thing?" or "reliance on something in the future?"[1]

How about the belief that your employer shows confidence and support in you? Or the belief that performing certain tasks in a certain way will earn you specific rewards in return? Or that you are free to express your opinions and feelings in a candid, two-way environment? Or that the company will be open with you, sharing important information whether it is good or bad?

According to one study, trust is made up of the following tenets:[2]

- A belief in the integrity, character, and abilities of others
- A feeling of confidence and support shown by an employer
- A commitment to perform as agreed
- A commitment to openness, including the disclosure of relevant information, feelings, and opinions

Recently, the Research Foundation of the International Association of Business Communicators (IABC) released its study, "Measuring Organizational Trust," which included a trust index, a list of elements required to achieve trust with employees. The factors are ranked; the closer to 1, the stronger the correlation between the factor and both desired outcomes—job satisfaction and operational effectiveness:

1. Concern for employees (exhibition of empathy, tolerance, and safety): .91
   - Example: "Top management listens to employees' concerns"
2. Openness and honesty (amount, accuracy, and sincerity of information shared): .88
   - Example: "I have a say in decisions that affect my job"
3. Identification (sharing common goals, values, and beliefs): .84
   - Example: "I feel connected to my organization"
4. Reliability (consistent and dependable actions): .80
   - Example: "My immediate supervisor follows through with what he/she says"
5. Competence (coworkers' and leaders' effectiveness): .75

• Example: "I am highly satisfied with the organization's overall efficiency"

The actual survey results from the IABC trust study are equally revealing. For example, the three statements that garnered the most responses were:

1. "My immediate supervisor is sincere in efforts to communicate with team members."
2. "My immediate supervisor keeps confidences."
3. "My immediate supervisor keeps commitments to team members."

The lowest responses were attributed to these three statements:

1. "I receive adequate information regarding how organizational decisions are made that affect my job."
2. I receive adequate information about how I am being evaluated."
3. "I receive adequate information regarding the long-term strategies of my organization."

In other words, the importance of the immediate supervisor as a communication channel cannot be overstated. Employees *trust* their supervisors, which is not the same as *liking* them. These results also suggest that companies do a lousy job of explaining how company strategy will affect employees' jobs and how they will be evaluated on the work they do in support of those strategies.

Studies repeatedly show the importance of building employee trust. The "Trust in Employee/Employer Relationships" study listed the benefits of a trust-based relationship according to study participants. These included:

• Increased productivity and growth
• Greater organizational credibility

- Increased repeat business and customer loyalty
- Better decision making
- A more productive relationship between employees and employer[3]

Trust is a key communication element because communication is one of the few ways for an organization to build trust with employees. Open communication, shared decision making, and broadly disseminated information all require a solid communication foundation. And here's a nice added benefit: More communication tends to equal greater trust.

Involvement

Gone are the days when an employee was content to show up in the morning, sit in his or her cubicle pushing a pencil for eight hours, take two coffee breaks and a lunch break, then go home. Along with the death of traditional loyalty went the complacency of employees satisfied to do what they were told with little or no sense of the bigger picture.

Today, employees want to know they make a difference, that they fit into the overall plan. They want to believe that their brainpower is appreciated by the organization, beyond the scope of the tasks outlined in a job description.

In other words, commitment comes from the *opposite* of the old axiom, "I don't want to get involved." Employees *desperately* want to be involved!

Involvement is critical to the development of trust. According to the Watson Wyatt "WorkUSA 2000" study, giving workers a greater voice in decision making is a key factor in the creation of trust. (This was the opinion of more than 90 percent of the employees responding to the survey.)

Companies have used many techniques to encourage employees to become more involved. Surveys, audits, and focus groups allow employees to share ideas and articulate what needs fixing, driving changes in the organization. Employee councils—both general and initiative-specific—are convened to give employees a more direct voice in planning. Intranets and other online tools have expanded the potential for involvement, with employees participating in knowledge-sharing forums and experiencing greater involvement in decision-making processes.

Role Knowledge

If the company does not provide you with the knowledge or resources you need to know how to do your job—and how your job fits into the organization—you are not likely to be committed to the goals and objectives the organization has set. The best part of work is feeling satisfied that you've accomplished something well that makes a genuine difference.

Job Satisfaction

In addition to trust, commitment happens when employees are satisfied with their jobs. The factors that influence job satisfaction are trust, the employees' immediate supervisor, and compensation. We have already addressed trust, so let's look at the other two factors:

1. *The immediate supervisor.* Nothing beats face-to-face communication between the immediate supervisor and an employee. This is the source of information about what the company expects of employees at the micro level—the work they do on a day-to-day basis. It is the supervisor who translates information coming from higher levels of the organization so that it makes sense on the job. A good supervisor (even if he or she is not a very nice person) can lead to satisfied employees. However, supervisors who do little to help employees understand their roles can create an environment of dissatisfaction.
2. *Compensation.* The compensation factor in job satisfaction has little

to do with the actual amount an employee earns, and everything to do with the perception that compensation is fair and consistent. Most employees can tell you how much salary they earn, but they couldn't tell you what their total compensation is, including the value of their benefits, vacation time, and other noncash compensation. They can learn any time they want to if that information is available online. Further, they can learn how compensation works at the company, why some jobs are worth more than others, and what their potential earnings would be under a variety of scenarios.

The Employee-Stakeholder-Profit Chain

None of this would be relevant to leaders if these factors did not result in bottom-line profitability. But consider Figure 2-1 on the next page, which shows the relationship between internal issues and external performance.

This model begins with the employee dimension, with key communication inputs leading employees to an understanding of the business and the environment in which it exists, trust in management of the organization, and knowledge of requirements for doing their jobs. These inputs result in commitment to the organization and its goals, along with job satisfaction.

Employees who are satisfied with their jobs and committed to organizational goals are likely to produce quality work, whether their job involves making a product or providing a service. Their comprehension of the marketplace in which the company functions also tends to make them brand ambassadors, that is, enthusiastic representatives to stakeholders of the various things the organization stands for.

Stakeholders (represented in the stakeholder dimension) interact with the organization at a variety of levels, most of which are influenced by product/service quality and knowledgeable, supportive employees. Customers are more likely to conduct repeat business

Figure 2-1. Relationship between internal issues and external performance.

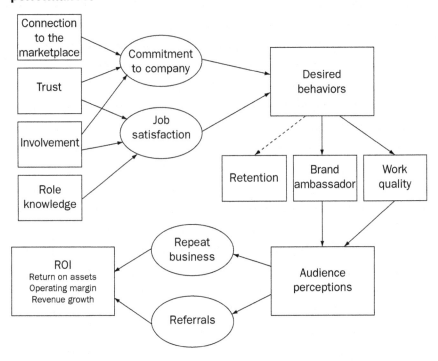

with the organization and refer business to others. Noncustomer stakeholders—such as shareholders, media, the financial community, or local communities—are also more inclined to lend their support or, at the very least, not create obstacles, such as boycotts, strikes, and other hindrances.

The intersection of internal communications and external performance occurs in two places in this model:

1. *Communication focusing on "trust" and "connection to the marketplace."*
   The nature of this communication can be reporting on news, activities, and success stories. It also can be explanatory in nature, such as feature articles in print publications that illustrate concepts, overview information in dedicated intranet sites, and training programs that cover core material (notably in connecting employees to the market-

place, where education about company finance, among other topics, could pave the way for other communications later).

2. *Communication that reports on the outcomes of customer referral, customer retention, employee retention, and stakeholder support.* Keep employees updated on the results that matter to them—which exceed those that matter to Wall Street—such as customer referrals. Customers make referrals when they are so pleased with their dealings with the organization that they believe they are doing their friends and colleagues a favor by referring them. Rising referral rates reflect satisfied customers, which can be attributed to dedicated employees. Little explanation is required for this kind of communication, which simply keeps employees updated on these performance measures. (Of course, a celebration over good numbers is not out of line—in fact, it's consistent with the idea of recognizing employees in order to reinforce desired behaviors.)

Proof of the link between role knowledge and profitability comes from a study that determined employees in high-performing organizations gain a better understanding of organizational goals and their role in achieving those goals. The study revealed that employees in 72 percent of high-performing organizations had a good understanding of the organization's overall goals, 51 percent understood how their work contributed to achieving the goals, and 55 percent understood the means used to evaluate their performance.[4] Those are significantly higher numbers than for other organizations that are not high performers.

In other words, if you concentrate on ensuring that employees are committed to the organization, the business will prosper.

Notes

1. *American Heritage Dictionary of the English Language,* Fourth Edition.
2. J. Mishra and M. A. Morrissey, "Trust in Employee/Employer Rela-

tionships: A Survey of West Michigan Managers," *Public Personnel Management,* 1990.

3. Ibid.

4. "IABC/Watson Wyatt Study," Watson Wyatt Worldwide, IABC and the IABC Research Foundation, 1999.

CHAPTER THREE

Types of Employee Communications

NOT ALL COMMUNICATIONS to employees are the same. The types of communications can be broken down into four categories:

1. Communications required by law
2. Human resources communications
3. Business communications
4. Informal communications

Although business leaders need to be cognizant of each type of communication, they focus primarily on the last two. Business and informal communications afford leaders their best opportunity to get employees on board with company strategies and objectives. However, the tone established by the leader influences *all* communications. It is important, therefore, for the leader to review each of these categories and understand the nature of the communications that occur within them, as well as the overlaps that occur between them.

Communications Required by Law

Some things must be communicated. The government requires it, and being out of compliance can lead to penalties. Most information that a company is required to communicate is related to human resources, and the human resources (HR) department should be on top of these. Some are simple bulletin-board postings; others require substantial efforts to comply with the law.

(Not every legally required communication falls under HR's jurisdiction. Some communication, for example, is required if the company deals in hazardous substances. These companies usually have a department called Environment, Health & Safety, or something similar. This department is obligated to comply with these laws.)

The most onerous legally required communication falls under a 1974 act of Congress called the Employee Retirement Income Security Act (ERISA). It is because of ERISA that an organization produces a series of documents called Summary Plan Descriptions (SPDs), which articulate the provisions of all defined benefit and defined contribution plans. The requirements for these documents—from the types of words used and how they are formatted to how to distribute them—are explicitly stated in the statute.

Another set of complex communications falls under the Comprehensive Omnibus Benefit Reconciliation Act (COBRA), along with other tax-related legislation. And there are other laws and regulations that dictate internal communication. A company is even required to communicate with employees if it is planning to close a plant.

In fact, there is hardly a law or regulation in existence that does not require some sort of disclosure or compliance on the part of an employer. Punishment for failing to comply is often a part of the law.

What laws an organization is required to obey depends on several factors, including its location (state laws vary), the number of employees, the type of organization (such as for-profit, nonprofit, not-for-profit, educational, or governmental), and the type of business. But once again, the company's HR department should be on top of this.

The fact that a company will comply with the laws and regulations is a given. The question is: *How* will it go about complying? The company can do the bare minimum the law requires, or it can apply its general communication philosophy to the effort. It's up to the leader to make clear to the HR department how these things should be done.

The laws and regulations that include communication provisions clearly articulate what needs to be communicated and how. That doesn't mean that you are limited to what the law says; it means that you cannot do any *less* than that. But why would you want to do more than the law spells out?

It isn't a question of how much work is involved, but the philosophical approach you take to communicating with your employees. You won't run afoul of the law if you restrict yourself to what the law requires, but you probably won't score points with your employees, either. In fact, if meeting requirements is more important to you than focusing on the *reason* you're communicating, you could wind up with disaffected and confused employees.

Let's look at the example of a summary plan description (SPD). To comply with the law, a company simply needs to publish a document that fulfills the law's requirements. No doubt, you have seen plenty of these documents. They comply just fine, but employees hardly ever use them. These documents are thrown out or tossed into drawers. Rather than try to use these documents—which certainly were not prepared with employees in mind—employees needing information about one of their benefits plans will pick up the phone and call their HR representative. A communication effort that actually kept employees and their needs in mind would preclude the need for employees to take up an HR representative's valuable time.

At Allied Gate & Fence

In order to comply with regulations, Allied distributes updated SPDs to its employees each year. The effort begins by recognizing that the goal is not only compliance but also helping employees to understand and appreciate their rights and obligations under the provisions of each plan. Ultimately, employees should be able to use their plans without mistakes or confusion.

As a result, the goal is *not* to produce a document but to develop a useful and usable tool employees can use. Because Allied's HR department has conducted research with employees, it knows employees' concerns and issues. This leads HR to recast the approach to the document. Keeping the specific language of the law in mind, HR sets out to communicate the following information about the plan:

- The nature of the plan
- The advantages of the plan for employees
- Do's and don'ts
- Penalties for violating the rules
- Costs

The communication that results from Allied's approach certainly complies with the law, but it takes a step further in recognizing the employee's perspective. Thus, rather than simply cranking out a document for the sake of compliance, the company has enhanced its relationship with employees and created greater understanding and appreciation of the benefits the company provides. The effort was the same; only the outcome was different.

Human Resources Communications

While legally required communications almost always fall under human resources, not every HR-based communication is legally required. In general, human resources' communications are any that focus on the employee as an individual rather than on the work the employee does in support of organizational goals.

These communications fall into several categories:

- Benefits
- Compensation

- Career
- Social

Many larger companies employ communications professionals who work full-time in the human resources department. They spend all their time producing communications about compensation and benefits. For most companies, a department dedicated to HR communications is an unreasonable luxury. They either outsource this type of communication (human resources consulting firms maintain communication practices to service the HR communication needs of their clients) or count on their employee communications departments to include HR communication in the scope of their work.

As with legally required communication, company leaders are rarely involved in HR communications. But, as with legally required communication, the overall tone set by company leadership will color the way HR communication is handled. Ultimately, you are responsible for the success or failure of an HR communication campaign, since the communication culture of your organization rests in your hands.

Why do organizations pay employees? Why do they provide medical, dental, vision, disability, and life insurance coverage? Why do they host holiday parties and company picnics? Why do they present employee of the year or president's award recognition? Any HR person worth his or her salt knows the answer: to attract and retain the best employees who will execute the company's strategy and to compete for those employees in a market where your competitors also pursue the best talent.

This rationale should inform the approach HR takes to communicating compensation and benefits issues.

Benefits Communication

Most leaders view benefits communication as a necessary evil, a costly and mundane chore companies are obliged to perform once a year. When approaching benefits communication with this mind-set, organizations lose a number of opportunities to:

- Reinforce the value of benefits, thereby enhancing an employee's understanding of his or her total compensation, which contributes to job satisfaction and commitment to the organization, as well as employee retention.
- Strengthen employees' connection to the marketplace. Simply telling employees that their share of medical benefit coverage is rising will create resentment and concern. Instead, your communications can educate employees about the state of health care costs, what health care benefits cost the company, how the benefit affects the company's competitiveness, how employees can become advocates for change (in support of lower health care costs), and other marketplace factors can only help employees understand the reasoning behind any changes (such as increases in the contribution employees must make). Remember, employees don't need to *like* something in order to understand it and accept it. Candid communication promotes greater trust.

Compensation

Most organizations limit their compensation-related communications to information about bonuses, notably nonmanagement profit-sharing plans. Talking about pay in general, though, seems to make most companies uncomfortable. It is a private matter; people are sensitive about it. Speaking candidly about pay could create resentment and feelings of unfair treatment.

Certainly, each individual's pay is a private matter. However, organizations should be up-front and open about their compensation philosophies. After all, while pay is not a contributor to employee commitment, a belief that compensation is managed fairly and equitably most definitely is a factor driving trust and job satisfaction.

Communicating a Compensation Philosophy

Say little or nothing about compensation and employees will view their pay as an entitlement (which, of course, it is) and nothing more. Explain the link between compensation and performance, and pay becomes a motivator for everything from improved quality to employee retention.

Communicating compensation issues begins with a statement that articulates your organization's beliefs about pay. For example:

> To maintain our competitiveness, we recruit and retain the best employees by offering competitive compensation programs that motivate and reward employees for supporting and advancing organizational goals and objectives.

There are several nuances to this seemingly simple statement:

What Was Said	The Message
To maintain our competitiveness . . .	We don't just pay the minimum to save a few bucks. We view pay as a means of competing and invest in it appropriately.
. . . we recruit and retain the best employees . . .	Compensation is designed to attract the very best. It is so good that once an employee works here, he or she will never want to work anywhere else.
. . . by offering competitive . . .	Go ahead, look elsewhere and see if you'll find a more lucrative employer.
. . . compensation programs . . .	There is more to compensation than just your base pay. We offer a number of programs that will boost the total value of your compensation in exchange for your efforts.
. . . that motivate and reward employees . . .	Compensation is a two-way process. Our programs are designed to get you focused on what is important to the company. You scratch our back, we'll scratch yours.
. . . for supporting and advancing organizational goals and objectives.	Compensation is linked directly to how your efforts affect the bottom line. If you help us win, you win.

A statement like this makes it clear that the company views compensation as a business driver and not a necessary evil. The company will not hesitate to reward employees, since the rewards are *quid pro quo* for employees who help increase the company's value. Further, employees know they can participate in programs to boost their income, whether it's a profit-sharing plan or a one-time reward for making a suggestion the company implements.

Next, employees need to understand the elements that make up their total compensation. There are usually three elements:

1. Base pay
2. Incentive pay
3. Benefits

Employees who fail to appreciate the components of compensation could leave the company for a competitor who offers more base pay, even if their *total* compensation will be less than they were earning with you! It's this goal of creating an awareness of total compensation that leads many organizations to crank out an annual benefits statement, a personalized summary of each employee's total compensation, including the value of any retirement or pension, stock options, bonuses, insurance plans, and any other forms of recompense. These days, with the advent of intranets, it is possible to offer a benefits statement on demand, so that employees can see the value of their compensation at any time, rather than waiting for an annual snapshot that must be printed and distributed.

Most organizations base their pay on salary studies that help to determine what competitors are paying their employees, pay structures by geography (salaries are higher in San Francisco and New York than they are in Omaha and Tucson), and by profession. (You can commission a study or you can obtain studies already prepared by several leading human resources consulting firms.) The goal is to establish "external equity"—a fancy way of saying you want to be competitive. The results of a salary study are factored into a salary structure to ensure so-called internal equity within the organization. The study and the results should never be kept secret from employees. Rather, communicate the study results to employees and update them on any adjustments you have made to the salary structure based on the results. Let employees know that you're working to ensure that they have the best pay package possible. You can use your normal reporting vehicles to communicate—such as the company newspaper or intranet news page—along with special communications—for example, a face-to-face update by the CEO or head of HR at an all-hands or managers meeting.

Be sure your communication focuses on both internal *and* external factors. For instance, many companies talk about the competitiveness of their salaries but fail to address the fact that more important positions are paid more than less important jobs. You should let employees know that many factors contribute to a final compensation figure, such as the following:

- The level of knowledge or skill required in the position
- The education level required
- The amount of responsibility shouldered by an individual in that position
- The amount of experience required
- The number of people supervised within the position

Most jobs are paid within a range that includes a minimum, a midpoint, and a maximum. Employees should understand their grade, where they fall in the grade, and the implications of achieving the maximum pay within the grade—that is, no more merit increases until the employee moves into a new higher pay grade. For many employees, commitment levels diminish when they find they cannot possibly earn any more money, no matter how much they contribute to the company. Educating employees up front about maximum pay—and what employees need to do to move up to a higher grade—can prevent employees from building resentment against a company they perceive to be stingy and unwilling to reward dedicated effort.

In addition to base pay, employees are eligible for merit increases, the means by which they move up within their grade. Here, too, employees should be well informed about the nuts and bolts of merit increases. For example, you should communicate that merit increases:

- Must be earned and are not automatic
- Reward employees' performance within the salary structure
- Are based on a number of factors, including external market conditions
- Are guided by a merit budget and a matrix that determines the potential range of an increase

Again, employees who received a 1.5 percent merit increase could feel a building resentment toward a company that fails to properly reward them for all their hard work. Understanding the factors that led to merit increase decisions—along with attendant knowledge about alternative ways to boost income (such as a suggestion program that pays a percentage of the money saved or earned as a result of a suggestion's adoption)—can offset such reactions. In fact, effective communication about the conditions that led to a small merit budget could also motivate employees to address the situation so next year's merit budget will be substantially higher.

Communicating Bonuses

Whether a company is offering stock options to high-level employees or a profit-sharing plan to the rank-and-file, it needs to communicate *proactively*. What is the point, after all, of telling employees there will be little or no profit sharing this year *after* the year is over? The idea is for employees to work in a manner that will achieve the levels of performance that cause the profit-sharing plan to kick in.

Any bonus is a reward for performance that enhances the company's bottom line. Based on the type of business you are in, the contributors to a profit-sharing or nonmanagement bonus plan can include items such as cash flow return on investment, inventories, sales, new patents, contracts signed, average tons per hour, or new products introduced. If employees have no clue about the company's performance in the areas that lead to a bonus, they cannot adjust their work to make improvements.

At Allied Gate & Fence

At the beginning of the year, the nonmanagement employees at Allied receive a booklet that explains "Partners for Success," the company's nonmanagement bonus plan. The booklet explains that two factors go into the bonus plan: company profit and individual performance.

"If the company's after-tax profit is less than 90 percent of the plan, no bonuses will be paid." The plan is explained in simple terms. Employees know what they must achieve to get a bonus. They also know that the closer to 100 percent of the plan they get, the more money will be added to the bonus fund.

The booklet also explains how each individual's bonus will be calculated, based on his or her performance evaluation rating. In fact, employees can use the intranet to calculate how much bonus they will receive based on their current job grade, current company performance, and their last evaluation. Then, they can manipulate the tool to figure out how much more their bonus will be if they can improve company performance and get a higher performance evaluation.

Each month, management at each company facility tacks posters to the employee bulletin boards showing how the company performed in the previous month in the areas that determine profitability. While these posters are printed at headquarters and distributed throughout the company, each facility manager supplements the posters with updates about local performance. For example, at the Alhambra ornamental fence–manufacturing facility, plant manager Brenda Franco uses a simple computer graphics program to show the defect rate. Employees know that defects cut into profits. If defects are still running high, employees turn their efforts to reducing defects in order to improve profitability and improve the odds of earning a bonus. Other communications (including departmental meetings) are used to reinforce these ideas at the local level.

The same principles apply to communicating bonus programs at higher levels of the organization.

Special Rewards

Most companies offer additional compensation programs, even if many of these programs are not viewed as part of the compensation effort. For example, Allied Gate & Fence pays a bonus to employees who refer a friend or relative to a job opening (assuming that the new hire stays with the company for at least six months). Depending on the level of the job filled, an employee can receive anywhere from $500 to $5,000. While this incentive is part of a recruiting effort, it is still compensation, a way employees can supplement their base pay. There is nothing wrong with communicating both aspects of the program and including it in the list of means by which employees can increase the total amount they take home.

Other kinds of special rewards that are common in business include:

- Bonuses for making suggestions that are implemented.
- Bonuses for inventions that receive patents.
- Reward associated with a one-time recognition, such as an annual president's award or a smaller-scale recognition program. (At Allied Gate & Fence, employees can be nominated to receive "Something Special," a recognition for performance above and beyond the normal day-to-day work routines. Payment is made in gift certificates good for dinners or merchandise valued between $50 and $200.)

- Retention bonuses, paid during a layoff or other difficult time to lock in the company's highest-performing employees.

Whatever programs you offer that put money in employees' pockets, be sure to lump them into the compensation category so employees are aware of every possible way they can add to their base pay and appreciate the breadth of the company's programs. Employees appreciate the company's total compensation efforts far more if they understand the scope of the program.

Employee Stock Ownership

Company stock represents one more category of compensation that companies offer. The idea behind stock ownership seems like a good one. Employees who *are* owners will *act* like owners.

Unfortunately, the reality is a far cry from the ideal. The vast majority of employees who acquire stock through a stock purchase program own so little that it doesn't register. An increase or decrease in the company's fortunes makes virtually no difference to their overall financial health; nor do they suffer if the company experiences a downturn.

(Of course, if employees' retirement nest eggs are wrapped up entirely in company stock—as was the case with Enron employees whose 401(k) matching contributions were paid in stock and who were encouraged to invest their own contributions in Enron shares—the situation is different. But in that case, employees' efforts to help the company meet its goals and objectives were academic, given the actions taken at the top, which were beyond the employees' control.)

There is nothing wrong with encouraging employees to invest in their own company. Your communications, however, should be realistic. Telling employees they "own" the company doesn't ensure that they will buy into such a fatuous argument. Front-line employees who own shares aren't likely to jump out of bed every morning

bursting with enthusiasm, itching to get into work so they can enhance shareholder value. In other words, this level of ownership is
simply not relevant to a front-line worker.

So, what *do* you tell employees about investing in company
stock? Tell them that their stock means they have a *stake* in the company's future (which is a different argument than claiming they are
"owners"). Make sure to address these things:

- The opportunity to invest in company stock is another way the
  company allows employees to share in the company's success. It
  gives employees a common stake in that success.
- What does success mean? Without information about the company's goals, employees may believe a stagnant share price is a
  sign of failure, while the company sought investment to expand
  the business (which could keep share prices flat during the
  expansion). Employees need to know the company's goals and
  how it gauges success.
- Employees need to know what they can do to influence the outcomes the company is seeking from the investments it has received. Achieving this degree of understanding means that
  messages need to be relevant at the level where individual employees do their work; generic pronouncements in the all-
  employee publication won't do the job.

Career Communications

Communications that help employees with their careers are closely
aligned with compensation communications. These messages and resources help employees succeed so that they can earn more pay and
be eligible for better compensation programs. (Who wouldn't want
the same kind of compensation executives get?)

The materials you provide to employees about their careers
should mirror the concepts and programs human resources has established. For example, some companies have career sites on their intra-

nets. These sites include career paths, which help employees to determine the skills and experience they need to move to the next level on a current path or to jump to a different path altogether. If certain skills are required, links take employees to training programs offered inside the company or classes offered by local universities or other institutions that qualify for repayment under the company's tuition reimbursement program.

Social Communications

At some level, most organizations recognize the social nature of work. If it is not integrated into work-related communications (as I suggest it should be), it is at least acknowledged through company picnics, holiday parties, and other non-work-related activities.

The more employees feel that they are part of an organization that cares about them as people, the more likely they are to feel satisfied with their jobs (a critical element of commitment, don't forget). Among social activities to communicate, you can include the following:

- Opportunities for employee involvement in company-sponsored community events, such as Toys for Tots or community housing projects.
- Employee services, such as discount tickets to movies, sports, and cultural events.
- Special games and contests. One company for which I worked had a Halloween costume contest; another sponsored an ugly-tie contest. It is all in good fun, costs next to nothing, and adds a dimension to what motivates employees to dedicate their efforts to achieving company goals and objectives.
- Birthday and service anniversary parties and lunches.
- Non-work-related educational opportunities, such as brown-bag lunches featuring speakers from outside the company, like local politicians or retirement-planning specialists.

Business Communications

Your human resources department should handle most of the legally required communication. It will also manage HR-specific communication. Your job as a company leader is to set the tone to ensure communications are not merely an expense that regrettably must be absorbed but are strategically aligned with business objectives and ultimately influence employees to support organizational goals.

The one category of communication where you have a *direct* role is in communicating to employees about the business. It is entirely up to you as a leader whether internal communications is a lowly staff function or a vital management function that affects everything from product quality and customer satisfaction to employee retention and your company's reputation.

Most of this book deals with communicating business to employees. In summary, however, business communication includes the following:

- Reporting business news to employees
- Connecting employees to the marketplace in which the company operates, including customers, consumers, marketplace trends, competitors, and the impact of the economy on the business
- Ensuring that employees are able to obtain the knowledge they need from other employees when they need it
- Ensuring that employees know the company's goals, its strategies for achieving those goals, and what it expects from employees
- Helping employees understand their role in the company's performance and how they benefit from helping the company succeed

Informal Communications

A great deal of unplanned, informal communication happens in an organization. This form of communication is not designed to achieve any particular objective. It is not intended to promote the company's plans, goals, or expectations. It simply happens—around coffee machines, in carpools, in hallways, or at lunch. It also represents one of the most common ways that information and knowledge move within an employee population. In most communication surveys conducted within companies, the preferred source of information might be an immediate supervisor, but the actual source is most often identified as the so-called grapevine. In many companies, employees even believe the grapevine to be more accurate than the formal communications that are handed down from on high.

Work is social. (We will revisit this concept in greater detail in Chapter 11.) Organizations are made up of people, and people talk with one another. You cannot stop it, nor should you try. But that doesn't mean that you cannot influence the conversations.

Grapevines fill a void. Information (like space) abhors a vacuum. In the absence of trusted communication from a reliable source, secondary and tertiary sources of information rush in to fill the hole. One way to suppress the grapevine is to ensure that employees have accurate information about the issues that concern them from sources they can trust.

At Allied Gate & Fence

The intranet at Allied Gate & Fence includes a page called The Rumor Mill. Here, employees are encouraged to post any rumors they may have heard about the company. Furthermore, employees are encouraged to respond to the rumor based on what they know.

Initially, management was uncomfortable with the idea that responses to rumors would come from unofficial sources. As it turned out, however, the employees who posted replies *were* official sources. That is, they worked in the departments that owned the accurate information; they knew what they were talking about. What's more, in the rare instances where an employee posted an inaccurate response, employees working in departments with correct information were quick to respond, noting that the reply was wrong and citing the authoritative response.

The result of maintaining this system: Rumors dry up incredibly fast at Allied Gate & Fence.

The Allied Gate & Fence model requires a leap of faith by management that employees will behave responsibly given access to an open forum like The Rumor Mill. A more common approach is for employees to submit rumors one-way through a submission vehicle (such as a form on an intranet, an e-mail to a Rumors e-mail box, or a paper form sent through company mail). The input is routed to the appropriate authoritative source for an answer, which is then posted in whatever vehicle ensures the broadest distribution. Time is the biggest drawback to this system—by the time a manager crafts a response and routes it through the various approvals, the inaccurate information at the heart of the rumor will have spread beyond control. Of course, it isn't difficult to establish a system that ensures answers within twenty-four hours, as long as those tasked with generating the answers understand that it is a requirement and not an ideal that can rarely be achieved.

Promoting Hallway Conversations

I once saw a manager approach two employees who were standing at the coffeemaker engaged in conversation. The manager, a stern look clouding his face, told them, "You need to stop gabbing and get back to work."

I took the manager aside and informed him, "They *were* working."

Machines do not pass on knowledge and information. It's a person-to-person activity. (Chapter 11 discusses how to use electronic networks like an intranet to enhance this informal communication process.) At Allergan Inc., a pharmaceutical company in

Irvine, California, the hallway walls of a new research and development facility were made of dry erase board. If two scientists met in the hall and began a conversation that led to an idea, they could begin sketching the chemical formulas or mathematical equations right there where inspiration struck. Casual hallway conversations aren't frowned upon at Allergan; they're encouraged!

Many companies have promoted informal conversation as a communication tool. Steve Jobs, Apple Computer's CEO, for example, used to have coffee and donuts set up in the hallways on a given day. His goal was to lure employees out of their offices so that they would talk to one another.

Semiformal Communications

Informal communication can also occur in semiformal settings. Departmental meetings are a good example. A manufacturing team meets every Monday mainly to discuss safety but also to address any other issues that may arise. In this setting, employees may ask their supervisors questions about company-wide initiatives and announcements or about rumors they have heard. Employees may also talk among themselves. Depending on the organization's communication environment, these sessions can leave employees feeling well connected to the organization and satisfied with the answers they get or they can wind up feeling disoriented, confused, snubbed, or unappreciated. Company leaders have the ability—and the responsibility—to establish a climate in which supervisors are equipped to answer employee questions with accurate information that localizes the issues.

CHAPTER FOUR

Communications Planning

IMAGINE SHOWING up at work, sitting down at your desk, and asking yourself, "What shall I do today?" You open the *Wall Street Journal,* read an interesting article about a new business practice, and say, "Well, first thing, we'll implement this new idea." Next, you recall an item you saw on *Moneyline* about an emerging market. "Do we have any products for that marketplace?" you wonder. "If not, I'll get R&D on it right away."

The scenario is absurd. It's a slipshod, unplanned, random approach to running a business. If you tried to manage your company in this manner, you would be collecting unemployment in six months. Among all that is wrong with this picture, the most glaring problem is that it doesn't adhere to any kind of a plan.

Creating a Strategic Communications Plan

As a business leader, one of your primary accountabilities is to develop a plan for your business. Circumstances change rapidly, so you and your team routinely update your plan. But still, you must have a game plan for where you are going and how you will get there.

Your communications with employees should be managed no differently:

- Your communication efforts should follow a strategic plan.
- Your communication plan should be aligned with the company's strategic plan.

Your organization's strategic plan—the one you or your company's leaders work on every day—is designed to achieve your company's mission through the strategic management of your employees, what they do when they come to work and how they use the company's various resources and assets. Senior managers are accountable for achieving the mission within the areas for which they are responsible. They, in turn, hold *their* managers accountable for their part of the equation.

(You have a mission statement, don't you? And if your mission statement reads, "Provide excellent service to our customers in order to generate a return on the investment made by our owners," scrap it and get a *new* mission statement.) A mission statement should articulate what your company does to generate return on investment. *All* for-profit companies want to produce great stuff to earn more money! What is unique about your organization? Wal-Mart's mission statement, for example, is: "To give ordinary folk the chance to buy the same things as rich people." The pharmaceutical company Allergan's mission is to focus "on specialty pharmaceutical products for specific disease areas that deliver value to customers, satisfy unmet medical needs, and improve patients' lives." A mission statement should make it easy for employees to determine whether the work they are doing supports the company's mission.

Communications need to support these efforts. If your editors beat around the bushes trying to sniff out stories to write because they don't have anything to put in the magazine, they aren't following a strategic communication plan. If your company doesn't *have* a strategic communication plan, the internal communication department's first task should be: Create one! Without it, you cannot hope to turn your workforce into an integral element of your company's overall strategic plan.

There are two distinct types of communication plans; you'll need your communicators to engage in both of the following:

1. A general plan
2. Special communication plans

The general plan is the roadmap for ongoing communication within the organization. Like the strategic plan that guides your business, the ongoing plan can have a fairly long life span, usually between one and three years (although communicators and leaders need to be ready to alter the plan as conditions and circumstances change). It covers the communication channels, media, and messages for your day-to-day activities, including regular face-to-face meetings, publications, online communications, and multimedia.

When issues or events occur that require a special, dedicated communication effort, you need to operate from a plan constructed specifically for that issue or event. Consider the issues and events in the following list; each requires a plan to ensure that communications meet goals and objectives unique to the situation but still support the company's overall mission:

- Plant closing
- Layoff
- Acquisition of a company
- Bankruptcy filing
- Entry into a new line of business or market segment
- Labor conflicts
- A crisis, such as an explosion or a death on-site
- Reaction to adverse regulation or legislation

The process for building a strategic plan is the same for your ongoing plan and your situation-specific plans. Consulting firms and communication associations offer a plethora of planning models. Several templates are available from various associations and consulting firms. Some have as few as four steps, some as many as ten. All are worthwhile, as long as they include each of the following elements.

Background

Every communication plan should begin with a review of the organization. It should ask questions such as: Who are we? How did we get to where we are? Where are we going? What is our vision for the organization? Our mission? What values do we expect employees to embody in their work for the company?

(You have a vision statement, don't you? A vision statement articulates an image of what the organization will look like if it achieves its mission. My favorite mission statement comes from Disneyland: "The happiest place on Earth." If everybody does what they are supposed to do, Disneyland will *be* the happiest place on Earth. President John F. Kennedy also promoted a brilliant vision: to send a man to the Moon and return him safely to Earth before the end of the 1960s. Employees who can close their eyes and *see* the vision have an easier time aligning their work with that vision.)

The background section should also outline the need for the plan. The need will depend on whether your plan is for ongoing or situation-specific communications. For ongoing communication, consider the needs that might arise from the following circumstances:

Situation	Need
Your reputation among several key audiences has been damaged by revelations of unacceptable accounting practices.	A communication plan must help employees understand the source of public mistrust and identify ways in which employee efforts can help rebuild the company's reputation.
Your merger two years ago failed to produce the expected results, and we were forced to close down several business units and lay off a significant number of employees.	Employees need to understand how the organization arrived at this point. The plan must help the organization move forward.

Situation-specific communications will address more urgent, time-sensitive needs, such as the following:

Situation	Need
You are closing a major manufacturing facility and sending the work offshore.	Retain employee commitment to the organization in the face of layoffs. The plan must explain the rationale for the decision, show what is being done for affected employees, and help employees understand what is in it for them to support the change.
You are acquiring a company.	Employees on both sides—current employees and those working for the target company—need to know whom they will be working for when the acquisition is complete. The plan needs to paint a picture of the new organization and help employees on both sides understand where they fit. The plan also must address any negative consequences of the acquisition, such as layoffs or mandatory transfers.

Situation Analysis

The second phase of your planning focuses on identifying the actual issues the plan must address. At the heart of this analysis is the separation of causes from symptoms.

At Amalgamated Pulp & Paper

The vice president of human resources has grown increasingly aware that morale among the company's workforce is dangerously low. In an effort to improve morale, he launches an intensive, three-month campaign called Beat Consolidated, aimed at helping Amalgamated regain the number one ranking it held in the marketplace before Consolidated Paper Mills assumed the top spot through the acquisition of a smaller competitor.

The campaign boasts banners, posters, and a wide variety of other collateral material, such as table-tent cards, mouse pads, and key chains. Employees attend rallies. Status reports are published illustrating the company's progress on a week-by-week basis. The intensity of the campaign has the desired effect: Employees become pumped up.

After three months, the campaign ends as scheduled. Without the constant barrage of the campaign, the excitement employees felt for ninety days begins to dwindle and morale sinks back to its previous state.

What was wrong with the approach the Amalgamated vice president took to boosting morale? He focused on the symptom. The fact is, employees were not suffering from low morale because they were number two. The vice president didn't have a clue why morale was bad; he simply thought that introducing some excitement into their lives would fix it. But the root causes of employee dissatisfaction had not been addressed. In Amalgamated's case, morale was low because of a series of takeaways—the company store was closed, a couple of prized benefits were dropped from the benefits package, and the company switched its vacation policy so employees could no longer carry their unused vacation days over to future years. Employees still had to deal with the takeaways well after the Beat Consolidated campaign ended.

A situation analysis, then, can identify the *causes* of the situations the communication plan is designed to deal with. This analysis will be a fairly brutal exercise in self-examination. What are the circumstances behind the issues you're trying to address?

Goal

Now that you have established the foundation for your communication plan, it's time to move into the elements of the plan itself. First and foremost among these are the goals. A situation-specific plan can have a single goal—for example, "Retain 95 percent of our top-performing employees during the upcoming layoff"—or more than one goal. Your ongoing plan will probably have several goals that are aligned with the elements of the company's business plan.

Goals can be defined as the big-picture results you are trying to accomplish. Retaining 95 percent of your top-performing employees during a layoff is a well-stated goal. Note that this goal includes no communication elements. Communication can be applied to help achieve the goal, but communication in and of itself isn't a goal. Not all the approaches taken to achieve the goal will be communication goals. For instance, in the case of our effort to retain employees, you could offer a retention bonus (a bribe, so to speak).

Some examples of goals for which communication plans can be developed include the following:

- Win the election.
- End the strike.
- Return to profitability within three quarters.
- Defeat proposed legislation that would adversely affect our business.
- Introduce a new product.

A goal is not specifically measurable, but you will know that it has been achieved if the effort has been successful. You *did* retain 95 percent of your top-performing employees; your candidate *won* the election; the strike is *over;* after three quarters, you *are* profitable.

The rest of your plan will flow from the goal(s).

Audience Analysis

Before we move on to the next major elements of a plan, we need to identify the audience for the messages we're going to create.

Audiences? you ask. The audience is employees!

It is, indeed, easier to segment external audiences than it is internal audiences. There are media, investors, the financial community, customers, consumers, vendors, and so on. Even within these audiences, you can begin to break down the groups into more concise segments. Take media, for example. There are local media and national media. There are daily newspapers, weekly newspapers, local and national television and radio, and the trade press. You can engage in the same exercise for any external audience.

You can segment internal audiences just as easily. Within the employee category, you can target messages to the following:

- Managers
- Supervisors
- Professionals (e.g., doctors, engineers, programmers)
- Headquarters staff
- Field personnel
- International staff
- Collective bargaining employees
- Salaried and hourly employees
- Front-line workers

As you can see, there is no shortage of ways to classify employees by their segment. With your goal in mind, you need to ask which segments are the targets of your message. Look at the goal we have been using as an example—the retention of 95 percent of the top-performing employees during a layoff. Where are your top-performing employees? Are they hourly production workers? Certainly you *have* top-performing employees on the production line—if you grade on a curve, they're easy to find! But they are also easy to replace (particularly in a slow economy), and training is not a major investment. No, the top performers you are concerned about are in other parts of the organization. They may be your top salespeople, your most important scientists, the marketing managers you rely on the most. In your desire to retain as many top-performing employees as possible, you might target some messages to the entire employee population, but you should focus the most intently on the professional and managerial ranks.

Once you have identified your audience, you need to assess them. What will they find relevant? What media are most appropriate? (For employees who go into the mines, the intranet probably is a lousy option, since they aren't likely to have access to it.) What messages will be most receptive? (Chapter 13, which addresses measurement, explores ways to obtain answers to these questions.)

Strategies

Strategies are general directions you take to meet the goal. One dictionary defines strategy as "an elaborate and systematic plan of action."[1] Good definition.

Every goal requires multiple strategies. By way of example, let's return again to our effort to retain top-performing employees. The company will most likely embark on several strategies designed to retain these vital employees. Some of these strategies will have little or no communication component, even though they are designed to send a message. For example, many companies pay retention bonuses to employees, essentially bribing them to stay with the company and put up with the negative environment. A retention bonus definitely sends a message: "You're so valuable we're willing to pay you extra to lock you in." But there is no role for a communicator to execute this strategy.

So, let's come up with a strategy that requires good communication:

Show high performers the value of staying with the company.

Your communication needs to reach the audience before any of them make a decision to quit. It needs to grab their attention, which has been distracted by the prospect of the layoff. It needs to be relevant, rather than simply noting, "Everything's going to be okay for everybody if we all just stay the course and see this through as a team." It needs to relate specifically to the high performers in their work environment and clearly state what's in it for them if they stay. If you can do that, they won't quit and you will have achieved the goal.

Objectives

Objectives are the measurable things you do to achieve a strategy. One dictionary offers this definition: "Something to be worked toward or striven for."[2] I admit that objectives and goals can be synonymous (and they are, according to some dictionaries). But for our purposes, the *strategy* is the general plan; the objectives are the steps you take to execute the plan.

We can have many objectives for the strategy of demonstrating the value of continued employment, such as the following examples:

- Present a compelling and appealing vision of the company that makes it a place of choice to work—you'll *regret* it if you leave and then see what the company became because you're no longer part of it. This is a big-picture objective.
- Show each identified high performer what his or her compensation will potentially look like in one, five, and ten years based on the projected success of the organization, accounting for the career paths of high performers, stock options, and other incentives. This is a ground-level objective, focused on the employee, making it even more relevant.

It is here, in the objectives phase of the planning process, that you will establish your messages. Messages are the most critical element of any communication. Without defining the message, your communications can stray off-topic, create confusion, or suggest multiple possible meanings. (One analysis of the 2000 U.S. presidential election suggests that George W. Bush had a strong message while Al Gore had *no* message. Consequently, the American public was able to define Bush while Gore remained an enigma.)

Start with an overall message statement, a concise articulation of the primary message your plan needs to share with all audiences. For example, you will need a message to support your broad communications to employees aimed at retaining your best workers. Then, create one- or two-sentence messages targeting each of the audience segments you have identified. These messages should affirm what it is you want each audience segment to understand.

Tactics

Now that you know the objectives you must achieve, you can determine the tasks that must be done. These are actions, things you actually *do*. You can employ several tactics to achieve your objectives, such as the following:

- An intranet site that articulates the vision
- A brochure that offers highlights of the vision
- A special intranet feature for only high-performing employees that allows them to model their income in the short-, mid-, and long-term and compare their potential at the company to what employees at the same level earn at competitors
- A worksheet that summarizes short-, mid-, and long-term compensation

Note that it is here, in the tactics part of the plan, where you determine the media you will use to get your message to your audience segments. This approach contradicts the idea of selecting media based on their price. Switching from a print publication to digital online delivery, for example, might save a few dollars, but it won't necessarily help achieve the objectives in support of strategies that lead to the realization of a goal. Sometimes print is more appropriate. Some of the attributes to consider when selecting media include speed, two-way characteristics (can you get feedback?), and the ability to convey a complex message.

You cannot ignore cost, of course, and budgeting falls under the tactical part of your plan. After all, you cannot calculate how much a communication will cost until you know how you are going to communicate.

Finally, you need a method for determining whether your effort succeeded, which leads to the last element of a plan.

Measurement and Evaluation

You cannot simply assume that your communication succeeded. You must perform an assessment that shows to what degree your efforts worked. If your measurement efforts show your communication failed, you know you have to go back to the drawing board and try a different approach. (Chapter 13 addresses measurement in detail.)

Notes

1. *American Heritage Dictionary of the English Language,* Fourth Edition.
2. Ibid.

CHAPTER FIVE

Traditional
Communication Tools

MOST PROFESSIONAL communicators enter the business because they are skilled at producing communication tools, such as words, publications, videos, or Web sites. This is the fun stuff, the production of communication *stuff*. Often, it is this focus on their craft that leads company leaders to believe communication is not strategic, and that it has little to do with the bottom line. Chester Burger, a venerated public relations professional, once noted that you rarely see the CEO eating lunch with the head of employee communications because the CEO simply has no interest in the effective use of white space or the pros and cons of serif versus sans serif fonts.

Yet, without the stuff, it's difficult to get a message across. In fact, it is impossible. So, despite the fact that the tactics come last in the communication–planning process, it is important to know what is available and how it can best serve your company's interests.

When you follow a strategic planning process, you find yourself selecting media (that is, tools) based on how well they will help you achieve your goal.

At Amalgamated Pulp & Paper

Tyler Cunningham is vice president of corporate communications. He is proud of the fact that he has eliminated print from his internal communication program. Asked about his rationale, he explains, "The company needs to cut costs, and I wanted the communications department to do our part. By eliminating print, we're saving a lot of money."

The problem is that only 40 percent of Allied's employees have access to e-mail or the company intranet. "Not a worry," Cunningham asserts. "We send a weekly e-mail to all supervisors explaining the key news and information they need to pass on to their employees."

Theoretically, this isn't a bad idea. Realistically, it fails to recognize that not all supervisors communicate equally. Some have good, natural communication skills; others struggle. Some are motivated to share information with their employees; others believe knowledge is power and hold it close. Information, therefore, is distributed unevenly throughout the organization—there are information haves and have-nots. Trust deteriorates as a result, and morale begins to sink.

Communication tools should never be selected based solely on how much they cost. The most important measure is how effective they are. The value of achieving a bottom-line business goal can far outweigh the expenses associated with a print publication, even if that publication is considerably more costly than publishing the same material to an intranet.

Knowing which tools to choose requires an understanding of each tool's strengths and weaknesses, what they do best, and where they fit in a strategic employee communication process.

Face-to-Face

Human beings are hard-wired to send and receive communications in a face-to-face setting. Most people are aware that much of the information gained in communication is derived from nonverbal cues. Posture and body language, tone of voice, facial expressions—these all communicate at least as much as the words themselves (and often more). Without the face-to-face component of communication, information recipients are left to interpret an incomplete message, one without facial expressions or tone of voice.

It has been suggested that any communication that is *not* face-to-face is a corruption of face-to-face communication. That is, it is inherently defective because it lacks the characteristics that allow people to interpret those nonverbal features of the message.

Face-to-face communication, despite its essential characteristics, has fallen into disuse because of the proliferation of online communication tools. It is easier to send everybody an e-mail message than to convene a group meeting. It is less confrontational to chastise a colleague from the isolation of a keyboard than it is to articulate a problem with him or her face-to-face. Professional communicators have not struggled to maintain a balance of face-to-face communication, partly because they're enamored with the new technologies and partly because they have never felt comfortable with face-to-face as a formal tool. After all, a communicator can control exactly what a page in a magazine or on a Web site says and looks like, but once an executive begins to speak, the communicator has lost that control and is left to cross his or her fingers and hope the executive says the right thing in the right way. (I knew a company president who, at a meeting of business leaders, suggested from the lectern that anybody convicted of any drug offense should be executed. How do you plan to deal with a loose cannon like that?) And not everybody is a skilled face-to-face communicator, including many of those who have ascended to the top of the corporate ladder. Consistency is dicey, too. Not only is it impossible to ensure that two people will deliver a face-to-face message in exactly the same way, it is difficult to ensure that *one* person will deliver a message the same way *twice*.

The diminishing use of face-to-face as a strategic communication tool is a dangerous trend. Leaders intent on developing strong organizations that perform beyond expectations need to understand that face-to-face at every level of the company must serve as a key communication tool. That person-to-person connection and opportunity for real-time interaction cannot be replaced by any other tool or combination of tools. Trust is the primary outcome of face-to-face communication; employees who can associate a message with a person—a *leader*—trust the message because they trust the person who delivered it.

Face-to-face communication already occurs in your organization. In most cases, though, it is not planned communication. Every time a manager dresses down a worker while colleagues stand by nervously and watch, that manager is sending a face-to-face message. But, is it the kind of message you want sent? It's certainly not strategic—it doesn't help employees get to the point at which they are ready and willing to support the organization's goals with their well-focused efforts.

Whether face-to-face communication is effective in your organization depends on several factors. For example, does an environment of trust already exist? If employees have learned to be skeptical of all messages, they will look askance at face-to-face messages, especially those delivered by the company's leaders. Do employees already feel involved in the company's communication processes? If so, they will be receptive to face-to-face engagements; if not, nobody likes to be lectured to. Effective communication is multidirectional. Are meetings a regular part of your culture? If everything is communicated in print and e-mails, face-to-face encounters can feel alien and uncomfortable.

You don't need to put up with a culture that discourages face-to-face. As a company leader, nobody is in a better position to drive cultural changes than you are. At FedEx, supervisors are held accountable for face-to-face communication. They must spend a certain amount of time in formal face-to-face meetings with their direct reports a specified number of times each month. Failure to do so results in a hit to the supervisor's performance evaluation. Remember, culture is best changed when reward and recognition are at stake.

Nobody is born knowing how to handle a face-to-face encounter designed to influence employees. Consider why employees are promoted to supervisory positions. It's not because they displayed masterful supervisory skills. Most often, it's a career track, a reward for a job well done. Thus, a good worker suddenly put in the position of managing employees needs help—he needs to acquire the skills to allow him to communicate face-to-face with his employees. Similarly, senior managers have rare opportunities to make an impression with a variety of audiences—not only on employees but also on investment analysts, key customers, and a variety of other constituents. Standing in front of an audience making key points in a meaningful way while advancing PowerPoint slides is another skill executives are not born with. When face-to-face communication has such a significant impact on business performance, it should not be left to chance.

The role of face-to-face communication varies depending on who is doing the communicating. The three layers of face-to-face communication are handled by the following personnel:

- Senior management
- Middle management
- Front-line supervisors

Senior Management

The organization's leaders are responsible for painting the big picture. These are the people with the view from 30,000 feet, who comprehend how all the pieces of the company fit together, and how those pieces can be put into play to address marketplace conditions. They decide how the organization must change in order to address marketplace changes. Therefore, employees—who need to know that leaders are leading—expect to hear from senior management about that big picture.

Leaders should cover the following topics:

- What are the conditions driving decisions?
- Where is the company going?

- How is the company going to get there?
- What will the company look like if it is successful?
- What's in it for employees if the company succeeds (which assumes that the company will rely on employees to get it there)?

These messages can be delivered in a variety of settings—and they should be. Leaders should take advantage of every opportunity to spread the gospel, ensuring the same messages are delivered within the context of the audience. Venues for leaders include the following:

- *Large group meetings.* An annual employee meeting for all employees—or, at least, all those who are able to attend—affords company leaders the opportunity to look and act like leaders. Consider the State of the Union, in which the president of the United States addresses both houses of Congress and the Supreme Court, as well as the nation. Rarely does the president come off looking more presidential. At large group meetings, you can offer a summary of all your key messages—where we are, how we got here, where we're going, how we're going to get there, what roles employees are expected to play, and what rewards await them for fulfilling those roles. Here is the chance to utter phrases that can be repeated in subsequent communications, to launch important initiatives, and to issue calls to action.
- *Town hall meetings.* Town hall meetings are similar to large group meetings, but with a few distinct differences. First, they tend to be less formal. Attendance is generally voluntary; employees who *want* to hear from the leaders attend; those with no interest in the topic or who are too busy with other priorities are excused if they stay away. Town hall meetings often have themes—discussion of quarterly sales results, focus on a challenge the company faces, the introduction of a new leader, or an explanation of a strategic imperative. Finally, town hall meetings are more focused on questions from the audience than on missives from leaders. The president, CEO, or business unit leader issues a few opening remarks, then opens the session to questions.

Usually smaller than those attending an all-hands meeting, the audience comes ready to ask questions and is anxious to get answers from the people at the top.

- *Managers meetings.* Many companies hold monthly or quarterly manager's meetings, an excellent forum for helping managers understand the messages they need to deliver to their reports. A mix of a large group meeting and a town hall meeting, managers meetings are characterized by an overview of company performance during the recently ended period and a look ahead. The focus is on meeting the managers' need for information to help them communicate downward. Leaders should concentrate on how the company's various operations are expected to perform during the upcoming quarter and how those actions fit into the bigger picture. Give much of the program over to questions from managers; they need all the clarification they can get if they are going to cascade accurate and consistent information down to their employees.

- *When visiting an off-site facility.* Employees at headquarters are far more accustomed to seeing senior management than those working in off-site locations, including remote offices, manufacturing plants, retail outlets, and distribution centers. Still, company leaders often visit these locations, usually for meetings with the company's local senior representatives. Leaders should never pass up an opportunity, when making off-site visits, to meet with the facility's employee population (or, at least, as many of the local employees who might be available for a meeting). In these settings, it is important for senior leaders to adapt their messages to the local environment. You should have a solid understanding of what the people who work at the facility do, how they contribute to the company's bottom line, and how they can play an even more significant role in the future. Know the statistics pertinent to the facility—production output, sales figures, contracts signed, or other key performance indicators. Your job in these meetings is to rally the local troops to the company's larger vision in a way that is meaningful to them.

- *When wandering around.* Hewlett Packard popularized the idea of "management by wandering around," which turned into an acronym, MBWA. I remember during a focus group asking employees of a manufacturing company about their most meaningful encounter with the organization's management. "It was when our division president was on my floor," said one employee. "He poked his head into my cube and said, 'Hi, Nancy. How are things going?' I didn't even know he knew who I was!" This kind of face-to-face communication serves as a form of recognition in addition to an opportunity to make top-level messages meaningful to employees in the most direct manner possible. It is more than idle chitchat. Take advantage of the intimate nature of one-on-ones to convey key messages and ask whether employees have any questions you can answer. I escorted one executive on his first MBWA trip; he was terrified. The former advertising executive who had risen to the number two spot in the company would be visiting a group of craftsmen and he was afraid they would eat him alive. Imagine his surprise to find the workers were thrilled to have such a senior-level executive taking the time to visit *them*. They queried him about company plans and listened intently to his answers. He was so delighted with the visit that he couldn't wait to schedule another one.

- *Recognition events.* A company where I worked had a president's award program. Like all recognition programs, the purpose was to shine the light on employees and teams who reflected the kinds of behaviors management wanted all employees to emulate. The winners were ushered one-by-one into the president's office where they were presented with a check, shook the president's hand, exchanged a few words, and were ushered out. My question upon witnessing this mode of presentation: "Why would anybody want to win?" That's the idea of such recognition, isn't it? Employees should be so exposed to the benefits of winning that they turn green with envy and say to themselves, "Next year, *I* want to win that award. What do I have to do to guarantee I'll be one of the winners?" The following year, the awards were presented at an all-hands meeting at which the president made introductory remarks about the company's goals and its key values, and that these outstanding employees exemplified the kind of effort required for the company to reach its destination. The winners were also immortalized in a high-quality brochure, and they and their spouses attended a ritzy dinner with senior management and *their* spouses—a dinner that was covered in the company publication. All these activities were designed to reinforce the desirability of winning so that employees would focus on the kinds of efforts that would make them eligible for consideration the next time the competition rolled around.

- *Breakfast (or lunch) sessions.* "Breakfast with Bill" or "Lunch with Larry" are common activities throughout the business world. In these informal gatherings, a small group of employees are selected to dine with the top dog. The president or CEO may open with a few selected comments, reinforcing key messages or reporting on progress. The bulk of the session, though, is Q&A—with a twist: The employees aren't the only ones asking the questions! You can take advantage of these sessions to find out how well employees are assimilating your messages and how well they understand the company's core strategies. Of course, most of the questions should come from employees, who should even be invited well before the meeting to solicit questions from their coworkers.

Middle Managers

The role of the middle manager—a role that is diminishing as technology enables greater networking of employees—has been to serve as a conduit of information. Leaders deliver information to middle managers who are expected to communicate it to their troops and, ideally, the troops provide intelligence to middle managers that they should communicate back up to management. In many organizations, though, information freezes in the middle. In some cases, middle managers believe that information and knowledge represent their power base; they become stingy with it because relinquishing the information they have diminishes their power. In other cases, middle managers simply don't have the skills necessary to fulfill the role of information channel. The reason, though, doesn't matter much if the end result is the same: inadequate communication.

When executed well, on the other hand, communication from middle managers plays a vital role in the process of cascading information from the highest levels of the organization to the lowest. It is the middle manager who explains to front-line supervisors (and often directly to employees) what the messages from leaders mean to the business unit, the plant, or the operation for which he or she is responsible

The company's senior business leaders should never assume that middle managers know everything *they* know. Leaders must provide middle managers with details, resources, and tools to help them communicate with *their* direct reports. (It is for these kinds of tools and resources that senior management can turn to its communications department, which is addressed in more detail in Chapter 12.)

Providing the resources isn't always enough; sometimes middle managers also require a push. Hold middle managers accountable for communicating face-to-face with their direct reports. Insist that they add the business unit/division/plant context to the broader messages dispensed by the company's top leaders.

Forums for middle managers to address their employees face-to-face include the following:

- *Staff meetings.* Nothing is worse than a staff meeting without an agenda. Managers everywhere hold staff meetings every week (or every month) because they think they should, even if they have nothing important to say. However, a regular staff meeting is meaningful if it is used to convey the business unit's progress toward contributing to the company's success and what the unit can do to improve its efforts.
- *Wandering around.* Middle managers should practice the principles of Management by Wandering Around as much as executives. The same guidelines apply, too: Feel out employees to see how well they understand their role in executing the company's business plan, then deliver the key messages that explain or reinforce their commitment to the plan's achievement.

- *One-on-one.* Middle managers have many opportunities for one-on-
  one sessions, ranging from meetings to get updates from their direct
  reports to performance evaluations. Managers can use these sessions to
  make sure their reports understand their part in making core business
  messages meaningful in the workplace and to answer any questions
  their reports may have about the meaning or substance of the messages.
- *Team meetings.* Middle managers often lead cross-functional teams that
  are assembled to address a short-term issue. These meetings are yet
  another venue for managers to explain how the team's efforts link
  with the company's strategies as articulated by senior management.

Front-Line Supervisors

The farther down the line a message is communicated, the greater
the responsibility the individual doing the communicating has for
adding context to the message that started at the top. It is at the front
line that employees turn to their supervisors and ask the most significant question in the communication process: "So what?" In
other words, "What does this have to do with me? How does it affect the work I do and how I do it? Why should I care? What's in it
for me and my coworkers in this department if we take the trouble
and make the effort to embrace the message?"

The fact that supervisors represent the front lines of communication means that they should also be the focus of significant communication efforts. They need the resources, information, tools, and
training to ensure that they're able to translate messages, answer
questions, and build employee trust and commitment.

At Allied Gate & Fence

After adequate consideration, Allied's leaders have decided on
a drastic overhaul of the company's merit increase program.
The project leaders are highly paid—so highly paid, in fact, that
their compensation is driving the price of contract bids so high that

Allied cannot win against lower-bidding competitors. Fence designers, however, are paid so low that competitors and other businesses are routinely luring the best designers away. To address both problems, merit increases for project leaders will be suspended, while those for designers will be accelerated.

Communicating this change will be dicey. For project leaders, merit increases have been routine for so long that they perceive them to be entitlements. They will be miffed not only at the lost income but at the fact that their subordinates will get monster salary bumps.

The goal of the communication effort to introduce the change is simple: Let designers know their salaries will rise up to the level of their peers in other companies so they won't defect while avoiding a sense of disaffection among the project leaders. Among the various communication tools developed to introduce the change is a simple laminated card, small enough to fit into a shirt pocket. On one side of the card, a list of the reasons for the change has been printed. On the other side appears a list of the key elements of the change. These cards are distributed to the supervisors to whom project leaders and designers report. Upon announcement of the change, employees approach their supervisors to ask what's going on. Even though they have been briefed, supervisors are able to refer to the card to avoid missing any important points.

Face-to-face opportunities for supervisors include the following:

- *Daily briefings.* Particularly in a manufacturing environment, shifts often begin with a briefing to cover the daily production goals, safety issues, and other important topics. Supervisors can also use these briefings to relate their unit's progress toward meeting plant goals, and then tie those goals to the company's strategy, reinforcing front-line employees' importance in the larger scheme of things.
- *Staff meetings and performance evaluations.* The same opportunity that middle managers have (see previous discussion).
- *Wandering around.* While this may seem to be similar to the MBWA

activities of middle and senior management, it is in fact more important because it happens more often. Front-line supervisors don't need to find the time or a reason to walk among their employees; they do it as a routine part of their job. Thus, supervisors need to be ready at any time to answer employee questions; they also must be prepared to take advantage of any occasion to chat up an employee about how his or her job affects the department's performance and how, in turn, the department's accomplishments drive plant or business unit achievements and, ultimately, the success of the entire organization.

Guidelines for Face-to-Face Communication

In all of these settings, leaders routinely fall into traps that they should strive to avoid. In addition, there are guidelines for leaders to embrace in their face-to-face communications.

Executives routinely toss jargon around in the boardroom, but that same jargon can befuddle front-line employees. You should never talk down to employees, but simplicity is still an admirable goal. Using simple language with employees can help make your position clear.

Another trap is to focus on numbers. Numbers can be powerful, but only if they are meaningful. Peppering your talk with numerous figures from the 10K can obfuscate your message and heighten distrust.

Leaders should talk to employees, not read to them. Employees *want* leaders who lead. A leader who looks down and reads from a prepared text (probably not one that he or she even wrote) does not inspire that kind of allegiance.

You should practice your talk before you deliver it, whether it is before a large audience or with a single employee. Salespeople practice their sixty-second elevator pitch. Similarly, you should know exactly what message you are delivering and how to deliver it before you go out on your MBWA rounds or stand up at the town hall meeting.

When engaged in Q&A, don't answer questions to which you don't know the answer. Many leaders believe they will look weak and uninformed if they say, "I don't know." Nobody, not even the most cynical employee, expects you to know *everything*. If you don't know the answer, say so. But promise to find out, and get the employee's name and contact information so you can keep that promise.

Use other media to spread your messages beyond the face-to-face audience. Your "Breakfast with Barry" sessions, for example, can be transcribed into simple Q&A and posted on bulletin boards, published in a newsletter, or distributed to supervisors to share with their direct reports.

Print

Some pundits go so far as to suggest that any communication with employees *must* be face-to-face; anything less is a waste of time, money, and energy. Print, they say, has no power. The notion is, of course, absurd. Consider the power of "Common Sense," the pamphlet written by Thomas Paine that served as a rallying cry to American independence, or the Declaration of Independence itself. Print can be very effective indeed. In fact, the research study by Watson Wyatt Worldwide, IABC, and the IABC Research Foundation found that ongoing print publications for all employees are the most effective media for in-depth and complex communication, according to 70 percent of the 913 organizations participating in the study.[1]

Contrary to popular belief, print is not dead. It has been more than ten years since we have heard the predictions that we were well on our way to a paperless office. (Those predictions implied that the paperless office was only a decade away.) In fact, we use more paper in our offices now than we ever have, up by some 30 percent over a decade ago. Why? Because we all print out e-mail messages and Web pages, and other computer-generated documents.

And why do we print these rather than simply reading them on the screen? A review of the reasons helps support the notion that print has an important place in the communications toolkit.

Portability

Print is portable. I still do not see people taking their computers to the beach. (When you get drowsy and toss your paperback into the sand, you are not taking a major risk. Would you be willing to do the same with your $500 e-book?) Print goes anywhere, and it doesn't take up much room.

Not every communication needs to be portable, but consider the following reasons you would want people to be able to transport communications:

- It is important that they be able to share the communication with family or domestic partners.
- You have employees who spend little time in the office and will be more likely to absorb communications if they can take them along on their travels.
- The material is lengthy and employees would be more inclined to read it when they have sufficient time.

There are more reasons, but you get the idea.

Readability

Ask most people what they like about print and they will tell you that they can actually *read* it. The readability of paper is, in fact, the reason we print out all those e-mail messages and Web pages.

You probably already intuitively know that computer screens are hard to read. The headaches or eyestrain that you have experienced after spending long stretches in front of the monitor is all the proof you need. It is useful, however, to know *why* computer screens discourage reading:

- *Reduced blinking.* When you look at a computer screen, you see glowing light. Our eyes, on the other hand, are conditioned to see *reflected* light. If you spend too much time looking at glowing light, your blink rate drops to as much as one-fifth of normal. Reduced blinking means your eyes do not receive adequate lubrication, resulting in itching and burning, along with that headache you seem to feel coming on immediately behind your eyes. The flicker rate of the screen only exacerbates the situation.

- *Scrolling.* Scrolling through text (whether in an e-mail client, a Web browser, or a word processor document) causes the following two problems:

  1. *Moving lines*—Think about a television set when the vertical hold goes bad. Those bars scroll from bottom of the screen to top (or vice versa). Do you stare fixedly at the middle of the screen as the bars roll by? Certainly not. Your eyes latch onto one bar and follow it to the top, then drop to the bottom of the screen and follow it back to the top. This is an example of the human inclination to follow a moving line. Physiologically, we are similarly inclined to view a page of text that way—following a line of text while advancing page-by-page. This conflicts with the intellectual part of us that wants to pay attention to the meaning of the words on the page.

  2. *Scrolling induces nausea*—It is the same phenomenon as motion sickness—too much information transferred from the eye through the optic nerve to the brain. The brain sends a signal to the body asking, "Please, knock it off." It is not as pronounced a case of motion sickness as you might experience in the backseat of a car on a mountain road, but it is still unpleasant—and you don't want your readers to feel like they're going to vomit while reading about your company's strategy.

- *Text size.* We have a built-in mechanism for dealing with text that is too large or too small: We move it either closer to or farther away from our eyes. I have yet to see somebody lift a monitor and move it back and forth to adjust the size of the text. Instead, because of the fixed distance between our chairs and the location of the monitor on our desks, we must adjust our eyes to the screen.

As a result, the computer screen tends to be a good vehicle for delivering short, timely information, but it is a lousy tool for delivering long material—unless your intent is for employees to print it out. Print is inherently more readable.

Permanence

Owners of Web pages can easily remove pages from the server where they were stored. Anybody who tried to retrieve one of those pages would find it missing and (with certain technical exceptions) not be able to find it again. Print, on the other hand, may yellow a bit, but it stays the way it was when you got it. Stick it in a manila file folder, stuff it into a file cabinet, and it will be there when you need it in ten years.

Authority

Anybody can create a Web page, but it takes considerably more thought, work, and resources to produce a good print document. Holding something in your hands creates a tactile sensation that is missing from the computer screen. Knowing that it was produced by powers with the ability to print lends documents an additional tier of credibility.

You Can Write on It

Another reason so many people print documents from a computer is the desire to annotate the text with notes, underlines, and other scribbles. Try *that* on your monitor.

Accessibility

Finally, one of the most critical aspects of print is the fact that anybody who can read can access it. You don't need to worry about whether they have computers, access to the intranet, or e-mail addresses.

Based on these characteristics, it becomes easy to see print's strengths. Its weaknesses, though, could lead you to select other media to meet your needs. For example, print is:

- *Passive.* You cannot interact with print beyond turning pages. Some communications require interaction, which can be managed face-to-face (with normal, conversational give-and-take, question-and-answer periods, group breakout sessions, etc.) and online communication (through the use of message boards, chat rooms, e-mail lists, etc.).
- *Linear.* Readers have no choice but to follow a print document along its linear path, from a beginning to the middle to the end. Of course, readers can start where they like, but only within the context of the document's linear structure. Some communication works better when employees can chart their own paths through it.
- *A single medium.* Print is limited to text and still pictures. Often, sound and moving images make information more clear and more compelling.
- *Pushed.* Print is *pushed* at employees; it lands on their desks whether they want it or not. And it is merely human nature to pick up a print tool and flip through it. Think back to yesterday when you arrived home and found a catalog in your mailbox. It may have been from a company you have never heard of selling products in which you have no interest, but you still flipped through it. It took only a few seconds. However, it can be a challenge to find just the right information in the right print document when you need to *pull* it.

A variety of print tools are available as communication vehicles. Each serves specific purposes and should be selected based on how well it fulfills the objectives it is designed to meet. This next section explores the various print options available to you.

The Employee Magazine

For years, the employee magazine has been a hodge-podge, a smorgasbord of content about everything and anything under the sun. In the organizations that use the magazine in this manner, it is probably the flagship internal communication vehicle. But an employee magazine works only in the context of its strengths and the objectives that it is created to achieve.

The nature of a magazine—its dimensions (mimicking that of magazines found on newsstands and bookstores); its better paper stock; its elegant design; and, in most cases, its broad all-employee distribution—points to higher quality as a key characteristic. Meanwhile, a magazine has, in these days of digital communication, become an inadequate means of communicating news. Given the ability of the intranet (including e-mail) to communicate news almost as soon as it breaks, why would anybody consider delaying the distribution of news for weeks while a magazine is in production? The monthly "news magazine" has become an oxymoron.

When you consider print's strengths, though, the uses of a magazine to achieve communication objectives become more obvious. Let's explore how a company magazine can align with strategies designed to meet business needs.

Your intranet can contain all the data employees can stand (and then some)—and it should. But no employee is going to read all that material. It takes as long to read a page of text today as it did one hundred or five hundred years ago. The discomfort produced by the glowing, glaring computer monitor doesn't help matters.

Print, remember, is easy on the eyes. If people are going to read anything that is lengthy, it is going to be in print. Simply stated, then, a company magazine is the place for feature-length content, anything that offers detail, depth, analysis, or context. Some of the content to consider for the employee magazine includes:

• *Connection to the marketplace.* Your magazine can include features about competitive activities, detailed explanations about the current state of the economy and its impact on the business, and in-depth profiles of customers.

- *Company strategy.* Employees turn to supervisors to localize company strategy, to understand what it means to them where they perform their work, day in and day out. However, employees still want to know the big picture—they want to believe that the company's leaders are smart, that they know what they're doing, and that they have good reasons for putting the company through major change or taking it in a new direction. To that end, management visibility is important. Face-to-face communication is vital, but time is too limited in face-to-face encounters to provide the kind of detail that makes a strategic initiative understandable and compelling. Print affords the opportunity for features that explain the strategy, that provide real-world examples and case studies that bring the strategy to life, and management question-and-answer sessions that address all key questions, not only those asked in a face-to-face venue.

- *Recognition.* The fact that print has substance makes it an ideal venue for employee recognition. Employees can take a magazine in which they have been recognized home to share with loved ones; that is much more meaningful than printing out a page from the intranet.

- *Sharing with family.* There is more to this idea of sharing a company publication with family than recognition. There is a sense of connection to the company. Good magazines are placed on coffee tables for neighbors and families to read. A sense of pride leads people to display their company publications at home, and that pride has a way of rubbing off. Furthermore, if an employee is under stress as he or she learns to cope with a new company strategy or initiative, it is easier for family members to understand if they can read the company magazine article that explains the nature of the change.

- *Context.* Every now and then, Hewlett Packard's late, great *Measure* magazine ran a feature story that had nothing to do with the company, the industry, or the marketplace. One brilliant piece the magazine published profiled Southwest Airlines. The focus of the story was "What can we at HP learn from Southwest's success?" It was a compelling and fascinating piece that drew parallels between Southwest's operational success and areas where HP had room for improvement. It ran several pages and drew broad readership. You have to wonder how many people would have read the article if it had been available only as a "pull" piece on the intranet.

To summarize, then, the employee magazine's strengths rest in its ability to communicate the following:

- Image
- Length
- Detail
- Context
- Material of value away from the office

The Employee Newsletter

A newsletter is a step down from a magazine. It is generally published more frequently, boasts lower production values—such as one- or two-color printing instead of four-color—and it is printed on less expensive paper. Newsletters also tend to be shorter—four or eight pages instead of the sixteen, twenty-four, or thirty-two that typify employee magazines. Thus, newsletters are best for shorter items. If the intranet is ideal for short items, why waste resources on a newsletter?

Good question! In some cases, there may well be *no* reason to produce an employee newsletter. On the other hand, consider the plight of Allied Gate & Fence.

At Allied Gate & Fence

The intranet at Allied has finally arrived. Dedication by a team of communication and information technology (IT) professionals has helped to evolve the intranet from a collection of static informational pages into a dynamic tool for sharing knowledge, communicating news, and providing access to job-critical information.

The problem is that not everyone at Allied has access to the intranet. Security concerns keep the intranet hidden behind the firewall, limiting access by the traveling sales force. Then there are the union employees working in manufacturing facilities, where the company has opted not to put kiosks.

To address the have-nots, Allied's communicators decided to produce a biweekly newsletter. The tool is not an expensive proposition, since it is printed one-color on newsprint. It covers much of the material that appeared on the intranet, focusing on the information, news, and other tools that these employees need.

These items are not among those that require timely dissemination, which are distributed to supervisors for subsequent communication to employees. Rather, these are the news items supervisors would be unlikely to take time to communicate but may be of value to employees.

Newsletters can serve other functions as well, such as the following:

- Business unit leaders can use newsletters to communicate information to employees of a division that is best pushed or requires careful reading.
- Putting key information in print reinforces the information published online. Repetition increases retention and ensures that employees less inclined to use the intranet still learn what the company wanted them to know.
- A newsletter can serve multiple audiences. A sales or merchandising newsletter, for example, can be published for members of the sales force as well as the customer representatives with whom they interact (and who, as nonemployees, do not have access to the intranet).

- Newsletters provide nonheadquarters facilities, including labor-intensive operations ranging from factories to oil fields, with another means of getting local information into the hands of employees—particularly those without access (or with limited access) to electronic tools. A variety of information types are appropriate in local newsletters. They update employees about local achievements, especially those that help the company meet its goals. They also recognize individual accomplishments, helping others understand the kind of performance plant managers expect. Finally, these local newsletters are an ideal place for that type of communication that seems so unimportant as to be comical: personal information such as sports scores (for example, a company softball league), employee birthdays, birth announcements, marriages, and obituaries. Employees who work together get to know one another. Especially at the plant or factory level, these people go out together after work, have coworkers over to one another's homes for weekend barbecues, and share one another's lives. Paying attention to this social aspect of work can help increase job satisfaction (which leads to greater trust). In fact, you can consider producing a local newsletter for headquarters, too.

Other Periodicals

Depending on the communication needs you identify, you can authorize the production of any number of other publications that capitalize on the positive characteristics of print. Among those that have produced results for companies are:

- *Management journals.* Among the communication media meant to help managers with the managing part of their jobs, management journals are the most abstract. Rather than dealing with the realities of day-to-day work, these higher-end publications address issues common to anybody managing other employees and responsible for achieving business-focused goals. Topics appropriate to this kind of vehicle might include motivating employees and coping with radical change. Reprinting articles from external journals (with permission, of course) can also be useful, as can articles about management styles of intriguing figures from outside the company. The management journal at the oil company ARCO (now part of BP), for instance, once featured an interview with Tom Landry, the late coach of the NFL's Dallas Cowboys, in which the taciturn leader answered questions about leading a football team. The author suggested lessons managers of the oil company's departments could learn from Landry's management style.

- *Sales and merchandising updates.* As management journals target managers, these slim and inexpensive newsletters are aimed at sales and merchandising staff to keep them up-to-date on new products, promotions, and campaigns. In these days of intranets, e-mail, Lotus Notes, and other electronic and wireless communications, these printed publications are for employees in the field without routine access to online resources.

- *Marketplace compendia.* Does senior staff have the time to read every external periodical that contains useful information? Communications staff can read through these publications, extracting articles of interest to management, summarizing the articles in a regular publication, and enabling managers to read the complete text of those articles in which they are interested (by requesting complete copies or using the intranet to visit the complete story online). These tools are useful in print for executives who travel routinely and do much of their business-related reading on airplanes; creating a printable version online is another approach to making the hard copy available. (In any case, be sure the company has attained the rights to reproduce the complete article and is not in violation of the publisher's copyright.)

Irregular Publications

Irregular publications are those that have a name and an identity but are produced on an as-needed basis.

At Allied Gate & Fence

The employee communications department at Allied Gate & Fence maintains a supply of letter-size paper sheets printed with the title, *Management Briefing*. The rest of the page is blank. Whenever a major announcement is pending, the department quickly produces the text to fill the page using a desktop-publishing tool. This copy explains the issue, and then provides managers and supervisors with a list of questions their employees might ask and the answers they can provide. The bulletins also offer advice for applying the local spin to the information provided.

The print version is important at Allied because many supervisors work in the field on job sites and in the company's factories where the product is manufactured. The desktop-published text is photocopied quickly onto the preprinted stock, giving the publication an identity that is immediately recognized when managers receive it. It is published only when an announcement is imminent that may cause concern or distress among employees. Supervisors know that they should read the material as soon as they receive it. It is their early-warning system and their resource to help them manage the issue among their direct reports.

Employee Annual Reports

The annual report provides the vital investment audience with a summary of the company's performance over the previous year and its outlook for the upcoming year. Shareholders are not the only audience that benefits from the annual report; in fact, for most companies the annual report is the most important document produced all year. Customers, strategic partners, vendors, legislators and regulators, the financial community (including analysts), and the media all rely on the annual report. For employees, though, the annual report has limited value.

Employees *should* read the public annual report, particularly those employees who own company stock through the 401(k) plans, stock options, or stock purchase plans. However, a vital element is missing from the annual report from employees' perspective: How did their contributions affect the company's performance, and what is expected of them in the year ahead?

Many companies have produced a special annual publication, the employee annual report, to answer these questions. The employee annual report does not have to display the same kind of production values typical in a shareholder's report, which often serves as the company's showcase publication. Even if its production values do not measure up to those of the public annual report, the employee version is a celebration of employee contributions to the company's accomplishments. Furthermore, like the annual report, the employee report makes the link between employee efforts and the performance that resulted, adding context and meaning to the cold financial statements in the shareholder report. Finally, employees gain a better understanding of what the company hopes they will accomplish in the coming twelve months.

Special Publications

You can produce a publication whenever you need one; it does not need to be a periodical. Brochures, minimagazines, or flyers can all serve a purpose, particularly when you need an issue to stand out.

At Allied Gate & Fence

A cost-reduction program at Allied is nearing its completion. Employees have been encouraged to suggest cost-containment ideas based on their unique knowledge of their jobs and departments. Employees with access to the intranet submitted their ideas online, while others dropped paper forms into old-fashioned suggestion boxes.

Now, management wants to recognize the best ideas, the ones that will be implemented. Tossing them on the intranet is inadequate; it gives the recommendations a sense of transience, or nonimportance. Instead, the company's management opts to publish the best ideas in a two-color brochure, permanently enshrining the ideas and making them substantial, worthy of such treatment. This treatment leads other employees to sense there is genuine value to the recommendations, and that the company's leaders take them seriously and employee contributions genuinely matter.

Collateral

Not everything you print will be a publication. You can print posters, for example. Want everyone to know the deadline for enrolling in their benefits? Posters taped to bathroom doors are a sure-fire way to have that assurance. There are also table-tent cards and other attention grabbers. I once managed a project that involved printing popcorn boxes that contained key information about the relaunch of an intranet. (The whole marketing campaign was based on a movie preview theme.) Another time, we distributed laminated cards to supervisors that contained key talking points; they were designed to fit in shirt pockets.

Once again, I remind you to go back to your strategic planning. What you want to accomplish comes first. How you accomplish it comes next. The tools you use come last, and should be designed to most effectively achieve the objectives.

And whatever you do, don't dismiss print from your toolkit. Print still rocks.

Video

Video magazines aimed at employees were all the rage a few decades back. Today, it seems only companies rolling in money produce video for their employee communications. It's just too costly, and besides, what with the intranet, who has the time?

These are arguments I just don't buy. First of all, there's value to producing things people can see and hear instead of read. And second, your intranet is an ideal platform for the distribution of audio and video. But it's not the *only* platform.

Consider this scenario: Forty percent of your employees work in manufacturing facilities. They don't have their own computers. The company has provided kiosks with access to the intranet, but they're only used for those things employees *have* to use them for, such as self-service benefits enrollment. Will employees read the company news on the intranet during their breaks as the company hoped when the kiosks were rolled out? After working for three straight hours with your hands, would *you* want to go to a keyboard and type? Most likely you'd want to drink a cup of coffee while chewing the fat with your friends.

A print publication is problematic, too. Employees won't read it while they're working; their supervisors won't let them. Because they're hourly, they're not inclined to take a publication home to read.

At several organizations, company news and other messages are communicated to this audience through closed-circuit TV monitors set up in break rooms, lobbies, and other key areas. Some even situate these monitors on the factory floor in high traffic spots. They're not showing live TV, but something like a PowerPoint presentation that plays continuously. One slide contains a safety reminder, another an important story about a new company initiative, another a news item about a new product launch. Interspersed between company messages are weather, general news, sports, and other items. Watching the entire thing takes two or three minutes.

And here's the compelling part: They're compelling! Factory workers actually stand around and watch these continuous broadcasts until they've seen all the messages (a couple of minutes), which means they've got all the main information you wanted them to get.

And that's just one use of multimedia. Here are some more.

Message Retention

Raytheon, the Massachusetts-based defense contractor, conducted studies that determined multimedia increases retention. Say something in text and employees remember only so much of it, and only for so long. Make it audio and retention increases. Make it video, and retention increases yet again.

Thus, key messages are introduced in text. Then employees can click a link to hear the CEO talk about it. Later, they can catch a video where another executive reiterated the message at a meeting. Message retention skyrockets.

The idea of message retention was behind all those videos I used to produce when I worked in the communications practice of human resources consulting firms. You can't explain all the details and nuances of an employee retirement savings plan in a fifteen-minute video—that's what print is for—but you can make the main points that you want people to remember; you can *sell* those points so employees *will* remember them.

The Next Best Thing to Face-to-Face

Face-to-face is great, powerful, dynamic, important. It's also impossible to implement as a pervasive element of your internal communications program for your company's leaders. They can't always be everywhere engaging in face-to-face communication with everyone.

Video fails badly at the interactive, give-and-take parts of face-to-face communication. There is no active listening on the part of the speaker. But it works quite well at going beyond the small percentage of your communication that is conveyed in your words. Tone of voice, facial expression, body language—it's all captured in video.

We used to videotape the quarterly managers meeting held at company headquarters and edit it into a watchable one-hour program, then send it to offices where managers worked outside of our headquarters city. (We also solicited questions for the company's leaders from managers in remote locations so they could participate, then get the answers to their questions on the tape.) Remember that old phone company slogan? It's the next best thing to being there.

What Employees Are Used To

Employees watch a lot of TV. They're accustomed to getting information that way. It makes sense to communicate to them that way. Even though diminished communication budgets and the accelerated growth of the Web have all but done away with employee video magazines, they can still work.

Aetna, the insurance company, produces a monthly video magazine for employees. Employees watch it by clicking a link on the intranet and viewing the streaming media file. Because the video appears in a very small window in less-than-optimum conditions, Aetna is able to produce the video with lower production values than would be required for TV broadcast. That saves money. But it still allows an anchor to introduce stories—interviews, features, etc.—in a format that is familiar and easy for employees to digest.

Unable to accommodate streaming media due to bandwidth restrictions, General Mills opts instead to Webcast over its intranet. The difference is that instead of individual files being pulled on demand through the intranet by individual employees, one file is being broadcast at one time. Employees check the online schedule of upcoming broadcasts and make sure they're at their desks when a video or audio is going to be presented. These include everything from recordings of meetings to a new-hire orientation video.

Note

1. "IABC/Watson Wyatt Study," Watson Wyatt Worldwide, IABC, and the IABC Research Foundation, 1999.

CHAPTER SIX

Online Communication Tools

COMPANIES HAVE EMBRACED a variety of online tools for employee communication—embraced them so fervently that they have dismissed other communication vehicles. Print is too expensive. Face-to-face is too time-consuming. *Everything* can be communicated by e-mail or a Web interface.

Indeed, research shows that intranets can enhance return on investment considerably, primarily through altering the way work is accomplished and generating substantial productivity improvements. (An intranet is the Internet captured inside your organization and leveraged to the organization's benefit. It includes e-mail, a Web interface, and other tools such as file transfer and network news.)

Your intranet is a powerful tool, but it cannot do all your communications. After all, regardless of how dynamic online communication tools are, they are still merely tactics. Choosing to communicate everything over an intranet means abandoning strategic planning. You no longer choose the best tool to achieve objectives with specific target audiences. While an intranet can do some things exceedingly well, there are others it simply cannot do well at all.

What Can an Intranet Do?

The intranet can do whatever the Internet can do. For example:

Improve access and speed of delivery. Look at nearly any internal communication audit. Invariably, one of the biggest complaints is that information is hard to find and that news reaches employees late. The intranet can store unlimited volumes of information and deliver news almost instantaneously.

Go global. Ever send publications to worldwide locations? The intranet eliminates drop-shipping as a routine part of the internal communication mix. At Levi Strauss, the company's always-up-to-date fact book is available at the same time to media relations representatives in the United States or in the United Kingdom—U.K. reps are not hampered by time zones to receive accurate information from the U.S. headquarters.

Inspire collaboration and interaction. E-mail has long been considered the "killer app" of the Net. Discussion groups thrived long before there was a World Wide Web, and instant messaging is infiltrating the workplace faster than any medium in history. These tools allow individuals to engage each other and work together.

Integrate information and transactions. Policy documents about, for example, company travel can be linked directly to the page where employees can book their flights, rental cars, and hotels. A page providing information that a customer service rep might need can include a link to a related element of a customer satisfaction improvement initiative.

Deliver multimedia. Audio, video, and animation are relatively easy to incorporate on an intranet (given enough bandwidth to handle it).

What Can't an Intranet Do?

Despite these wonderful features, the intranet is not a panacea. Some things the intranet cannot do include the following:

Replace face-to-face. Sure, you can stream or Webcast video of meetings—that is a great use of the medium. But it is *still* not a face-to-
face encounter with a live human being in the real world.

Replace print. If you think print is passé, consider how often you print
out e-mail messages or Web pages. That is because print is easier
to read than your computer monitor and much of the content *delivered* on the screen was not designed or written to be *consumed* on
the screen.

Push. E-mail is the only electronic form of communication you can
push at employees. Everything else on the intranet sits and waits
to be pulled. If you want everybody to know something—such as
a benefits enrollment deadline, news about an acquisition or a layoff, or details of a product launch—you won't get that message out
if all you do is publish it to a Web page.

Planning Considerations

When deciding what elements of an internal communication program to move online, it is common for many communicators to
benchmark what other companies are doing. Identifying best practices can be illuminating, but blindly implementing them can be a
mistake. Keep in mind that the amazingly cool intranet element you
saw on the Cisco Systems intranet was developed to address a Cisco
Systems need within Cisco's environment. If your organization does
not have the same need and the same culture, duplicating the feature
can be a waste of effort.

If you must benchmark, you would be much better off to
benchmark best *principles*. That is, how did best-of-breed companies
go about figuring out what to put on their intranets? How did they
go about getting the work done? Measuring the outcomes?

In any case, before you put *any* communications on your intranet, review some key considerations:

Access

Do all your employees have access to the intranet? If not, what classes or categories of employees have access?

If you can identify the category of employees with access, then you can develop communications that accommodate their special needs. These might include:

- Managers
- Headquarters employees
- Specialists

Those without access could fall into classes such as the following:

- Employees at nonheadquarters facilities
- Factory workers
- Field employees

Culture

The company's culture will be critical in determining how effective online communication can be. (By the way, I define culture as "the way things are around here.")

How trusted are communications currently? And by which parts of the employee population? If employees don't believe what management tells them in all-hands meetings, the intranet—a sterile environment compared with face-to-face—could conceivably make things worse. How do employees want to receive their information? If you have conducted a communications audit that includes a gap analysis, you may have asked this question for various company issues: "What is your *preferred* source of information? What is your *actual* source of information?" For many issues, the immediate supervisor is the preferred source, and the most credible. To begin publishing that information online won't enhance credibility, but giving supervisors a place to get the information to communicate to their employees *can* improve consistency and *heighten* credibility. Will supervisors support their employees spending time online? There still are plenty of companies where supervisors tell their employees, "Get off the intranet and get back to work!" (Sad, but true.)

One of the best ways to get the answers to these questions is to conduct a communication audit to help you figure out which of your communications will be most effective online. Unless every employee has access to the intranet, be sure to use a paper-and-pencil approach to the audit; otherwise, your only feedback will come from the segment of the population that already uses the system.

Intranets Solve Problems

We already know from broad research the sources of general dissatisfaction in organizations. (There may be other unique conditions in your company. You may know intuitively what these are, or you may need to do some research.) Dissatisfaction arises from a few things we have already discussed and a few that we haven't. Let's look at them one-by-one and explore how the intranet can improve your current traditional processes for addressing them:

Speed

Nothing is worse for an employee than learning vital company news from some source other than the company. Have you ever learned that your organization has made a major announcement while listening to the radio news on your commute home? Has a neighbor ever asked if you are going to survive a layoff about which you have not yet been told by the company?

The reason for the lag—at least, for publicly traded companies in the United States—is often disclosure requirements from the Securities and Exchange Commission. Companies are not permitted to communicate with *any* audience, including employees, until financial markets have been informed. Timing being everything, many companies wait until after stock trading has ended for the day before making major announcements. On the East Coast, that means after 4 P.M. By the time the markets have been notified, the media has the information but employees have already started heading home for the day.

Compound this with the fact that most employee communication vehicles are scheduled periodicals, and the channels for as-needed announcements are often less than efficient, and you can see why breaking news so often is delivered to employees through non-company sources.

The intranet provides an obvious solution: You don't need to wait for a scheduled periodical, nor do you need to arrange a massive desk-to-desk distribution of paper (a regular means of communicating breaking news before electronic networks offered a more instantaneous solution).

But the solution is *not* simply to publish the news on a Web page. That presumes employees will make an effort to go *look* at that particular page. One of the most important characteristics of any Web environment—internal or external—is its pull (receiver-driven) nature. Visitors to the intranet extract only what they're interested in; they ignore the rest. As a result, vital news requires two concurrent approaches:

1. Publish breaking, vital news on the home page.
2. Alert employees about the news by e-mail.

Far too many intranets are driven by the technology that underlies them rather than the functions for which they are designed. For example, many portal solutions hide the news under a tab called (not surprisingly) News. Employees must click the News tab to see any news. Of course, employees who have come to the intranet for any purpose *other* than reading news simply will not click that tab. The solution is for the home page to serve as the front page of the newspaper as well as the navigation tool for the rest of the intranet. (If your architecture and navigation are good, you won't *need* an entire page to show employees how to get to the information for which they came looking!) Since most employees start their journey on the home page, they will inevitably see the news whenever they open their browsers.

And what of those employees who, as the news breaks, have no particular need to use the intranet? They learn about the news because the news is *pushed* to them. Remember, e-mail is the only online channel that allows you to push content at employees.

Communicating the news online should never be the end of your communication. Remember not to forsake print and face-to-face.

Access to Information

Another common complaint is that employees do not have access to the information they need to do their jobs. The intranet is a no-brainer approach to providing that access, but you cannot assume that the various departments that own the information will publish it merely by virtue of the fact that they have their own intranet sites. It is up to you, the communicator, to identify the kind of information employees need. Start with the greatest common denominators from your research and work with the departments that own that information to make it available.

In addition to information all or most employees need, you will find that classes of employees need specific information. These classes can be defined by department, specialty, or job category. One good example I have found in virtually every organization: administrative assistants. They need to know the processes for getting various things done. In one company, this was addressed by an enterprising administrative assistant who built a page featuring links to all of the various resources that answered questions most commonly asked by administrative assistants. That is a serendipitous approach. It would be better to know the importance of this information to administrative assistants and plan to make it available through simple navigation tools on the intranet. As for department-specific information—that is, content employees in one department need that is owned by another department—establish the systems that allow the two departments to get together.

Sense of Fairness

The intranet should include all policy documents and manuals so that employees can easily review them and recognize the consistency with which policies are administered. Don't simply shovel these online in their paper format. Ensure that employees can find the information they are looking for in as few clicks as possible. One way to do this is to provide multiple pathways through the information. Consider benefits materials, which in print are restricted to a linear path, usually plan by plan. On an intranet, however, you can build a timeline, a chronological listing of life events (from birth to death and everything in between). An employee having a baby can click on "Having a baby" and learn what benefits she is eligible for, what workplace rules apply, what is allowed and what is not.

Similarly, they can learn about salary levels, the requirements for attaining a particular level, and even link to information about how those levels apply in the departments where they work.

Recognition

Recognition is a huge motivator in the workplace. It should be one of your first objectives on your intranet: Build recognition into the system.

The easiest part of this is to integrate the intranet into existing recognition programs, so employees can instantly see the most recently recognized workers, learn the criteria for recognition, and even submit themselves or coworkers using an online form. The harder part is developing entirely new online recognition programs.

At Allied Gate & Fence

On Allied's intranet named Gateway, the home page features a weekly "Hero," an employee's picture linked to a brief bio and an explanation of what that employee does. This employee generally is one who would never otherwise be recognized, one of the silent majorities of workers who do their job but never stand out in a crowd. In addition to providing an avenue of recognition for them, this feature introduces employees to each other. The weekly Heroes feature is one of the most widely read features on the Allied intranet, and frequently introduces employees to other employees they might never otherwise have met—employees who may have knowledge of value to them. Allied's communicators have also created a "Pat on the Back" page where any employee can recognize another employee or team for its efforts. There is no committee to determine the appropriateness of the recognition, and there is no cost. It is just an "atta-boy," a simple form where an employee can enter the name and department of an employee who helped out, along with brief narrative about what the employee did to help, and a submit button. The recognition automatically appears. This is another popular page—employees *love* to look for their names and the names of their friends in company communications.

Success stories represent one more form of recognition, one in which the employee communications department can be more intimately involved. Given the lack of limited space on the intranet, you can write as many success stories as you like (or have time for). You can even solicit contributions from employees. These can appear anywhere on the intranet—on a "Success Stories" page, on a recognition site, within the departments where the work is done. This is made possible by the kind of database programming inherent in online production.

Communicating the Company Strategy

It would be hard to help employees figure out where they fit in the big picture if they didn't understand what the big picture was. A company can use its intranet in a variety of ways to address strategy with various employee audiences.

A Dedicated Strategy Site

The easiest place to start is to construct a site dedicated to the company's strategy. Few companies have such a site because no single department is responsible for the strategy, and the executive team that set the strategy rarely undertakes the construction of intranet sites. If you need to make the strategy site a component of an employee communications section, go ahead—as long as employees view the site as an independent resource.

Treat the area as a separate entity with its own navigation. The top-level page should clearly show navigation to the contents of the site while also displaying the key elements of the strategy. If there are four planks to the company's strategy—for example, customer acquisition and retention through better customer targeting and improved customer satisfaction, focused research into a particular area of inquiry, reduced inventories, and acquisition of small companies to fill in market gaps—each of these planks would serve as a link to more information.

What kind of additional information? That depends on how strategy is implemented in your organization, but some considerations include the following:

- Org charts, contact information, and updates from teams dedicated to implementing the plank of the strategy.
- Links to current activities (including content of other intranet sites) directly related to the plank. For instance, the customer re-

tention plank could include a link to a page on the sales site where sales reps share ideas for keeping customers.

- Links to discussions about the topic.
- Audio or video of any executive speeches dealing with the issue.
- Statistics about the issue. For example, looking again at customer retention, you could show the cost of losing a customer, the cost of acquiring a new customer, and the potential return on investment from a retained customer versus a new customer.
- Marketplace data, including competition and demographics.

Links from Related Sites

Although it makes sense to build a dedicated site, you have to wonder how often employees will visit it. The trick to making these sites vibrant is to ensure that real-world content links to it.

Let's say your company has a research and development (R&D) department with a site on the intranet. The site is a resource for the scientists working in R&D. A section of the site is dedicated to a particular field of research. The section includes a link to the part of the strategy site associated with research, helping the scientists working on the project understand how their day-to-day work fits with the company's strategy.

News

Any news that appears on the intranet home page that relates to company strategy should include a link to the relevant strategy on the strategy site.

Metrics

One of the best standing elements to include on your home page is an overview of company performance against key strategies, especially if certain thresholds must be achieved for bonuses to kick in.

Simple charts or rows of numbers that show top-line results can link to detailed explanations and background detail.

Integrating Traditional Internal Communication Vehicles onto the Intranet

Undoubtedly, you already had communication vehicles before you launched an intranet. You shouldn't seek to transfer your existing communications to the intranet; rather, you need to integrate your existing communication channels with the intranet so each leverages its strengths.

For example, if you have a monthly print publication that you want to stop printing and put online, don't simply begin publishing a monthly publication on the intranet. Articles can appear whenever they have been written (and approved). Your monthly publication schedule was based on budget, employee tolerance for frequency of information, and other criteria that have no bearing online.

But more to the point, you should consider whether you really want to give up your publication at all or merely recast it in light of the intranet's capabilities. You can limit your print publication to the longer articles that employees won't read online, because they will print them out anyway. Each full-length print article could include the following:

- Links to related content on the intranet—for example, the sites of departments involved with the project covered in the story
- Links to additional resources on the intranet—for example, photos for which there was no room in the magazine, the complete Q&A of an interview only excerpts of which appeared in print
- A scheduled online chat with the subject of the interview

In any case, your goal should be to take advantage of the strengths of each medium. Ultimately, your audience should have a hard time telling where one medium ends and another begins; that line should be significantly blurred. The magazine and the intranet could each stand on its own, but they are stronger because they are supported and supplemented by the other.

With this general guideline in mind, let's look at some of the more common traditional internal communication components and how to integrate them with your intranet.

Employee Magazine, Newsletter, or Magapaper

If you continue to produce a print publication, there is nothing wrong with archiving the print contents on the intranet. After all, how productive is it for you to search for articles in your publication morgue when an employee calls? It makes much more sense to let employees search for articles from back issues. It is also valuable for employees conducting a search on a topic to be able to find content from back issues, even if they didn't know articles had been published that would be useful. An archive of print articles, though, is different than simply posting print articles to the intranet and calling it an online publication. It is a print publication that happens to have been digitized.

If you are intent on eliminating your print publication (or if management has given you no choice), don't treat the intranet as a replacement. Instead, reinvent the way you deliver news, features, and other information to take advantage of the intranet's characteristics. For example:

- *Make the intranet home page the front page of your publication.* Provide a review of the most important news (a headline, a short who-what-when-where-why paragraph, and a link to the full story), a feature or two, key metrics, marketplace updates. Most portal packages allow you to designate a section of the portal page to this type of information.
- *When readers link to the complete text of the story, they should be able to use*

the story as a launching pad to other related information. Include links to related articles in your archives, related departmental or other sites, interactive discussions, and even links to external World Wide Web content.

- *Invite discussion about the article.* Integrate threaded discussion capabilities directly into the article, allowing employees to share additional insights and ask questions, enhancing the spread of knowledge among the employee population.
- *Incorporate interactivity and multimedia into the publication.* You can include video interviews and interactive quizzes, for example.

One more point about items appearing in your publication (or your news site): Let employees contribute news. Your employees know what is going on in their work areas. To be sure, not every item they submit will be an appropriate item for publication, but many will be. You can turn every employee into a correspondent by including a simple link that invites employees to submit a news item. You will receive far more interesting material than if you simply make calls to find out what is going on or wait for stories to come to you. Any employee reading the news who thinks about an activity or accomplishment or news item in his or her department will be inclined to click the link and spend twenty seconds tapping out a note.

All-Hands Meetings

Use the intranet to promote all-hands meetings. As part of the promotion, include the opportunity for employees to submit questions in advance. This will accommodate employees who cannot be at the live meeting, including those from off-site facilities. Use a question submission form on the intranet.

If your intranet has the infrastructure to support it, Webcast the meeting to off-site facilities. Archive the video as a stream for employees who cannot watch it live (such as those in incompatible time zones). Webcasting requires adequate bandwidth, but if you have this capability, it is not an outrageously expensive proposition.

Following the meeting, prepare a news article about the highlights for your home-page news listing. The complete article will include all of the Q&A, access to the streaming video, and any documents used at the meeting (for example, memos or PowerPoint presentations).

Birthdays, Brides, Babies, Bowling Scores

If ever the intranet was the perfect place for something, it is this employee communication staple for showcasing promotions, transfers, retirements, retiree obituaries, new hires, weddings, babies, company sports league results, and so on.

I am the last person to suggest that this is a waste of time. As much as many people argue that communicators need to focus 100 percent on business-related matters, I would argue that this *is* business related. Employees with whom you work might start out as colleagues, but later they may become friends. Making that social aspect of work a little more evident can increase job satisfaction and, by extension, commitment. Besides, people *like* to read this stuff. If you are already publishing it and try to take it away, you will hear complaints.

Thanks to the intranet, though, you don't have to dedicate anywhere *near* the kind of time to this communication it requires in print. For example, you can have a page created with hooks to the Human Resources Information System so that current anniversaries, promotions, transfers, and the like are automatically posted, set to update weekly. You could also invite employees to submit birth announcements and other such notable information through a content-publishing interface: Select the appropriate type of information (sports league score or wedding announcement, for instance), the salient information, and any dates, and it appears automatically on the page.

Create and maintain this page, and I would be willing to bet it becomes one of the top-visited pages on your intranet.

Q&A

Another staple of employee communications is the submit-your-question program. The employee communications department takes the questions and distributes them to appropriate subject-matter experts for an answer that appears in the company publication. With the intranet, employees don't need to wait for the publication to get an answer. Given support from senior management, you can remove employee communications from the mix. Make sure your subject-matter experts check the discussion forum every couple of days to answer any questions in their area, and you can let employees post the questions themselves.

News

One nice thing about a print publication is that everything is conveniently situated in one place. The nature of the news does not matter—news issued via press release to the media, marketplace news, or news from outside sources can all be found between the covers of the magazine.

On the intranet, news is everywhere. On some systems, you would need to follow dozens of links to find it all. Press releases are on one site, news generated by the employee communications department is on another. News acquired from Factiva or Luce or some other external wire service is in another place. Competitor news is somewhere else, and who knows where to find marketplace news? And let's not even talk about news generated by factories and non-headquarters locations!

If you want employees to have access to news, ensure that they can do it from one place regardless of the nature of the news.

As for the news you want every employee to see, consider placing articles on more than one page. Using content management systems, news briefs can be tagged for inclusion on any number of pages. For example, an article about a competitor working in the financial services marketplace in Ohio could appear on the "Competitor" news brief page, the "Ohio" news brief page, and the "Financial Services" news brief page.

Finally, make sure news is posted while it is current; don't wait for a publication date. Do not accept anybody telling you that you cannot, because there is always a way. And remember, the intranet is a tool to help employees do their work; it should be adjusted to make that possible. If you have room for five news items on the home page, drop the oldest into archives whenever a new item is ready. You can also feature a link to additional news items, but recognize that these cannot be important items because most employees will not follow a link to more news. They will pay attention primarily to the news on the home page, which argues for an e-mail newsletter to push at employees, perhaps weekly, covering *all* the news published to the intranet. Your e-mail newsletter—part of the intranet—will feature a headline, a who-what-when-where-why sentence or two, and a link to the full story on the intranet.

Once readers are on the news page, offer a couple of other conveniences, such as:

- Let employees print out a page of all of today's (or this week's) news items so they can read it on the go rather than be tethered to their computers.
- Let employees download a summary of the news to handheld devices such as a Palm Pilot. You can even make this feature available in a wireless configuration so employees away from a computer can still stay in the know.

Make It Viral

Online communications can get into the hands of employees who may not otherwise see it. The way to achieve this is through a viral approach. (The term *viral,* in this context, means that your employees distribute the news for you.) Include a link that invites employees to "e-mail this article to a colleague."

Communicating to and from Managers and Executives

There is no understating the importance of managers and supervisors in an organization. Nearly any communication audit will show that, in most cases, the immediate supervisor is the preferred source of information. Even when employees are *not* seeking information from their supervisor, the supervisor's ability to do his or her job will have a more direct bearing on job satisfaction than nearly any other factor.

As noted earlier, in most organizations, supervisors are not selected based on their management skills but rather are promoted as a reward for excellent work in their nonmanagement jobs. Some managers have a built-in ability to manage; others struggle. The resources companies provide to help these people become effective managers is inconsistent at best. But the intranet can help in several ways.

Manager's Toolkit

This is another one of those sites that does not automatically belong in any single department's jurisdiction. Since employee communications often undertakes efforts to improve management and supervisory communication, I suggest that this is an employee communications effort—even more because the communication between managers and employees is one of the most common day-to-day communications. If a company is not influencing its managers' ability to communicate, the intranet may be the impetus to get started.

The manager's toolkit is a one-stop shopping resource for managers and supervisors. Simple, clean navigation should make it easy for managers to find what they are looking for despite the many different kinds of content that could be available here. A few basic categories should include:

- *News for managers.* Anything a manager needs to know to do his or her job well. This would include policy changes, changes to reporting structures, or the introduction of new processes, such as the switch to an online form from a paper form. You can enhance the value of this section by including news and features from outside the firewall, such as relevant articles from human resources publications on improving management or supervisory skills.
- *Tools for managers.* Any interactive form on the intranet for managers should be accessible with one click from this section, regardless of where the form actually resides online. This would include performance evaluation processes, new-hire forms, or job requisition forms, for example.
- *Information for managers.* Any guidelines, handbooks, or manuals that are aimed at managers belong here.
- *Press kits.* Okay, they aren't really press kits, but they are the management equivalent. This would be a standalone document providing links to all resources for short-term issues. Let's take the issue of a major change to compensation policies. Here is where managers would find an overview of the change, background documentation validating the need for the change, an FAQ (frequently asked questions), statistics, talking points for addressing the change with employees, and a guide to holding a meeting about the subject. Even if much of the material was created by the compensation department and resides on its intranet site, you can still consolidate links to all relevant information in this one place.
- *Link to employee data.* Managers should be able to use a link on the site to find information about the employees who report to them—how many days of vacation they have taken, how many sick days, that sort of thing. It is much easier than calling HR to find out, and the information is just sitting there in a database!
- *Management discussions.* If you host discussion groups, you cannot go wrong by giving managers and supervisors a place to talk about managing. This is where one supervisor can post a message asking if any other supervisors have ever dealt with a particular issue.

- *Training materials.* Offer links to any training resources, including streaming media, designed to train employees to manage other employees. Include a catalog of management-related live training opportunities, which could be a subset of an existing company-wide online training catalog.
- *Management newsletter.* Take one or both of two approaches here. You can let managers/supervisors subscribe to a regular (weekly, biweekly) newsletter that offers tips and advice on managing. You can also push a newsletter to all managers, whether they think they want it or not, advising them of any new content on the manager's site. You can also use this newsletter to push major news they will need to know to answer employee questions (pointing them to the comprehensive resources on the intranet Web site), along with any news the company wants communicated (or reinforced) in a supervisor-to-employee setting.

Be sure to cross-link where it makes sense. For example, a job requisition form (which a manager would fill out to staff a new position in his or her department) would include a link to the policy manual text outlining the requirements for requisitioning a new employee.

Executive Content

One of the greatest challenges any communicator faces is convincing the executive management of a company to use the intranet. Many executives see the intranet as a tool for employees lower down the pecking order.

But trust me: Those same executives will flock to the intranet if there is content that meets their unique needs. At Sears, only executives had access to interactive, dynamic executive compensation information, which the executive team used frequently, getting them accustomed to using the interface. In addition, they had to view the news headlines on the home page to get to the executive compensation site.

Can you create a secure site only for executives that contains resources and information they really need? Remember, the trick is to make the online content more convenient or easier to use than the old way of obtaining the same information.

Executive Chat

You may be surprised to hear it, but many executives who conduct chats with employees *love* the exercise and the results. The challenge is to get them to try it in the first place.

The first executive chat I heard about was from Sears. Former CEO Arthur Martinez maintained his own site on Inside, the Sears intranet. His site included a newsgroup for asynchronous discussion, an idea submission, and a variety of other two-way tools. (It also included some top-down material, including a column Martinez wrote about what was on his mind and an overview of his executive team and what he expected from them.)

The chat room was open during specified periods when Martinez hosted chats on specific topics. Later, Sears' new CEO, Alan Lacy, resumed the chats. In fact, one was scheduled for September 12, 2001, on quarterly sales results. Of course, one day after the September 11 terrorist attacks, nobody wanted to talk about sales, so the CEO used the session to address employee anxieties and fears. The discussion ranged from questions about any Sears employees who may have been killed (none were) to security measures being taken to protect employees to travel policies in light of the attacks. Research that followed suggested that employees felt a lot better about the company and their jobs following the CEO's candid answers to their questions.

The next time I heard about a CEO chat, it was from Jerry Stevenson at EDS. The EDS chats are an extension of a live program called "Straight Talk." Under the program, executives traveling to EDS field offices took time to meet with employees to bring them up-to-date on company issues and to answer questions. Adding chat allowed management to conduct "Straight Talk" sessions in reverse—employees, regardless of their location, could come to an executive. (The first "Straight Talk" chat was held with the company's vice chairman because he was the only member of senior management who knew how to type.)

Since then, I have spoken with representatives of many companies who use chat to this purpose. Let's run down the scenario for successful executive chats:

Elements of Executive Chat Sessions

Choose a theme for every chat. It could be a quarterly update that is scheduled regularly. It could be a topic of current interest to employees, such as a new-product introduction or the company's response to a regulatory challenge. It could even be a hastily convened chat to address a crisis.

Next, promote the chat. Use all your existing communication resources, including any appropriate print vehicles. Let people know the time the chat will be held, what it is about, and how to log in. Also, ensure that employees know that they can submit questions in advance, and explain how they go about making those submissions. This is important for the following two reasons:

1. It allows employees who cannot be at their desks to participate when the chat is happening to submit their questions anyway.
2. It gives the CEO some questions to answer at the beginning of the chat, before anybody has been able to type a question into the system.

When the chat begins, a moderator kicks things off. This individual sets the ground rules and introduces the executive. The following is a sample scenario:

> *Mike:* Welcome to the third in our series of quarterly chats with Ed Smith, Acme's chief executive officer. I'll be your moderator for the chat. Just so you know

how this works, the questions you enter will come to me, and I'll select questions to pass on to Ed. I'll read them out loud, then Ed will dictate his response to me, which I'll type to you. If you have any questions about the chat, just send a private message to me and I'll get to you as quickly as possible with an answer.

The theme of today's chat is improving relations with customers. I hope you all had a chance to read Ed's column about this subject in the magazine that was distributed last week. So, with that, let's open the questions.

Gary Franklin: Hi, Ed. I work in retail merchandising, and we're out with the customers on the front lines. We hear a lot, but nobody at headquarters ever asks what we've heard. If the messages customers pass to us got up to your level, I think we could go a long way toward improving customer relations.

Ed: You're absolutely right, Gary. In fact, I have to say I'm surprised that your observations aren't being solicited. I'm making a note right now to ask Lou Campbell, my marketing VP, to make sure we develop a process to get this kind of information from you and your fellow retail merchandising reps on a regular basis. Hearing exactly what customers are saying in the field is one of our most important monitoring methods.

Mike: Here's a question that was submitted in advance from Beverly Green, a sales analyst in our Midwest Division . . .

It works much better if the executive can speak off-the-cuff while the moderator (or even a typist, as some companies do it) takes dictation.

Make sure the window for the chat is limited. It is very difficult for employees to sit at their desks and read plain text for too long. Ninety minutes is about the maximum length.

Also, make sure the moderator selects a range of questions. His job is not to pick the easy questions and help the CEO avoid tough ones. Rather, his job is to ensure that the questions selected are on topic and that a range of employees have the chance to be heard. It'll be rare that every question is asked. You need to set the expectation early that the chat lasts only ninety minutes and that only a selection of questions will be taken. But if every question looks like a slam dunk to the audience, the entire chat will seem like a whitewash and a waste of time, and few employees will want to participate again next time.

After the chat, make sure employees know how to get to the archive so they can reread what was said (and those who were unable to attend have an opportunity to read it for the first time).

Finally, conduct research after the session is over to assess employees' opinions about the chat. Determine whether employees felt it was useful and candid.

Taking Executive Chats Beyond the CEO

Most companies that hold executive chats limit them to only the president or the CEO. Some, though, have expanded beyond that one individual. EDS holds chats with various members of the executive team. Other companies have made the chat utility available to division or business unit chiefs to hold similar chats with only the employees of their units.

Don't forget the fundamental strategic approach to your effort. You are not doing it because chat is a cool utility and you think it would be a great way for your executives to communicate. You are doing it because communication challenges exist that chat could help you meet. Once you adopt this philosophy, it becomes easy to figure out, in your organization, where benefit could be derived by putting executives and employees together in a chat room.

President or CEO Site

Notice that the chat archive for Sears is part of Lacy's own site. Companies with well-maintained, current CEO sites go a long way toward removing the ivory tower stigma from the top executive, personalizing him and making him more accessible to the employee population, while requiring the CEO to invest only a little time in the effort.

Consider the CEO site as a great way to dispense with that worthless old standby, the CEO column in the print publication. The column's frequency coincides with the publication's (monthly, for instance), is written long before the magazine reaches employees' hands (so it cannot be too timely), and is usually very broad in scope (so that all readers can relate to it). The CEO intranet site can be current, with articles posted while the information is fresh. It can be focused. But to be effective, it must be maintained. Old content on a CEO site, addressing issues resolved long ago, will inspire employees to avoid the site at all costs.

Consider the following content for the CEO site:

- A regular update or letter from the CEO on whatever is on his or her mind.
- An overview of the management team: who reports to the CEO, what do they do, and what does the CEO expect from them.
- A Q&A, allowing employees to submit questions to the CEO. (Employee communications can manage this function.)
- Idea submissions, allowing employees with suggestions or ideas to submit them. (Again, this function can be managed by the internal communications department.)
- Announcements of upcoming face-to-face meetings, CEO luncheons, or online chats.
- Archives of chats or Q&A sessions from luncheons, for example.
- A poll to let the CEO find out how employees feel or think

about a particular issue. (Former Sears CEO Arthur Martinez, for example, published a poll on his home page, asking, "Where do you think we should focus our efforts to battle the competition?" Choices included merchandise, marketing/advertising, service, e-commerce, among others.)

- The executive's chat room.

Communities of Practice

Every company has hidden communities, employees who share subject-matter expertise or common goals but don't know one another. If these employees could be introduced to one another, they could form an overt community available to other employees who need to tap into that expertise.

Here is an example set in a company that makes photocopiers. Unknown to the company, a core group of employees has unique knowledge about toner. Management might scoff at the idea. There is, after all, no toner department; there is no vice president in charge of toner. The company simply *makes* toner. They buy the raw materials, mix it in a factory according to specifications, inject it into toner cartridges, and sell the cartridges to customers.

Elsewhere in the company is a sales rep who receives a call from an irate customer. "We've had your technical rep out here five times to fix our copier, but the toner *still* smears on the paper. We're using *your* paper. If we cannot get this problem fixed, we're canceling our contract and going with your competition's product."

Odds are that if the tech rep has not been able to fix the problem on five earlier visits, he won't be able to fix it on the sixth. Count that as a customer lost.

Now, add to the mix a toner community of practice (CoP). One member of the CoP is in the R&D department. Another works in sales. A third is in manufacturing. A fourth is in customer service. They all happen to know everything there is to know about toner; each has a different perspective based on the nature of the work he or she performs. Give that community a site on the intranet. What goes on the site?

- Biographies of each member of the community.
- Access to any documents the CoP members have created, such as memos, reports, or PowerPoint presentations.
- Links to valuable resources on the intranet or out on the World Wide Web.
- A secure discussion area where the members of the CoP can communicate with one another. Anybody can *read* the discussion, allowing him or her to identify the best person to call to address the problem.

Now, the salesperson at risk of losing a customer can contact the toner CoP with his or her question. The tech rep member of the CoP asks about the climate where the copier is located. The desert, the sales rep replies. The CoP member replies, "The lack of humidity can have an effect. You could introduce a humidifier to the room, or switch to different paper that will hold the toner better in dry climates."

Of course, this is a hypothetical example; I don't really know a thing about toner. The question is, What areas of expertise have hidden communities in your organization that could become a visible asset if provided a CoP site on the intranet?

Employee Home Pages

At one telecommunications company, employees are encouraged to create their own home pages. While there are no restrictions to prevent an employee from posting photos of their vacation, a drawing made in school by a child, or a piece of poetry written in the employee's spare time, the primary use of the home pages is work related. It is on these pages where employees indicate, for example, their knowledge areas, interests, special skills, or second languages.

There are a couple of benefits to the employee home page concept. First, if two employees are scheduled to work together on a project but have never met, they can check one another out on their home pages. "Oh, he likes baseball and dogs. I like baseball and dogs, too. We're going to get along great!" That initial discomfort can be erased in a two-minute scan of a personal home page.

More beneficial, though, is the idea that anybody can conduct a search of the home pages looking for employees who speak particular languages, have college degrees in particular areas of expertise, or have experience on certain projects. At the former US West, the Webmaster noted that employees who have created home pages are being tapped for interesting work, while those who have not are being overlooked.

The intranet's multimedia and database capabilities give us an opportunity to communicate in ways that were never available before. Let's briefly review some of the uses of each technology.

Multimedia

Video is nothing new to employee communication efforts. On-demand video, however, is a new feature of the intranet. Multimedia—sound, video, and animation—can be retrieved by employees when they are ready for it. This just-in-time approach to multimedia not only serves the needs of employees but also reduces video production costs by eliminating the need to produce and distribute cassettes.

Live multimedia is equally useful. Employees in field offices can watch live broadcasts of headquarters-based meetings with only a fraction of the investment required to deliver the same content over closed-circuit television.

Databases

We've already addressed some fundamental uses of databases, but we haven't talked yet about using databases to offer employees customizable content.

Your company most likely has loads of data sitting in its databases. Consider sales data as an example. You write an article about quarterly sales results that explains the most important data to the greatest common denominator among your employee audience. Anybody who needs more specific information needs to dig into the data on their own.

Or, you could create a utility to supplement your article, allowing employees to manipulate the data visually. A map of the country features dots of different colors, each color representing a different kind of customer. Employees can use pull-down menus or checkboxes to specify the kind of information they want: "Show me all our retail customers who usually spend over $5 million annually on our products but have not placed an order in the last 90 days." The map redraws, extracting information from the database. Next a smattering of purple dots appears across the entire country, representing only mid-sized mall-based boutiques, allowing the reader to determine something is happening in that marketplace. Or a cluster of many colored dots hovers over Chicago, indicating a problem with the sales office in that region. We're talking about instant visualization of data.

Again, I've never actually seen anything like this on an intranet—but I should. For an example of a more trivial nature, look at the baseball hitting chart on the Major League Baseball Web site. It's exactly the same idea—a way for readers to visualize how a hitter is hitting based on the criteria of interest to the reader.

There's another use of databases implemented recently at IBM on the employee directory. Each employee listing includes various database fields. There's a field for second languages, one for books read, one for fields of subject-matter expertise, one for jobs held, one for college degrees earned, and dozens more. Now, anyone viewing an employee's directory listing can learn all these things about that employee—or, if you conduct a search for employees who speak a particular language, you'll find links to the appropriate employees' listings.

CHAPTER SEVEN

Ongoing Communication

ORGANIZATIONAL COMMUNICATION is often reactive. Company newspapers (and now intranets) cover the news, reporting things that have already happened. There is nothing wrong with telling employees what has happened; it is irresponsible not to. If you do not report on events, employees will learn about them through other channels. Accuracy can be questionable, and even if the information is presented correctly, it is not prepared with the employee audience in mind. Employees who hear reports about the company from the public media, for example, are left to speculate about the impact of the news on their departments or their jobs.

As important as covering the news is, however, it is not the most important aspect of employee communications. Communication that produces business results needs to be ongoing, providing regular, updated information about everything from the company's plans to expectations about how employees will contribute to the success of these plans. Employees need to know about the environment in which the company operates and the factors that could affect the organization (and their jobs). It is two-way, encouraging employee involvement. It reinforces the behaviors that will drive the company's strategies. That is much more than simple reporting. It is:

- *Analytical.* It explains the rationale behind decisions management makes, the conditions that led management to make those decisions, and the results the company's leaders expect to achieve. It assumes that employees are intelligent adults who can understand these issues. For many leaders, that's a tough adjustment to make. In order for employees to decide to commit their energies to the organization, they need to believe that the organization trusts them. Knowing the company treats them as adults is a significant component of earning that trust.

- *Two-way.* Communication that moves only from the top down is not communication; it is informing, instructing, ordering, and reporting. To be communication in the true sense of the word, though, both parties need to engage actively in the process. Communication derives from the agreement of the sender and receiver about the message. One river *communicates* with another when they join together to form a new, larger river; they become common. To reach that kind of commonality in organizational communication, the sender of the message needs to listen as much as talk. In the academic study of public relations, educators have introduced the notion of *two-way symmetrical communication.* To achieve this ideal, the outcome of the communication is balanced between the sender's desired result and the receiver's. If the leaders of the company convince employees to support an initiative that ultimately leads to layoffs, that is not symmetrical. The leaders win, but the employees lose. If, through a process of communication, leaders and employees agree on certain behaviors that will achieve the results the leaders want but also improve working conditions and job satisfaction, that is a *win-win* and symmetry is achieved. Symmetry rarely occurs in a one-way, top-down environment.

The rest of this chapter explores the various types of issues that leaders need to communicate continuously.

The Marketplace

When I was growing up, my father didn't know much about the marketplace in which his company operated. He knew his job. He was an estimator in the production design department of a major film studio. (This was back in the days when the studios still produced the movies they released.) He knew that the designers would send artist's renditions and blueprints to him, and (based on his background as a construction contractor) he would estimate the costs so the producer could calculate production design expenses into the film's overall budget. If the budget was too high, he would often calculate ways to lower the cost. That is what he did, day in and day out. He didn't know about the impact of the economy on a typical family's entertainment expenditures, or how rising ticket prices were affecting movie-going patterns. He didn't worry about the impact of cable television on the frequency with which people went to the movies. The company saw no reason to education him and his fellow workers about issues such as the gradual transition to independent production companies.

That was fine. Most companies operated like that. This was back in the days when the deal was still implicit: Do your job and you'll retire with that gold watch and pension. Under those circumstances, employees didn't need to know much, and they derived their sense of involvement from activities outside of work. For my father, that fulfillment came as a leader in a thriving Boy Scout troop. For others, it was church activities, family, or hobbies.

The deal came to an end in the 1980s. Investors gorged on mergers and acquisitions, sucking profit out of the parts of companies that were profitable and spinning off the rest. Employees who used to know the companies that employed them found themselves in a state of perpetual confusion, uncertain who would own them next week or if they would have a job when they became part of another larger organization. While the binging of the 1980s is a thing of the past, it has left a legacy of job insecurity. No company can assure an employee that it will be able to employ him or her for the next thirty years. In the wake of corporate malfeasance among companies like Enron, Tyco, and WorldCom, many companies are even finding it difficult to credibly promise to pay out retirement income from employees' own investments.

In such an environment, employees want and need to understand the forces at work on the company. They not only want to be able to predict the changes in the wind but also to take whatever actions they can to affect those changes; they want desperately to be *involved*. They are not content to perform their discrete tasks in blissful ignorance of conditions that will affect their futures. They not only want to make a difference, they want to have the information they need to figure out *how* they can make a difference.

Leaders need to implement two critical components of this involvement:

1. They need to ensure that employees understand the dynamics of the marketplace.
2. They need to provide channels through which employees can act on their knowledge and leaders can incorporate employees' ideas into the business plan.

According to research by Watson Wyatt Worldwide, IABC, and the IABC Research Foundation in 1999, high-performing organizations are more successful than other organizations in communicating with and educating their employees. Seventy-seven percent of high-performing organizations' communication programs focused heavily on helping employees understand the business. Conversely, only 64 percent of organizations that do not perform highly consider business education to be an appropriate focus for internal communication.

Communicating the Dynamics of the Marketplace

Business leaders do not make decisions based on whims. In some organizations, though, you'd be hard-pressed to convince employees that management-led change isn't arbitrary and capricious. What else should employees think when they don't have the same background information that led management to make the decision?

In the command-and-control structure of organizations structured in the industrial economy model, lower-level employees trusted management to make decisions in the way that rank-and-file soldiers trust the generals to make decisions about their platoon's next action. In today's companies, employees wonder, "Who the hell is running this place?"

You are already paying dearly for the intelligence that drives your decision making. You will receive much greater value for your investment if you share that information. Employees—with the help of their managers and supervisors—are equipped to understand how that information relates to the work they do and how they might be able to adjust their processes or behaviors in light of the information. They are, in fact, far better equipped to make those decisions than the company's leaders, who simply cannot be intimately familiar with every process that powers the company's engine.

Think about it: Could you walk down to the shipping and receiving department this moment and do the job of a shipping or receiving clerk? You wouldn't have the first clue about the processes involved in logging in shipments and getting them to the right recipient, or how to load those trucks with the product so that it would get to the right customer on time, or who needs to sign what form. That is not your job. But given information about the importance of reduced inventories in a slow economy, or the need to deliver product in a more timely manner, that shipping clerk might just have an answer. After all, it is what he or she does every single day.

The Customer

Employees must know who the company's customers are. They cannot possibly produce the products or services to meet customer needs, help customers solve their problems, or innovate on behalf of the customer if they don't know who the customer is.

Your sales force can be a vital source of information about customers. These are the troops on the front line, the ones who spend more time with customers than they do with fellow employees or management. Most communication to sales reps is traditionally one-way, top-down. The company tells them what to sell, and they inform them about the marketing and merchandising programs the company has developed to help them sell. What the customer *thinks,* though, is knowledge that resides in the heads of the sales reps. A good salesperson, after all, knows how to *listen.*

As a communicator working for a pharmaceutical company, I made sure that I (or a member of my staff) spent a full day each quarter in the field with a sales rep. We went into the doctors' offices and heard what the doctors' concerns were, how they viewed our products against our competitors', how the economy or regulation or insurance companies were affecting their businesses.

We reported on these visits in full-length feature articles in the company magazine. We also profiled customers in every issue of the magazine. These were brief overviews presented in outline form; each profile contained the same categories, including how the customer felt about the service he or she received from our company, the value of the products against competitive offerings, and the key issues the customer faced in his or her practice. The same information can be presented through other media, notably intranets (which didn't exist when I worked for the pharmaceutical company). Intranets make it possible to archive information so that employees can learn about many customers, not only the one per month we were restricted to in print because of space limitations. (Intranets are addressed in detail in Chapter 6.)

In business-to-business companies, you can also glean a great deal of information about your customer from the trade publications that cover the customer's business.

Some other channels for creating the link between employees and customers include the following:

- Videotaped interviews are particularly useful in companies with video magazines.
- On-site visits are beneficial for customers who would *love* to come into the company and meet face-to-face with employees and tell them how they can improve the relationship. Consider making brown-bag lunch sessions open to any employee, and then report on the dialogue through your formal communication channels.
- Summaries of reports submitted by field sales reps about issues customers are facing.
- A general overview of customer segments and issues presented during new-hire orientations.

It is equally important to let your employees know when the customer changes. At a toy company, for example, the increasing divorce rate (a demographic trend) represents a shift in customer profiles. There are, for example, more single parents, many of whom are competing with one another for a child's affection by spending more money on toys. Improving medical innovation and health care lead to more grandparents who live longer. Children of divorced couples who remarried found themselves with multiple sets of grandparents (adding step-grandparents into the mix).

The customer profile goes through a variety of changes based on factors ranging from regulation and legislation (to whom can you legally sell a regulated product?) to shifts in trends (eight-year-old girls are now buying earrings from retailers that cater to their tastes), to the economy (customers who spent liberally during a strong economy pinch pennies when the economy weakens). Employees need to understand these changes if they're going to innovate within their work space on the customer's behalf.

Levi Strauss offered employees an innovative way to understand customers via its intranet named Eureka. The communications department established relationships with customers representing different geographic regions and demographic groups, publishing those interviews quarterly on the intranet. Any employee wanting to know about fashion trends and preferences from a teenager in the Pacific Northwest could click a couple of links and either read the interview or, in some cases, watch the streaming video of the interview. The information presented straight from the customer's mouth could inspire a fashion designer to try something new, a marketer to take a different approach to marketing the product—even laborers who stitched clothes together at the company's plants had a better understanding of why they were producing the kind of clothes they were, increasing their commitment to the company and its products.

The Competition

Nearly as important as knowing the customer, employees should know the companies competing with you for their business. Make sure employees have access to static information about these companies. Your intranet, for example, can include a section in which your competitors are profiled. For each competitor, include the following:

- Name of the company.
- Address and phone number.
- Number of employees.
- Financial data, including sales and earnings.
- Segments in which the company competes directly with yours. This is an important category, because not every competitor competes with you head-to-head. Consider the pharmaceutical company where I worked. The company managed a skin-care division. Several companies competed with our skin-care division, but parts of those companies targeted marketplaces where we did *not* compete. These parts of the business, then, weren't competitive threats to *our* business.
- Key competitive products.
- Market share for competitive segments and products.

An advantage of using your intranet for this information is that you can provide links to competitors' Web sites, one way to ensure that the view your employees have of the competition is current. For example, each product that competes with a product your company makes should include a link to the competitor's page on the World Wide Web that positions that product to the customer segment. Access to this information is useful to a variety of employee groups, such as marketers, advertisers, and customer relations representatives. If a competitor is gaining market share, employees throughout the organization may want to see how that competitor is portraying its products. That intelligence could spark an idea in the unlikeliest of places—an idea that could bring customers back to your offering.

In addition to snapshots of the competition, you should keep employees up-to-date on competitive news. Again, intranets have proven a boon to this effort. Many intranet home pages include a section called something like, "About the Competition." These headlines are generally culled from wire service reports and press release distribution services. (Factiva, for example, is a joint venture of Reuters and Dow Jones that provides subscribers with news feeds on topics of interest to the subscriber from a variety of sources.) Knowing what the competition is up to can help employees identify opportunities within their work spheres to meet competitive threats head-on.

Like knowing the customer, knowing what the competition is up to—and how well it is succeeding—also prepares employees for change. If the company's leadership decides that acquiring another company is the best way to address a challenge from the competition, for example, employees won't be surprised when that acquisition is announced.

Remembering that repetition is an essential part of communication, you should take advantage of other channels to address the competition. Consider some of the following options:

• *Publish a monthly competitive report in any print publications you produce.* A competitor profile might appear in each issue of a company magazine, featuring a quick overview of the competitor, including strengths and weaknesses.

- *Include a competition segment during regular all-hands or managers meetings.* The CEO or COO might address the top two or three competitive issues that have arisen since the last meeting, any that the leadership is anticipating, and provide updates on continuing issues.

- *Invite employees to submit any intelligence they gather about the competition.* Sears, Roebuck & Company and EDS are among the companies that provide space on the intranet for employees to report what they have learned about competitors. Consider Sears as an example. Let's say, hypothetically, that a buyer meeting with a sales rep from a sporting goods manufacturer hears about a new marketing innovation that Target is about to introduce. That employee can enter the information into a text-entry field on the intranet. With the click of a button, management now has access to information about a key competitor not available anywhere else.

The Economy

Economic conditions have the potential to affect the business as much as any other factor, sometimes more. Most businesses are affected by recession, yet it is not unusual for employees not to even know what a recession *is,* even though they hear it referenced on the news repeatedly.

Economic news should be part of the news-reporting mix. Of course, you do not need to ensure that employees see all the economic news; they do not have the time to absorb the entire contents of the *Wall Street Journal* or *MarketWatch.com.* It is incumbent on your business to make sure employees hear about any economic news or news about economic trends that have an impact on your business.

The kinds of economic news to consider reporting, based on the nature of your business and how the economy affects it, include the following:

- Recession-related issues
- Unemployment trends
- Major swings in the markets that affect your business
- Consumer confidence reports
- Key economic indicators, such as gross domestic product, productivity, producer prices, inventories, and orders (released to the markets on a regular basis)
- Foreign influences on your nation's economy

You do not need to go into great detail about these figures. In fact, if you take advantage of your intranet and a news-feed service, you can simply provide links to wire service stories about relevant economic news. It gets more complicated if you rely on print. Consider a single page of a monthly publication (or one page per month of a publication produced more frequently) that covers the key facts. All you need to communicate is the news itself—for example, "Consumer confidence dropped .3 percent last month"—and how it relates to the business—for example, "This could lead to slower sales for our consumer products; as a result, we need to redouble our marketing and merchandising efforts in order to reach our targets for the quarter."

In addition to news of the economy in general, employees need to see the company's financial news. Quarterly earnings and other financial data should be part of the news mix.

Government Issues

Most business is regulated to some extent by federal, state, and local government. Many industries—such as pharmaceutical, energy, and financial companies—are far more heavily regulated than others. New regulations and changes to existing rules can have a significant impact on the company, its performance, and how it does business. Often, leaders fail to inform the workforce that a new regulation has been proposed. When the regulation becomes the rule and the company must change the way it operates, employees are caught by surprise.

To prevent this kind of surprise, regulatory and legislative reports should be another category of news conveyed to employees. You can go a step further when the news is about proposed legislation that could adversely affect the organization. Your employees, in particular those who are committed to the organization's success, stand ready as an advocacy group. You can mobilize them to write letters to their legislators that can ultimately influence whether a bill reaches a vote and, if it does, the outcome of the vote itself.

Aetna, the insurance company, is one example of a company that routinely informs its employees about governmental activities that could affect the insurance company's ability to achieve its goals. The "Aetna Issues" page of the company's intranet, AetNet, includes the following categories:

- *State Government Watch.* News about financial regulatory and legislative activity in each of the states where Aetna does business.
- *Issues Center.* A review of all of the key issues Aetna faces from government.
- *State Presence.* The government relations—that is, lobbying—efforts Aetna maintains in each state where it does business.
- *Member Success Stories.* Features about how people insured by Aetna have affected the course of legislative or regulatory activities.
- *Grassroots Volunteer Program.* Information on how employees can become actively involved in supporting Aetna's interests among government agencies and legislatures.

The site also features a hot-topics box where the most important news is presented, the means for employees to contact their legislators (via an external service called Capitol Connect), and external links to sites on the World Wide Web (such as sites that provide information on legislative activities). The tagline for Aetna's government-focused site conveys the rationale for every company offering this kind of news and information: "A well-informed, motivated workforce is the most powerful competitive weapon we have!"

Business Literacy

For many business leaders, the idea of communicating complex business material—such as financial information, market-share data, and economic trends—to line employees makes little sense. Even if these employees *are* intelligent individuals, it does not mean they have MBAs. CEOs, of course, need to understand this kind of information. An employee working on the factory floor needs a different set of tools for him to do his job. Hence, even if you communicate all this information, most employees won't understand what it means.

This may be true, but it certainly does not *have* to be that way. You can take two approaches to ensuring that employees understand the significance of the business information you share:

1. Use the skills of your professional communications staff to interpret the data into language all employees *can* understand. This will be important as you communicate with supervisors, who will need to explain what the numbers and trends mean to the employees at the local level, working in their departments. (Communicating to supervisors is addressed in Chapter 4.)
2. Make sure employees have the background to understand those numbers and trends as well as you do.

You may laugh at the idea of workers on the factory floor or the oil patch absorbing the rows and columns of a balance sheet with the same acumen of a chief financial officer. But there are compelling reasons to strive for this level of comprehension, not the least of which is this: *Employees cannot affect what they cannot understand.*

Are inventories a concern? An employee in the shipping and

receiving department who grasps the numbers and understands the situation might, based on knowledge of his or her job and the processes that drive it, come up with a way to adjust schedules to improve the flow of parts into the company and finished products out to customers. But if all the information he or she receives relates to the success of the company's softball team, and all he or she is expected to do is the job as outlined in the procedure manual, this employee will never know that the opportunity exists to make a difference to the company's success. In other words, this employee will never be able to apply his or her unique job knowledge to larger company issues. And while that shipping-receiving clerk *can* learn the nuances of a profit statement, it is not likely that company leaders can learn every bit of knowledge that occupies the brains of every single employee across the enterprise.

Teaching employees how to read and interpret critical business data is known as *business literacy*. Providing them with the actual numbers so that they can apply what they know about business to their jobs is known as *open-book management*. There are plenty of books you can read on this subject, and consultants who would be thrilled to help implement an open-book management program for you. For purposes of this discussion, though, we will leave it at this: You need to implement processes and programs that help employees learn what they need to know about the numbers and trends that underlie the company's performance. Employees (like anyone else) cannot fix what they cannot measure.

Some of the means of educating employees include the following:

Training

There are few classes you can offer your employees that will provide a greater return on investment than those that will help them to understand the business and how their work affects the company's performance. Your training department can put together classes that teach the fundamentals of business, such as how to read the annual report. You don't need to reinvent the wheel; classes abound with titles like "Business finance for nonfinancial professionals."

You can develop tiers of classes, one for managers and directors, one for line supervisors, and one for rank-and-file employees. These distinctions recognize the level of comprehension employees at different levels bring to a class. A director or manager with a college education and experience at the management level already has some background, while line employees may have none. (Don't underestimate the rank-and-file, though. These people manage their 401(k) plans and personal investments. Many spend more time with the financial pages while drinking their morning coffee than they do with the sports section.)

Your goal is not to produce MBAs but to develop a workforce that can translate the numbers so they can adjust their efforts to improve the company's overall results. Lest you think this is a pipe dream, look at the case of Springfield Remanufacturing Corp., a company on the brink of failure when a business literacy and open-book management culture was introduced. One news reporter covering the company's turnaround was skeptical that the overall-clad workers he saw on the factory floor genuinely understood the business of the company. He selected one at random and shoved a microphone in his face. "What is the value of that piece of machinery you're working on?" he asked. Without missing a beat, the grease-stained worker looked up at him and asked, "Do you mean the cost of raw materials or the value of goods sold?"

Communicating bottom-line business performance alone is not sufficient. Anybody who has ever managed a plant or factory knows that employees need to know the metrics the company uses to measure its performance. Units produced, units shipped, and other site-specific performance is equally (if not more) important to employees in terms of managing their own efforts than overall business results. But these employees also need to understand how their local performance ties in to the achievement of overall business goals. If they do not, all the talk from company leaders about macrolevel strategies is merely irrelevant rhetoric.

Consider the company that assesses business success on formulas so complex that the average employee, no matter how thorough his or her understanding of business, cannot comprehend how his or her endeavors can possibly affect it. "It's a black box," one business leader told me. "It's influenced more by the sale of real estate than anything an employee can do." This kind of measure is certain to serve as a disincentive to employees who figure their efforts do not count for much and cannot possibly influence business outcomes—so why bother? There is *always* a way to accurately show how bottom-line business performance depends on employees doing their jobs at their local work sites.

An Intranet Business Literacy Site

Your intranet can serve as an always-open library with always-available resources on the business. A business literacy site can include the following:

- Glossary of terms
- How-to guides for reading the annual report and other financial data, including leading economic indicators
- Overviews of all key demographic groups upon which the company depends for business
- Capsules of key customer segments

In fact, the intranet's business literacy site doesn't need to contain all original content. In addition to material generated uniquely for the site, you can also provide links to other parts of the intranet where information on customers and competition resides, and to external World Wide Web resources (such as the Conference Board's economic reports).

Articles

One of the benefits of print is that people actually *read* it. As noted in Chapter 5 in the Print section, research proves that people are far more likely to merely *scan* information on the computer screen. Since you're going to maintain some kind of print vehicle to leverage its strengths (aren't you?), you can use it to enhance business literacy by:

- *Offering a regular feature about an aspect of the business.* The feature could be the meaning of continuing operations, the definition of depreciation and how it relates to the company's activities, or the difference between overhead and assets for which the company pays overtime.
- *Covering the news behind the numbers.* For those numbers that are important to the company's success, report on the latest updates. You should treat employees no differently than the financial community—analysts, institutional investors, and the *Wall Street Journal*—in terms of reporting quarterly and annual performance.

At Amalgamated Pulp & Paper

Management has determined the need to lay off 10 percent of the company's headquarters staff. In a case of bad timing, the company's leadership will announce the cutbacks at about the same time the new company cafeteria is to be opened. It is a state-of-the-art cafeteria, with a waterfall for ambience and gourmet foods. It is clear that employees will resent the cafeteria. They would have been content to continue eating at the old high-school-like cafeteria if it meant a colleague or two could have kept their jobs.

Anticipating the negative reaction from employees, the internal communications manager recommends communicating *proactively* the difference between overhead (such as an employee's salary) and a physical asset (the company would be paying for the cafeteria for the next ten years). By doing so, she argues, employees will understand that the cafeteria and the layoff are mutually exclusive. The company's leadership resists the idea, asserting that this communication would create a fire where there was none.

The day the cafeteria is opened with a ribbon-cutting ceremony, employee resentment bubbles over. The company winds up producing the communication *reactively.* While this is better than not communicating the business rationale at all, Amalgamated could have avoided any disgruntlement at all by ensuring that employees understand the business foundations for both decisions and that no jobs would have been saved by scrapping plans to build the cafeteria.

Products and Services

It is downright embarrassing when your employees cannot talk intelligently about the products and services that represent the company's core offerings. The fact that so many employees *cannot* is a failure of leadership. The old expectation—"They work here, don't they? They should know what we sell"—doesn't wash. Business is complex, and employees will best understand the company's offerings if the company makes a concerted effort to introduce them.

The intranet is an ideal place to maintain a repository of information about all the company's products and services. Because databases can underlie your product site, it becomes easy to develop cross-referencing that can, for example, lead a salesperson to identify a new sales opportunity based on what a customer has already bought.

One financial services company was developing such a database designed to provide all marketing information on every one of the company's thousands of products. Here, an employee could find everything from the sixty-second elevator speech to PDF files of four-color brochures for each product, or look up the appropriate product based on the needs of a customer. Of course, the repository also included all product specifications and contact information for everyone, from the product manager to the sales manager.

Product Launches

A product launch is a cause for celebration—and education. Limiting the festivities to the product team also restricts the ability of other employees to serve as ambassadors of the product to the communities with which they interact. Imagine an investor relations manager who couldn't extol the virtues of a new product to the investment analysts who cover the company. While most employees don't interact with constituencies as influential as Goldman Sachs analysts, they do have certain influence with buyers, vendors, social groups, members of trade or professional associations, even neighbors and relatives. In any case, it sends a sad signal when an employee, asked about a product launched with fanfare by the company, cannot endorse it because "I really don't know anything about it."

Additionally, sharing the pride of launching a new product instills pride in the workforce at large; they feel as if they are part of the introduction. Any communication at the worksite level that helps employees understand the role they played in the product's development—or will play in its success in the marketplace—serves to affect company morale. You cannot be a mindless cog in an industrial machine when you are an integral part of the company's engine of success.

CHAPTER EIGHT

Communicating Bad News

IF ORGANIZATIONS FALTER at any aspect of communicating, it is in the act of communicating bad news. Leaders resist sharing bad news with employees for many reasons. For example, because they're afraid of losing their top-performing employees, leaders withhold bad news to keep them on board. Some leaders hope that they will be able to solve the problem before communication is absolutely necessary. Many leaders are just plain uncomfortable talking about bad news.

Then, there are those who view the vast mass of the employee population as being unable to cope with bad news, believing them to be too low-level, too unsophisticated.

If you have found yourself uttering these rationalizations, make a trip to your plant floor, or the retail floor, or the mine, or the fields, or wherever it is your front-line employees do their work. Pick some workers at random and talk to them. Do it now. Go on, put the book down.

So, how did it go? If your experience is the same as other senior leaders, you were surprised. When viewed as individuals instead of as part of a collective, it is easy to see that these are people who probably can understand and cope with bad news as well as anyone. They are (with a few exceptions) mature adults who manage household finances, pay mortgages, and own rental properties. Some refurbish classic cars in their spare time. Some are active in Boy Scouts or Kiwanis or Rotary or Elks. Some help their spouses run a business.

Imagine how it must feel to an employee who finally learns bad news that has been withheld by the company's leaders. What must that feeling do to the degree of trust that once existed between the employee and the company? The fact is, communicating bad news, when done effectively, can *increase* trust, ultimately leading to heightened employee commitment. Employees, remember, do not need to *like* what they hear; they only need to understand it and believe the company was candid and honest with them.

In any case, employees will find out about bad news even if the company doesn't share it with them. No employee believes all the news from the company will be rosy all the time. As for the bad news that does occur, they will hear it through that grapevine that is so much more effective when there is no authoritative source of information. They may hear it from the media. And the Internet has spawned a new source of information for employees to find details online. (Many of the online sources are less than flattering to companies. Web sites like The Vault and F★cked Company provide news with a sardonic spin to which many organizations would take umbrage.) You might as well be first to communicate, ensuring that employees hear the real story and taking advantage of the opportunity to enhance the bond of trust you share with your employees.

A Plan Is Needed to Communicate Bad News

No matter what kind of bad news you are communicating, your communication should be geared to get the desired results: trust, continued commitment to goals, and a focus on the tasks that need to be performed regardless of distractions, no matter how large. Communicating bad news effectively begins with a plan. In fact, your bad-news communication plan shouldn't be different from any other communication plan in using the same steps. As in any other communication plan, you need to begin with a goal. For example, if you are communicating a layoff, your goals might be to maintain productivity while retaining key employees. In a reorganization, you will seek employee support for the outcomes you have established. For a merger, your goal is for the reshaped company to get off to a fast start. You will issue a call to action when faced with a competitive threat. If you are launching a new identity, your goal is for employees to embrace and reflect that new image. And if you're trying to affect a change to the company's culture, your employees should drive that change. Strategies, objectives, and tactics all flow from your goals.

If you are communicating well, you need never ask: "How do we communicate this bad news?" You simply communicate the way you always do.

Basic Guidelines for Communicating Bad News

While there are nuances to each of the categories of bad news, you should adhere to some general guidelines regardless of the nature of the news.

Tell Employees First

Let employees know the bad news as soon as you can, and certainly before it gets to external audiences. (This presumes that you aren't required by regulation—such as SEC rules—to communicate first to financial markets.) Don't wait for all the facts. The media will cover the bad news before you have all the facts, and the grapevine won't wait for complete information. Tell employees what you *do* know, and make it clear that the information is not complete; you'll provide updates as quickly as possible when new information becomes available.

Don't simply share with employees the same information you will distribute to the media or other external audiences. Craft messages specifically for employees that address the impact of the news on them.

Among your employees, you should share the news first with supervisors if at all possible. This will prepare supervisors for the questions their employees will ask of them, specifically in terms of how the news will affect their departments or their jobs.

Once the media begin covering your news, ensure that employees can see what the media are saying. The creation of a spot on your intranet that highlights media coverage—and provides links to World Wide Web sites where employees can read media stories for themselves—helps show that the company has nothing to hide. It can help prevent rumors from spreading later, after employees have read media coverage on their own that the company hasn't acknowledged.

Deal with Rumors

Have a plan for dealing with the inevitable rumors that will arise as events unfold. Ideally, you already have a mechanism for addressing rumors, such as a rumor center on your intranet. If not, you should establish a process for identifying rumors and responding to them quickly, before they spread through the grapevine and become accepted as fact.

Be Candid and Comprehensive

Start off by telling employees what happened and how it happened. Don't leave it at that, though. Be sure to cover the following information:

- What alternatives were explored to address the problem?
- What decision was finally made?
- What process was used to make the decision?
- Who made the decision?
- What were the difficulties in making the decision?

- How does the decision align with the company's values, mission, or vision?
- How will the decision affect the company?
- How will the decision affect employees?
- What does the company need and/or expect from employees for the decision to be effective?

Be sure to sympathize with any deleterious impact the decision will have on employees. Although employees might not like negative effects, they will respect a company that clearly cares enough about its employees to articulate how difficult it was to make the decision.

Focus on the Future

While you need to show concern for employees who are affected—for example, in a layoff, explain what is being done for those employees who are leaving—your focus should remain on the outcomes the company seeks as a result of the decision it has made. Concentrate on the vision for turning the situation around. Talk about the rewards and recognition employees can earn by keeping their eyes on the goal.

At the same time, you should avoid making promises you may not be able to keep. For example, don't project the outcome of the decision management has made if you aren't 100 percent certain that the company can achieve the outcome. If there is any chance the desired results won't pan out, don't assure employees that they will see that result.

Be specific about what employees need to do to contribute to the problem's solution, including any targets that must be reached. For example, if sales must increase by 15 percent, say so.

Be Visible

Too often, leaders go into hiding when employees are digesting bad news. Leaders need to be visible and accessible when the company is coping with bad news. It may not be the most pleasant aspect of your job, but it is the reason why you are a leader.

There are many ways to achieve visibility. Management by Wandering Around (MBWA) is one. Senior leaders should be seen eating in the cafeteria and talking to employees at their job sites.

Visibility can also be attained online. Executive chats represent one good example of how a senior leader can be visible to all employees at once without leaving his or her office.

Evaluate the Results

Like any other communication plan, you will want to know how well your bad-news communication worked. Ideally, the results will indicate that while employees don't like the news, they *do* understand the situation and the company's plans for dealing with it.

Types of Bad News

There are several types of bad news to consider, such as the following:

- Layoffs and other employment-related news
- Business performance news
- Externally generated news
- Crises

Layoffs and Other Employment-Related News

News that directly affects employees is often the kind of news we most want to avoid disclosing. The announcement of an impending layoff will demoralize workers faster than nearly any other type of news. Yet, it is this type of news that most needs to be communicated effectively if there is any hope of retaining employee commitment during this difficult time.

A workforce reduction is as traumatic an experience as an organization can have—and it seems more and more organizations are experiencing the trauma on a regular basis. Layoffs don't occur all of a sudden—at least, not in the eyes of management, which has been trying long and hard to find a way out of the situation without resorting to job losses. But denying that a layoff is likely (or delaying an announcement) leads to different perceptions by employees than those held by management.

Management usually delays in an effort to retain key employees—those top performers we've talked so much about. By insisting that layoffs were not on the table, management hoped to lock these employees in while they found a way to implement reductions among less vital parts of the employee population.

Employees, of course, knew what was coming. The media had been reporting on the company's financial situation for months, and lately the press has been predicting layoffs as the only remaining solution. The top performers never find it hard to land another job, even when the economy is suffering, so many of them left the organization anyway. As for those who would eventually become the targets of the layoff—the less critical employees—work performance began to suffer as fear of layoffs set in and employees spent more time talking about it, spreading rumors, and generally brooding.

Information abhors a vacuum. In the absence of authoritative information, employees made their decisions based on the information they had—which came from the media and the grapevine. News stories predicting the layoff were more credible than management's pronouncements that layoffs wouldn't happen.

Management would have been better served in this instance to answer honestly:

> "We're hoping to avoid layoffs, we're making every effort to address the financial situation without affecting our workforce, but we simply don't know if we'll be successful. There are too many factors in play, including our sales over the next quarter, interest rates, and a number of other indicators. We'll keep you advised as soon as we know more.

In the meantime, avoiding layoffs starts with producing excellent products our customers will want to buy, so your efforts will be critical to our success."

Benefits Changes

Benefits reductions are not as traumatic as layoffs, but they are nevertheless serious announcements. They affect all employees and often serve to underscore deeper problems in the organization.

You cannot make employees happy about reducing their benefits. Your goal when communicating benefits takeaways is to gain acceptance. Guidelines for communicating benefit changes include:

- *Explain any new choices employees may need to make.* Let them know the differences between their options. For example, they may be able to move from a PPO to an HMO, so you need to explain the differences. Employees may be able to continue making the same contribution to their health-care coverage but get less in their plan, or increase their contribution to retain the elements of their current plan. Be clear about the options.
- *Explain the reasons for the change.* Any communication of a benefits reduction needs to incorporate an element of education focusing on the true cost of health care to a company and the impact of those costs on product pricing and competitiveness.
- *Tell employees what they can do to hold their costs down.* Let them know that the less often that they get sick, for example, the less the company will spend on health care, which could reduce costs. Thus, everything from proper diet and exercise to smoking cessation can have an impact over the long term on health care costs.
- *Don't let human resources be the scapegoat for bad benefits news.* The initial announcement should come from senior leadership.
- *Make sure human resources representatives are equipped with answers to the questions they will be asked.* In your communication planning, try to anticipate all the questions employees may have.

• *Use multiple media to communicate.* Face-to-face is always the best choice, but you can also distribute print and populate the intranet with appropriate information (including an FAQ—a frequently asked questions document).

At Amalgamated Pulp & Paper

In an effort to hold the line on health-care costs, Amalgamated has introduced a utilization review (UR) program to its medical benefits program. (Under a UR program, an insurance company's health-care specialists review a doctor's recommendations and authorize insurance coverage for only as much health care as the specialist deems necessary. The goal is to reduce the number of days an employee stays in the hospital and the number of unnecessary procedures.) Unwilling to confide in employees the reason for the new policy, based on the belief that employees would neither comprehend the situation nor care about the effect on the company, the organization has chosen to introduce the plan as a benefit. "You'll avoid unnecessary medical procedures," the company told employees; "we're doing this for you."

Employees saw through the lie immediately. Not only did they resent the new hoop through which they had to jump, they also resented the company for making such a blatant and clumsy attempt to justify what they viewed as an impediment to getting needed health care.

At Allied Gate & Fence, the same UR program was introduced in a different fashion:

At Allied Gate & Fence

Throughout the year, Allied's HR department has been keeping employees up-to-speed on the health-care crisis in the United States. Through regular updates in the company's print publication and on its intranet, HR has shown how costs have been rising. Employees know how much the company pays for its employee medical coverage, and the small percentage absorbed by employees. Charts and graphs project the cost over the next couple of years, and simple models explain how the company needs to increase the cost of its products and services to customers to absorb the increase—and how those increased costs will affect the company's ability to compete in the marketplace.

In addition to this explanation, the company has offered employees a way to get involved. Links on the intranet provide access to advocacy sites where employees can write their legislators or sign petitions protesting insurance company costs, the tort system that allows for frivolous medical-related lawsuits, and other avenues of activism.

The introduction of a UR program comes as no surprise to employees who have been monitoring the situation through the company's ongoing communications for many months. The company apologizes for the inconvenience the UR may cause, noting that it was the least onerous option (the company opted not to increase employee contributions). Finally, the communications note that there *are* some advantages to the UR, which has been known to prevent unnecessary surgeries and excessive hospital stays. But the crux of the communication remains focused on the connection to the marketplace the company has worked so hard to establish and the impact of the UR program on employees.

Business Performance News

If your company's performance is going to improve, you must rely on employees to help make it happen. Thus, they are a key audience with whom you should candidly share news about faltering business performance.

As the example of Amalgamated Pulp & Paper has shown, sometimes the best way to learn how to do something is to see how it is done badly. In terms of communicating poor business performance, there are hardly any worse examples than the widely reported e-mail message from the CEO, distributed to managers of Cerner Corporation's Kansas City managers. Cerner had been one of *For-*

tune's 100 best companies in America to work for, but you would be hard-pressed to tell from the e-mail CEO Neal Patterson distributed, which was widely reported and reprinted in U.S. newspapers and Web sites:

I have gone over the top. I have been making this point for over one year. We are getting less than 40 hours of work from a large number of our KC-based EMPLOYEES.

The parking lot is sparsely used at 8 A.M.; likewise at 5 P.M. As managers—you either do not know what your EMPLOYEES are doing; or YOU do not CARE. You have created expectations of the work effort which allowed this to happen inside Cerner, creating a very unhealthy environment.

In either case, you have a problem and you will fix it or I will replace you.

NEVER in my career have I allowed a team which worked for me to think they had a 40-hour job. I have allowed YOU to create a culture which is permitting this. NO LONGER.

At the end of next week, I am planning to implement the following:

1. Closing of Associate Center to EMPLOYEES from 7:30 A.M. to 6:30 P.M.

2. Implementing a hiring freeze for all KC-based positions. It will require Cabinet approval to hire someone into a KC-based team. I chair our Cabinet.

3. Implementing a time clock system, requiring EMPLOYEES to "punch in" and "punch out" to work. Any unapproved absences will be charged to the EMPLOYEE'S vacation.

4. We passed a Stock Purchase Program, allowing for the EMPLOYEES to purchase Cerner stock at a 15 percent discount, at Friday's BOD meeting. Hell will freeze over before this CEO implements ANOTHER EMPLOYEE benefit in this Culture.

5. Implement a 5 percent reduction of staff in KC.

6. I am tabling the promotions until I am convinced that the ones

being promoted are the solution, not the problem. If you are the problem, pack your bags.

I think this parental-type action SUCKS. However, what you are doing, as managers, with this company makes me SICK. It makes me sick to have to write this directive.

I know I am painting with a broad brush and the majority of the KC-based associates are hard working, committed to Cerner success, and committed to transforming health care. I know the parking lot is not a great measurement for "effort." I know that "results" is what counts, not "effort." But I am through with the debate.

We have a big vision. It will require a big effort. Too many in KC are not making the effort. . . .

I STRONGLY suggest that you call some 7 A.M., 6 P.M., and Saturday A.M. team meetings with the EMPLOYEES who work directly for you. Discuss this serious issue with your team. I suggest that you call your first Meeting—tonight. Something is going to change.

I am giving you two weeks to fix this. My measurement will be the parking lot: it should be substantially full at 7:30 A.M. and 6:30 P.M. The pizza man should show up at 7:30 P.M. to feed the starving teams working late. The lot should be half full on Saturday mornings. We have a lot of work to do.

If you do not have enough to keep your teams busy, let me know immediately.

Folks this is a management problem, not an EMPLOYEE problem.

Congratulations, you are management. You have the responsibility for our EMPLOYEES. I will hold you accountable. You have allowed this to get to this state. You have two weeks. Tick, tock.

> Neal . . .
> Chairman & Chief Executive Officer
> Cerner Corporation
> "We Make Health Care Smarter"

Can you imagine the feeling managers had in their guts when they received this missive? Patterson didn't want managers' ideas. He didn't address the reasons for the problem, if he knew them at all.

He didn't discuss a process for fixing the problem. He just said, "Here's the bad news, it's your fault, I'm punishing all of you now and I'll punish some of you even more. Now fix the problem for me." It is a classic case of how *not* to communicate bad news.

Patterson's approach to addressing his problem is an extreme example of leaders who believe employees should live and breathe the company's vision merely because they are getting a paycheck. If performance is suffering, Patterson (and you) should adhere to the following guidelines:

- Find out the underlying root cause of the problem. (In Cerner's case, why is the parking lot not full early in the morning or late in the afternoon? Is it because employees are taking work home? Or are employees leaving early because they lack commitment to the organization and only do as much as they need to to get by?)
- Explain the performance problem and how it affects the business.
- Explain the desired state of affairs.
- Make it clear how employees contribute to the vision.
- Do not simply mete out punishments, such as closing the employee recreation center. Let employees know what the rewards are and how they can reap those rewards.
- Give employees a forum for contributing their own ideas about how to address the problem.

Externally Generated News

Some bad news has its genesis outside the organization. Often, the media report an event or disclosure about the organization. The company's lawyers counsel leadership to stay mum on the issue. "We'll take care of it in court," they say.

The attorneys may well be able to address the legal concerns in court. Meanwhile, the fallout from your silence could have consequences farther-reaching than anything the legal system might have forced down your throat.

At Amalgamated Pulp & Paper

A law firm filed a class-action lawsuit against Amalgamated, claiming that one of the company's paper products contained an ingredient that made customers violently ill.

Following legal advice, the organization enacted a "no-comment" policy on the issue. "Anything we say can be used against us in court," the general counsel insisted. "If we don't say anything, nobody can ever claim we admitted to anything."

Employees are among the audiences noting the company's silence. Several wonder if the silence belies guilt. Even those who know the product couldn't possibly have caused any harm are distressed at the company's apparent lack of compassion for customers who may be suffering. Most of all, though, employees are confused about the company's lack of response. They don't know what to tell their family, friends, and neighbors when asked about the lawsuit. Finding themselves in a position where all they can do is stammer, they begin to resent the company's lack of trust in them.

By the time the lawsuit goes to trial, the company has lost 20 percent of its high-performing employees, who have defected to more candid and trusting competitors. Morale among those who are left has plummeted, affecting product quality and customer perceptions of the organization. Profits have fallen and the company's reputation has taken a measurable hit.

How could Amalgamated have dealt with the news of the lawsuit? How about a statement like this:

"A class-action lawsuit filed against Amalgamated claims that an ingredient in our professional-grade laser paper has penetrated the skin of users and caused a number of illnesses.

"It is Amalgamated's policy to never discuss pending litigation publicly. However, we wanted our employees to know where we stand on this issue.

"First, the company sympathizes with those who are suffering regardless of the cause.

"Our products, however, are 100 percent safe. Our papers contain no ingredients that can cause an illness, and no change has been made to our manufacturing processes that would account for a sudden outbreak of illnesses among people using our paper. We consume over 10,000 reams of this grade paper internally for our own photocopying and computer printing purposes and no employees using the paper have reported any illness. Employees using our laser paper can continue to feel secure and safe. However, any employee who is uncomfortable using the paper is welcome to switch to our lighter-grade all-purpose office paper while the legal matter is being resolved.

"Our media relations policy is in effect for this lawsuit. Should you be contacted by a member of the press for information about the lawsuit, please point them to the media relations department without further comment.

"If you have any questions, please direct them to your supervisor."

The company made no admissions. It expressed concern for an affected constituency, displaying compassion to its employees. It allowed employees to take action based on their own comfort levels. And it ensured that employees had answers and knew where to go for additional information.

Crises

The lawsuit illustrated in the Amalgamated case study was foisted on the company by an outside source—a law firm. If the lawsuit had been unexpected, it could have been classified as a crisis.

Some crises arise when a public (like customers) have an issue with the company. Many crises can be averted through the practice of issues management. (In order to "manage" an issue, you must know what it is before it boils over into a crisis. Then, you can engage the interested public groups to find common ground and identify solutions. This is the heart of public relations.) Sometimes, though, issues arise too quickly to manage. Exxon, for example, had no time to address the issue of tanker safety when the *Valdez* began pouring oil into Alaska's Prince William Sound.

Employees are often a neglected audience during a crisis, despite the fact that they represent one of the most affected of all groups. They will be identified with the company in crisis by everyone from friends and neighbors to vendors and partners. They may well have a part to play in handling the crisis. And how they behave could have an impact on the reputation with which the company emerges from the crisis.

There are, in fact, several types of crises, such as the following:

- *Meteor crises* are those that cannot be anticipated. They are random, senseless, and impossible to predict. In most meteor crises (so named because they seem to fall from the sky), the company is a victim. Still, the confidence various audiences have in the organization is at risk. Whether the organization is seen as innocent or guilty, blameless or culpable, depends on how it responds. Examples of meter crises include a workplace shooting, a product tampering, or an accidental fatality on the job.
- *Predator crises* occur when somebody with an issue raises it publicly. Generally, the organization is not a victim in a predator crisis, which usually results in damaged reputation and credibility. An employee disclosing confidential documents that contradict the company's stated position is a predator crisis. (This was the case when an employee of a tobacco company gave boxes of documentation to a television news magazine.) A labor dispute with a union that goes public is a predator crisis, as are lawsuits and boycotts.
- *Breakdown crises* represent a failure of the company to perform—it is something the organization does to itself. Product liability or a safety accident can represent breakdown crises if they occurred because a company policy was ignored or a shortcut taken around proper procedures.

In any crisis, organizations strive to achieve specific objectives, such as:

- Presenting and maintaining a positive image of the company
- Presenting timely, accurate, up-to-date information
- Remaining accessible
- Monitoring communication channels to catch misinformation early
- Maintaining constituent support
- Surviving the crisis

For employees, we can add to this list:

- Maintaining productivity and profitability
- Minimizing the distraction the crisis is causing
- Retaining key employees
- Ensuring that employees reflect well on the company in their interactions with other constituent audiences

A Step Beyond Communication: Mobilizing Employees in a Crisis

Most of a company's communication during a crisis will serve the first three objectives: maintaining productivity and profitability, minimizing the distraction, and retaining key employees. Not many organizations, however, consider that employees who support the company could become a force to be reckoned with.

At Allied Gate & Fence

Allied's CEO learns that a local congressional representative is planning to introduce legislation that would require gate and fence installers to be bonded. Since installers never enter homes, the requirement is absurd, but the congressional representative is capitalizing on fear that sprung from media coverage of a crime committed by a fence installer. The installer in question was an independent contractor, and not an employee of a reputable company like Allied.

The CEO videotapes a brief message to employees; the message is digitized and made available as a streaming media file over the company's intranet. Employees learn about the video through a brief e-mail. In his message, the CEO explains the situation and expresses his outrage that anybody would paint his employees with the same brush used to paint a lone criminal. Adding insult to injury, he says, is the notion that Allied could be penalized when it has never done anything wrong. At the end of the message, he invites employees to visit a site on the intranet where they can sign a petition.

By the end of the week, nearly five thousand employees had signed the petition which says, in effect, "We work in the gate and fence industry, we're conscientious people who are proud of our efforts, and we vote." The signatures are placed in a newspaper advertisement in the congressional representative's home district.

Within days, the legislation is withdrawn.

You can mobilize employees to any number of tasks if they believe in the cause and the objective is consistent with their own interests. In the previous Allied Gate & Fence example, employee pride was at stake, not to mention some of the company's profits and productivity. Employees can write letters, join a company speaker's bureau, and talk to their friends, neighbors, and family.

Carrying this notion one step further, employees often want to know what they can do to help during a crisis. Imagine the employees at Union Carbide when poisonous gas leaked from a plant in Bhopal, India, and killed thousands of people. Or imagine the employees of any airline when a plane crashes. Employees may be willing to staff a volunteer center, answer telephones, or even take part in a cleanup effort. Most employees probably won't, but for those who do desire to be part of the company's solution, it shows that the company is thinking of them when it offers information about what employees can do to pitch in.

In any event, employees will want information, and they will want it from the company. Several years ago, a life-flight helicopter transporting a patient to a hospital went missing in the mountains of New Mexico. A communicator from the hospital attended all the sheriff's department briefings, drafting e-mail updates and sending them to employees directly from the sheriff's station. Employees knew they would get information fastest and most reliably from the company instead of from a third party.

Your Intranet in a Crisis

Part of the job of answering employee needs during a crisis can be dealt with in advance. If you have an intranet, you can set up crisis templates that include the kind of information that never changes, such as contact telephone numbers and media relations policies, for example. The rest can be filled in whenever a crisis emerges.

The intranet can serve as an extraordinary crisis communication tool. Consider the following uses:

- *Information aggregator.* An intranet crisis page should (among other things) provide links to all relevant information that resides elsewhere on your intranet. For example, in a product recall, one link directs employees to general recall policies. Another link might direct employees to the manufacturing procedures for retrofitting recalled parts when they arrive. A third links to the official language of the recall. A fourth summarizes media coverage of the recall.
- *Listing of how to help.* List the various opportunities for employees to lend a hand.
- *Rumor center.* Post official responses to any rumors that have surfaced. You can also consider letting employees contribute rumors they have heard so you can deal with them fast, before they have an opportunity to spread.
- *Updates.* Whenever new information is available, publish it on the in-

tranet. (You can also send an e-mail bulletin notifying employees that the update has been posted.)

- *Executive chat.* In a crisis, employees want to hear directly from leaders. Consider a live, real-time chat as a means of reaching all employees at one time. (This was the approach Sears, Roebuck & Company CEO Alan Lacey took after the September 11 terrorist attacks, leading employees to feel a deeper connection with an organization that was sympathetic to their feelings and concerns.)

In addition, your intranet can serve as a resource for the employees who manage the crisis. A crisis management site that sits ready for action when a crisis strikes can contain the following:

- A document archive, including document management so members of the crisis team can check out, revise, and check back in documents like statements and press releases
- An image archive—for example, facility photos or executive mug shots
- Travel schedules for all members of the crisis management team
- A message board where team members can communicate with one another

CHAPTER NINE

Communicating Change

CHANGE HAPPENS. How many times have you heard that change is the only constant? How often have you read Machiavelli's quote about change being the most perilous activity leaders can undertake?

In business, change occurs more rapidly than in almost any other venue. Companies change their long-term strategies in midstream to correct for changes in the economy or the marketplace, new technologies, and a host of other factors. Change can range from short-term budget adjustments to acquisitions, divestitures, and mergers—and everything in between.

Some change happens to your company whether you want it to or not. Other change occurs because you desire it. In either case, the success of the change depends on planning and communication. Successful change doesn't happen simply because you want it to. Change must be supported by effective internal communication. Otherwise, how do people know the company wants them to change? How can they understand why they should go along with the change? Or exactly how they are supposed to change?

Change Management

Change management involves people in the organizational change process; it builds commitment to the outcomes of change and supports employees' ability to deal with change. These processes and outcomes are functions of communication, not as an exchange of information but rather as influence to achieve change and build relationships.

Most business change efforts fail. Many factors account for these failures, but resistance is the primary reason. Management frequently views resistance as the enemy, as destructive, disloyal employee efforts to block or alter the change upon which management has embarked.

Reasons to Resist

People resist change for many reasons, such as the following:

- *Self-interest.* Employees get comfortable with the way things are for many reasons, but none is more compelling than the success they have achieved under the status quo. Employees have advanced to positions of authority, they have earned rewards and recognition, or they have launched new products or implemented new programs based on existing systems and processes. Employees often perceive that change will threaten continued success.
- *Fear of the unknown.* Employees know how things are done under the status quo. Will they be able to learn the new systems or acquire the skills required to work within a new environment? Will they be able to fulfill a new role?
- *Conflicting beliefs.* People may sincerely believe that your decision to change is wrong. They may view the situation from a different angle, or they may have aspirations for themselves or the organization that are fundamentally opposed to yours.
- *Lack of trust.* People may not trust you. This has little to do with the change effort and more to do with the efficacy of your ongoing communication efforts. But if there is no trust, employees will suspect the motivation behind your decision to change.

Whatever the reason, some resistance is inevitable. Even if your employees believe that the change through which your organization is going is a good idea, they may still resist it.

Resistance can be overt or covert. Open, observable resistance is the easiest to deal with. You can see it, assess it, and figure out how to overcome it. It is the covert resistance that is dangerous. People pay lip service to the change in meetings then go back to work and passively resist. Covert resistance is impossible to manage because it cannot be confronted. It must be flushed out into the open where it can be managed.

Overcoming Resistance to Change

The following three elements underlie any communication plan to overcome resistance to change:

1. *The desire to change.* No one changes unless they are motivated. Motivation requires a compelling reason to change—one that takes into account the four levels of communication addressed earlier (logistics, attention, relevance, and influence). Employees must believe that the outcome of the change is more desirable than standing still, and that the change will result in benefits not possible under the status quo.
2. *The ability to change.* If employees are motivated, they must be assured they will get the help they need to develop the requisite skills. One thing that holds people back is the ingrained beliefs and behaviors that cause them to doubt their ability to change.
3. *The permission to change.* Those in power and authority must grant permission for people to change. The corporate culture must be conducive to the change.

Underlying any strategies to overcome resistance must be an openness to share information, to communicate about the change thoroughly, frequently, and honestly. So, how do you manage change?

Establish a Sense of Urgency

People need a reason to change, to do something different. If your communication efforts already focus employees on the marketplace, establishing a connection between employees and the conditions that underlie your business, much of this work is already done. If not, you will need to expend considerable effort in making a compelling case to employees that the current situation is worse than the unknowns associated with change.

Create the Vision for Change

Once people understand the sense of urgency, employees will want to know where they are going to be led. They will want a clear direction to a better future, and they expect the company's leaders to provide that vision. Failed change efforts are characterized by plans and directives but no vision. For employees to share this vision, it must be clear and understandable. You and your team—and, ultimately, your managers and supervisors—should be able to communicate it in less than five minutes.

Communicate the Vision

Don't keep the vision secret. The leader's first task is to communicate the vision every day—aggressively, frequently, and face-to-face. Furthermore, leadership behaviors must reflect the vision.

Empower Employees to Implement Change

Leaders must open the door for employees to innovate processes and work methods that support the change in their jobs without being hampered or trapped by the old way of doing things. Leaders must remove obstacles, especially the showstoppers. They must ensure that the systems, structures, and processes in the organization are aligned with the new vision and strategy.

Create Short-Term Wins

Employees need to see results within fairly short time frames, usually within twelve to twenty-four months. Short-term wins validate the effort and maintain the sense of urgency. It is equally important to recognize and reward these short-term successes. Reward and recognition shine a spotlight on the behaviors the company desires in support of the change.

Embed the Change in the Organization

You must connect the new employee behaviors that reflect the spirit of the change effort with bottom-line business success, showing that the new ways are here to stay.

Communicating Change

Planned communication is essential during each of the three critical phases of change. There is nothing magical about these phases. They are simply signposts on a timeline: before, during, and after the change initiative. Your communication efforts during these phases should play the following roles:

Counselor

In the world of public relations, the professionals who work with clients are not known as consultants. Instead, they are counselors. In many instances, this is merely a label—they don't actually provide counsel as much as follow client instructions. But the idea is correct. As counselors, communicators can review company plans and advise management about the best means to communicate them—or, when appropriate, let management know that no method will effectively communicate an unsound message. For example:

- You cannot successfully communicate a bad change initiative.
- You cannot motivate employees to embrace business practices that are contrary to their own interests.
- You cannot convince employees to support a change by explaining only the big picture.
- You cannot make employees feel good about a change that negatively affects them.

At Amalgamated Pulp & Paper

Amalgamated has spent millions of dollars on a quality improvement process. The employee population has been inundated with communication materials. Every employee was indoctrinated through intensive training. The entire structure of the organization was jiggered to accommodate steering committees, improvement teams, and other groups dedicated to weaving quality improvement principles into the company's fabric.

The only people who did *not* go through the process were at the highest levels of executive management. When the company faced its first real test of the process, management had a clear decision to make. Push product out the door that did not meet requirements (the benchmark of quality under the program was "conformance to requirements") or embargo the product, then find and fix the root cause of the problem.

Management didn't balk. They shoved the product out the door. Instantly, the time and money invested in the quality program became a waste. Employees saw a clear distinction between the rhetoric of a superficial quality program and the behaviors for which they would be rewarded. Employees would emulate management's behaviors.

If the company's leaders had understood the impact the message their actions sent, they could have made it clear at the outset that they, above all other employees, would have to walk the talk. They would have known better than to roll out the quality program if they didn't intend to live it themselves.

Counseling should be aimed at managers as well. Knowing why change fails, communication efforts can equip managers with the tools and concepts to ensure success.

When a major announcement or change initiative is launched, the preparation of the team one-on-one ahead of time will allow managers to deal with objections, shock, and anger, and discover why people react that way. When things are changing, a good manager will take the time to deal with people and their fear of change and help them understand the reasons and benefits of change.

Managers also should be counseled to be honest. Lies and prevarications will almost always be found out. If employees ask a question the answer to which is not available yet, managers should say, "I don't know yet" or "That's still confidential," but promise to let employees know as soon as they can.

Actions are more important than words. Managers cannot be seen to be saying one thing and doing another. If standards of behaviors and values are communicated, the manager's own behavior must mirror the spoken word.

Unless a manager goes looking for bad news, it probably will not get there. As you move up the hierarchy, feedback is filtered and bad news softened. Managers (and leaders, for that matter) need to seek out the rumors and squelch them immediately with plain simple language.

Managers should never underestimate the intelligence of employees. How many managers are heard to say, "They won't understand," and gloss over issues at a team meeting? Employees deserve a rationale for decisions; during a change, it is critical. If things aren't going well, employees will probably be the first to know. Encourage managers to involve employees in finding solutions.

Managers should know which communication channels to use for different kinds of change-related messages. E-mail is probably the source of most inappropriate choices of communication channels today. Keep e-mail broadcast messages to a minimum, if not nonexistent, when communicating change. There is too much emotion and too many feelings involved to risk a cold, impersonal channel like e-mail. Encourage managers to do it face-to-face.

Interpreter

Once a decision has been made, employees need to understand that decision and its implications. It is easy for employees to listen to grand explanations of big-picture change, but these overviews have little to do with the work an employee does at the front lines. A key role of communication is to equip employees to enact change at the level where they work in support of the broader changes outlined by the company's leaders.

George Washington was a master of translating big-picture concepts into action at the local level. Washington was not a man of lofty ideas; he left those to the likes of John Adams and Thomas Jefferson. When the leaders of the American Revolution espoused the notion that people should be able to worship as they please, Washington put an end to the celebration of Pope Day among his troops. (Pope Day was an annual anti-Catholic festivity.) Thus, Washington was able to show what a lofty idea meant to his "employees," at the level where they did their daily work.

Facilitator

Communication efforts need to establish a common understanding of the change throughout the entire employee population, from the CEO to the guy who cleans the urinals.

Producing communication tools is certainly one way to do this, but equally important (if not more so) is establishing the channels for dialogue that promote greater understanding. These channels include:

- Q&A mechanisms that allow employees to ask questions and get answers from subject-matter authorities
- Forums that allow employees to talk among themselves, exchanging ideas and sharing knowledge

Cheerleader

All the slick publications, videos, intranet sites, and meetings in the world won't drive change without two critical factors: reward and recognition. In the quality improvement example cited earlier in this chapter, it was obvious to employees that they would be rewarded by executive management for emulating its behavior, which contradicted the principles of the change effort.

Obviously, the reverse is true, too. If employees see other employees being rewarded for behaviors that reflect the principles of the change initiative, others will modify their behaviors so that they will have a chance at reaping the same types of rewards.

The communication effort needs to lead the charge, waving those pompoms for the employees and teams who mirror desired behaviors.

Reporter

Employees need to know if the change is working. It is up to communicators to tell them.

If your goal is to improve customer satisfaction, how much more satisfied are customers today than they were when the initiative kicked off? If your goal is beating the competition, how are you doing? If your goal is the successful integration of an acquired company into your organization, how well is it working?

To report on the right things, you need to have *benchmark* measures that reflect the state things were in before the initiative was launched. Presumably, these status quo benchmarks are the *reason* the company is changing. Inventories are too high, customers are pissed off, market share is eroding, shareholders are selling off, or innovation is stagnating.

Analyst

Is the communication effort resulting in the desired behaviors? Are those behaviors leading to the change? Measurement is a critical aspect in any communication effort, but it takes on new meaning in a change effort.

Communication Principles for Change

Every communication strategy should be built upon some fundamental principles that should not change as it is implemented. Here are some fundamental principles that might apply for a change communication strategy for you:

- The primary communication channel is face-to-face.
- Secondary communication channels will be electronic and Web-based for timeliness and ease of access and used for knowledge sharing (unless, of course, your organization doesn't provide access to online communication tools to a significant portion of your employee population).
- Print can be used as support materials—for example, for employees to share with families—and as reference.
- Key communicators of vision, the case for action, and strategic priorities in the change process are the senior leaders.
- Key communicators of operational information in the change process will be line supervisors and managers.
- Communication processes will be a balance of conveying information while listening to and seeking feedback.
- People don't change unless they believe there is a good reason

to do so—that is, you need to make the case for change or a compelling vision.

- People are more open to change if they have a say in how the organization, and they as individuals, need to change.
- People are also more likely to change in the manner desired if they understand how they are being asked to change (behaviors and measures), have been provided with support (opportunities to express their responses to change, as well as education and training), and are acknowledged for changing (rewards, recognition).
- Change communication will be, wherever possible, timely, open, and honest and will provide information as early as possible after it becomes available.

Face-to-Face Communication

Face-to-face communication of change is effective because of the following reasons:

- It is immediate, dynamic, and interactive.
- It encourages involvement, which builds buy-in and commitment to change.
- It is the best and most immediate way to get feedback.
- It clarifies ambiguities and misinformation.
- It enables the participants to notice the nonverbal cues that add to the richness of the communication and the messages.
- In a group or team setting, it makes the change meaningful at the local level and enables consensus, compromise, and problem solving.
- It permits immediate influence and persuasion.
- Complex messages can be explained, questioned, and clarified.

Leaders

Times of change do not need absentee leaders. The visionary champion who leads by inspiration, motivation, and personal example will be the leader of successful change. When you embark on change, follow these guidelines:

- Expect fear of the unknown and plan for it. There will be stress, tension, and confrontation. Be honest, straightforward, and respectful.
- Don't be afraid to talk about failure, midcourse adjustments, or "bugs" that the project team will work through during the project. In fact, create the expectation that these will be a normal—and expected—part of the project. Tell the truth.
- In clear terms, communicate the case for action. Communicate the vision, rationale, impacts, and benefits throughout the project.
- Don't focus too much on the processes and too little (or not at all) on the people; you increase the likelihood and degree of resistance.
- Provide honest information that anticipates questions and concerns.
- Help employees understand the effort and their role, and encourage them to participate in—or not resist—the project or transition effort.
- Be honest about what you expect from your communication. Communication won't make miracles out of unrealistic deadlines, inadequate budgets, invisible leadership, constantly changing targets, lack of training and education, unclear roles, and other problems of many reorganization or transition efforts. The old adage "garbage in, garbage out" is applicable.
- Develop key communicators throughout your organization. Provide leaders, managers, and interested employees with the necessary coaching, training, and support tools.
- Make use of best practices from other companies that have embarked on similar projects, but remember that what worked for other companies might not be appropriate for your corporate culture.

- Create platforms to deal with the issues that people are afraid to talk about, such as confusion, prospective job loss, or discomfort with disrupted routines.

Line Managers

Most change is managed at the departmental level, where employee's translate the big-picture change into actions affecting the work they do. This kind of change is communicated by a blend of employee involvement and managers who are accountable for the ultimate decision making. Someone must be accountable for the decisions that are made, and it is the role and the responsibility of line management to do that. This places an onus on line management to communicate its decisions in a timely way, after having sought input into those decisions, and to explain the rationale for those decisions.

Formal organizational communication plays a critical role in this part of the process. Most managers are not great communicators. In times of change, managers don't have communication as a top-of-mind issue when decisions are being made. The organization's communication efforts should support managers through the change process by coaching, mentoring, and helping to plan their approaches to implementing change in their departments.

When decisions are made, when announcements are needed, your communications plan should include a strategy and course of action for the communication process. The spokesperson, however, should be the person in authority, in this case, the line manager.

Supervisors

Most important day-to-day information should come from the immediate supervisor. This should include information about work team or unit activities, plans, and performance, as well as individual impacts of the change—especially when it is bad news. There is no substitute for the immediate supervisor when communicating difficult news on the personal level.

Your communication efforts should ensure that supervisors are well informed, have access to the right information when they need it, and have the skills to communicate sensitive information in a respectful manner. Supervisors need coaches, too.

The immediate supervisor has credibility and a personal relationship with individual employees. This strength should be played to through the communication of change. The supervisors should be the most well-informed people in the organization. They provide the local perspective of change and the insights about local impacts.

What their supervisor says and does influences most employees' opinions of management. The supervisor is one of the most important influencers during change, and the success or failure of a change effort can depend on the acceptance and support supervisors have for the change.

Undercommunicating and Overcommunicating Change

Invariably, during a change effort, there is frequent criticism of communication. The criticism is usually one of two comments: There is too much communication or there is too little communication. The following table shows the consequences of each:

Undercommunicating Change	Overcommunicating Change
Information vacuums thrive, and fill with rumors.	Counteracts rumors, unreliable messages.
	Keeps the truth up-to-date.
Reinforces pretense of business as usual.	Changes culture faster.
Leaves problems unattended.	Uses new information routes.
Normal channels malfunction.	Reduces fear of openness, honesty.
Questions go unanswered.	Counteracts skepticism, mistrust.
Ideas and opportunities are lost.	Corrects ambiguity, uncertainty.
Morale fails.	

Clearly, you are better off overcommunicating, since the results can only serve the cause of organizational change.

CHAPTER TEN

Managing Communication Overload

INTERNAL COMMUNICATION is not solely a matter of formalized messages designed to fulfill a strategic imperative. Employees also need to communicate with each other. The fact is, regardless of what an employee does for a living (doctor, lawyer, accountant, facilities manager, purchasing agent, engineer, training specialist, or investment broker), it is likely he or she spends most of her time communicating. Employees who communicate well tend to get good assignments and advance through the organization, succeeding in their careers. Those who don't . . . well, they don't. It should be incumbent on the organization, therefore, to ensure that employees have the tools to succeed as individual communicators.

Unfortunately, the increasing number of messaging channels has made it harder and harder for employees to know how to communicate effectively.

According to one study ("Messaging," conducted annually by the Institute for the Future on behalf of the study's sponsor, Pitney Bowes), the average knowledge worker (as opposed to a worker engaged primarily in physical labor) in the United States manages more than two hundred messages a day. On average, 39 percent of knowledge workers are interrupted by a message six times or more per hour. Twenty-seven percent are distracted by the volume of messages with which they must deal, while 19 percent say they are over-whelmed by messages. (Among high-tech workers, the numbers jump considerably.)

The issues that have led to the so-called message meltdown are many and varied, including:

- *The individual nature of messaging.* Companies cannot mandate the tools employees will use for messaging. It is a highly individualized decision.
- *The additive nature of messaging tools.* Each new messaging technology is added to the mix. When e-mail was installed, fax machines weren't simultaneously removed. There are at least sixteen different messaging processes available to workers today, ranging from regular postal mail to pagers to instant messaging.
- *Geography.* People who live in different parts of the world have embraced different preferences. For example, in the United States, which has multiple time zones, e-mail is desirable, while in the United Kingdom, which has one time zone, cell phones are preferred.
- *Expanding work responsibilities.* The average knowledge worker is involved with (on average) seventeen projects per week, each of which requires messaging.
- *Increased mobility.* Telecommuting and other nontraditional work arrangements have led to an increased need to stay in touch and access information.
- *The state of the organization.* The larger the organization is, the greater the likelihood that multiple messaging systems will spring up. At Fortune 1000 companies in 2000, for instance, the average worker coped with fifty daily e-mail messages compared with only eighteen in small companies.

While the expansion of messaging systems is problematic, e-mail alone has created a problem worth addressing. According to a 2002 study (conducted by Rogen & Goldhaber Research Associates, which analyzed responses from 1,500 executives), one-third of all e-mail messages received are irrelevant to the job being performed by the worker. In a workforce of 100 people, that works out to 15,000 hours lost to dealing with irrelevant e-mail, or $420,000. Scale up to 5,000 workers and you are looking at 750,000 lost hours worth $21 million in productivity. Meanwhile, face-to-face communication—so important for bad news and messages designed to persuade employees—is declining as e-mail volumes increase.

Why is there a rise in business e-mail? Not even considering spam, the reasons include:

- Employees who copy everybody they can think of to make sure it is widely known that they have taken the action promised (also known as "covering their asses").
- Supervisors who want to avoid confrontation. Employees have received negative performance evaluations and even been laid off by e-mail.
- Without thinking, employees click "reply to all" instead of "reply," sending a reply to everybody who received the original message rather than just the intended recipient.
- Employees reply without editing the original message, creating longer-than-necessary messages that are difficult to wade through.
- Management thinks that because e-mail is cheaper than other messaging methods, it should replace all of those other channels.

Who Is In Charge?

Who is responsible for establishing and guiding the way people message within your organization? Human resources? IT? Administrative services? The mailroom? Odds are, nobody has that responsibility.

There is only one possible explanation for the lack of centralized messaging management in our organizations: Management doesn't think it is worthwhile. Managing how employees pass messages among themselves is seen as off-radar, something that simply happens. Targeting resources, such as time, money, or personnel, to help employees message effectively is just busywork and doesn't grow the bottom line.

That, as we have seen, is nonsense. Messaging is at the heart of many of our organization's critical success factors, ranging from productivity to innovation. Messaging is the infrastructure for innovation!

Now we know better. What we know is that message meltdown won't get better unless someone is in charge. In fact, it will only get worse.

Messaging Is Communication

Most messages that employees receive and send are not the same type that we have been addressing throughout this book. However, it is still communication. "Message mission control" will be more at home in the communication department than anywhere else in the organization.

Communication departments represent the formal effort an organization makes to get all audiences to share common ideas, goals, objectives, beliefs, knowledge, and information. That is the communicator's job; it is what we're skilled at. Nobody is better positioned to help others in the organization acquire those skills than communicators are.

It is not IT's job. IT's job is to make sure the wires connect the boxes and that the data flows between them the way it should. (I don't mean to oversimplify, but IT builds and maintains the systems that transmit and process data; they are not responsible for the input.)

It is not human resources' job. HR is there to attract and retain the talent needed if the organization is to meet its goals.

It is only partly the job of training, since there is much more to it than training.

Integrating Messaging Into the Communications Department

Adding responsibility for organization-wide messaging to an existing communication department is no simple task. It requires planning. Your communications staff will probably be able to handle much of the work with existing resources, but you may also need to increase staff and budget to accommodate this newly defined work.

Start with a Goal

Figuring out how to fit message mission control into a department begins with setting a goal. This goal, much like those in any communication plan, is an overarching statement of the big-picture end result you are seeking. A goal might be one of the following:

- *For a company where e-mail is the dominant issue.* Improve internal e-mail usage so that it is a productivity-enhancing tool rather than a drain on productivity.
- *For an organization seeking to improve messaging habits.* Employee messaging contributes measurably to individual success and the success of the organization.
- *For a company seeking to address broad messaging issues.* The spectrum of messaging tools and the way they are used by employees serve the organization's needs and are the basis of innovation and productivity.

Determine Strategies

Let's discuss the first goal of improving internal e-mail usage so that it becomes a productivity-enhancing tool rather than a drain on productivity. Of course, every company will identify different strategies based on their own unique circumstances, capabilities, and culture—so don't limit yourself to these examples. But these examples give you an idea of how to state strategies that will, in the next step, serve as the foundation for measurable objectives:

- Recognize and reward best practices.
- Reinforce desired behaviors.
- Adopt technologies that address key issues.
- Establish policies and guidelines to alleviate the worst problems.

Assign Measurable Objectives

Objectives are the measurable results you will seek from each of the strategies you have listed. Let's look at the example of reinforcing desired behaviors. Some objectives you might set include:

- Put all employees through training on messaging fundamentals.
- Include a messaging tip in every issue of the employee newsletter.
- Create and launch an awareness campaign.

Develop Tactics

This is the part of any strategic communication plan that communicators like best—it is the part where they get to make communications stuff! (This expertise is one of the main reasons you have a communications department. Chapter 13 discusses how to staff the function and how to use it.) For example, let's tackle the awareness campaign objective. Tactics are the things you will actually do, such as:

- Developing and distributing posters for company bulletin boards and table-tent cards for cafeterias and break rooms
- Creating an online game with prizes to be deployed over the company intranet

- Holding a contest for the top best practices submitted by employees
- Creating a supervisor communication package to aid supervisors in pushing the messaging message

Consider that these four tactics are only examples, and they focus on only one objective. If I came up with four tactics for each objective and three objectives for each strategy, I would have forty-eight tactics to work on, or forty-eight *things* to do. And you will probably have more than three strategies and so on—you could end up with *hundreds* of tactics. Hence, there is a need to budget for message mission control as an independent company strategy.

Ongoing Communications

The work that is most familiar to communicators is the production of formal communication stuff. While this is fun, visible, and important, don't be lulled by thinking that just because your message has been communicated, it has been absorbed and acted upon.

It is important to remember that, ultimately, the only reason we communicate to employees is to influence them. Thus, your communications need to be considered in the larger context of an overall message mission control.

This reminder is not meant to diminish the importance of communication products. They shine the light on the effort, convey its importance, and serve as reinforcement. With that in mind, let us look at the communication tools you can use to push effective messaging in your organization.

Your communication plan needs to accommodate the following two seemingly incompatible mandates:

1. *Change the messaging culture.* Culture in an organization is, simply, the way things are, the way things get done. Changing the culture means

making a change to the patterns of behavior, the ethical code, the presumptions of what succeeds and what fails. This kind of change is usually gradual and evolutionary in nature, and it rarely happens because of a program. Remember quality improvement? How many employees saw it as the "program of the month"? How many companies have integrated the principles of the Crosby QIP or the Deming quality program into the fabric of their organizations?

2. *Create employee focus on the issue and the solutions.* In order to encourage employees to change their behaviors, you need to articulate the problem, present the solutions, and show employees what is in it for them to make an effort to do things differently. You cannot succeed at this with stealth communications—you need a program!

You can have this cake and eat it, too, by treating the program as a short-term launch of a longer-term culture change effort. At some point, the slogans and logos vanish, but the imperative to handle messaging differently continues to be a part of all your communications.

Your continuing communications such as newsletters, video magazines, e-mail bulletins, quarterly meetings, or intranet news coverage can be your most dramatic communications force for change. Since these vehicles address the way things are, continuous reinforcement of good messaging habits will begin to seem like the normal state of things to those who pay attention to your publications and other tools. You should use these tools both to spotlight any introductory change campaign you undertake and to begin integrating desired behaviors into the status quo.

Print

Assuming you still have print communication, you can use it to accomplish the following:

- *Tell longer stories.* The simple fact is that most people don't read on the screen. They scan. (Or they print out what they want to read.) Use your print vehicles for longer features you want your audience to read, including success stories and features that focus on employees and teams that exemplify sound messaging habits. Focus on the *outcomes*—that is, the successes achieved by employees or teams as a result of adopting desired behaviors.
- *Provide details.* Your print publications are a good place for detailed analysis, explaining the rationale for a behavior-change initiative. Cover the statistics, the impact of message anarchy on the organization, and the steps the company will take to address the issue.
- *Report on progress.* Seeing progress reported in print makes it tangible. Offer a regular report on key measures you have selected, such as the reduction in volume of weekly e-mails or the reduction in time spent handling e-mail.

E-Mail

If you have an e-mail bulletin or newsletter, add content that focuses on messaging, which could include:

- A regular messaging tip—for example, "How to write a good e-mail subject line"
- Progress report
- Recognition of employees or teams who have adopted positive messaging habits
- Announcement of any new initiatives, policies, or events

In the spirit of good messaging habits, keep these articles very short and provide links to your intranet where employees can obtain additional information or complete details. For example, if your e-mail bulletin includes a messaging tip, include a link to the messaging section of the company intranet.

Intranet

Use ongoing elements of your intranet—the news coverage on the home page, for example—to reinforce messages being delivered through other vehicles.

- Report on statistics from outside.
- Provide progress reports.
- Highlight employees and teams.

If you have a section of your intranet dedicated to managers and supervisors, enhance it with information about how to work with their direct reports to improve messaging in their departments.

Video Magazine

There is little time in video magazines and their frequency (usually quarterly) makes it difficult to convey anything timely. Still, you can work at least one message about messaging into each edition. Try a feature story one quarter, a quick tip the next, then a brief news item about new research results, then a management interview about productivity that mentions (but is not entirely focused on) messaging as one way to improve the bottom line.

Face-to-Face

There is no reason you and your management team cannot reference messaging in any all-hands or large group meetings. Hearing directly from the top can send a strong message. Senior executives in these meetings should reference other communications—for example, "Be sure to read the article in this month's issue of *Insight* magazine"—but they should also personalize the issue and clarify expectations—for example, "I don't want to see one e-mail cross my desk that has 20 CCs of people who don't need the information. No more cover-your-ass e-mails. Period."

Special Communications

You can create special materials to cover the campaign that you develop to launch the change initiative *and* communications that focus on messaging *after* the launch campaign has ended.

Launch Campaign Communications

A launch campaign is designed to shine the light on this new internal effort to gain control of organizational messaging. As such, it is entirely acceptable to create a look and feel for the campaign such as a logo, slogan, or catch phrase and design standards.

Most of your communication vehicles should *not* be tied to this campaign. Once the campaign has run its course, many employees will toss out the materials they received, even if they include worthwhile information and resources. Thus, your campaign materials should be limited to those that create *awareness,* not those that educate or inform. Awareness collateral can include posters, table-tent cards, giveaways such as mouse pads or coffee mugs, or banner-ad-like promotions on your intranet. Remember, the campaign is to alert employees that something new is happening.

Other Special Communications

Beyond the limited scope of an introductory campaign, you will most likely spend much of your time during the first several months in your new message mission control role creating special communications designed to educate and inform. These can include the following:

Brochure. This is a highlights booklet that covers the basics of good messaging. Why produce this in print when it can (and should) just as easily be housed on the intranet? Because the brochure is *pushed* at every employee—nobody needs to make an effort to *pull* it from a Web site. Seriously, how many employees will voluntarily go look at a messaging Web site if they don't need to? This brochure should be a keeper, something that finds its way onto a desktop or a bookshelf or into a drawer for future reference. In fact, thinking about it as a reference guide is a good approach—for example, "The Allied Gate & Fence Company Employee Messaging User's Guide."

Supervisors' materials. Resource material for supervisors can include guidelines for group messaging, information about incorporating messaging behaviors into performance reviews, and information about how to reward and recognize employees for their good messaging habits.

Intranet messaging center. In addition to housing information, the messaging center will also be the repository of tools and resources employees can use to improve their messaging practices. Include in this center the following:

- Policies
- Guidelines
- Articles about messaging
- Samples
- Templates
- Links to related material (including resources on the World Wide Web)
- Tools—for example, start a mailing list, download the instant messenger software, upload an attachment
- Best practices

Contests. It is amazing what people will do if they might win a T-shirt or a baseball cap. Of course, your prizes can be a cut or two above that. Award a monthly prize to the best messaging innovation or the most effective use of messaging in the organization.

Best practices knowledge sharing. One contest you could launch would randomly select a best practice for reward from among those that have been contributed in an online knowledge-sharing forum. Invite employees to contribute their messaging best practices; then pick one a week (or one a month) at random. It is the possibility of winning a prize that will motivate employees to contribute.

Recognition program. If employees are not rewarded and recognized for adopting new behaviors, their behaviors will never change. It doesn't matter what else you do—communicate until you run out of ink, cajole, beg, introduce new tools, cite the statistics, or pray. Habits are habits, and culture only changes when employees are compensated somehow for doing what you want them to do (or punished for retaining old habits).

Two kinds of rewards should be applied to changing messaging habits: compensation and special rewards.

Compensation

Employee pay is based on performance evaluations. These evaluations need to include a messaging component. Those who adopt the company's new messaging practices will receive higher merit increases, bonuses, stock options, or raises than those who do not.

Special Rewards

Most organizations have some kind of reward program to compensate employees for a job well done. These programs often blur the line between reward and recognition, but they are characterized by the fact that the employee receives a tangible reward.

You can consider two classes of special rewards for your messaging effort:

1. Existing rewards can be presented to employees who exemplify the best messaging behaviors.
2. You can implement a short-term messaging-specific reward

program. For example, employees could vote for the best "messager" in their departments and one winner from each department would get the prize.

In addition to the recognition inherent in any tangible reward, you can recognize employees who do great messaging in many ways, such as:

- Feature articles in your existing publications or intranet about how effective messaging led an employee to achieve a success in a task or assignment.
- Senior management can single out employees who message effectively for recognition at all-hands meetings.
- Do you have an annual president's or chairman's award? Make sure you shine the spotlight on the messaging habits of the winners, or even select a winner solely based on good messaging habits.
- Develop a messaging recognition competition with categories like "Best E-Mail of the Year," "Best Voice Mail Message," and "Best Voice Mail Greeting."
- Let employees submit names of employees whose messaging impresses them. They can use a "Messaging Heroes" intranet site to submit the names. This kind of recognition does not even require someone to approve the winners. A submission could automatically add the employee to the list of messaging heroes.
- The message hero of the month could receive a special parking place, his or her picture in the newsletter (or on a poster, or on the intranet), and a certificate.

A Cross-Functional Effort

While message mission control may be housed in your communications department, one department alone cannot manage messaging.

A total message mission control effort must involve a cross-functional effort that includes the following:

- Training and development
- Human resources
- Executive staff
- Information technology

Training and Development

Employees cannot embrace good messaging behaviors if they don't know how. That is where training and development comes in.

Depending on the severity of the problem in your organization, you can work with training staff to create a mandatory all-employee training program or establish a voluntary class that employees can choose to take (or to which supervisors can elect to send their employees). This should be a short course that covers the following:

- The problems.
- How the problems affect the organization.
- How the problems affect employees.
- Good messaging habits. (This should represent about 70 percent of the class.)
- Rewards for complying.
- Disincentives for failing to comply.

Another task for the training department is the new-hire orientation. New hires should be indoctrinated into the company's desired messaging practices before they have a chance to learn bad habits from long-term employees who haven't started to comply with the company's new messaging focus.

Human Resources

Reward and recognition only happen when HR makes them happen. It is in HR that decisions are made about criteria for bonuses, merit increases, performance evaluations, and other reward programs, along with most recognition efforts.

Work with HR to identify the key elements of reward and recognition in your organization. Which are the most influential in terms of employee behaviors? Find ways to build messaging practices into these programs. For example, most organizations' performance evaluations are facilitated using a form completed by a supervisor. The form lists criteria for various levels of performance. Amend these criteria to include messaging practices consistent with the goals, strategies, and objectives you have set for improving messaging in your organization.

In some organizations, HR may be reluctant to alter existing criteria to accommodate a single issue. That is why it is so important to have support from company leadership and IT.

Company Leadership

Leaders need to pay more than lip service to the idea of message mission control—they must be absolutely committed to it. Leaders can articulate that commitment many ways, ranging from interviews in existing communications to pronouncements at all-hands meetings. Most important, though, will be the commitment expressed when message mission control is introduced.

Imagine a CEO who says, "This is a new function within the communications (or organization development or HR) department. We have committed resources to this effort because it is vital to our success. We're buried under messaging and something must be done. I expect every department to lend its full support to the message mission control effort." Now imagine a department blowing off message mission control when an employee directly involved in the effort seeks to partner on an element of messaging in the workplace.

Information Technology

Many of the approaches you will take to get a handle on message meltdown will involve the deployment of new technologies and enhancements to others. You need to partner with IT to turn these ideas into reality.

"Pull" Messaging: Mailing Lists and Message Boards

As we have already discussed, copying hordes of people to e-mail messages they don't need is one of the prime reasons employees receive too much e-mail. Sometimes it is a cover-your-ass mentality that leads to the excessive copying; sometimes it is a sincere belief that all those recipients might actually need this message.

You can eliminate nearly all of this overload by implementing tools that remove the "push" factor from the equation. Right now, the sender "pushes" those messages to the many recipients who don't want it. The alternative is "pull," and it works in a variety of circumstances.

The following case study is one example:

At Allied Gate & Fence

Several departments are able to use the all-employee e-mail mailing list. One of these departments, the employee services department, sends notification to employees whenever the department obtains a block of tickets to sell at a discount to employees.

Employee services adopted the all-employee mailing list as part of a paper-cutting initiative; e-mail meant they wouldn't need to print and distribute notices every time tickets became available.

As a result, employees would receive e-mail messages notifying them of every event, from baseball to opera. Employees who love opera would welcome the e-mail. Those who hate it, though, would find the message contributing to their overload.

To resolve the situation, the employee services department cre-

ated a page on its intranet site that allowed employees to create
a profile by checking off the kinds of events about which they would
like to be notified. Employees who didn't like opera simply didn't
check the box. Now, whenever the employee services department
receives a new block of tickets to the opera, the e-mail notification
goes only to the list employees who specified they like it.

This form of customization is based on employee profiles, the
equivalent of letting them subscribe to certain kinds of information
while rejecting others. Information guru Tom Davenport once noted
that there is no such thing as information overload because as an
information-hungry society, we can stand all the information we can
lay our hands on—*about the stuff we're interested in.* It is only when
we are forced to slog through material we don't care about that we
experience overload. The method described in the previous case
study ensures that no employee suffers overload from employee services; they will *only* receive information that they are interested in.

Let's review the main methods of providing "pull" tools to employees and how they alleviate message meltdown.

Mailing Lists

At PricewaterhouseCoopers, the accounting firm, approximately
five hundred employees subscribe to a mailing list called The Kraken
(named for the mythical sea monster in a poem of the same name by
Tennyson). The mailing list is known as their premier knowledge-
sharing forum, despite the availability of a complex and expensive
knowledge database. The vast majority of Kraken messages ask questions: Does anybody know . . . ? Does anybody have . . . ? Has anybody ever done something like . . . ? While the mailing-list software
is about as unsophisticated as it can be—poor archiving, no indexing—and users can get as many as fifty Kraken messages a day, it is a
resounding success.

Why? Because the five hundred people who use it are the ones who *want* those fifty messages every day. Those message aren't overload if they are useful. The tens of thousands of other PricewaterhouseCoopers employees who *don't* want those messages never need to bother. Only those who *subscribe* ever see the messages.

The Kraken is so successful that it is spawning similar mailing lists at PricewaterhouseCoopers focusing on other areas of the business.

None of this would come as a surprise to workers at Microsoft, where status is often determined based on which mailing lists to which an employee has been added.

One-Way or Multidirectional

Many lists are one-way. List owners can send messages to subscribers by sending an e-mail to the list address, but if a subscriber sent a message to the list address (or replied to an e-mail received from the list), it would go only to the list administrator. Another option is to set the list up so that *any* subscriber can send a message to the whole list. (That's how the Kraken is set up.) The idea is to facilitate an exchange of ideas via the list.

To reiterate, the advantage of a mailing list is that only those who want them will receive the messages from the list.

Opt-Out vs. Opt-In

There is another way to set up mailing lists. Start by automatically subscribing all employees to the birthday list and let those who don't want to receive such messages *opt out*. They would do this by unsubscribing from the list.

There is much debate over whether it is better to automatically opt everyone in and force those who want to opt out to take deliberate action, or whether it is better to make everyone who might be interested take steps to subscribe. For employees, this is less of an issue than it is with external audiences. The choice you make will depend on your culture and your system capabilities.

Managing Lists

Odds are that your company's internal mail server already has the ability to create lists. In fact, you may already have active lists in existence. Your challenge is to adapt the technology to your message meltdown issues.

Start by identifying the worst offenders among the classes of messages going to all employees or to large numbers of workers. These would be your first candidates for lists designed to alleviate message overload.

Some companies complain there are too many messages hitting everyone's in-box notifying them of a birthday or a birthday party. Try creating a list for birthday announcements in your organization. Set a policy: Birthday announcements *must* be sent through the list. Anybody who wants to know about birthdays or birthday parties must subscribe. Those who don't subscribe will no longer see birthday announcements hit their in-boxes.

List Indexing

Several mailing-list software packages allow you to set your mailing list to the index option. At PricewaterhouseCoopers, this means that instead of receiving fifty separate e-mails each day, an employee would receive *one* e-mail that lists all of that day's messages at the top, then includes each message, in the order it was received, in the body of the e-mail.

Indexing makes it easy for a reader to scan the list of messages for those that are of interest, then scroll to those messages, ignoring the rest. Another indexing method shows *only* the message headers and provides the means to retrieve those in which you are interested.

At Allied Gate & Fence

Allied's facility in Des Moines faced massive e-mail overload as employees sent e-mail to the all-employee list about everything from lost-and-found items to after-work activities. The company solved the problem by requiring all such notices be sent to a list address where they were indexed and forwarded to all employees as a once-a-day listing of all such e-mails. The number of messages the average employee received each day was dramatically reduced by this simple use of a list.

Customizable E-Mail Newsletters

Subscriptions can be used not only to sign up for an e-mail bulletin but also to manage the contents an employee receives.

I subscribe to an e-mail newsletter from a research company. When I subscribed, I was presented with a series of options. I checked the ones I was interested in. Now, each issue of the newsletter contains a lead article (which the company determines is its key message for the month), along with a series of other articles based on my preferences. As a result, the newsletter I get is different from those received by other subscribers, except for the hard-coded lead article.

Here is how it works:

Each article is stored in a database. When the list is instructed to send a monthly newsletter, it looks at each subscriber's profile and retrieves articles from the database that match. These are assembled on the fly (or "dynamically"), and then sent to each subscriber.

If it sounds complex, that is only because most communicators do not use databases. It is actually fairly easy to set up. Now, an employee could visit a "Profile" Web site and select the kinds of announcements they want from any number of categories. As the communicator, you can hard-code the material you believe *every* employee should see, but the balance of the newsletter would include only those items that matched the employee's profile. An employee working in Division A wouldn't have to see miscellaneous news from Business Unit B.

The advantage of a profile-based newsletter is that employees will find material in their copy of the newsletter completely relevant.

Message Boards, Chat Rooms, and Instant Messaging

These tools offer alternatives to e-mail, voice mail, and other vehicles for messaging; we'll discuss them in more detail in Chapter 12. The trick is to ensure that each tool is used based on its strength, and that new vehicles aren't thrown into the mix without a strategy for how they will be utilized. In Appendix A, we'll review some proposed guidelines for the use of each medium as a means of reducing message meltdown.

Unified Messaging

When you talk to IT about various ideas for alleviating message meltdown, you may hear some talk about unified messaging.

Unified messaging provides a single point of access to voice, fax, and e-mail messages. Users are not bound to a single tool to retrieve their messages, either; they can get them from a telephone, a personal computer, and the Web. Different types of messages are identified with icons representing the way it was sent; for example, a telephone icon might represent a voice mail message.

Employees away from the office can get to their messages over an Internet-connected Web browser or by using a telephone user interface (TUI). Employees call a number to get into their unified messaging system; then they listen to any messages, replying to those that warrant a response. Messages can be forwarded, as well.

Lotus Development Corp. recently ratcheted up the notion of unified messaging, suggesting that truly unified messaging would incorporate any messaging device—including, for instance, text messages. Furthermore, unified messaging should be accessible over any type of device, including PDAs.

Since most of us haven't experienced unified messaging, it is difficult to imagine that it is a serious alternative. However, market researcher Frost & Sullivan figures organizations will spend more than $5 billion on unified messaging by 2005; the Polaris Group guesses it will be more like $6.3 billion.

Waiting for Technology to Catch Up

Unified messaging depends on two technologies that work now, but could work better. The first of these is text-to-speech (TTS). When you listen to your e-mail or your fax headers over the telephone, TTS software reads the text and produces the words you hear.

The second technology, speech recognition, is how the telephone system converts your spoken words into text that appears in the e-mails or faxes you send.

A host of other technologies will find their way into unified messaging, including Internet voice mail (IVM), the session initiation protocol (SIP), and XML (Voice XML is an emerging standard for speech services).

Changing to a New Messaging Culture

Before anything can change, you must have the right tools in place. The focus on quality improvement in the 1980's provides a good example.

It would have been a pipe dream to think that employees would adopt quality principles without certain tools. For example, there were teams that set goals and established measures. There were templates employees could use to apply principles to their own efforts. A common language was introduced (mostly acronyms, like DIR-TFT—Do It Right The First Time, but also definitions, like "conformance to requirements" as the definition of "quality"). And quality goals were written into performance expectations, meaning an employee's pay was directly tied to how well he or she did at improving quality.

Messaging is no different. You can tell employees repeatedly how serious a problem messaging is; how much it is costing; how it is hurting profitability, productivity, and competitiveness. You can list everything employees are doing wrong. But if employees do not have the resources to do things right, it will all be for naught. And to complicate things, the tools must make life *easier* than those they are currently using! One of the reasons e-mail has become so pervasive is because it is so darned *easy.*

Some of the tools to put in place have already been covered in earlier lectures, but let's review them in simple categories here.

Alternatives

This category of tools covers those you want employees to use *instead* of e-mail or other channels (like snail mail). These include:

Instant messaging. IM is the utility that allows you to send a quick message instantly to the desktop of anybody already in your buddy list who is logged into the network.

Message boards. Themed spaces on your intranet where employees can exchange information, knowledge, and ideas about issues related to the theme. These boards are asynchronous (not real-time) and require employees to make the effort to visit them.

Peer-to-peer. This represents a relatively new approach to online communication. Most people associate peer-to-peer with Napster and the music file-sharing resources that have followed. What it really means, though, is that no server is required; if you can connect to one person on the network, you'll automatically connect to everyone that he or she is connected to. How does this relate to messaging? Take a look at Groove, developed by Ray Ozzie (the guy who invented Lotus Notes), which is designed to facilitate collaboration without a server. It includes an e-mail-like utility and a chat feature, and is ideal for project teams.

Mailing lists. Employees can opt in to the lists that contain the kinds of messages they want to get, or you can opt them in automatically and allow them (in most cases) to opt out. Mailing lists can be based on profiles of employees—for example, their level, the type of work they do, their location, their business unit, or their profession.

Employee Publishing

Many messages that contribute to the problem find their way into e-mail because employees simply don't know where else to put them. Creating places for employees to add their knowledge or information would preclude them from using e-mail.

At Allied Gate & Fence

A chain-link buyer at Allied meets with a sales rep from Chains 'n' More, who nonchalantly observes that your competitor, Total Fencing, has launched a compelling initiative for sales reps. A few years back, the buyer would have had no formal venue for sharing this information with the company. In the past year, though, the Allied intranet implemented an alternative, a place where employees can contribute any competitive intelligence they have picked up. It is handled on a special intranet page where employees complete a simple form. The employee communications department reviews the output once a week, creating a list of the most important findings; the list is circulated to senior management. Anybody can visit the page and search for information based on key words.

That is the idea behind employee publishing: providing employees with a specific place to contribute specific information.

The following are other methods for encouraging employees to publish their knowledge for sharing throughout the organization:

Communities of practice (CoP). Create a site on the intranet for employees who share a common area of expertise. Generally, members of a CoP don't work for the same department. This site can include the bios of these experts, their calendars, their memos and reports, and a place where they can engage in discussions with one another. The message board is restricted to them for posting, but *any* employee can read it; that is how they find the right person to talk to about issues they are facing related to that area of expertise. Communities of practice were covered in more detail in Chapter 6.

Blogs. The word *blog* was created by mashing together "Web" and "log." Blogs are Web-based diaries or journals. Rather than create a site to which they publish their entries, bloggers use a blog utility by setting up a blog and then simply pasting their entry into a form and clicking a publish button. Why let employees do this? Consider an engineer who reads several engineering publications, attends local association chapter meetings, and travels to a conference. She uses her blog to provide short updates about what she has learned. Other engineers who find her posts useful would make it a habit to read her blog, gaining from that one resource the benefit of all the publications she reads and meetings and conferences she attends.

Of course, message boards also allow employees to publish themselves, as do personal home pages and/or management of the information on an employee's directory listing.

Messaging Management Tools

Messaging preferences vary by geography. According to research, North Americans prefer e-mail but the British would rather engage in text messaging. Why? Because in the United States, we deal with four different time zones, while in merry old England, there is only one. In North America, therefore, we prefer asynchronous (that is, not real time) messaging, while the British find real-time communication to be more effective. When you are sending a message to a fellow employee, how do you know where they are so that you can send the message by the preferred channel?

Here is another situation that might cause you to consider how you will send a message. When you are traveling, odds are you cannot retrieve your e-mail at will. You must wait until you get into your hotel, then dial in (long distance) to the Remote Access Server, hope for a connection that works, then deal with the torturously slow download speeds you get over a dial-up connection. On the other hand, you *can* check your voice mail frequently. How do you let colleagues who may want to contact you know you are traveling and that they should leave a voice mail rather than send an e-mail? Auto-responders do not work, since your colleagues hear from you *after* they have sent an initial message!

The answer is to establish a means by which employees find out what they need to know about you *before* sending a message. Ideally, this is the directory listing. It is not difficult to give employees the means of indicating their preferred method of contact at any given time.

Of course, there are other tools you could use to let employees see the current status of those with whom they usually share messages. For example, a portal could include a "container" for a list of regular contacts and their current location (which each employee sets for him or herself). Ideally, an employee would enter a message and address into appropriate fields, and the message would automatically be routed through the best channel. (It would be converted via text-to-voice software to a voice-mail message, for example, if you want to get your messages over the telephone.) Your IT department can help to identify a method for employees to set their messaging preferences.

The trick is to get employees to use the directory page as a messaging tool *before* they send a message. That is where culture change comes in. With the right tools in place, you can start to consider how to encourage employees to change their behaviors.

CHAPTER ELEVEN

Organizing, Budgeting, and Using Your Internal Communications Department

AS A LEADER, your communication role is to set the tone for proactive, candid, open communication that is designed to foster trust, enhance role knowledge, improve job satisfaction, and heighten employees' commitment to the company's goals. You establish the communication mandate.

But just as you rely on specialists to handle the company's legal issues and accounting chores, nobody expects you to produce newsletters or to maintain intranet sites. For that work, you rely on your employee communications department.

Communications is not an end; it is a *means* to an end. If your internal communications don't contribute measurably to the company's achievement of its business goals, why is it getting even a nickel of the company's hard-earned money? Thus, you set the agenda and your internal communications department executes it based on the skills and expertise you have sought when staffing the function. Typically, an employee communications department does the following:

- Produces ongoing communications, handling all the writing, editing, and production
- Manages special communication projects as they arise
- Provides counsel within the organization on issues with internal communication implications
- Measures the results of its efforts to ensure it is meeting expectations

An effective internal communications department—one that helps you to achieve the business results shareholders expect of you—depends on many factors, including:

- Where it reports
- How much influence it has
- How it is structured
- What kind of expertise it contains

Where to Put Employee Communications?

Most departments in a traditional organization chart are fairly consistent across business. Accounting and the controller's office report through the finance department to the chief financial officer, for example. Market research is part of a product development group. Employee communications, on the other hand, seems to be a department without a common home. In some companies, it is part of human resources; in others, it belongs to public affairs or corporate communications. There are companies in which the employee communications department reports to legal, finance, or a variety of other departments.

None of these solutions is optimal for the internal communications function.

Human resources. Both HR and employee communications address the same audience, making HR—at first glance, anyway—the logical home for internal communicators.

Most HR management expects its communications department to support HR goals, which is hardly unreasonable. The senior HR leader operates her department based on goals she received from her boss (usually the president or CEO). All of the work done in her organization logically should support those goals.

The role of an employee communications department, however, transcends HR. Consider, for example, the role that employee communications plays in a merger or acquisition. The department's goals would hinge on getting the two organizations to mesh as quickly as possible, establishing the new merged company's identity in the minds of employees, and kick-starting the newly formed organization into high gear. If internal communications is subordinated to the HR agenda, the communication effort will focus instead on compensation and benefit issues; operational matters fall outside of HR's scope.

Public affairs or corporate communications. A corporate communications department routinely addresses external audiences, covering community relations, investor relations, government relations, corporate public relations, and media relations. Typically, media relations is the largest component of a public affairs department. Leaders of corporate communication departments often are so focused on these external audiences that they fail to appreciate the importance or intricacies of internal communications. (Many media relations professions look down their noses at employee communications, viewing the function as either a stepping-stone for beginners who want to grow up to become media relations professionals or the last stop for aging communicators unable to cope with the pressures of a media job.) Even in corporate communication departments with a deeper appreciation of the importance of employee communications, internally focused messages are often subordinated to external priorities. ("We can't tell that to employees; it's *different* from what we told the press!")

So where, then, should employee communications report?

Ideally, the function should report directly to the CEO, for whom employees are a critical audience. In this relationship, the CEO is one link removed from employees through the department that manages the processes employed to reach them. There is little risk of messages being watered down or filtered as they pass through layers of management with different concerns and agendas. And the internal communications department will know exactly what is happening and why, giving the team the ability to translate correctly for all audiences.

Of course, most CEOs won't embrace this recommendation. They already have too many direct reports and too many competing demands on their time. Few internal communication managers report to the CEO. However, you would do well to consider the notion of a chief reputation officer (CRO), whose status in the company is equal to that of the chief financial officer, the chief operation officer, the chief information officer, and the general counsel. The chief reputation officer maintains either solid or dotted-line reporting relationships to all departments whose job it is to communicate with constituent audiences; that is, those with a direct impact on the company's reputation. The CRO sits at the management table, is privy to top-level discussions and decisions, and has the CEO's ear. She is able to ensure that all departments receive the information they need and coordinate their efforts to ensure that each of their respective audiences get consistent messages designed to achieve audience-specific communication objectives.

Ultimately, where the internal communication function reports is not as important as the degree of support the department enjoys from the company's leaders. If the leaders set a strong agenda for communications by articulating its expectations, the management of the function to which communications reports will ensure that the department has the resources and backing it needs to meet those goals.

A Seat at the Decision-Making Table

The highest-ranking internal communicator needs to have a seat at the leadership table where decisions are made. You need communication input about the effect on employees of decisions you are making and how the decision will be communicated—*before* the decision is made. Communications will be far less effective if the department is treated as hired guns brought in to clean up the town after the town council's decision to go along with the cattle baron's demands backfires and the town is overrun with gunfighters, gamblers, and other lawlessness!

In that perfect world to which I alluded earlier, this seat will be occupied by a chief reputation officer. However, even if your highest-ranking communicator is only a manager, make certain that he or she is invited to leadership meetings where key decisions will be made. Since you wouldn't make a legal decision without counsel or a financial decision without input from an accountant, why make a decision about what to communicate without a communicator's advice?

At Amalgamated Pulp & Paper

The manager of employee communications walks nervously into the office of the chief executive officer. He has been in this office only a handful of times, and it still intimidates him. He also fears that direct conversation with the CEO is going over the head of his boss and his boss's boss.

The CEO informs the manager that the leadership team has decided to embrace a new focus on the organization—on shareholder value enhancement. "Shareholder value will drive everything we do," the CEO explains; then he launches into an overview of the foundations of the shareholder value approach.

The communications manager listens patiently, taking notes. The CEO wraps up, noting, "I'm counting on the employee communications department to make sure every employee in this company understands and buys into this philosophy."

"Well, that will certainly present some, um, *challenges*," replies the communicator. If he were bolder, he would have said, "That's not a realistic expectation."

The CEO, who has been excited by the shareholder value concept, blanches. "Challenges? What kind of challenges?"

"Well, sir, consider the average employee on the factory floor welding iron gates. I don't think there is a communication approach that will succeed in getting that front-line worker to the point that he can't wait to jump out of bed in the morning so he can come to work all fired up about enhancing shareholder value."

"But most of those employees have company stock," the CEO argues. "In the 401(k) plan, in the profit-sharing plan, in the employee stock ownership plan. It's in their own self-interest to grow shareholder value."

"Yes, sir, it is. But that front-line employee doesn't own that much stock and never really touches the shareholder. And where is the customer in all of this? We've been telling our front-line workers for years that the customer is king."

"The customer has to be satisfied if shareholder value is going to grow," the CEO explains, frustration clearly growing.

"Yes, sir, that's true, but it's still a roundabout message to the average worker. What we'll be telling employees is that everything we do is designed to increase the wealth of the people who own the company. That contradicts our mission and value statements, and will probably leave some employees feeling confused and disoriented."

As the communicator explains the problem, the CEO begins to realize that the philosophy of shareholder value may be sound on paper, but will, indeed, be difficult to translate into action for most employees. Not that it can't be done, mind you; but how will a focus on enriching owners synch up with previous messages, and how will that apparent conflict affect employee trust and, by extension, employee commitment?

If only the CEO had had this counsel when the chief financial officer first brought shareholder value to the table, but the decision was made without input from any internal communications staff.

Amalgamated would probably have taken a different approach had the communication department been represented at the discussions that led to the adoption of the shareholder value initiative. (And they would have been wise to do so, since a focus on shareholder value has been blamed for much of the mind-set that led to the corporate scandals plaguing companies like Enron, Tyco, Adelphia, and WorldCom. The focus on achieving profit for owners is believed to have outweighed ethical concerns or a focus on customers.)

Structuring Employee Communications

Wherever the employee communications department resides, the structure needs to include a relationship between the department and the highest levels of management. Communicators must have access to readers if they are to deliver to employee audiences the messages you want delivered, achieving the results you want achieved.

There are more logistical structure issues to be addressed in assembling an internal communications department. How the department is organized often reflects its charter. If, for example, the department is viewed as a hands-on producer of communication tools like newsletters and Web pages, the structure is more likely to be based on craft specialties. The department will have editors, writers, and production specialists for functions such as layout, design, artwork, or photography. While these skills are certainly needed in an internal communication function, structuring based on skills is not the best way to ensure that a department helps the company attain business results.

Several companies have opted for a client-focused approach to the department's structure. There is a team that supports the corporation, one that works with HR, another that serves operations, and so on. The small size of a communication staff means every employee serves multiple clients, but the focus remains squarely on the business needs of the various components of the organization.

A matrix model is also popular in communication functions. Under this design, functional characteristics such as writing or editing are wedded to project (or product) needs to form a grid (or matrix).

The best approach will depend on your organization, its culture, its structure, and the priorities identified for internal communication.

The scope of your organization is another consideration in structuring the department. If your company is global or national, should the function be centralized or decentralized? In a decentralized organization, communicators report to plant managers, field officers, and international managers. When the department is centralized, communicators are still situated in facilities around the world, but they all report to one department (with dotted-line responsibilities to their client base).

Whatever the structure, the department needs to form linkages with other departments on which they need to rely to do their jobs. Employee communications will deal directly with several departments. For example, few employee communications departments maintain their own printing operations. The department will work either with an internal print shop or with the purchasing department to acquire the services of an outside vendor. The department will also work with designers (internal or external), photographers, artists, and a host of other service suppliers. The department also will interface with the parts of the business it serves. And when writing articles and other materials, communicators will interface with virtually every corner of the company. Employee communications is one of the most interdependent functions in the organization.

What the Department Does

What do they do, these communicators, besides take a seat at the decision-making table and dispense their advice about the communication implications of decisions the company's leaders make?

Communication Counselors

If you hired well, your communicators have the same degree of expertise in their field as accountants, attorneys, IT professionals, or compensation and benefits specialists have in theirs. They are expert in audience research and analysis, message creation and delivery, and the use of communication to achieve measurable degrees of influence.

This expertise applies to more than company-wide communication. The employee communications department can serve as a consulting agency within your company, ready to assist with any communication issues that arise, whether they are company-wide or department-specific. Some real-world examples of communicators counseling within the organization include the following:

- A new vice president was appointed to a key business unit. Although she had a solid reputation within the company, her background was completely different from the scope of her new responsibilities. The employee communications department helped her to prepare her initial meetings and other communications with her new team. The result: employees who had been skeptical about her qualifications to run the department were now supportive and ready to work with her.
- Two departments were having difficulty working together; hostilities were reaching the boiling point. The communications department identified the disconnects between the two departments and developed the means for dialogue and mutual understanding. The result was that the two departments ended their conflict and began working together.

Communications Planners

By working with you and other leaders, communicators can translate company goals and issues into an action plan that covers ongoing communication and special projects. In my days managing internal communications, I used a color-coded chart to ensure that all communications were tightly focused on business issues. I assigned each company goal and issue a different color: development of innovative new products might be green, while improving customer satisfaction would be red. Across the top of the chart was each of the twelve months in the plan year. Along the left-hand side were the various communication tools the company had in place. In each box, I would list a communication that would reinforce a goal or address an issue, ensuring that each color was represented at least once for each month. I maintained the chart on a dry erase board so that it could be updated and amended, particularly if a new issue arose.

Ongoing Communications

The employee communications department will devote much of its effort to maintaining the day-to-day communications that occur within the organization in support of company goals. These include the following:

- Any regular publications, such as a monthly magazine or a weekly newsletter
- Maintaining and updating the internal communication component of the company intranet
- Planning any face-to-face sessions, such as quarterly managers meetings or town hall meetings
- Feeding supervisor communication resources, such as an intranet's "supervisor toolkit"

Project Specialists

In addition to the day-to-day communications the department handles, your communicators will be called on to develop communications for one-time or short-term activities. These can be as simple as a brochure commemorating the winners of the president's award to a full-scale communication plan to support a merger or a company reorganization.

Media Experts

Need a brochure? A video? A page on the intranet? Your internal communications department most likely has the expertise to produce these communication tools. Among the skills your staff should have are the following ones:

- Writing (for print, online, speeches, and AV).
- Editing.
- Layout and design.
- Publication management.
- AV production.
- Photography, artwork, and printing. (You don't necessarily need photographers and artists on staff, and it is unlikely that your communications department will own a printing press, but your staff should know how to identify and work with suppliers, whether they come from inside or outside the company.)
- Network infrastructure. (Your communicators should know enough about the nuts and bolts of the online world to make good decisions about the use of company bandwidth and to work well with their partners in the IT department.)

Measurement Mavens

Finally, your communication staff should be able to apply the tools of communication measurement to assess the effectiveness of their efforts at helping the company achieve its business goals.

What should you look for in a communicator to manage your internal communications function? The following is a solid job description you could use in your recruiting efforts:

As manager of our employee communications department, you will play a key role in providing communications consulting to employees at all levels in meeting business objectives, plus developing and executing communications plans that build trust between employees and management. In this role, you will independently manage projects and lead a virtual communications team in a matrixed team environment. You will serve as reporter, consultant, and distiller of information to electronic media, affinity groups, business groups, and one-on-one audiences. (Customers include employees, leadership team, business area leaders, corporate office, and local community relations partners.) You will lead the ongoing efforts of a communications team of five employees, as well as respond to immediate issues and needs as they arise.

Qualified candidates will have:

- A generalist communications professional background with eight-plus years of senior-level communications experience, plus a demonstrated ability to develop and lead internal communications for another organization with a reputation for excellence in communications
- Team-building skills, as well as strong interpersonal, writing, and visual communication skills
- Strategic development skills coupled with agility for rapid response to fast-surfacing issues
- Experience designing, planning, and managing communication projects to deliver value-added solutions on time and within budget
- Experience managing a communications team and a budget of at least $1 million
- Outstanding oral and written communication skills and the ability to build and maintain relationships with peers, other employees, and senior management as well as a variety of internal and external constituencies
- Executive presence, poise, persuasiveness, and the appropriate confidence to earn credibility

- Outstanding communications consulting experience to effectively listen to and counsel internal clients on ways employee communication can help to meet business needs
- A bachelor's degree (minimum) in journalism or organizational communication
- Accreditation by a reputable and acknowledged communications-focused professional association (IABC or PRSA preferred)

Budgeting for Employee Communications

How much money should you spend on employee communications? Several approaches have dictated the amount available to spend on the function, ranging from what it cost last year to a zero-based budgeting approach.

Neither is an ideal methodology for funding a function that will spell the difference between success and failure for your entire enterprise. You are far better off adopting a "future-based" budgeting plan. Under this approach, you align the expectations you have of your internal communications function with the vision of your organization. In other words, budgeting is a function of the communication-planning process addressed in Chapter 4.

Looking at your long-term vision, what does the organization need to focus on in order to get there? What strengths and weaknesses characterize the company, and what constraints would hinder progress toward that vision? Based on the answers, establish communication priorities. What would it cost to implement communications to achieve the highest-priority action items? Include the cost of ongoing communications as well as special projects.

One of the advantages of this approach is that it won't lock you in to existing communication tools. Far too many organizations maintain a regular monthly all-hands meeting or a continuing quarterly publication because "We've *always* done it this way." The way something has always been done is backward looking. When you plan forward, you may well find that a quarterly magazine no longer meets the company's needs as expressed in the list of high-priority action items.

Who pays for what is another consideration in budgeting. Three categories of communication each dictate a different funding source:

1. *Ongoing communication.* Employee communications should budget for its ongoing communications, such as the maintenance of intranet content or production of a monthly employee magazine.
2. *Client-based efforts.* If HR approaches employee communications to produce a campaign designed to explain reductions in medical insurance coverage, should employee communications pay for the collateral material it produces? As in any consulting organization, communications charges HR the cost of producing those materials.
3. *Special projects.* This is the most difficult category. As situations arise such as mergers, divestitures, reorganizations, and crises, the money to produce communications must come from some source. It is, of course, impossible to anticipate a crisis. Typically, if you budget for a crisis and it doesn't occur, that piece of the budget isn't allocated again for the next year. (The maxim of "use it or lose it" dictates a great deal of corporate spending.) The solution could be to establish a discretionary fund maintained by the communications department or the CEO for special communication projects that emerge. In any case, the department should never need to suspend a communication that has been planned as an element of support for business goals to find the dollars to communicate an emerging issue.

CHAPTER TWELVE

Enhancing Employee-to-Employee Communication

WHAT IS AN ORGANIZATION? According to one dictionary definition, an organization is a group of persons organized for a particular purpose. Or, to put it another way, it's a collection of humans who get together based on mutual interests (the performance of duties in support of organizational goals) and who share a common culture.

An organization is more than a set of bylaws, financial reports, or org charts. It is a group of *people*. To artificially deny the social aspects of the workplace is to inhibit the transfer of information and knowledge and to hinder the organization's ability to outperform and innovate.

Your challenge is to harness the social nature of work to the benefit of the company. One of the primary advantages of the social side of work is that it is the primary conduit for the transfer of knowledge. Knowledge management (KM) is probably one of the most overused and least understood business terms to emerge in the past fifty years, but that situation shouldn't prevent you from employing its best principles.

For our purposes, KM is the way an organization manages the knowledge that it has, or its intellectual capital. Why should knowledge be managed? Because employees *need* knowledge to do their work, and they don't necessarily know where that knowledge can be found when they need it. This was always true, but it is absolutely vital now that we live and work in a knowledge economy where so many employees are knowledge workers.

There are two types of knowledge. Tacit knowledge is that which is swimming around in somebody's head, available only when that individual knows that somebody else needs it—and only if he or she is willing to share it. Latent (or explicit) knowledge is that which is written down in manuals, handbooks, memos, or databases.

Knowledge management is based on two principles: knowledge transfer and knowledge codification. Transfer means that the knowledge is passed from the person who has it to the person who needs it. Codification means that it is written down—it undergoes a metamorphosis from tacit to latent, so anybody who needs it in the future has access to it even if the individual who originally had the knowledge has retired and left the company.

How can the knowledge transfer that happens informally through the network outperform the expensive and sophisticated knowledge databases implemented by IT departments? Consider the characteristics of knowledge databases compared with those of an informal social work-focused network as outlined in the table on page 222.

Encouraging Face-to-Face Interaction

Innovation is nearly always the serendipitous result of employees interacting with one another as people, not forced together in some artificial construct, such as a meeting or task force. Innovation is more likely, then, when leaders provide an environment and drive a culture that encourages interaction.

Formal Knowledge Databases	*Informal Work-Focused Networks*
A repository—Employees need to know to look through its deposits of documents, historical archives, and data collections.	*Demand-driven*—The network kicks into gear when someone needs information or the knowledge it contains.
Closed—The knowledge selected for the database is deemed by an authority to be *the* correct information.	*Open*—Employees tap into the knowledge accumulated by various fellow employees, which offers alternative ideas and viewpoints.
A collection—Collections, whether they are on shelves, in files, in a computer database, or on the Web, rely on taxonomies to help users figure out where to find information they seek. Taxonomies are inherently nonintuitive; that is the reason librarians need college degrees to figure out the Dewey decimal system.	*A conversation*—Conversations are natural exchanges of information, based on a common language and a common understanding of the issues at hand. Misunderstandings can be clarified quickly, and the experience can lead to further fruitful exchanges.
Focuses on teaching—The information stored in databases and file cabinets must be read and absorbed for users to glean anything from them. If a user needs clarification or additional information, he or she must figure out where that data might reside. And don't forget that a user needs to *learn* to use the system to learn the information it contains.	*Focuses on learning*—An employee seeks out another employee to learn what that employee has to offer. She wants to extract the information she needs, and rarely does the individual who has the desired information resort to lecturing to pass the information along. If you consider the growth of instant messaging (IM) in organizations, it is easy to see that knowledge and information exchanges are short, personal, and productive.

At Allied Gate & Fence

In an effort to expand into a new market, Allied has acquired a small but reputable company called Signature Garden Boundaries. Signature specializes in gates and fences for home gardens, distinct from the much larger installations common to Allied.

Beyond the need for the two companies to begin working and thinking as one, Allied's leaders recognize that Signature's specialized focus requires knowledge that has not been required for the fences that surround homes and public facilities. Similarly, Allied employees probably know things that could be of use to Signature workers.

The dilemma that Allied faces is how to facilitate the transfer of that knowledge. The company considers a variety of approaches. The chief information officer recommends the development of a database into which both companies could dump their expertise.

In the end, management opts for a Knowledge Fair. Each Wednesday, two departments set up booths in the cafeteria courtyard. Employees of the department operate the booths, displaying samples of their work, such as photos of projects they have completed. Employees from other departments are able to stop by, examine the work, and ask questions. Employees of the newly acquired Signature are strongly encouraged to visit the Allied booths, while equally strong suggestions are made to Allied employees to stop by the Signature booths.

The results are astounding. Most comments overheard at the ongoing fair start with words like, "I didn't know anybody knew how to . . ." and "You mean, you know how to do *that?*" Management is delighted at the speed with which the two companies begin figuring out how to leverage their knowledge and resources, and even recommend how to reconfigure the company's departmental structure to capitalize on synergies.

Creating Communities Online

Knowledge transfer that occurs face-to-face is the best kind, but in organizations that have grown beyond a single building, it is not practical on an ongoing basis. For that, companies need to build knowledge networks that transcend space. Fortunately, intranets have given us tools that make it possible to transcend not only space but also time.

Take the case of Buckman Laboratories, a specialty chemical company based in Memphis, Tennessee. The company, an early adopter of online knowledge communities for its employees (the network is now known as K'Netix), has been considered a paragon of knowledge management. *Fast Company* magazine writer Glenn Rifkin told this story from the Buckman KM lore:

> Dennis Dalton . . . is based in Singapore as managing director of all company activities in Asia. According to the K'Netix archives,

Dalton sent out a call for help: 'We will be proposing a pitch-control program to an Indonesian pulp mill,' he wrote. 'I would appreciate an update on successful recent pitch-control strategies in your parts of the world.'

The first response came three hours later, from Phil Hoekstra in Memphis, and included a suggestion of the specific Buckman chemical to use and a reference to a master's thesis on pitch control of tropical hardwoods, written by an Indonesian studying at North Carolina State University.

Fifty minutes later Michael Sund logged on from Canada and offered his experience in solving the pitch problem in British Columbia. Then Nils Hallberg chimed in with examples from Sweden; Wendy Biijker offered details from a New Zealand paper mill; Jos Vallcorba gave two examples from Spain and France; Chip Hill in Memphis contributed scientific advice from the company's R&D team; Javier Del Rosal sent a detailed chemical formula and specific application directions from Mexico; and Lionel Hughes weighed in with two types of pitch-control programs in use in South Africa. In all, Dalton's request for help generated eleven replies from six countries, stimulated several 'sidebar conversations' as participants followed-up on new knowledge they'd just learned—and catapulted Dalton into position to secure a $6 million order from the Indonesian mill.[1]

That couldn't happen with traditional org chart-style command and control. It happens when there's community to support the transfer of knowledge. Between generating knowledge to win contracts, solve customer problems, and compete more effectively, it's easy to see how, over the years of K'netix's existence it has generated a $500 million net profit for Buckman.

(Incidentally, Buckman has set up a site dedicated to knowledge management. You can find it at http://www.knowledge-nurture .com/.)

One more benefit of virtual knowledge communities is that

they cross boundaries—organizational and geographical. There is a great anecdote about a company that made satellite dishes. One division made outrageously expensive dishes that were launched into space on satellites. Another made cheap dishes that were bolted onto roofs so consumers could watch satellite television. These divisions were archetypal corporate silos. Because they functioned in entirely different markets and because they employed entirely different technologies, they were isolated from one another.

Fortunately, the company had a message board for engineers. One day, a message appeared on the board. It was from an engineer in the television division, complaining that a forty-nine-cent filament in the dish was fizzling in hot, dry climates. Repair crews had to climb up ladders to rooftops in order to replace it. Could anybody help figure out how to keep it from happening?

One reply saved the company millions of dollars, not to mention a damaged reputation. It said, in essence, "I can't help solve the problem, but boy, am I glad you pointed it out! I work in the aerospace division, and we're about to send a dish into space with the same filament, and it'll be *pointed at the Sun*." (It would have been murder to send a technician up on a ladder to replace that forty-nine-cent item!)

So, let's review the business case for establishing virtual communities:

- Employees can talk to each other directly, minimizing the distortion that occurs when messages are passed through channels.
- It equalizes all employees; everybody has access to the same pool of knowledge.
- It also democratizes the submission of knowledge, because anybody can publish. (Has the person with an answer to your question ever been an administrative assistant you've never heard of and you never would have guessed had that kind of knowledge?)
- It is available twenty-four hours a day, seven days a week.
- It is available wherever the employee happens to be.

- It does not need to be accessed in real time.
- It communicates in the language that is most suitable to the user (important for global companies).
- It crosses organizational boundaries.
- It is demand-driven.
- It increases productivity, such as time-to-market and speed with which customer (and other audience) issues can be addressed.
- It improves morale. (Would you rather work for a company that is characterized by its org chart or one that reflects its communities?)

Let's examine some of the key approaches to online communities.

Message Boards

"We're shutting down our intranet message board."

That is what a client told me. The message board had been on the intranet for a while, but it was not being used very much, and when it was it was mostly so employees could complain and whine.

What went wrong?

Let's look at the problems with this message board, and what could have been done to prevent this outcome:

It Didn't Have a Theme

It was simply "the message board." It was as though the company said, "Here's a place for employees to come talk about whatever they want."

You won't find anything like that on the Net. Every message board on the Net has a theme, a focus that helps people to figure out where they can go to talk to the kind of people they want to talk with about the kind of stuff they want to talk about. Want to talk about how to grow roses? There are message boards for that. Want to talk about how much you hate the character of Wesley Crusher on *Star Trek*? There are message boards for that. (Really. I'm not making this up.) Want to talk about corporate globalization and its unsavory effect on local culture? Guess what? There are places to talk about that. But try as hard as you might, you won't find a place to talk about any old thing that crosses your mind.

That is the idea of a virtual community—a place where like-minded people can share ideas, information, and knowledge. And that is what works on intranets.

What kinds of themes should you consider for your intranet? There are two ways to look at this:

1. For the most part, you need to make certain that your themes focus on real-world business issues.
2. The themes need to be topics employees really need to talk about.

You can slice and dice your themes several ways. For example, what kinds of employees do you have who need to talk to one another? Where do you have employees who share subject-matter expertise but do not work in the same department? Some ideas include:

- Engineers
- Sales staff
- Administrative assistants
- Accountants
- Trainers

You can also create message boards for members of cross-functional project teams, for discussions of business initiatives such as quality improvement or customer satisfaction, and for people who work in the same department but are not all in one geographic location.

For example, one administrative assistant needs to know how to speed up a requisition for office equipment. He asks if anybody has ever managed to get a new PC in less than the usual four-week time frame. Another administrative assistant discovered a trick that got a PC delivered in ten days, and she shares it with the admin who asked. Administrative assistants are a fabulous test audience for a message board because they need to share their knowledge.

One organization shut down its pilot message board. Even though it had a theme, nobody was using it.

"What was the theme?" I asked.

"Employee diversity," I was told. "It's an important company-wide initiative."

"And a noble one. But is it an issue about which employees need to share knowledge and information?" I replied.

"Well . . . no."

This message board was doomed to failure.

When you launch a message board, it needs to have a topic that employees have a burning need to discuss with one another.

If the competition is a serious issue at the company, a discussion group on competition would probably be popular. If people are talking about the competition around the water cooler, it is likely they would be willing to talk about it in broader, more virtual communities. Competition is a good starter discussion group.

It Didn't Have a Moderator

Too many people think a moderator is the equivalent of a Web police officer. Wrong. The moderator is an enthusiastic member of the community who wants to see the message board succeed.

Consider a group for sales reps. The best choice for a moderator is a sales rep who is already engaged in some informal e-mail lists with other salespeople, exchanging leads, sharing ideas for selling products, telling stories about how he or she got a foot in the door. This person loves the idea of knowledge sharing and wants more.

Why recruit this character to moderate a sales discussion group? Because he or she wants it to succeed, which means this person has a low tolerance for anything that happens in the message board that would derail the conversation. This sales rep will keep the discussion on track and focused.

Of course, you can have more than one moderator in a group, which is a particularly good idea for very active groups. Develop a set of guidelines for moderators that includes:

- Any hard-and-fast rules, such as a ban on sexually explicit remarks that could result in legal consequences
- Guidelines for moderating a group, such as how often messages should be checked
- Technical information, such as how to delete a post if a particularly heinous message screams for removal

Incidentally, a moderator is not a censor. He or she does not read posts before approving them for publication. The delays inherent in such a process dramatically diminish the value of the message board. Instead, the moderator is reactive, dealing with messages after they have been posted.

There Were No Incentives

Why should people share their knowledge in a message board if there is no incentive to do so? Particularly, if they perceive that they were working just fine without taking the extra time to try out a new computer application?

Incentives come in many flavors. Simple incentives include things like prizes. I participate in an intranet discussion forum that is part of the Intranet Journal. As an incentive to participation, the forum draws the name of someone who posts a message each month and gives that person a prize. You could also pick the best post (that is, the most valuable or useful bit of knowledge that was shared).

Bob Buckman used a different type of incentive. In the early days of his knowledge-based message board K'Netix, Buckman de-livered a speech that made his expectations clear: "Those of you who have something intelligent to say now have a forum in which to say it," he told them. "Those of you who will not or cannot contribute also become obvious. If you are not willing to contribute or partici-pate, then you should understand that the many opportunities of-fered to you in the past will no longer be available."

The incentive was obvious: You would not only continue to have a job if you used K'Netix but you would also thrive in the organization. If you didn't use it, you would probably be better off seeking new employment. The carrot-and-stick approach might sound draconian, but it works. In fact, if you want to change the culture of your organization to one in which people share knowl-edge simply because that is the way things are done, you must change the reward and recognition system. Job security is an excel-lent incentive.

It Wasn't Promoted

Like anything new you want people to try, you need to market your message boards. You must tell employees how their participation will make their lives easier, help them get work done faster, and help them to create new contacts and expand their resources.

Don't limit promotion to the launch of your message boards. It should be an ongoing process. If you have a print publication, con-sider adding a feature that explains how an employee solved a prob-lem or capitalized on an opportunity by posting a message and then receiving a reply in a message board. Make it a regular feature. You can also build success stories into other articles. If you are explaining how a product team was able to launch its product three months ahead of schedule, include the story about how a message board post received an answer to a question overnight that would normally have taken weeks. In other words, make the message boards part of the company's storytelling culture.

Should You Allow Anonymous Posts?

"We don't have a very trusting culture," one communicator said. "If message boards were to succeed on our intranet, employees would have to be able to post anonymously."

This is *not* a good idea.

Remember, for the most part, these are *work*-related resources. If you post a message on a board and I read it and find it valuable, I may want to contact you for more information, or pick your brain about other related issues. Helping employees establish relationships with other employees who would otherwise never find one another is one of the goals of knowledge management. But if your post is anonymous, this will never happen.

It is far better to commit to a hands-off policy when it comes to reacting to a post you don't like, or (not to put too fine a point on it) management must grow a thicker skin. As a leader, you should recognize the value of the trade-off: In exchange for putting up with some uncomplimentary messages, you will have better productivity, better profitability, increased competitiveness, reduced turnover, and improved morale.

In addition, the culture that would lead employees to *want* to remain anonymous, one that has instilled them with a fear of speaking their minds, will begin to turn around. This culture shift can only have positive implications for the organization as the bond of trust between employees and the organization improves.

There are, however, some times when it is appropriate to allow anonymous messages. You may, for example, inaugurate a short-term message board during a traumatic change, such as a layoff, a reorganization, or a merger. There is nothing wrong with a message board where employees can ask questions about the things they are most concerned about or to express their deepest fears. This is a message board that probably *should* be anonymous. It is a judgment call. But for the most part, employees' names should be attached to their messages.

Short-Term Groups

You can use message board technology for anything that makes sense, including short-term discussions. The U.S. General Services Administration used a limited-time message board to encourage employee dialogue about how to fix problems in the agency, leading to an overhaul that succeeded largely because employees felt ownership of the changes—the changes the agency implemented had, after all, emerged from their conversations.

Let's consider the IBM experience. With tens of thousands of employees scattered around the world—many working in nontraditional teams in which they didn't regularly see their managers or supervisors—the company wondered how to spark employee involvement in addressing key issues the company was facing. The answer was "World Jam," a three-day knowledge-sharing and idea-generating event on the company intranet. The company generated a list of discussion topics; an intranet site was created for each one. Message boards, chat rooms, and forms for submitting ideas were included along with general overviews of the issues. Over the three days, thousands of ideas were generated. Several were put to use immediately; others were targeted for study. Vice presidents participated equally with front-line employees. Approximately ninety thousand employees contributed to the online discussion, from about ninety countries. The event was so successful that IBM developed an offshoot for a more limited population, called "Manager Jam," and (as of this writing) is in the process of developing a "Sales Jam."

Non-Work-Related Message Boards

The vast majority of your message boards should be work related, but nobody ever said work should not be fun. Companies have employee picnics, holiday parties, and a host of other special events. Some set up employee recreation centers. Many companies offer employee clubs, ranging from car clubs and book clubs to religious groups and gay-and-lesbian clubs. The reason for all of this is that, at some level, somebody recognized that work is social. If companies are going to ask employees to dedicate so much of their lives to work that they don't have time for a life outside of work, it is only fair to help them live part of their nonwork lives while in the workplace. This is the notion of "work-life integration."

Message boards are a natural extension of this philosophy.

You can set up message boards for each of the clubs or employee social groups that already exist. (This is a logical idea, since the vast majority of Internet users participate in an online community that is a virtual extension of a physical community to which they already belong, such as their church, the PTA, or some other social group.)

You also can set up some online-only social opportunities, such as a recipe exchange or a book discussion group.

But classified advertisements represent perhaps the most common non-work-related message board in the business world. Here, employees offer their used cars and bikes, litters of kittens and puppies, vacation rentals, cast-off computers, and other odds and ends for sale or rent.

Classifieds are a common feature in many companies, and it makes sense to move them to a message board environment. From the company perspective, it means no employee is dedicating work time to managing the classifieds. It is also a great way for employees to become accustomed to using the message board interface. Finally, employees have one more opportunity to meet each other through channels that are likely to connect people who might otherwise never connect.

Other non-work-related message boards that are appropriate in a work environment are of an affinity nature, such as a Hispanic Workers Association, a Women's Network, or a Gay and Lesbian Employees Association.

Measuring Effectiveness

No communication effort should go unmeasured, including message boards. I have heard many people say that it is easy to obtain anecdotal evidence of their effectiveness, but that a quantifiable number is impossible to come by.

Don't tell that to Bob Buckman. The CEO of Buckman Laboratories (whom I promise I won't mention again after this) told an audience that his message boards are responsible for half a billion dollars to his company's bottom line since he first launched them. How did he arrive at that number? By monitoring the discussions, he has been able to determine:

- The dollar value of sales that were finalized thanks to knowledge passed on in the forum, such as a $6 million contract for pitch-control chemicals in Singapore
- The dollar value of existing customers who didn't take their business elsewhere when they had a problem thanks to employees resolving the problem quickly and efficiently over the knowledge message boards

This type of measurement has convinced Buckman that message boards are worth any risk they might pose.

Here are some approaches you can use to measure the effectiveness of your message boards:

Quantifiable Measurement

You probably don't have the time to read every post in every message board to assess its value. Instead, pick two or three hard-core work-related groups. Pick one from each category of groups (one job related, one issue focused, and so on). Monitor the posts carefully for one month. Assess the value of the messages, which can include:

- Any actual sales completed because of information passed from one employee to another.

- The value of reduced cycle times: What is it worth in hard dollars if a project is completed in half the usual time? What is it worth if a product reaches market three months earlier, and ahead of a competitor's offering?
- Offset costs: The following scenario isn't difficult to imagine: A project team was about to spend a bundle of money on a test conducted by an outside research lab. However, a post to a message board revealed that another department in the company already had the required equipment, so the company saved nearly $100,000 as a result.
- The value of a customer whose business was at risk but was ultimately retained because his problem was addressed using information obtained in a message board.

Other real measurable results will make themselves apparent when you see them. Now, multiply those results by twelve. You can assume that similar messages are being posted every month, not only the month when you happened to be watching. Then, multiply that by the total number of work-related message boards. It will give you a realistic idea of the bottom-line value of your message boards.

In addition to this method, you can use focus groups, surveys, and anecdotal evidence (which is discussed next under Qualified Measurement) that reveal a hard-dollar value. For instance, you may hear in a focus group that a frustrated employee was considering an offer from another company, but after a particularly satisfying work experience in a message board, decided to stay. That is a reduction in turnover, which is a quantifiable measure.

If you don't know the value of a particular outcome, somebody in your company does! Take the issue of employee retention. In your recruiting department, somebody knows what it costs to lose and replace an employee (in some industries, the average is 1.5 times one year's salary for the position being replaced). All you need to do is find the person who knows that value and ask. (If you don't know whom to ask, post the question on the appropriate message board.)

Qualified Measurement

Not all of your measurement needs to result in hard dollars. Even the most reputable communication measurement experts will tell you that qualified measures are an entirely valid tool for assessing effectiveness.

To assemble evidence supporting the value of your message boards, you can assign the following techniques to your communications staff:

Focus groups. Assemble a group every month to discuss message boards, including opportunities for improving their effectiveness. Record a summary of the group's comments. You can also discuss message boards as an element of a focus group convened to talk about other issues. For example, you can ask a group that gathers to provide feedback on a business initiative about how much the message board has contributed to the initiative.

Surveys. If you conduct a regular communication audit or work-environment study, start adding message boards to the mix. If you have a regular poll on your intranet, dedicate a question now and then to the value of message boards. You can even issue a survey dedicated to message boards.

Anecdotes. If you hear a success story about a message board, jot it down and store it with others. Ultimately, you can create a document that lists one success story after another. Include those that you used as write-ups in your company publications.

Taken together, these hard-number and soft results will provide overwhelming evidence of the value of your message boards.

Real-Time Chat and Instant Messaging

So far, the communities we have been talking about have had one characteristic in common—they are all *asynchronous*. That is, they don't take place in real time. Any kind of message board involves leaving a message, then checking in later to see whether anybody has left a response. E-mail communities are clearly not real-time, since you have to wait until the recipient(s) check their e-mail and then write a reply.

There are ways to build communities that take place in real time, involving the immediate give-and-take of messages between multiple participants who are all at their desks at the same time.

There is great potential value to real-time communities—but the value is limited. You will discover that most of the communities that you create or support are more effective in the asynchronous mode. When you are not forced to be at your desk at a specific time, you are able to participate more frequently.

Given that there is broader participation in asynchronous communities, why would you want to consider real-time efforts? Consider the following advantages:

- From a purely practical standpoint, real-time communities can have a significant impact on the volume of e-mail in your organization. The more your employees can engage their communities in search of quick answers and fast facts, the less e-mail they'll need to send.
- Real-time communities tend to be more personal and, in business environments, more cordial. There is something detached about typing a message to a message board; in a chat room, you're actually typing to a real person who is going to respond immediately, so you tend to be more solicitous.
- The fact that real-time chat is more personal means that individuals participating in it will be more likely to establish bonds and be more inclined to work together.

A variety of real-time methods exist, including:

Chat. If you have ever taken part in an America Online chat room, you've taken part in a chat. You enter a room populated by other individuals. You have a screen that is usually divided into two parts (some chat clients employ multiple screens): One part allows you to enter your text, the other shows all the words that you and other participants have entered.

You type your message into your window, then either click a Submit button or hit your enter key. Your words appear almost instantly in the larger chat window.

Often, these messages fly fast and furious; in some Internet chat rooms—many of them functioning under the Internet Relay Chat (IRC) protocol—you must type quickly on the keyboard to get your message posted to the conversation so that it makes sense in the context of the overall dialogue.

Instant messaging. Instant messaging (IM) is just like chat, except that it is limited to a one-on-one conversation rather than an entire group. However, if you have ever watched a teenager instant message, you know that you can have several IM sessions going on concurrently.

IM works when you build a buddy list, which is a list of individuals with whom you'd like to be able to talk online. Your list will show which of your buddies are at their desks and which are away. If you want to initiate a conversation with a buddy, double-click his or her name in your buddy list and the appropriate windows open.

Chats Among Employees

Many companies have dismissed the idea of letting employees chat online. Even if they subscribe to the idea of message boards, most are disinclined to let people simply talk to each other in real time. While they can take part in newsgroups when they have the time, chats require that they participate when the chat is happening, even if they have other work they should be doing.

The challenge is to apply chat to a genuine business issue rather than try to find a business issue that will let you use chat. I have heard many communicators say something like, "Chat is a very cool tool and I'd love to have it on our intranet. What could we use it for?" That is the wrong approach. The right approach is to say, "We have a need to brainstorm a solution to a business problem. We don't know which employees might have viable solutions, and our employees are scattered across the country. It would be important to capture all of the comments that are made so we could analyze and distill them. Hey, a chat room would let us do *all* that."

In other words, the business need precedes the tactical solution.

With that in mind, let's look at some of the circumstances that would suggest live, real-time chat as a solution:

The value of real time. As noted earlier, there is something particularly personal about chatting with other people when you *know* they are sitting at their desks at the same time you are.

The ability to capture what people say. The text of a chat can be automatically set to "save."

The desire to prevent "herd mentality." In face-to-face meetings—and even telephone conversations—dominant personalities tend to take control, leaving others to follow their leads. Although chat does not completely eliminate this herd mentality, it certainly minimizes it. The force of somebody's physical presence or tone of voice is not a factor—only the power of his or her words.

Why not telephone conference calls?

The biggest argument against chat is that the telephone is much easier. Everyone has one, you don't need to know how to type to use it, conversations are much faster, and you can actually hear the real voice of the individuals who are speaking.

All of which is true—assuming there are only a few people on the call. By the time you have up to six or more, the telephone becomes unmanageable. People keep interrupting one another and it becomes difficult to keep track of the conversation. And just *try* to

take notes about everything everyone says! Of course, you can record the conversation, *then* take notes. You can even use the telephone conferencing system by which an operator takes requests to
let people talk one at a time. But these techniques disrupt the conversational nature of the conference call, and they can run into some
serious money, too. At that point, you are better off with chat.

Guidelines for Effective Employee Chats

Most of the employee chat rooms that fail do so because they are
aimless. One telecommunications company had a chat room open
twenty-four hours a day. It had no theme. It was merely a place
where employees could go to chat. The company hoped employees
would pop in and meet one another. Only a few die-hard chat fans
used it, though, and their conversations were pointless (except for
those that were flat-out negative).

Like discussion groups, chat rooms need to have a purpose. (For
details on how to use a chat room specifically for leaders to engage
in communication with employees, see Chapter 6.) I have not found
a good reason to open a chat room twenty-four hours a day. No matter how large a company is, it does not have enough people to sustain
momentum in a chat room on an ongoing basis. It takes the entire
Internet or the entire subscription base of America Online to generate that kind of participation.

Let Employees Schedule Chats When the Need Arises

Any employee should be able to schedule a chat. A company can
create an online utility that allows an employee to set the time, date,
and topic. The employee should also be able to enter a list of employees that he or she would like to participate in the chat (if the
chat is going to be limited to a small group, such as a project team)
so those employees receive e-mail notification or an announcement
is generated to appear on a list of upcoming chats.

Schedule and Announce Special Chats

This is the approach IBM took with its World Jam event. Chat rooms were announced for real-time engagements along with the asynchronous newsgroup discussions. Employees knew in advance the nature of each chat room and when it would be active. You could use this approach to invite employees to brainstorm, to offer feedback, or to share their knowledge on a particular issue. It is also a great way to allow employees to express themselves under certain circumstances. On September 11, 2001, for instance, it might have been useful to let employees jump into a chat room to convey their feelings and offer each other real-time support.

Regularly Scheduled Chats

Employees could know that a chat takes place every Wednesday at 4 P.M. EDT among, say, sales reps to discuss new issues and competitive intelligence. Anybody who is available at that time is welcome to jump in; others can read the transcripts. This is also an effective way to bring more employees from distant locations into events such as weekly or monthly "brown-bag lunches," where participants listen to a speaker and then engage in conversation about the speaker's topic.

Succeeding with Chats

The following guidelines can ensure that these types of chat rooms do not flounder:

Communicate and train. Like newsgroups, chat rooms should be treated as business initiatives, not merely new technology that has been rolled out. Ensure that employees understand at launch *and* on an ongoing basis the reason for chat rooms and employee obligations to use them professionally.

Use a moderator. No chat room should mirror the kind of anarchy that exists in so many public chat rooms. The moderator behaves much like those in newsgroups—reactively, to keep the conversation on track and deal with any problems or issues that might arise.

Use easy software. While the software should be technically sound, it is also important that employees not struggle to use it. Test the software you bring in-house with a group of employees who are *not* your power-user base.

Announce chats in advance. Ensure that the right employees know the chat is coming so they can make plans to be there.

Take questions or comments in advance. Employees who simply *cannot* be there may still want to participate. Have questions and comments sent to the moderator so that he or she can incorporate them into the conversation.

Summarize results. Produce a short document that captures the most important information that arose out of the chat. Ensure that management members sees it so they know that this is not some kind of technical time waster, but that it is generating genuine business value.

Instant Messaging

The number of people in the U.S. workforce using IM is up 34 percent over a year-earlier figure, according to a study called "Instant Messaging in the Workplace" released by Jupiter Media Metrix. As of September 2001, 13.4 million people were using IM, up from 10 million in September 2000.

For most people, IM is that tool kids use to hold conversations over the Internet with friends who live a block away. My fourteen-year-old daughter can IM simultaneously with ten to fifteen friends. And perhaps it is because IM is most popular among children that management shrugs off its workplace potential. But that potential is huge.

How It Works

IM is a one-to-one chat. You maintain a buddy list, which contains a list of all the people with whom you want to IM. You can add new people to your buddy list and put them into categories, such as "HR," "Engineers," or "Project Team." When you want to chat with one of them, simply double-click the name and a window will appear on your screen. Type your message (and keep it short), and then hit Enter (or click the button), and your message will pop up in a window on the monitor of the individual you selected.

Someone wants to chat with you? A window will pop up on your computer—unless you set your IM software to "away." You can even set the away message; for example, "I'm in a meeting; back by 3 P.M." That message will appear on the screen of the individual sending you a message (which they would do only if they did not notice that your icon on their buddy list showed that you were away).

Why IM Reduces E-Mail and Builds Productivity

Employees use e-mail to contact other employees because it is more efficient (in most cases) than leaving a voice mail message. You make the call and discover the person you wanted to talk to is not at his or her desk, so rather than leave an inefficient voice mail, you fire off an e-mail. But you still must wait until your colleague replies to your e-mail message before you can move on, using the information for whatever you needed it for.

With IM, assuming your colleague is at his or her desk, you can get the answer to your question right now. And because the nature of IM is *short*—short messages, short replies—most exchanges happen in a heartbeat. Problem solved, employees move on. Fewer e-mail messages are left, so work is done faster.

IM is making inroads in many organizations that have found applications for it based on its strengths. Call center employees use instant messaging so that they can get answers to customer questions without ever having to put the customer on hold. In one company, approximately 30 percent of the telephone bill is attributable to employees on one continent calling employees on another only to find the employee is not at his or her desk. This prompts the caller to leave a voice mail message, which results in another call. Now, the company requires employees to IM an employee on another continent (at no cost) to ensure that employee is at his or her desk. The company's telephone expense has dropped dramatically.

Note

1. Glenn Rifkin, "Buckman Labs Is Nothing But Net," *Fast Company*, June/July 1996, p. 118.

CHAPTER THIRTEEN

Measuring the Value of Internal Communication

YOU CAN MAKE three measurements during a typical communication process. First, before you develop a strategy you can benchmark the status quo. If, for example, your goal is to improve job satisfaction, you need to know the current level of satisfaction. Without this baseline, how will you ever know if anything has improved?

Second, you need to assess the validity of the communication plan you have developed. You need to test it with a sample of the audience for whom it is intended.

Finally, you need to find out if it worked. This is the most critical phase of measurement. It is not my intention to dismiss the first two, but practically speaking, most companies don't have the time or budget to spend as much time researching as they do communicating. But if you do nothing else, you need to know that your communications are paying off, that they are influencing outcomes consistent with your company's bottom-line goals.

The first measure is the one that points out the need for communication. You need to find out how things currently are before you can use the tools and strategies of communication to fix them. One method for obtaining this information is through a communication audit or environmental survey.

You can go about conducting this study several ways. Most experts recommend a three-step process:

1. *Focus groups.* Speaking directly with a group of employees can reveal some trends about the company's communication strengths and weaknesses. You should conduct these sessions with at least three groups—first-line employees, supervisors, and managers. Depending on the size of your company, you may also want to cover different locations, for example, plants versus offices or international offices.
2. *Executive interviews.* Your communicators should spend time with you and other leaders in the organization to ensure they understand the company's issues, initiatives, and other matters that leaders believe need to be communicated.
3. *Survey.* Using the results of the focus groups, craft a questionnaire to develop statistical information about the state of communications in the company.

Your survey can use several techniques, including multiple choice ("What's the most difficult kind of information for you to get when you need it?") and gap analyses ("What's your preferred source of information about company performance? What's your actual source of information about company performance?").

The results of this process should help you identify what the company is doing well and where it can improve its internal communication efforts to support organizational goals and objectives.

Assessing the Prospects of a Communication Plan

Once you have developed a communication plan, don't simply launch it and hope for the best. Test it with your audience to ensure that it hits the mark.

Here are two quick case studies to show you how a pilot test can work. The first deals with a change to a compensation program.

At Allied Gate & Fence

Remember Allied's efforts to communicate a change to its merit increase program (presented earlier in the book)? Managers were paid too much and installers were paid too little. The result was that installers were leaving to work for higher-paying competitors, but high managerial compensation was boosting bid prices into the stratosphere, so the company was losing the vast majority of its bids. The change to the merit increase program, while dramatic, was meant to bring pay in line with industry standards so that contract bids would be reasonable and installers would not be eager to defect to competitors.

Before Allied's communication department introduced the change to the merit plan, they determined that peer opinion leaders were the greatest potential obstacle to the program's success. Employees would turn to these people and ask, "What do you think of this? Is this for real, or is it a load of crap?" The responses these individuals gave could make or break the program.

To counter the potential damage these employees might cause, the communications staff convened a meeting of about thirty-five people identified as peer opinion leaders. Of course, they didn't know that was who they were. They couldn't look around the room and say, "Hey, this is a room full of opinion leaders like me!" The meeting was positioned as a pilot test and they were told that they had been selected as representatives of the general employee population.

The CEO joined the communicators for the presentation of the entire communication plan to the group, explaining the reason for the communication and showing them mock-ups of print material. They walked through the phases of the plan, showed mock-ups of proposed collateral, and then asked for feedback.

The peer opinion leaders told the CEO and his communicators what they thought employees would believe and what they wouldn't, then offered suggestions on changes to make the program more credible. The communications staff incorporated nearly all the suggestions peer opinion leaders offered, even some they were less than thrilled with. When the communications rolled out, peer opinion leaders throughout the company felt a sense of ownership of the plan. When employees turned to them for their opinions, they expressed their support, the most critical element in the program's success.

The second example focuses on a benefits enrollment campaign.

At Allied Gate & Fence

Allied's benefits department developed an online self-service benefits program. The process included a tight integration of the enrollment process—the completion of forms—with information about benefits plans and communication about changes.

The enrollment process would be a huge cultural shift for employees accustomed to using paper forms. Many employees had never been on the company's intranet before.

Allied's communications department assembled a cross-section of employees from across the United States as a pilot group. The pilot group was given access to all the same content employees would receive when the enrollment period began. They were also sent mock communications about changes using the same channels that would be used with the entire population.

The feedback communicators received helped them with everything from adjusting the steps people would go through to complete the enrollment to the positioning of change statements. The rollout's success was attributable largely to the input obtained from those who participated in the test.

You don't need to limit pilot tests to one-time or special programs. Even if you're planning a redesign of a monthly print magazine, you should test the design with the employees who will be using the magazine.

What to Measure: Communication Tools

Communicators spend far too much time measuring how much employees like their publications, intranet pages, and e-mail bulletins. The real focus of measurement activities needs to be on how good the company's communications are at helping leaders sleep at night.

That doesn't mean that a company should not assess the effectiveness of its communication tools. After all, if the tools are awful, employees will never pay attention to the communications in the first place. Therefore, there is value in measuring the effectiveness of the tools. However, a company should not spend all its measurement efforts in this area.

For all of your communications, regardless of the medium, there are certain measures you can identify fairly easily:

- *Cost per audience member.* Divide your communications budget by members of the audience.
- *Readability.* Calculate the grade level of your writing and determine how that stacks up against the reading level of your audience.
- *Distribution.* Find out when people received specific communications. Use the sample to assess the delivery system.
- *Audience penetration.* Identify the subcategories of employees, such as executives, supervisors, specialists, line employees, or union employees. Note which of your media or channels are designed to reach those subgroups.
- *Media mix.* Determine the type of media you use to ensure that you are achieving an appropriate balance.
- *Content analysis.* Ensure that your communication vehicles are being used to address company issues and objectives.

There also are measurement techniques you can use for each type of channel.

Measuring Print

Back in the days when nearly all employee communication was printed, reader response cards were popular measurement tools. Personally, I never liked them. First of all, the only people who ever responded to them were your readers. People who *didn't* read the publication never sent in response cards. They never got to the point of opening the publication to find the cards in the first place! Second, there is nothing scientific about who responds. You might be able to identify some trends, but you won't be able to state with certainty that the results reflect the opinions of the entire employee population.

Finally, most reader response cards address superficial issues, such as "Did you read all, most, or only part of the publication?" "Do you find the design appealing, do you not pay attention to the design, or does the design need improvement?" "What was your favorite article in this issue?"

Frankly, I don't care how much an employee likes a publication. I only care that employees were influenced by the contents in a manner consistent with the goals associated with producing that content in the first place.

Again, this is not to suggest that there is no value to inserting a reader response card in a print publication. But if you do, you should craft your questions to solicit feedback you can actually use to improve the publication's odds of capturing attention and being relevant.

Some questions to consider asking, and some sample answers (actual choices will depend on your publication and your company) include:

- When do you read the publication? (As soon as it arrives. When I have time. At home.)
- What parts of the publication are you able to relate specifically to your job? (President's column. Financial reports. Ethics column. Customer profiles. Organizational announcements.)

- How easy is it for you to find the information in each issue of the publication that you're most interested in?
- What compels you to open the publication? (The cover story. The items listed on the cover. Desire to find pictures of people I know in the publication. Need for updated financial information. Curiosity. I read it because I work here and I should know what's going on.)
- How credible is the information in the publication? (Very believable. I take it with a grain of salt. It's corporate spin from start to finish.)
- Which article(s) in this issue were *most* useful to you in your job? (List articles and features.)
- Which article(s) in this issue were *least* useful to you in your job? (List articles and features.)

Measuring Face-to-Face Communication

Measuring face-to-face communication is trickier than any other channel. You're not measuring a product generated in a communications department; instead, you're measuring the ability of supervisors and leaders to communicate. That is, you measure their effectiveness in order to identify the kinds of training required to improve their abilities so that they can support your organization's communication strategies.

You need to decide whether you will ask only the people with whom supervisors and leaders engage in face-to-face encounters to evaluate their bosses, or whether you will ask those delivering the messages to evaluate themselves.

Finally, you must decide whether your evaluations will be absolute or relative. Absolute evaluations determine how good or bad the communication is. You can use an absolute evaluation to record improvements after the supervisors or leaders have undergone training or counseling for their face-to-face communication skills. A relative evaluation ranks the speaker's skills, which means even a bad speaker will be able to identify his or her best trait. This approach is less threatening to the supervisor or leader than an absolute assessment, if not quite as useful.

A relative evaluation would look for a ranking of best skill (1) to worst skill (10) for such issues as:

• Giving clear instructions
• Soliciting employee input
• Conducting staff meetings
• Providing feedback

An absolute evaluation would, for instance, use a scale (1 to 5, 1 being strongly disagree, 5 being strongly agree, and 3 serving as the "no-opinion" midpoint) for statements such as:

• "My supervisor effectively explains how company initiatives will affect our department."
• "My supervisor is good at speaking in front of groups."
• "My supervisor does a good job when conducting my annual performance evaluations."

Measuring Electronic Communication

The worst mistake communicators (and others) make when measuring the effectiveness of online communication is measuring hits. Hits, according to one communication measurement guru, is an acronym for "how idiots track success."

A hit is a record in a server log that shows how many files have been transferred to a browser from the server. What good does it do me to know that four hits were recorded when someone visited this page? Imagine how useless it is to tell your boss, "Our intranet got 50,000 hits this month!" So what?

You're better off recording unique visits, but even that is of limited value. Knowing that someone visited a page doesn't tell you whether it was the page they were looking for. They might have followed a link, looked at it, and said, "Jeez, this *still* isn't the information I want!" It doesn't tell you whether they read the page, what they did while they were there, how they got there, where they went next, or if they were influenced by what they read.

The limitations of recording traffic doesn't mean that you shouldn't do it. You can still learn a great deal from measuring site traffic, including:

- When people use your intranet most. Are there peak hours?
- Where people tend to start.
- The most frequently visited pages.
- What pages or sites you have created that employees are *not* visiting (leading you to launch an inquiry into the reasons: It is not interesting? It is not needed? It is not easy to find?).

Beyond statistics, though, you should look into the usability of your intranet. Usability refers to the ease with which employees can find what they're looking for and take advantage of the resources and applications available online. Volumes have been written about usability, but the main thing to know, according to usability guru Jakob Nielsen, is that intranets that are *not* usable can cost an average midsize company as much as $5 million annually in lost productivity. Some usability elements to consider are the intranet's search engine, navigation, content (readability, for instance), and applications (such as an expense reimbursement form or a benefits enrollment process).

What to Measure: Outcomes

Now we come to the crux of communication measurement. This is the research that shows management that communication does, in fact, support the bottom line and help you sleep better at night.

The first step in measuring outcomes is to know what your

communication efforts are supposed to accomplish in the first place. Earlier, we looked at a four-step strategic planning process. That process started with identifying a goal, setting strategies, then establishing measurable objectives. One of the most important reasons to go through this process is to know what you are going to measure to determine if your communication worked.

. I have served several times as a judge for the International Gold Quill communications competition sponsored by the International Association of Business Communicators (IABC), working both at the first-tier level and on the blue ribbon panel. My greatest frustration (shared by other judges) always occurs in the measurement arena. Entrants are supposed to show how they measured the successes of their efforts. Under the category of objectives, they list lofty and noble aims. Under measurement, they talk about meaningless results that have nothing to do whatsoever with the objectives. No kidding; we once had a submission where the measurement was, "Our president's wife sent us a letter telling us how much she liked it."

By now, of course, you know how absurd that is. It may have made the communications staff feel good to know that Mrs. President enjoyed the magazine, but what you really want to know is whether that magazine influenced anybody in a manner consistent with the objectives you set.

The following example is from Angela Sinickas, ABC, president of Sinickas Communications, Inc.—one of the leading authorities on internal communication measurement. (Visit Angela Sinickas's Web site at http://www.sinicom.com.) Let's say your goal was to improve safety on the factory floor. Your strategy is a cash award for employees if they meet a target for accidents over a certain period. You set objectives: By year-end 95 percent of the employees in the factory will know the maximum number of accidents allowed to be eligible for the cash award. They also will know, on any given day, how many accidents have occurred to date and the names of their teammates who have had an accident during the contest period.

Finally, you want 70 percent of the factory workers to agree (or strongly agree) to the following question on a survey: "If I see a co-worker operating machinery in an unsafe manner, I feel it is my responsibility to encourage him or her to change that behavior."

Now you have measured outcomes. It doesn't matter if those factory workers liked the poster, or read the entire brochure, or enjoyed the artwork, or thought the supervisor's speech on the topic was well delivered. All that matters is that you achieved the results you set out to achieve.

Other outcomes to consider include the following:

- Company performance
- Employee satisfaction
- Trust
- Role knowledge
- Employee involvement
- Employee commitment
- Productivity

How you measure outcomes depends on the kind of results you are looking for. You can, for instance, measure improvement over time. If your baseline research indicates that employees don't support the quality improvement initiative, you measure the groundswell of support that materialized after you have communicated. (For example, only 15 percent of supervisors included quality improvement goals in their performance evaluations before your communication, but afterward, 85 percent of supervisors are including these goals in the performance evaluations they conduct with their direct reports.)

Actual results are another solid measurement. Let's say the goal is to have 75 percent of your employees complete the new online benefits enrollment by the early-bird deadline. Did you achieve that result?

Finally, you can assess the gap between ideal and actual communication. Find out what your various audiences think you should be communicating, and how they want that communication delivered. Judge that against your actual communications to adjust your content mix and your approaches to delivery.

How to Measure

Now that you know what to measure, you must determine how you are going to do it. The following is a list of measurement tools:

Surveys

Surveys offer a great opportunity to track the opinions of the audiences we communicate with. Did we create awareness or knowledge? Were we able to persuade a group to change an opinion?

The ability to be precise when measuring awareness, knowledge, and behaviors has limits determined by the tools we use. We can track readership, Web-site hits, or observe behaviors such as meeting attendance or involvement. These are all good statistics but they are flat measures. They tell little about results and even less about causation.

Surveys can do the following two things:

1. Measure where you are at a particular point in time with respect to an opinion, a behavior, or knowledge. This provides a benchmark upon which you can plan and evaluate change.
2. Track what is changing over time.

Paralysis from Analysis

Surveys are not good for everything. Too many surveys in an organization create noise. They send mixed messages about what is important to the organization. Additionally, employees become blasé about surveys when the company is continually conducting them, leading many employees to stop taking the time to complete them. Surveys should always be driven by corporate priorities and relate to business performance. There should be excellent business reasons to do surveys and surveys should support business strategy.

The use of survey data can also be a problem. Survey data is not a measure of individual motivation. Mining data down to its smallest parts is not useful if it does not represent a prevailing attitude. Measure how groups behave together and look for prevailing results.

Current Survey Methodologies

The main survey methodologies currently used are online surveys and paper surveys.

Online Surveys

The online Web-based survey offers an invitation to respondents to participate by using an e-mail message with a link to a survey on a Web site. The invitation explains why the survey is being conducted and what will be done with the results. After completing the survey, the respondent clicks the Submit button, which enables the encrypted data to be sent to a database for tabulation and analysis.

The Pros

- You can reach geographically dispersed employee groups more quickly and more cheaply than paper-based surveys.
- You can conduct surveys overnight if you need fast turnaround and quick answers.
- Online surveys, constructed and administered with good software, are easier and faster to complete. In the first three days online, the survey will generate more than 70 percent of the total data collected.
- Response rate is higher and faster than conventional paper-and-pencil surveys.

- Data processing and analysis is much faster when you eliminate manual data entry (for telephone or paper surveys).
- Costs and data-processing time are independent of the number of responses. It doesn't matter whether you are surveying four hundred or forty thousand employees online.
- Collecting open-ended responses keyed in by employees is easier and cheaper (no transcription costs).
- Online surveying of employees is a fast, inexpensive tool for employee pulse taking, single-issue employee feedback, or full-blown communication audits.

The database compiles all the respondent data and the software tabulates and processes it. There is no risk of human error because the processes are automated. The reports are then prepared from the data.

The Cons

- Surveys attached to or as part of an e-mail message are cumbersome to manage and consume a large amount of bandwidth. There are still many people who do not understand how to attach a page of responses to an e-mail reply.
- Some organizations leave field staff offline with no access to a terminal or kiosk.
- Some employees are still suspicious of the confidentiality of electronic data submission even to an independent Web site. This perception is decreasing as employees' comfort with Web-based technology increases.
- The critical factors to consider for online surveys are the capability of the software and your survey expertise. There are many software packages that deliver nice-looking surveys, but the analytical capabilities are very limited (often to frequencies reporting, no graphs).

Online surveys have a bias. Those who respond online will be more likely to prefer electronic communication and less likely to prefer paper or faxes.

Paper Survey

The paper survey is typically delivered to employees directly by using internal mail. The fill-out time ranges from two to three weeks. It is sent back through internal and/or external mail. When received, it is entered either manually or by scanner into a database.

The Pros

- The paper survey can be sent to anyone.
- It gives the respondents time to think about their responses.
- The survey can be filled out over time.
- No technical knowledge needed.

The Cons

- Paper is expensive. You must print it, mail it, and input the data when it comes back.
- The response rate of a mail survey is lower than an online survey.
- Respondents can lose the paper surveys or treat them like junk mail.
- The time it takes to administer weeks out and weeks to return.
- Manual data entry takes longer and data entry by scanner is expensive.

Focus Groups

Focus groups are of particular value *before* you launch a survey. Although they provide *qualitative* rather than *quantitative* results, the trends and issues you identify can help you to focus your survey on the proper material. After a survey, you can conduct focus groups again to try to obtain the reasons employees answered the survey the way they did.

You can also get away with more focus groups than surveys. Since only eight to ten people participate and they are different people all the time, you're not going back to the well over and over again. I used to conduct monthly focus groups among employees in the companies for which I worked simply as a way to stay in touch. I always covered the key communication objectives we had been working on that month, then opened it up to participants to discuss any issues or challenges they were facing.

Conducting a focus group is not merely a matter of gathering a group of people and asking questions. Focus group facilitators should use a protocol to guide them through their questions. They must be able to handle dominating participants—the herd mentality quickly takes over in many focus groups; more passive participants simply agree with the more aggressive ones. Facilitators need to know how to keep people focused, how to probe, and how to leave one topic behind to move on to the next topic. In many instances, you are better off bringing in a professional focus group facilitator. (There is another advantage to using outside help—employees are more comfortable expressing themselves candidly to an outsider than to a company representative.)

Keep focus group participants at the same level. Don't mix vice presidents and administrative assistants in the same session.

Interviews

One-on-one interviews can be useful in identifying trends. Immediately following quarterly managers meetings, we used to call fifty managers who were selected randomly from the employee directory to ask what they got out of the meeting. We never drove respondents to the answers we were hoping to get, but our hope was that they would focus on the key message we wanted to get out. This is not very scientific, but if only a handful of respondents listed the same issue we had identified, we knew we had not communicated well and had to go back to the drawing board.

You can also conduct interviews with your organization's leaders to identify their issues (that is, figure out what's keeping them awake at night), and how they perceive communication can make a difference.

Anecdotal Evidence

It certainly never hurts to throw anecdotes into the mix. Conversations you overhear in the cafeteria, letters or e-mail you receive from employees commenting on your communication, stories told in meetings—these are all valid as means of supporting your assertions about the outcomes your efforts have achieved.

Other Measures

Based on your resources, you can use a variety of other measures employed by professional researchers. The following list is courtesy of Angela Sinickas, ABC, president of Sinickas Communications, Inc. and one of the best in the field:

Micro network analysis. If there is a breakdown in the communication loop among a small but important group of people, you can find out where the breakdown is occurring. Diagram communication interactions in that group to show where connections are working and where they are weak.

Decision-making analysis. This quantifies the amount of interaction required between different organizational groups to provide information needed for decisions, to make the decisions, and finally to execute the decisions. Using this technique, you can determine if some managers have a responsibility to communicate with too many or too frequently. (When their communication responsibility comes up against their other responsibilities, overwhelming communication activities may wind up taking a backseat.)

"Starch" study groups. Use these to analyze in detail your key communication media. This is similar to the Starch Test used in advertising research, which asks readers to recall which advertisements they saw in a magazine. Ask your audience members immediately after you distribute a publication what they remember from it. Then, distribute copies of it and ask them to review it item by item and respond to questions about what they recollect, why they skipped certain articles, and so forth.

Media effectiveness. Assess the effectiveness of the media used in the company: content analysis, media analysis, log sheets for in-box analysis of memos, e-mail, and voice mail; supervisor skill assessment; meeting assessment; and intranet site usage.

Measuring managers as communicators. Assess how well managers are handling face-to-face communication, particularly in terms of delivering company messages.

Knowledge tests. Ask employees how much they know about the subject or issue you have been communicating.

At Allied Gate & Fence

For all the research Allied's communications department conducts, none is more useful than the one-page quick survey distributed after every communication. Essentially, the same survey goes out after every issue of the company's magazine is delivered, after every managers meeting, and after new intranet sites are launched.

The survey features sixteen questions, four for each of the levels that need to be achieved for a communication to be successful at influencing audiences. Four questions deal with logistics—for example, ''Did the publication reach you in time to be useful?'' ''Was the publication readable?'' Four questions determine how effective the communication was at getting the employees' attention. Four more queried employees about the relevance of the communication. And four questions were designed to determine whether the employee's opinions or behaviors changed (or were reinforced) as a result of the communication.

The questions were mixed up so that employees couldn't follow the progression from logistics to influence. The results, however, were presented in those four categories, making it easy to determine where a communication failed so that corrective action could be taken.

The survey was sent to one hundred employees randomly selected from the HR database. While not scientific, this approach revealed any major trends (for instance, in one case, virtually all employees responding to the survey noted that the communication simply was not relevant to their work). The company's leaders paid more attention to these survey results than any others; the results pointed to the success or failure of specific, tangible efforts.

Messaging Policies

WHAT FOLLOWS are recommended policies for e-mail and other tools. You can even use this page as a template for your own policies. However, they are *generic;* they do not necessarily address your organization's culture, systems, or issues.

If you use these policies as guidelines, be certain to integrate the results of your research and employee input into the policies you create. Please note that these guidelines are *only* those that address communication and do not deal with legal issues, privacy, or use of e-mail for personal reasons. All these issues should be addressed in a general e-mail policy.

E-Mail Policies

Policies governing e-mail should be communicated as part of a general professional code of conduct and reinforced through ongoing communication.

When to Send an E-Mail

This guideline will depend greatly on the nature of your business. If your employees communicate with colleagues on other continents or in other time zones, the guidelines may differ than if every employee is in the same time zone. In general, though, e-mail should be used for the following purposes:

- A one-to-one or one-to-few communication in which information needs to be conveyed or a question answered.
- A communication in which some limited detail needs to be included. It is permissible to send an e-mail to request a meeting.
- A dialogue needs to take place that cannot occur in real time.
- You want to send a message quickly but you do not care how quickly you get a reply. If you need a reply quickly, use instant messaging or the telephone.
- The costs associated with a telephone call or a fax are an issue.
- The recipients are in other time zones or countries.
- You require a written record of the exchange with the recipient.

When *Not* to Send an E-Mail

E-mail should not be used when the exchange is better facilitated by a face-to-face meeting and such a meeting is practical. For example, performance issues should not be addressed by e-mail but rather by a face-to-face meeting. Other times to avoid e-mail include:

- When the conversation is confidential (unless both parties are using encryption).
- You require detailed answers. An issue with a vendor, for example, is probably best dealt with in real time, over the telephone or in person.
- You are delivering bad or negative news.
- You need a reply immediately.
- Your message is complex and better explained verbally (reading could lead to misinterpretation).
- You need to communicate simultaneously with a group of people, or need the benefit of group dynamics.
- The recipient indicates that he or she prefers another means of

messaging (for instance, when she is traveling and would rather get voice mail messages).

Writing Effective Subject Lines

Well-written subject lines make it easy for recipients to assess and manage their e-mail. Good subject lines are relatively short, concise, and explain exactly what the message is about:

Bad Subject Line	Good Subject Line
A question	How do I change my telephone number?
Meeting notice	Oct. 12 project team meeting
Press release information	New CEO press release information
Case update	Lawsuit depositions start today

Elements of an effective e-mail message include the following:

Brevity. Say what you need to say and nothing more.

Style. Be informal but remember: This is a business communication. Do not use all caps.

Receipts. Do not request receipts (which confirm that the intended recipient received the e-mail).

Priority. Exercise judgment in tagging your e-mail as high priority. If everybody does that, then *all* e-mails are high priority and we are right back where we started. Use this feature only for extreme situations in which a reply is urgently needed.

Knowing your audience. Are you writing to someone with whom you have been corresponding for a long time who already knows the context of your message, or are you initiating a dialogue with someone with whom you have never communicated before? Remember, date formats and other conventions change from region to region. (For instance, in the United States, 08/21/02 is the same as August 21, 2002, but in Europe, the order in which month, date, and year are presented is different!)

Identifying yourself. Do not assume recipients will know who you are simply because your e-mail address is in the FROM line. You can introduce yourself in the first couple of lines. (This would not apply for an ongoing exchange with a regular correspondent, of course.) All messages should include a signature, a standard block that appears at the end of your message that provides basic contact information: your name, e-mail address, telephone number, and other relevant information (pager or cell phone number, for instance). About four lines is the limit for a standard signature block.

Copying (CC'ing) Original E-Mail Messages

CC *only* those people who have a direct need for the information you are communicating in the e-mail, or from whom you need a reply. Do not CC anybody just because you think they might be interested or because they have some tangential relationship to the issue. Use a listserv mailing list dedicated to the project or the issue for messages that should be seen by everyone involved rather than using your personal e-mail.

Replying to E-Mails

Answer *all* the questions that were asked in the e-mail to which you are responding. Further, anticipate follow-up questions and answer those, too, even if they were not asked.

Do not "reply to all" unless there is a good reason for everybody who received the original e-mail to see your reply. Be selective about who receives your reply—only those who need the information should be on your CC list.

Do not forward an e-mail without the okay of the individual who sent the original.

Do not respond if you do not have anything to add. I hate replies that say, "Thanks!" Sure, it is courteous, but it is simply one more e-mail that I must deal with, and I wasn't sitting around waiting for someone to thank me!

Edit the message thread before replying. Some experts suggest eliminating the entire message thread, arguing that since the e-mail has already been sent and read, the initiator of the message already knows what it says. Other people argue for leaving it in because it sets the context for your reply. I opt for the middle ground. Leaving an entire thread in a reply can lead to very long e-mail messages and difficulty finding the latest entry. Leave in only those parts of the previous thread to which you are directly replying, and include an indication that these are quotes from a previous message. Here is how I do it:

>>What time will you be arriving?<<
I get in around 5 P.M.

Attachments

Do not attach unnecessary files. Ideally, you have an attachment utility on your intranet to which you can upload attachments (generating a URL to include in the body of your e-mail message), eliminating the need for *any* attachments.

Make sure recipients can use your attachment. I cannot tell you how many times I've received file attachments that only worked with software applications I did not have! If you absolutely *must* send an attachment, and the file is large, compress it. Use a utility like WinZIP or StuffIt to reduce the file size. Make certain your recipient has the ability to decompress the file.

Never open an attachment from someone you do not know, even if it was generated internally.

All-Hands E-Mail Lists

Authority to use all-employee lists should be extremely limited. These should be used only for official distributions of information all employees actually need. Other lists, such as classified advertisements or birthday celebrations, should be maintained on listserv mailing lists or delivered based on employee profiles that show an employee is actually interested in or wants to receive that kind of message.

Voice Mail Policies

We all use voice mail, and we all experience tremendous frustration dealing with the messages we get. But do we know how to leave an effective voice mail?

When to Use Voice Mail

- You need to leave a brief message on a single topic.

When Not to Use Voice Mail

- You need a written record of your conversation.
- You will need to refer to the information in the message more than once or twice.
- The information contained in the message is complex or technical.
- You need to deal with multiple topics.
- The information is sensitive, private, or confidential.

Leaving a Message

Leave a detailed message, but know what you are going to say before you start recording. Rambling messages are not necessarily detailed; they just *ramble*. Leave your return telephone number at the beginning *and* end of your message. Do not make someone listen to the entire message a second time because they missed your number the first time around. Likewise, people will often know what you are calling about and not want to listen to your entire message if they can give you a call. Read the number slowly.

Tell who you are; do not assume that your voice will be recognized.

Voice Mail Greetings

Your message should cover who you are, where you work, why you cannot take a call (such as "I'm in a meeting" or "I'm away from the office"), and how they can reach a live person if they need to. Also, request a detailed message and assure the caller that you will get back to them.

Update your greeting daily. Let people know whether you are in the office or out. If you are out, when will you return? People need to know so they can gauge when you will get back to them.

The following is my typical greeting:

Hi. This is Shel Holtz at Holtz Communication + Technology. It's Wednesday, August 21, and I'm in the office today but unable to take your call right now. Leave a detailed message at the tone and I'll call you back just as soon as I can. If you need to, you can reach me on my cell phone at 555-555-5555.

If callers can bypass your greeting, let them know how right at the beginning of your message. I cannot tolerate listening to long greetings over and over every time I call someone. I already know all the details, such as whom to call if my call is an emergency and I need to reach someone right away.

Fax Guidelines

Policies dictating the do's and don'ts of faxes as a communication tool should be included in a general professional code of conduct and reinforced through ongoing communication.

When to Send a Fax

There certainly continue to be uses for fax machines, even in this age when most of what was once sent by fax is now traveling by e-mail. For example, a fax is useful when sending a print document that does not reside on your computer, such as a page from a magazine or a completed form. Faxes are particularly useful for those who do not have scanners.

The balance between sending a fax and an e-mail attachment is a difficult one to achieve. It is a matter of judgment. Consider that an e-mail attachment will probably print more clearly than a fax, but it will also inhibit the recipient's ability to download all their waiting e-mail. As fax volumes decrease, you run less of a risk of tying up a fax line.

One businessperson likes to send a fax as an initial introduction, but turn to e-mail after the relationship is established. The header on the fax cover letter provides considerable information about the company the recipient may want or need, including telephone numbers, address, logo, professional affiliations, and other details.

When Not to Send a Fax

Don't you just love getting twenty- or thirty-page faxes? They tie up your fax machine, use a lot of paper and toner, and usually do not contain anything you couldn't have waited for until tomorrow. If it is that long, make certain that it is absolutely urgent that the recipient get it now; otherwise, use FedEx or UPS or whatever overnight courier service your company uses. (In some cases, interoffice mail will suffice.) When you *do* send that long fax, call first to make certain that it is okay to send it.

Cover Sheets

Use a cover sheet unless there is an existing relationship that precludes the need for one. Cover sheets should indicate who is sending the fax, the fax number it is coming from, a contact telephone number *and* e-mail address, the subject of the fax, the total number of pages the fax contains (distinguish the cover sheet: "Twelve pages plus cover"), and any information required to ensure the context of the fax is understood.

Instant Messaging Guidelines

As instant messaging (IM) makes its way into the world of business, it becomes important for employees to know the do's and don'ts of engaging in an IM conversation.

When to IM

You need a quick answer to a question and you can see on your buddy list that the person who knows the answer is online.

When Not to IM

Do not send an instant message if you know the exchange is going to be lengthy, complicated, or technical. If you become involved in an IM exchange that looks like it is going to be technical or detailed, suggest taking the conversation to e-mail or the telephone.

Create a Record

Copy and paste instant messages into a text editor or e-mail client (you can send it to yourself) to create a record of any important IM conversations.

Hit the Ground Running

If you initiate an IM conversation, start off with the question you are asking or the information you are seeking. Do not say, "Hi," or,

"Are you there?" The recipient will need to respond saying, "Hi, how can I help you," or "Yes, I'm here." (And if they're not there, you won't hear anything back anyway!)

Be Discreet

Do not say anything in an IM message you would not put in an e-mail. IM messages can be copied, pasted, and forwarded.

Adopt IM Shorthand

I have read arguments against using the shorthand teenagers are using with their instant and text messaging; it is unprofessional, the argument goes. To me, not using shorthand is a failure to recognize the fast, instant nature of these new media. There is nothing wrong with adopting these shortcuts, such as "RU there" and "Got 2 go." They are part of what make the tools so speedy and efficient.

Mind Your "Away" and "Back" Messages

Leaving your IM on when you are away from your desk is just plain rude. People see you on their buddy lists and IM you expecting a response, but you are not there and all they hear is a silence. Be sure to set your message to "away," even when you are only stepping away for a couple of minutes. Make it a habit.

Text-Messaging Guidelines

Text messaging—known formally as short messaging service (SMS)—is growing in popularity. (This is not instant messaging, which is from computer to computer, but rather used on handheld devices like cell phones and text pagers.) SMS is widely used—even more than e-mail—in countries where everybody is in the same time zone. Some guidelines for the use of text messaging include:

When to Use Text Messaging

Use SMS when you need to send a short message to an individual (not a group). Your message should not require an immediate reply, and it should not be overly important. The informal nature of SMS tends to diminish the importance of messages that would stand out if sent by e-mail or over the telephone.

When Not to Use Text Messaging

If you really need a reply immediately, try the telephone first. If you do not receive a reply by telephone and then by text message, there is probably a good reason. Your recipient is not able to reply. You have now left a text message *and* a voice message. He or she will get back to you as soon as possible.

Respect Schedules

Text messages, like instant messaging, are real-time. Just because you are working does not mean that your colleagues are.

Communicating Policies

Simply having policies is not sufficient, nor is merely distributing them. You need to undertake a campaign to make sure the importance of the policies is understood. Employees need to know where they can get more information. Training must be offered.

In other words, you need to undertake a communication campaign focused on spreading the word about the policies. It never hurts to have employees sign and return a copy of the policies; not every employee will read something they are signing, but many will. (This is particularly important if your policy covers legal issues. Check with your general counsel on this requirement.)

The Supervisor's Role

Communication about the cultural change you are seeking to drive around messaging needs to come from three places:

1. *Senior management.* The big picture about the issues and how important it is for everyone in the organization to take steps to address them.
2. *Process owners.* The steering committee, the Message Mission Control team, or whoever has been given responsibility for coming up with solutions needs to be heard.
3. *Supervisors.*

Immediate supervisors should be engaged in the change process so that they can fulfill a number of critical tasks:

Model behavior. If your boss does not adhere to new messaging standards, why should you? On the other hand, if you see that the messages you receive from your boss comply with the guidelines, you will be inclined to emulate that behavior.

Set departmental standards. Broadly defined standards issued from on high rarely resonate with people doing day-to-day work down in the trenches. The supervisor serves as a translator: "Here's what these rules mean to us." The supervisor, then, would need to help employees understand why new messaging guidelines are important, what they mean to *us* here in *this* department doing *this* work. Then, he or she needs to make it clear that the department will apply certain guidelines to its standard messaging. For example, there is great power in a supervisor saying, "If you have a quick question for me, IM me; don't e-mail me. Use the same standard for deciding how to get information from others on our staff, and even employees in other departments you need to communicate with."

Prepare relevant evaluations. Human resources may be responsible for the performance evaluation process, but supervisors conduct the actual evaluations. They need to be indoctrinated; they need to understand that the part of the performance evaluation dedicated to messaging is not a joke or an afterthought, and that they need to make a sincere effort to assess the messaging performance of their direct reports. Performance evaluations conducted only once a year are fundamentally worthless. How can an employee correct poor behavior if he or she does not find out it is not the *right* behavior until it is too late? For messaging habits to change (or any other bad habits, for that matter), employees need to receive regular feedback, along with suggestions for correcting their behaviors.

Communicate well to supervisors. How you get the message to your supervisors will depend, in large part, on the processes already in place for communicating to this critical group. You should, however, ensure that you provide supervisors with the following:

- An explanation for why policies and guidelines are changing and why new tools are being introduced
- Answers to questions they are likely to get from their employees
- Templates or other materials to help them turn broad guidelines into action items at the level where work is performed
- Access to resources to help them model behavior and teach it, where necessary
- A source they can use to get answers to any questions they may have

Selected Communications Resources

Associations

International Association of Business Communicators (IABC)
One Hallidie Plaza, #600
San Francisco, CA 94102
(415) 544-4700
Web site: www.iabc.com

Public Relations Society of America (PRSA)
33 Irving Place
New York, NY 10003
(212) 460-1490
Web site: www.prsa.org

Arthur W. Page Society
32 Avenue of the Americas
Suite S638
New York, NY 10013
(212) 387-4259
Web site: www.awpagesociety.com

Association for Women in Communications
780 Ritchie Highway

Suite 28-S
Severna Park, MD 21146
410-544-7442
Web site: www.womcom.org

Books

D'Aprix, Roger. *Communicating for Change.* San Francisco, Calif.: Jossey-Bass, 1996.

Kounalakis, Markos, et al., *Beyond Spin: The Power of Strategic Corporate Journalism.* San Francisco, Calif.: Jossey-Bass, 1999.

Sinickas, Angela D. *How to Measure Your Communication Programs.* San Francisco: IABC, 2000.

Wann, Al, ed. *Inside Organizational Communication.* New York: Forbes Custom Publishing, 1999.

Wood, Lecia Vonne. *Corporate Storytelling: Planning and Creating Internal Communications.* Loveland, Colo.: Grendel Press, 2002.

Web Sites

Holtz Communication + Technology
(The author's site)
www.holtz.com

Communication Ideas: Changing the Culture of Work
(Articles on employee communications)
www.communicationideas.com

Lawrence Ragan Communications, Inc.
(Articles, workshops, and publications related to internal communications)
www.ragan.com

Tudor Williams Inc.

(Presentations, articles, and a subscription e-mail newsletter on everything from communication measurement to knowledge management)

www.tudorwilliams.com

Sinickas Communications

(Tools and resources on measuring internal communication from Angela Sinickas, ABC, a leader in the field)

www.sinicom.com

The Measurement Standard

(A site dedicated to communication measurement)

www.themeasurementstandard.com

Index